A WOMAN'S EMPIRE

A Woman's Empire

Russian Women and Imperial Expansion in Asia

KATYA HOKANSON

UNIVERSITY OF TORONTO PRESS
Toronto Buffalo London

ISBN 978-1-4875-4560-4 (cloth)   ISBN 978-1-4875-4561-1 (EPUB)
                                 ISBN 978-1-4875-4562-8 (PDF)

Library and Archives Canada Cataloguing in Publication

Title: A woman's empire : Russian women and imperial expansion in Asia / Katya
    Hokanson
Names: Hokanson, Katya, author.
Description: Includes bibliographical references and index.
Identifiers: Canadiana (print) 20220186251 | Canadiana (ebook) 20220186332 |
    ISBN 9781487545604 (cloth) | ISBN 9781487545611 (EPUB) |
    ISBN 9781487545628 (PDF)
Subjects: LCSH: Women – Russia – History – 19th century. | LCSH: Women –
    Travel – Asia, Central – History – 19th century. | LCSH: Russians – Travel – Asia,
    Central – History – 19th century. | LCSH: Imperialism and science – Russia –
    History – 19th century. | LCSH: Russia – Civilization – 1801–1917. | LCSH:
    Russia – Territorial expansion – History – 19th century. | LCSH: Asia, Central –
    Colonization – History – 19th century.
Classification: LCC HQ1662 .H65 2023 | DDC 305.4094709/034 – dc23

We wish to acknowledge the land on which the University of Toronto Press
operates. This land is the traditional territory of the Wendat, the Anishnaabeg, the
Haudenosaunee, the Métis, and the Mississaugas of the Credit First Nation.

This book has been published with the help of a grant from the Federation for the
Humanities and Social Sciences, through the Awards to Scholarly Publications Program,
using funds provided by the Social Sciences and Humanities Research Council of Canada.

University of Toronto Press acknowledges the financial support of the Government
of Canada, the Canada Council for the Arts, and the Ontario Arts Council, an agency
of the Government of Ontario, for its publishing activities.

Contents

Conclusion 238

Illustrations

Acknowledgments

This book would not have been possible without the help of numerous people and institutions. A term at the Oregon Humanities Center and two separate summer sessions at the Russian, East European and Eurasian Center Summer Research Laboratory at the University of Illinois greatly aided my work. I received helpful audience feedback at my Humanities Center presentation and excellent assistance from Joseph Lenkart, the Manager of the Slavic Reference Service at the University of Illinois, and the whole SRS team. Dear friend and University of Oregon Slavic librarian Heghine Hakobyan was instrumental at every step of the way, assisting me not only in tracking down sources but also in communicating with her colleagues and contacts in Russia. In addition, her feedback was invaluable in helping me fashion more nuanced translations from Russian. A research trip to Russia was supported by research funds from the University of Oregon, as was the publication of the manuscript itself. Close friends and colleagues Jenifer Presto, Julie Hessler, and Anindita Banerjee read drafts and made very helpful suggestions. Kit McDunn was an attentive proofreader and researcher who helped improve the manuscript, and Maya Larson also provided helpful research assistance.

Collaborators on a cluster of articles in *The Russian Review*, Ingrid Kleespies, Valeria Sobol, Anne Lounsbery, Sara Dickinson, and John Randolph, gave helpful feedback on an early article. Various readers and interlocutors on conference panels helped give me insight and knowledge, including those already named, as well as Emily Laskin, Edyta Bojanowska, Catherine O'Neil, Jennifer Keating, David Powelstock, Olga Maiorova, Michael Denner, Robin Feuer Miller, Bella Grigoryan, and Emily Wang.

University of Oregon colleagues Susanna Lim, Roy Chan, Ryan Jones, Michael Allan, Ken Calhoon, Leah Middlebrook, Tze-Yin Teo, Katy

Brundan, and Dawn Marlan have likewise been supportive listeners and interlocutors on many occasions. Many colleagues both within and outside of the University of Oregon gave their support during writing circles, first and foremost among them Lara Bovilsky, Faculty Associate of the Faculty Writing Circle at the UO Center on Diversity and Community, and longtime office next-door-neighbour.

I also owe a debt to some of the many students whom I have had the great fortune to work with in one capacity or another and whose own research assisted mine, including Anna Kovalchuk, Peter Orte, Murad Jalilov, Maya Larson, Daria Smirnova, Alexis Gunderson, Verena Zabel, Elena Leonenko, Yuan Gao, Amanda Bird, Barbara Brown, Anna-Minna Pavulans, and Shona Allison. Daria also assisted me with Russian-language research.

Three anonymous manuscript readers gave me very helpful feedback, as did editor Stephen Shapiro and a member of the manuscript review committee at the University of Toronto Press.

I would also like to thank my parents, constant supporters of my work, my husband Steven Brown and son Gabriel Brown, for their love and support, as well as my brother Jon and sister-in-law Jocelyn Worrall. My parents-in-law, Verlin and Maryanne Brown, could not be more supportive, as are my sister- and brother-in-law Carrie and Ken Wallyn. Multiple nephews and nieces always keep life interesting, and longtime friends Leila O'Connell, Roxanna Gutierrez, Gordana Crnković, and Sonia Nazario always keep me grounded in the world.

A WOMAN'S EMPIRE

Introduction

Somewhere out East some new land has been opened up. They need people out there, they're looking for them right now and promising a lot of benefits. Why don't we go out there?[1]

These are the words with which Marfa Vasilievna, a character in Nikolai Karazin's novel *In the Distant Confines* (*Na dalekikh okrainakh*), published in 1872, exhorts her future husband to embark on a move to Central Asia.[2] The relative vagueness, but also openness, of that "somewhere out East" reinforces not only the vagueness of the "East" but also the equally open-ended implication that "people" (liudi) needed there include women alongside men. While Karazin by no means paints her as an admirable figure, Marfa Vasilievna freely rides around Tashkent on horseback and is "not at all enamored of the company of the local ladies," who arrive in a carriage "wearing round, straw hats, on which were set out entire flower and vegetable gardens."[3] Although the novel centres primarily on men's adventures and misadventures in Turkestan, Karazin clearly establishes the difference between boring ladies with straw hats evoking domesticated plants and independent women. Like the fictional Marfa Vasilievna, but unlike her in terms of their seriousness of purpose (as Elena Andreeva points out, Marfa Vasilievna is something of a flirtatious lightweight), a number of real Russian women travelled to and wrote about Central Asia and other Eurasian territories from the late 1860s to the turn of the twentieth century.[4] While these women were mostly unlike Karazin's self-centred protagonist, they steered between the Scylla and Charybdis of dull housewifery (at least during their travels) and actual physical danger, all the while intensely aware that the opportunity to travel to Russian-controlled Central Asia and the Russian Far East, borderlands such as those inhabited by Buriats and Uriankhai

Figure 0.1. The Russian Empire.

Source: Bill Nelson

(Tuvans), and parts of Mongolia, China, and Tibet – and farther afield, to British-controlled India – was a particular privilege. Their journeys correlated closely with Russia's imperial advances and aspirations at the cusp of the nineteenth and twentieth centuries, and their words were saturated by the particular imperial consciousness of that period.

This book investigates the complex relationship between women and empire in the framework of Russia's expansion into the farthest reaches of Russia's eastern frontiers. It examines the ways in which women "affirmed, naturalized and modified" the Russian imperial project, but also in some cases critiqued and problematized it.[5] As travellers, scientists, and writers, they were by no means monolithic in their identity, affect, or self-presentation; yet all of them participated in empire-building in a great diversity of ways, and most presented their own perceptions of their role in the project. And of course, they themselves were impacted by Russia's imperial expansion. As Sara Mills points out in the context of the British empire, "European" women who lived in colonial settings had complex and intersectional identities. Women who were oppressed or limited in one context could be privileged in another, and indeed, that very privilege depended on the imperial paradigms in which they operated as well as their own approach towards the composition of the society from which they emerged.[6] The lives of Russian women in the East, which was variously defined and imagined, or who travelled there, similarly, form an important but little-studied element of Russian imperial life. The multiple modes of their writing illuminate complex intersections between the issues of gender, labour, and colonial difference even as they underscore the distinctive imaginaries of new frontiers of expansion in the late nineteenth century. Unlike the earlier and adjacent imperial realm of the Caucasus, with its segmented and "familiar" spaces, the open horizons of the far less differentiated (in Russian minds) Central Asia and the Russian empire's furthest peripheries of India, China, and Tibet also provided room for women to add their unique perspectives and voices to the predominantly male canon of imperial letters, and in the process to continue to redefine cultural and professional arenas open to women.

The perspectives of Russian women who travelled to and wrote about Russia's eastern territories and peripheries during this period are varied, but in their common attempt to account for gender, they provide a self-conscious approach to the activities of the Russian empire. Because they do not write from the default, unquestioned perspective of men, they bring their own status into question as women – needing to explain, justify, or simply dare to assume a man's prerogative. Hence the experiences they describe bring the overall imperial project into sharper focus and delineate a status requiring justification or

Figure 0.2. Steppe and Turkestan Provinces.

Source: Bill Nelson

explanation – mainly to bring civilization, to impose the rule of law and legislate the freedom of women, but also to promote a rivalry with England, and to encourage science, such as botany, ethnography, archae-ology, zoology, and the like. It is also important to acknowledge that writing itself was a fundamental way to establish identity, perspective, and authority. Many of these women felt themselves to be representa-tives of an important civilizing force. Perhaps one of the most telling moments in these accounts is a travel narrative by Elena Apreleva, in which she describes the breakdown of order inside the first-class train car as she travels from Tashkent to Moscow in 1906 in the aftermath of the Russian loss at Tsushima. She paints the picture of a very nearly apocalyptic journey, forecasting, in effect, fragility of Russian imperial stability. The narrators of these texts constantly assert, in large and small ways, the importance and assuredness of Russian imperial longevity. If, as Benedict Anderson points out, nationalism depends on a reading public, these narratives asserted Russian national status, as headlined by Russian elites. To write, but also to depict, to collect, to categorize was to assert the rightness and inevitability of the Russian imperial project and the Russian civilizing mission.

As Mary Pratt noted in the context of the Americas, even in traditionally male spheres of activity such as science, women served as "central agents in legitimating scientific authority and its global project alongside Europe's other ways of knowing the world," meaning that travel literature by women played a significant role in the European imperial projects.[7] This travel included or overlapped with such fields as ethnography, botany, zoology, and other categorizing activities undertaken by "European" travellers and explorers. Other scholars have argued that women, although greatly affected by restrictions in education and occupation (even as these were also gradually easing), were able to take on the identity of "honorary men" during travel or expeditions, and thus overcome, at least temporarily, rules otherwise imposed on freedom of movement and expression.[8] Women travellers and participants in expeditions were able to play a role that otherwise was not available to women in their society, and their writing helped to create an imagined community that included women in such prominent, relatively independent, roles, at least for the period of travel they participated in. In turn, this increased freedom and status for these women depended on the kind of surveying, collecting, and ordering of the world that various imperial representatives were undertaking, and it did not necessarily significantly alter women's status in their own milieu; it also did not mean their contributions, however meaningful, would be recognized officially.

British women in Anglo-India have so far provided the paradigmatic model for studying and theorizing such writing. While the rich body of scholarship on the subject forms an important resource for thinking about Russian women in Asia, this book also underscores the differences between the two. Sara Mills has argued that nineteenth-century British women's activities in Anglo-India, such as writing, organizing charities, arranging the household, and so on, despite being glossed over as trivial, in fact "serve[d] as the supports for the imperial enterprise."[9] "[E]ven the writing of cookbooks and travel accounts are important elements in maintaining, affirming and contesting colonial relations," she notes, revising the concept of imperial activity to include work that "affirmed, naturalised and modified the imperial presence."[10] The Russian women addressed here, however, while also building the Russian imperial enterprise, were not primarily focused on domesticity and, in fact, often resisted it powerfully. They were usually acutely aware of their rivals the British and often compared Russian colonial efforts to those of England. Further, Russians rarely could put forward the kind of supremely self-confident image of themselves as civilizers that the British blithely did. Always needing to contend with the European image of Russians as lesser cousins in the European family, dependent for their status primarily on Russian military might, which had been shaken in the 1850s as a result of the Crimean War, and themselves thought semi-Asiatic, Russians approached their colonizing project from a different perspective than did the British, even if many of the results were quite similar. Virtually all of the women cited here made remarks about European misperceptions about Russia and Russians, and many also explicitly noted their view, commonly held among Russians, that the Russians treated ethnic others more fairly and humanely than did the British.[11] Much as there was a project to promote Central Asia as a space appropriate for Russians, there was also often a self-consciousness about such a project.

The real-life women who heeded the call to go East included one of the most remarkable Russian women ever to write a travel book, Elena Petrovna Blavatskaia, who lived and travelled in India on behalf of the Theosophical Society, which she founded herself. Combining her fascination with Hinduism and Buddhism with exploration of mesmerizing landscapes and cultures of numerous parts of the Indian subcontinent, and focusing extensively on women's rights, Blavatskaia existed on her own terms, travelling in her professional, Theosophical role and denouncing, via a published series of letters, British imperial practices in India while defending Russian imperial control of the Caucasus and Russia's ever-expanding movement into Central Asia. Another woman, perhaps her polar opposite, Varvara Dukhovskaia, embodied a completely different path towards the East. Dukhovskaia defined herself in great part as the wife of her prominent husband, who was already a general at thirty-six, celebrating her high spousal status in her memoirs, which described her travel and life at various postings in the Caucasus, Far East, and Central Asia. She represented the highest echelons of Russian power in her role as the wife of a general (later a governor-general), but also regretted the fact that her life was lived primarily in the imperial peripheries, even if she strove to make that deprivation a virtue, at least on paper. Undercutting her glowing picture of Russian noblesse oblige was her own depression and not infrequent resistance against her role in the imperial enterprise. The writer most called upon to perform the duties of a woman "civilizer" in a colonial setting, Varvara Dukhovskaia made it clear that she resented most social obligations, especially those involving receptions, greeting dignitaries, and appearing at various dinners and ceremonies. Charitable work that included her loves – music and writing – she seemed to enjoy, but mostly she presented herself as a long-suffering wife of an official who would prefer to be in her own milieu in Russia, rather than far-flung peripheries, except when she could portray herself as independent, bold, and adventurous.

Elena Apreleva, an imaginative writer, as well as an editor, accompanied her husband, an official, to Central Asia. She depicted some domestic scenes among Russians in Central Asia, but she removed her gender and her identity from the narrative by using a male pseudonym under which she published her "Central Asian Sketches," set primarily in Samarkand and Tashkent. She was as likely to focus on Central Asian women as Russian ones and never limited herself to a woman's perspective. Apreleva explored numerous aspects of life in Russian Turkestan in her quasi-fictional stories with a sensitivity, in many cases, about the changes wrought by the Russians on the local people and an attempt to present matters from their perspective. Several of her non-Russian characters are powerfully constructed and at times decentre Russians from the Central Asian narrative; her male pseudonym often results in a first-person plural narration, thus appearing to encompass the experiences and views of a married couple.

Several women were or presented themselves as explorers or chroniclers of expeditions, and while careful not to be seen as anything other than proper, prided themselves on being intrepid and unusual. Iuliia Golovnina's 1898 scientific expedition to the altitudinous Pamir mountains was not merely an undertaking of the Moscow Zoological Museum, but occurred against the background of native uprisings and contained extended commentary on the political control of Central Asia, including the boundary between Russian and British interests.[12] Shifting her attention from travelling and hunting to the individual Central Asian members of the expedition, Golovnina undercut the impersonality of her imperial narrative by focusing on the personal narratives of her servants.

In the same year, Anna Rossikova accompanied her husband to Central Asia on an entomological expedition along the Amu-Darya River. Her account underscores the class misunderstandings inherent in a meeting with exiled Cossacks, who resent their treatment by the Russian government, and reveals a change in Russian assumptions about local people when, after a terrifying storm, local Karakalpak fishermen provide both food and valuable information to the Russian travellers. The two groups ultimately met as equals.

Several women were active participants in early, often dangerous scientific expeditions, including Ol'ga Fedchenko, a botanist who travelled to Central Asia as early as 1868. She was the only woman among a large, primarily military contingent; the party was attacked more than once. After the untimely death of her husband, with whom she worked closely, Fedchenko edited a twenty-four-volume compendium of the findings of their joint expeditions, effectively solidifying his scholarly reputation. She was also an accomplished artist who documented the trip. Aleksandra Potanina, the daughter of a priest, was the most far-flung traveller aside from Blavatskaia, participating in expeditions to Mongolia, China, and parts of Tibet, as well as Russian and non-Russian Buriatia. Potanina began by assisting her husband and later published some of her own ethnographic work, much of which focuses on the lives of women, and was the first woman to give a scholarly talk at the Geography Department in Irkutsk.

Finally, Praskov'ia Uvarova, an archaeologist who was only able to become a professional after her husband's death, when she became head of the organization he had refused to allow women to join, published scholarly work primarily on the Caucasus, but in 1890 travelled to Tashkent for the second Tashkent exhibition, at the invitation of the governor-general of Turkestan. Her two-part published account of the trip, which displays her knowledge of the history and building techniques of Timurid Central Asia, was particularly focused on establishing her scholarly credentials, sometimes by denigrating those of male scholars or officials. Her writing indicates that in 1890 there was continued interest in travel accounts to Central Asia and much that readers still did not know.

Several other women are important to note even though they are only marginally mentioned in my study, and there are likely to be others as yet "undiscovered." Mavra Pavlovna Cherskaia (1857–1940) travelled with her husband in 1891 to the Kolyma region and after he died continued the expedition without him, including taking necessary scientific measurements.[13] Ol'ga Petrovna Lobri, a poet, wrote travel notes about Turkestan, published in 1899.[14] Maria Nalivkina co-wrote an ethnographic account of Uzbek women in the Fergana valley with her husband, Vladimir Nalivkin, published in 1886. The account was based on participant observation – the Nalivkins lived, dressed, and did the same work as the Uzbeks among whom they lived, in some sense "going to the people" in Turkestan rather than in a Russian peasant village.[15] Lidiia Poltoratskaia, the wife of the Semipalatinsk military governor, Vladimir Poltoratskii, took pictures of people and landscapes of the Altai while accompanying her husband on inspection tours and published her own album, *Al'bom tipov i vidov Zapadnoi Sibiri* (*Album of Types and Views of Western Siberia*) in 1879, as well as two accounts of her travels.[16] Non-Russian women writers also made their mark, such as Marie de Ujfalvy-Bourdon, who wrote *De Paris à Samarkand* (1880), as well as *Voyage d'une Parisienne dans l'Himalaya occidentale* (1887).[17] Isabelle Phibbs, an Englishwoman who travelled in 1897, wrote *A Visit to the Russians in Central Asia* and visited Russian dignitaries such as Aleksei Kuropatkin, then governor-general of Transcaspia.[18] St. George Littledale, a hunter and traveller, journeyed through the Pamirs from the Russian side with his wife, Teresa, in 1888 and 1890, hence predating Golovnina's trip, as Golovnina knew. Teresa Littledale's diaries and letters, although unpublished, are discussed and quoted at some length in scholarship on the couple; Littledale also acknowledged his wife's participation in the presentations he made to the Royal Geographical Society.[19] Other women, wives of officers, also resided in places then hardly visited by other Russians.[20]

Russia's Movement into Asia: "No Central Asian Lermontov"

Given Russian control of the Caucasus, the typical itinerary for Russians travelling to Central Asia was routed through the Caucasus, to Baku and across the Caspian Sea, thus reinforcing the connection between the two, with Central Asia as a kind of logical continuation of imperial expansion after the Caucasus. The railroad followed the same military routing as it expanded eastward. When the war in the Caucasus ended, there was a military culture already in place; Russia needed to control its border regions and keep trade routes open, and it had as a goal continuing to build rail lines eastward. Unlike the British conquest of India, at first carried out by a private company, Russians went into Central Asia first and foremost for military reasons, and rather than cheaply holding territory with local forces as the British did, had to use their standing army at high cost. Rail links were built first to strategic locations and only later to commercial ones.[21] Already familiar with Islam and with various styles of confrontation against, coexistence with, and assimilation of the native "other," Russian readers had a previous basis on which to encounter a new territory and new set of non-Russian imperial subjects, but the work of placing all of this new information into a readily available context remained to be carried out. Unlike the case of the Caucasus, in which most of this literary familiarizing was done by male writers, many of them canonical, primarily in the early nineteenth century, there was "no Central Asian Lermontov, no Russian Kipling," although there were first-class paintings by artist Vasilii Vereshchagin.[22] Numerous Russian writers in the first half of the nineteenth century had been military officers, a correlation that had mostly ended by mid-century. There was one particularly prominent imaginative writer (and prolific artist) of the later period, Nikolai Nikolaevich Karazin (1842–1908), who is now primarily remembered for his art rather than his writing, as well as a second, far-less-known writer, Nikolai Il'in.[23] Much that is written about travellers is treated primarily in strictly historical terms, and there is very little about women writers or travellers.[24] There is very little secondary material about Russian writers who wrote about Central Asia, and in fact even the primary texts of male writers, such as Karazin and Il'in, became quite obscure. Some exceptions to the rule, at least in regard to male writers, are Eleonora Shafranskaia's two books on the "Tashkent text" and Karazin, Elena Andreeva's book treating Karazin both as writer and artist, and Emily Laskin's dissertation on Central Asian Russian literature.[25]

In the second half of the nineteenth century, women writers of different kinds were more common than they had been earlier and brought a different perspective to various genres, including a more "heterogeneous" discourse of travel, as Sarah Mills terms it, since dominant forms of male travel discourse could not simply be reinscribed by women.[26] Women travellers increasingly played an active role in the latter nineteenth and early twentieth centuries in the pursuit of travel, helping to create the conditions for the cultural assimilation of the Central Asian conquest and opportunities to present the landscape of Central Asia (and beyond) to their readers. An important issue their identities as women brought to the fore was the topic of safety and security for Russians in the new territories. Depending on the circumstances, women's presence could serve as a kind of test of Russian control and assurance of "civilized values," such as when Iuliia Golovnina travelled through the Pamir borderlands or Varvara Dukhovskaia lived in a war zone in Kars or travelled in the vicinity of Andijan at the time of the 1898 uprising.[27]

As numerous scholars have shown, Russian imperial aims have long been tied to Russian literature, which typically celebrated Russian expansion. Dating back at least to the time of Peter the Great in the late seventeenth century, Russia's ability to command respect in Western Europe relied on the status afforded to Russia's military prowess. A continued expansion first south, then east, allowed Russia to style itself as a "European" power, a superior Christian civilization that was bringing enlightenment to Muslim, Buddhist, or pagan areas it continuously annexed. Russian national identity was nearly synonymous with Russia's military might, and typically even critics of Russia's autocratic form of government, such as the Decembrists, nonetheless supported Russia's imperial ambitions.[28] While France was long the model for a Europeanized aristocracy, with Russia's expansion into Central Asia in the second half of the nineteenth century, Russians increasingly compared the Russian empire to that of Britain, as the edges of each of their spheres of influence began to clash particularly in Afghanistan and in the high mountains of Central Asia. Though Russia had long been a contiguous land empire, while Britain primarily dominated with ocean power, British interests began to cross with those of the Russians as they moved inland beyond India and Afghanistan. As Hermann Kreutzmann points out, many high-level members of society in both England and Russia were involved, including explorers, military officers, diplomats, and nationally minded writers, such as Dostoevsky and Kipling; regardless of national origin, these groups shared many similarities of educational background and social status.[29]

During the eighteenth century, Eurocentrism had come to predominate among educated Russians, while terms to designate non-Russian groups within the expanding empire proliferated. While the terms inorodtsy (aliens), inovertsy (non-Orthodox), inozemtsy (foreigners) and iasachnye narody (payers of iasak, or fur tribute) were at first closely associated, even if they meant different things, after 1798 they began to be replaced by the category inorodtsy, designating, in the words of Iurii Slezkine, "congenital and apparently perennial outsiders" to Russians, which in turn became a juridical term.[30] Although they were sedentary and in the Western part of the empire, Jews were also labelled "inorodtsy" from 1835, probably because, as John Slocum notes, "the Russian authorities perceived both groups [Jews and eastern inorodtsy] as a dangerous alien presence within the body politic."[31] As Valerie Kivelson and Ronald Suny point out, Slocum challenges the idea that Russians were indifferent to the category of race since the category of "inorodets" designated not only a fundamentally different "other" but also one who could not be assimilated or "promoted" into a less othered category.[32] Islam and nomadism also began to gain negative connotations; Andreas Kappeler reports that by 1767, nomads were considered second-class citizens.[33] As Russia moved south through the Caucasus and trans-Caucasia, annexing eastern Georgia by 1801, taking Daghestan and Baku by 1806, it came into conflict with both the Ottoman Empire and Persia, as well as with the British and the French.[34] The conquest of the Caucasus and trans-Caucasia was long and bloody, ending only in 1859 with the capture of Shamil. As Kappeler points out, Russia lost tens of thousands of soldiers and up to one-sixth of the state's income in the Caucasus, while Russia's best generals were frequently defeated there.[35] Two Russo-Persian wars took place in 1804–13 and 1826–8, while in the western part of the country, Russia was attacked by France under Napoleon, defeating the French in 1814. Russia was also shaken by the 1825 Decembrist Uprising.

As Russia reached southward, it had an eye on what the British were doing further to the east. Both the British and the Russians were keenly aware of the territory that lay between the areas claimed by the two powers, particularly Afghanistan, as well as eastern Persia and the Central Asian khanates. The Crimean War (1853–6) put Russia and England on opposite sides of a military conflict. After the 1857 rebellion against British rule in India, the British crown took over rule of India from the East India Company. Once Russia finally "pacified" the Caucasus, it turned its attention to Central Asia. Prince Gorchakov, the Russian foreign minister, announced in a "note" of 1864 that Russia's goals in Central Asia were purely meant to obtain a secure border, and in fact, some of the logic of expansion was definitely due to the constant need to protect the border of land previously taken, thus leading to ever more expansion.[36] Imperial expansion, as Kivelson and Suny put it, "was motivated by a mélange of motives" – more strategic than either economic or religious, leading to the involvement of "ambitious men in uniform" who wished to make their careers and engage in adventures, and to compete against Great Britain in the "Great Game."[37] In quick succession, Russia took Tashkent in 1865, Kokand and Bukhara in 1866, Samarkand in 1868, and Khiva in 1873, the same year Russia and England signed a preliminary agreement about what would constitute the borders and sphere of influence of each. In 1877–8, Russia fought a war against Turkey, while in 1878, new disagreements about the status of Afghanistan led to the second Anglo-Afghan War, which lasted until 1880 (the first one had occurred in 1839–42). In 1881, Russia again expanded its territorial control, taking the Turkmen fortress of Geok-Tepe in what was widely considered to involve barbaric treatment of the defeated, including old people, women, and children. In 1884, Russia took the oasis town of Merv and, controversially, Pandjeh in 1885, which had been considered part of Afghanistan and hence in the British sphere of influence. A boundary commission was established and finally completed its work in 1895, much of which involved adjudicating borders in the Pamir mountains.[38] Against the background of the back and forth with England, Russia was continuing to build the Trans-Siberian Railway, construction of which was accelerated after 1880 and could, the

British reasoned, allow the Russians to quickly bring troops to areas uncomfortably close to their sphere of influence. Built to emphasize military priorities and not commercial ones, such as the transportation of cotton, the Trans-Siberian emblematized the Russian approach, which prioritized military and state goals, as opposed to British prioritization of commercial goals, as each enlarged its sphere of influence.[39] The Trans-Siberian was also a tool of expansion vis-à-vis China.[40] As a result of numerous factors, Russian Turkestan was the most archetypally colonial of all the Russian holdings. The people of Turkestan were the least integrated and treated the most differently from other peoples under Russian control, representing the most top-down colonial rule undertaken by imperial Russia.[41] An important consequence to the Russian conquest of Central Asia, of course, was its impact on the local people, who certainly suffered as a result of the combat itself and the imposition of Russian rule. As Alexander Morrison points out, due to difficult logistics, the steppe and desert campaigns tended to be on a small scale, usually fought "with no more than 5,000–10,000 men" – while such events as the taking of Tashkent occurred with only 2,000 soldiers.[42] These battles, while deeply impacting local people, also garnered little attention from historians, who dismissed the significance of wars fought against "savage" and "fanatical" opponents, "primitive 'asiatics' who did not constitute a serious foe."[43]

Colonization in Siberia, the Far East, and Central Asia led to conflicts over land, the crowding of local peoples and their decimation by disease; nomads in particular were gradually, over several centuries, killed, expelled, or surrounded by agricultural settlements and driven to more marginal land.[44] Alongside this drive to take over the former khanates and expand to the edge of territories controlled by China and Britain was an accompanying drive for scientific exploration and knowledge; these expeditions could be within Russian-controlled territories or range outside them to Mongolia, Tibet, China, and the like, so that Russian conception of "Asia" could be extremely wide and all-encompassing, and often therefore somewhat vaguely defined. Russia's Asia (Aziia) or Orient (East, or Vostok), certainly comprised the Caucasus, as well as such long-term Russian antagonists as Turkey and Persia. Russia first became a multi-ethnic empire by taking the khanate of Kazan in the 1500s. As Russian forces moved southward and eastward into Central Asia, Russia's Asia expanded. Not usually considered "Orient," Siberia too included many inorodtsy, and widened control in Siberia was a part of Russian imperial expansion. The Far East, including the Amur region, was a part of Russia's Asia, while many of the border areas – Buriat, Tuvan, Mongolian, Chinese, were subject to

Russian influence and some to Russia's territorial ambitions.[45] India, where Blavatskaia travelled, was both a completely non-Russian area, yet also the scene of the Great Game rivalry, with Blavatskaia's Russianness constantly evoking comparisons between the two empires. The Pamir mountains, on the border between Russian-controlled Turkestan and British sphere of influence Afghanistan, similarly evoked the Great Game. Because imperial expansion was a knowledge race as well as one for territory and influence, many explorers were competing not just with explorers from other countries but with their own countrymen. It is clear that Grigorii Potanin, for example, pressed on with his expedition despite his wife's illness, in part due to a rivalry with Przhvalskii. Most explorers also realized that Western designations of territorial borders did not always correlate with local people's own sense of their identity or homeland.

A Woman's Empire: Women in Russian Asia

The women who wrote accounts against the backdrop of these changes, depicted Central Asia in memoirs or literature or helped construct the Western archive of its people, fauna and flora were keenly aware of their roles and knew what it had taken to allow them to be in Russian-controlled Asia or places adjacent to them. Although recent scholarship has investigated the history of the Russian empire in the latter part of the nineteenth century, as well as how it was expressed in non-literary (and some literary) texts, there has been no study focusing in particular on how women took part in the project and how they saw themselves and their contributions, whether experientially in the case of those who took part in lengthy and uncomfortable expeditions or more observationally in the case of writers of literary texts or more typical travel texts.[46] Traditionally, one might think of a "woman's empire" as being the domestic sphere, and in fact, a number of scholars have attested to colonizers' desire, in non-Russian contexts, to set aside a designated women's domestic sphere separate from "the outside," a kind of slice of the home country in miniature. However, the women addressed in this study generally resisted the domestic, some of them quite vehemently, like Elena Blavatskaia and some more circuitously, like Varvara Dukhovskaia. They perhaps took for granted that Russia would prevail and come to completely control Central Asia but were generally far more interested in the process and interaction than in any kind of "finished product." While explorers Fedchenko and Potanina had to observe certain proprieties expected of women, their focus was on their work. Often, they saw themselves as explicitly different from British women. As Blavatskaia notes derisively in *From the Caves and Jungles of Hindostan*, the British lived separately from the Indians, unlike the visiting Theosophists: "We occupied three small bungalows, lost, like nests, in the greenery of the garden, their roofs literally smothered in roses blooming on bushes fifteen feet high, and their windows covered only with muslin, instead of the usual panes of glass. The bungalows were situated in the native part of the town, thus we were transported all at once to the real India. We were living in India, unlike the English who are merely surrounded by India at a proper distance."[47] Sara Mills describes the British propensity to attempt to carve out such separate spaces, an attempt that was unsuccessful, since, ultimately, "this distance is impossible to maintain and instead there develops what [Anthony] King has termed a third culture."[48] Both because (in this case) British living spaces were inevitably places where servants and others lived and worked, and because British women did not remain only in those spaces to begin with, there was ultimately no functionally separate English domestic sphere in India, even if there was an imagined one.

Arguably, women who participated in travel and expeditions were by definition not tied to a domestic sphere, although they had to navigate issues of femininity and domesticity during their travels. In fact, ultimately the typically male sphere of active empire building was also in part that of women, while the domestic sphere was ultimately not so separate from the public one, and at least for Russians in Turkestan, not necessarily so much restricted to women. Certainly, women who were part of any settled Russian population became part of a colonial sphere intended to be Russian, as they were building Russian society in newly conquered areas with their very presence, as a number of scholars have attested.[49] And Russians certainly also built Russian parts of established towns, with gridded, organized sections.[50] As Russians continued to settle in Central Asia, women doubtless had a role to play in "civilizing" the new society and in asserting its relationship to the capitals. In Russian Central Asia also this was a third culture or third space since, as Homi Bhabha has pointed out, "the colonial presence is always ambivalent, split between its appearance as original and authoritative and its articulation as repetition and difference."[51] In India, this third culture was Anglo-Indian, in Russia, arguably, "Turkestani."[52] Women like Varvara Dukhovskaia, wife of the Turkestan governor-general and before that the Pri-Amur governor-general, held what were official roles by virtue of marriage or family since wives and sometimes daughters of important officials were expected to serve as hostesses, patrons of charity and the arts, not to mention as examples of "appropriate womanhood." However, the women addressed in this study were not enthusiastic participants in what they considered to be the limited roles of Russian women in these circumstances. Dukhovskaia makes it clear that she participates in this process mostly under duress; she prefers adventure and travel, or being in European Russia, not building Russian society elsewhere. Such social roles are also expressed clearly, but quite critically, in Elena Apreleva's stories, in which well-connected noblewomen put on charity bazaars, hold lotteries, and bring assistance to the poor, but the stories are not told from their perspective, and indeed their undertakings are often somewhat estranged, either related by subservient males who are forced into the labour required to put them on or described from the perspective of a local figure to whom charity lotteries appear to be something immoral. Apreleva is far more likely to indicate the interconnectedness of the Russians and the Central Asians than emphasize their differences. The narrators of her stories do not identify with these nation-building Russian society women.

The women who participated in scientific expeditions or travelled relatively independently generally identified themselves as being separate from the domestic sphere or celebrated the ability to get away from the mundane; in fact, their biographers or other observers, in order to compensate for any lack in this regard, often hasten to emphasize these women's domesticity when "at home" in Russia or their domestic-oriented actions while in the field so that they do not appear too far outside of gender norms. Ol'ga Fedchenko, during an expedition, was praised for her hospitality and solicitousness to her husband, while Aleksandra Potanina's hospitality towards women students and other visitors was emphasized by those remembering her life in a volume of her work they published.[53]

With the presence of women in any endeavour in which they were newly participant, change occurred and was certainly proclaimed, and certainly there were women who focused more on creating a Russian domesticity in Turkestan. In Russian Turkestan, women "radiated civilization and permanence," Jeff Sahadeo points out, and their arrival in 1870, according to one longtime administrator, improved Russian social life.[54]

Gendered Rhetoric

Rhetorically, of course, the inclusion of women in expeditions could be seen to emphasize the expeditions' non-threatening qualities, in effect making them *more* scientific and less military. In the words of I.I. Popov, member of the Eastern Siberian section of the Russian Geographical

Society and future revolutionary, the participation of Aleksandra Potanina on Geographical Society expeditions changed their tenor, in effect increasing their efficacy:

> Before [Grigorii] Potanin, and even during his time, the expeditions of Przhvalskii, Pevtsov and others were more similar to military detachments than to scholarly expeditions. The locals reacted to them with fear and caution. But there was nothing for them to fear from an expedition in which a woman took part, where there was no military convoy; it was clear to them that such an expedition followed scientific goals, and not military ones. Thanks to such relations to the local people, Potanin could quietly pass among the aggressive Tanguts, hold conversations with fanatical Tibetans, and passed through areas where no European foot had ever trod and each time brought out rich material for scholarly work.[55]

In some cases, by literally embodying a gentler and less confrontational approach, women had an impact both on how Russian military and scientific groups were perceived and even on how they operated. Ol'ga Fedchenko, the only woman in a large expeditionary contingent in Central Asia, took over recording compass readings in order to make her expedition seem less threatening.[56] She also made artist's records of the sights and important flora and fauna, as the trip had no photographer; her art instructor, Savrasov, was the same as Levitan's. Popov also alludes to one of the singular advantages women had in these kinds of expeditions or travels: as women, they could often gain access to elements of women's lives that were inaccessible to male Westerners.[57] As Mills points out, one of the ways in which women played a role was by "contribut[ing] to the imperial task of revealing the secrets of the colonised country," which was fully embodied by the Nalivkins' participant observer study.[58] Race and religion, of course, also played an indisputable role, and these white "European," Christian Russian Orthodox women saw themselves as the default, civilized norm, indeed perhaps superior to European women in that role, at least in the case of Potanina, whose family members were concerned about unequal distribution of property and the rights of peasants, and Fedchenko, whose siblings were outright rebels against the system: for their activities, her sister was sent to Siberia and her brother was imprisoned. It would depend, of course, on how these women perceived themselves in this regard, but their commitment to the "civilizing" project was not necessarily any less vigorous even if executed more amicably and understood as necessary and motivated by the kinds of ideals that prompted Narodniks and Siberian separatists, nor if they resisted typically domestic roles.[59]

Potanina wrote approvingly of Russian efforts to win over the Uriankhai people (Tuvans), among whom she had travelled: "now already their relations with the Russians have become completely peaceful, and we notice the quick successes of our rapprochement (sblizhenie), a peaceful rapprochement, naturally worked out by life itself on the foundation of mutual relations and services. Last year one of our teachers visited the Uriankhai land from the Minusinskii okrug, with the sole goal of helping the Uriankhai population which was suffering from an epidemic of smallpox, with smallpox vaccinations. He was received as is the best guest, he was brought from one ulus to the next."[60] Potanina notably employs here the potentially more "feminine" rhetoric of teaching, "guest" relationships and healing, as well as the key Russian imperial term "sblizhenie," or rapprochement, which had numerous meanings although here is used primarily in its sense of "cultural uplift" or "enlightenment."[61] Although the Potanins' trips to Mongolia, which was part of China, were not aimed at physical control of the territory by Russians, they were aimed at trade and other benefits for Russia, and one can certainly have, it has been argued, an imperialist style of travel writing without a territorial agenda.[62] Iuliia Golovnina makes it clear in her book about the Pamirs, which formed the mountainous border between Russian and British territory, that military resources were employed to protect "lady travellers," especially when they had connections. The presence of women (the expedition also included a female photographer) elicited special responsibility on the part of the government, which assured the safety of travel "s damamy" ("with ladies") providing her expedition not only with a hunting team (essentially, special forces) but also two Cossacks to guard the female travellers.[63] Golovnina focuses much attention on how she handles the duelling requirements of a proper woman's appearance, hygiene, and skin care, with the need to be perceived as a fully responsible participant who could be counted on: "It is often supposed (priniato dumat') that not a single trip 'with ladies' can occur on time; so as to remove from myself such censure (narekanie), I hasten to assure the reader that on our trip holdups (ostanovka) were always **not** because of the ladies: our fellow travelers invariably had to do something urgent at the last minute."[64] The idea that women would be a drag on the efficiency of an expedition is likely evoked by the episode in Nabokov's novel *The Gift*, when the protagonist's mother's attempt to join his father's lepidoptera expedition in Tashkent is met with his insistence that she turn around and go home, back to St. Petersburg, an order she obeys.[65]

As Mills points out, another complicating aspect of women's writing was that it was read differently than men's, so that an account of a particular group of people or way of life might be read as ethnographic when written by a man, but merely as a domestic or travel account when written by a woman.[66] Arguably these issues are most salient in the cases of two of the women I address here, Elena Blavatskaia (more famously known as Madame Blavatsky) and Aleksandra Potanina. Blavatskaia's notoriety and propensity to embellish have often led to dismissals of her travel literature as "purple prose" or simply as problematically untruthful, a critique underscored by her often idiosyncratic and even morally questionable behaviour towards others, and therefore better left unaddressed or ignored.[67] In the case of Potanina, many commentators waver on whether she was actually an ethnographer or whether she was more of an assistant to her husband, albeit one who also wrote ethnographically flavoured travel accounts and stories and recorded the appearance of people and items with her drawings.

Another notable aspect of women's writing in these genres of the period is that women were typically never alone, partly due to the circumstances of group travel, partly due to the cultural customs and norms – with the "impropriety" of women being on their own during travel perhaps correctly justified at least in part by the real danger they might incur if they were alone. Therefore, much narration is in the first-person plural; sometimes the composition of this "we" can be easily determined, but sometimes it is rather vague. This aspect of women's lives in this territory, in particular, may help explain the frequent defaulting from a male narrator (matching her pseudonym) to a we-narrator in Apreleva's fiction, which is almost never defined in terms of its composition but seems to speak often from the perspective of a couple. Russian noblewomen rarely could be alone in a landscape or a social setting, so Apreleva's narrator, while officially and grammatically male, may be representative of women's typical social experience. The "we," however, also becomes extremely flexible, encompassing everything from an undefined "more than one person" to a couple, a family, or even ultimately much of the Russian-speaking world. Male travellers also often used "we," of course, but it was not one that necessarily encompassed women. The near impossibility of being alone in a landscape, as Sara Mills points out, also complicates the use of the sublime for women writers.[68]

Changing Tropes in a New Landscape

It is significant that the Golden Age of Russian literature took place during a major military expansion into the Caucasus in the early part of the nineteenth century; many literary texts from this time period, which coincided with Russian Romanticism, cemented numerous literary tropes and narratives, often originally deriving from European sources, into Russianized forms produced in the setting of the Caucasus. The landscape of the Caucasus, in particular, was codified in different ways, with the forbidding and cold mountains serving often as metaphorical warriors, sentinels, or turbaned heads, while the warmer valleys could often be seen as feminized and welcoming, or at least vulnerable, in part a testament to the political and ethnic differences in the North Caucasus as opposed to the Trans-Caucasus.[69] As the Russian empire continued its expansion, after the Crimean War and the defeat of Shamil, into Central Asia, the focus of Russian literature became more diffuse and its register turned to realism; although Tolstoy produced numerous pieces set in the Caucasus even until his latest years, most other writers turned their gaze elsewhere. Dostoevsky, for example, chronicled his imprisonment in Siberia and utilized it in such texts as *Crime and Punishment*; later he also produced political commentary and poetry on Russia's expansion into Central Asia. Turgenev focused primarily on domestic Russian issues, with an eye towards Europe, although he wrote his famous "Croquet at Windsor" in response to the Turkish suppression of the Bulgarians, a part of the Great Game tensions.[70] Chekhov made an epic trip to Sakhalin, writing as a doctor, scientist, and activist, but most of his work was set in "European" Russia, particularly the provinces. Goncharov's *Frigate Pallada* was notable for being focused on the Far East. Russian women writers, such as Karolina Pavlova, Nadezhda Khvoshchinskaia, Evdokiia Rostopchina, and Evgeniia Tur, generally did not write on topics of imperial expansion, although Elena Gan, the mother of Elena Blavatskaia, set a number of her tales in the Caucasus.

Writing on Central Asia, unlike the Caucasus and Trans-Caucasus, was mostly not literary per se, and much of it was done for very practical purposes. The telling of Russia's success in her conquest of Central Asia, perhaps because it happened far more quickly and decisively than in the Caucasus, tended to remain front and centre. For all that the Caucasian mountain dwellers had been seen as dangerous and other, they also fit into paradigms set up in Romantic literature, such as Byron's Turks or his Greeks fighting for their freedom. Orientalist paradigms based more on Near Eastern culture did not always fit Central Asian reality; Pushkin had already mocked "Oriental luxury" in *Journey to Arzrum*. Now faced with harsh and trying terrain and climate, and in the atmosphere of a dominating discourse of realism, available literary paradigms were more domestic and less given to idealization. Indeed, Turkestan was known for "self-absorbed and venal colonizers," as Jeff Sahadeo describes American Eugene Schuyler's view of them; literary and cultural critics like Mikhail Saltykov-Shchedrin satirized the corrupt, opportunistic bureaucrats in the newly settled territory.[71] His "Gospozha Tashkentsy" used motifs that were picked up across literary texts by other writers.[72] Saltykov-Shchedrin's texts described false enlighteners of the "wild East" in Turkestan, who instead of bringing civilization, were oppressive to peasants and filled their own pockets. The heyday of these literary "Tashkentsy," Eleonora Shafranskaia notes, was in the 1860s and 70s, when Tashkent, now "accepted by contemporaries as a part of Russia," "became an ambivalent image: the place of exile and a new 'eldorado,' and one that began to appear in various contemporaneous texts."[73] Shafranskaia makes note of the line "from Smolensk to Tashkent" in a parody poem in Dostoevsky's *Besy* (*The Possessed*), meaning all the way across Russia from west to east. Shafranskaia notes that some seemed to go to Tashkent for their career, some to make what appeared to be easy money, and others out of hopelessness, citing the case of the younger brother of Nikolai Leskov, who went to Tashkent in 1872, and having lived there less than a year, passed away.[74] Shafranskaia describes the many references to "Tashkent and Tashkenters," embedded in multiple texts and subtexts and even in "urban legends, gossip, whispers, rumors."[75] Mentions appear in such texts as Leskov's "Journey with a Nihilist," "Polunoshchniki," and Tolstoy's *Anna Karenina* with its character Vronsky, as well as in memoirs by N.A. Varentsov and literary work by Nikolai Karazin.[76] People who came to characterize Turkestan in writing, Shafranskaia notes, were first and foremost military figures, many of them ethnographers or vostokovedy; these were ultimately also the first "Tashkenters" in Saltykov-Shchedrin's characterization.

Alexander Morrison points out that information on the Russian military bureaucracy in Turkestan is hard to come by but that leadership positions tended to be filled by nobles and officers were stretched thin in terms of responsibilities, while life could be hard and not well paid for many; comparisons to the British bureaucracy in India often favoured the latter.[77] Hans Rogger called Central Asia "Russia's India and Algeria, the place where it was possible to build an empire and one's fortune."[78] Dostoevsky, in his *Writer's Diary*, showed enthusiasm for the Russian conquest, for which he was even willing to rethink his aversion to trains, finding them to be an appropriate way for Russia to effectively expand eastward since they could be used to revitalize the new Asian Russia.[79] He also took close notice of a Russian soldier who refused to betray his Christian faith, as Yuan Gao notes, which led him to underscore the need for Russians to control Central Asia in order to prevent what he considered barbarity.[80]

Figure 0.3. Vasilii Vereshchagin, "Zabytyi" ("The Forgotten [Soldier]"), 1871. Courtesy of Kartinnye Istorii, zen.yandex.ru.

The artist Vasilii Vereshchagin was certainly the foremost creator of Russian images of Central Asia. He chronicled the conquest in paintings that were both beautiful and disturbing, had great success showing his paintings in London and St. Petersburg, but was also criticized.[81] Vereshchagin was himself a participant in the conquest, although he also utilized genre conventions alongside his own knowledge. He "justified Russia's mission in central Asia by invoking Orientalist tropes about despotism, cruelty, fallen glory, and vice" but also "raised disturbing questions about the conquerors themselves," as one critic notes.[82] These "disturbing questions" in fact led to some of Vereshchagin's paintings, notably "Zabytyi" ("The Forgotten [Soldier]") being burned by Vereshchagin himself after the tsar disapproved of them, and some were also banned from being reproduced.[83]

Vereshchagin is alluded to often: Blavatskaia expressed appreciation for his depictions of India, Potanina was a great admirer, Golovnina mentions his depictions of Timurid buildings in Samarkand, while Uvarova defends "Zabytyi" by name in her "Journey to Tashkent and Samarkand." The painting is also described at length (without being named) in one of Apreleva's stories.[84] "Zabytyi" was seen as

Figure 0.4. Vasilii Vereshchagin, "Surprise Attack" ("Napadaiut vrasplokh"), 1871. Courtesy of Wikimedia Commons and the Yorck Project.

problematic because it showed a man who had to be left behind by his fellow Russian soldiers, but numerous commentators, including Uvarova and arguably also Apreleva, indicate that those who criticize do not understand the unforgiving conditions in Central Asia, where an effort to save one man could lead to the death of many others. Vereshchagin also created a powerful iconography of the Russian soldiers in their white shirts.

Russian Turkestan was very much a man's domain, and a military theatre, which makes it particularly meaningful to focus on women writers in this study. Not least, as scholar Fritjof Schenk notes, autobiographical material by women has been particularly overlooked as a source of information about the discursive construction of the Russian empire.[85] There is much to be gained, he notes, by examining the ways in which a member of the Russian elite understood the contours of the Russian empire, what was "near" and what was "far," how a woman memoirist might interpret the "civilizing mission" of the Russian government, and how she herself might perform as a *de facto* representative of the empire. The greater latitude in describing emotion, for example, can give insights into an experience that is otherwise characterized by writings far more controlled by restrictive genre and gender expectations. Even in non-autobiographical genres, such as Elena Apreleva's short stories, particular kinds of characters and issues are emphasized, not always in the way one might expect. Two of Apreleva's stories address the frustrations and disappointments of marriage not from a woman's point of view, but from a man's, and are closely inflected by the concerns and conditions of Russians living in Turkestan.[86] The writers whose work is studied here were keenly aware of, and in most cases wrote explicitly about, the Russian conquest and the Russian colonial project in Turkestan and often also emphasized the rivalry with England. Apreleva's Central Asian sketches extensively addressed the topic of Russian rule in Central Asia and its consequences, explicitly bringing up the question of nationalism and patriotism or civic duty (often called "grazhdanstvennost'"). At the same time, with the exception of the strongly Anglophobic Elena Blavatskaia, who critiqued the British in India at every turn, the women whose work is studied here definitely felt themselves to have more in common with other educated Europeans than with the local peoples of Central Asia, Mongolia, China, or India. Travel in these regions reinforced upper-class women's identity as "European," while Apreleva, who lived in Central Asia, interrogated the topic of the Russians in Turkestan.

It is also worthwhile to consider writings like these, written at a time when genres that have now solidified into geography, travel writing, and scientific writing were still fluid, and amateur lovers of nature and science could still contribute to scientific knowledge.[87] As Jeanne Kay Guelke and Karen Morin point out, "smaller lives and lesser figures" are no less important or revealing for understanding the rhetorical fabric and practices of a previous time we often think of as populated only by "the greats."[88] Further, the fabric of those who travelled, studied, and commented upon Central Asia, in particular, in this time period was extremely tightly woven and was transnational. For example, the Russian (Polish) officer-explorer Bronislav Grombchevsky met British officer-explorer Francis Younghusband in the Pamirs, and Ol'ga Fedchenko met and translated the work of British Orientalist Henry Yule. When in Tiflis, both the husband–wife British travellers the Littledales and the Golovnins, the Russian Pamir travellers, stopped to visit Dr. Gustav Radde, the curator of the Tiflis Museum and a specialist of flora and fauna of the Caucasus.[89] Uvarova worked on publications with Radde, while the Dukhovskois met with him in Paris while they attended the 1900 Paris Exhibition.[90] Both Praskov'ia Uvarova and Iuliia Golovnina, at different times, stayed at the home of General N.I. Korol'kov when they visited Tashkent, and Golovnina's husband met General Dukhovskoi, the governor-general of Turkestan, thanking him for his assistance in authorizing the trip.[91] The Golovnins also met V.F. Oshanin, the geographer and traveller and the friend and colleague of the Fedchenkos. Those who were well known and "important" were connected to those who were not; noble status and education brought disparate figures together.

For many women in Russia at the time, and for several of the writers examined here, women's rights were of particular importance, following the general interest in the "woman question" that had begun in Russia in the 1850s, 60s, and beyond; these concerns affected not only Russian women's sense of their rights and potential but also carried over in many cases (and helped to justify) Russian conquest, especially over Muslim populations.[92] Concern about the status of women varies among the writers considered here, but women's issues were often foregrounded in the study and presentation of Turkestan. When Aleksandr Geins, formerly an assistant to General Kaufman, the first governor-general of Turkestan, wrote up a catalogue to accompany Vasilii Vereshchagin's famous exhibit of Central Asian paintings in 1874, he emphasized the difficult life of women in Turkestan. Russian policy towards Muslims in Turkestan tended towards "ignorirovanie," or "disregard," but administrators struggled with the human rights component of this policy, especially as it affected women living under tight religious rules.[93] This aspect of the "civilizing mission" was prominent in the accounts discussed here, and in general women's rights were an important issue. Potanina's friends, when they created a collection of her work after her death, emphasized not only her scholarly ethnographic work on women's lives but also her support of other women teachers and students, and her example to them as a woman scholar; when she gave a lecture in Irkutsk at the Geography Department the writers of her biography noted: "I cannot not recall with what trepidation was met the news that Aleksandra Viktorovna would be giving a paper (delat' doklad). A woman in the department – this was an unknown sight for Irkutsk. She was very concerned, reading, but we worried no less, we young teachers and female gymnasium students, we felt that we were present precisely at an equalization of the human rights of women."[94] Potanina by all accounts attained expertise in her topic precisely by focusing on women's lives. It is clear that the writers examined here all considered themselves to play a role in, at a minimum, the success of Russia in Central Asia, the successful incorporation of the territories taken by Russia into the empire and into the sphere of places and experiences that could be considered a part of Russia.

Although many writers of this era used their knowledge of the Caucasus, both from a literary and a practical point of view, and depended on their readers' knowledge of it, in order to make sense of Central Asia, Central Asia was also a new space that was in many ways incommensurate with the Caucasus. Most writers emphasized Baku as the last familiar stop on the itinerary; once the Caspian had been crossed, they felt they had arrived in a new and completely unknown place. Likewise, in describing her travels to India, Blavatskaia also related readers back to the Caucasus and Romantic literature in order to offer comparisons of the two types of imperial and colonial relationships and to orient the reader to a less-familiar Oriental space. Women of the Caucasus had been highly stylized in Russian literature; native girls might be either sirens or victims, while Russian society women who found themselves in the Caucasus could be shown as engaging in society games, such as Lermontov's Princess Mary, or as potential kidnapping victims.[95] By contrast, the women of Central Asia and India depicted in these narratives appeared in numerous different ways, typically with more specificity and realism, given the tenor of the times. Most foreign visitors remarked, for example, that the nomad women were more independent than women in towns and villages, were more highly valued in their own society, and typically did not cover their faces, while Muslim women in the towns were treated with much less respect in their own milieu and typically had to cover up. The motif of the need to free Central Asian women from their bondage was widespread and appeared in all the accounts except Potanina's (who was primarily concerned about the oppression of Chinese women and girls, as well as Russian peasant women), Blavatskaia's, who focused on the need to free Indian women from oppression, and Ol'ga Fedchenko's, whose personal writing was quite limited.[96] The editor of Vladimir Nalivkin and Maria Nalivkina's ethnographic account on women of the Fergana valley notes that the woman question may have led them to focus particularly on women in their study.[97] Many of the women writers were women of the sixties or post-sixties years, with greater education and more opportunities than women of previous generations. Potanina, the daughter of a priest, had what was doubtless an entirely different life because of her education and her affiliation with her explorer husband.

Arguably the representation in these texts could be called something like "ethnographic Orientalism" – while many of the older tropes and patterns of Orientalism remained, such as seeing Central Asian and other people of the region as "other," categorizing them by appearance, and attributing some form of "backwardness" to them, there was some self-consciousness about these patterns, even an undercutting of them, and to most of the writers, facts as they saw them mattered, and specimens, artefacts, and examples, including photographs or drawings, were required in order to create a full picture. The constant collection of specimens, including human ones, as well as the increasing emphasis on artefacts and exhibitions, influenced the way Central Asia was represented. Vereshchagin, the most famous representer of Central Asia, notably displayed his paintings in a very deliberate way, organizing backdrop, arrangement, and captioning, and displaying them in and among various artefacts from the region, evoking both the realist styling of the panorama, which consisted of real-life objects in the foreground receding to a painted background, in *trompe l'oeil* fashion, as well as the ethnographic exhibition, a common undertaking in which Ol'ga Fedchenko, Varvara Dukhovskaia, and Praskov'ia Uvarova participated.[98] Fedchenko, as an artist herself, created her own artistic view of Turkestan, probably without having seen any of Vereshchagin's work. Vereshchagin's paintings also challenged the viewer's understanding of who was ultimately responsible for war, victory, defeat, cruelty, and the like; as Oleg Tarasov points out, his reliance on norms of photography was creating a "battlefield without a hero," along with other painters of his time.[99] And as Schimmelpenninck van der Oye points out, Vereshchagin, interestingly enough, depicted few women, a major staple of Orientalist painting of the Romantic period.[100] Vereshchagin's depiction of Turkestan was influential and affected how Russian Turkestan was seen and understood; his great notoriety meant that first-time visitors essentially saw the region through the lens of his paintings.

By this point, "Orientalism" has numerous meanings and a long history, while Russia's relationship with Orientalism and the "Orient" has its own special valences. For my purposes here, it should be said that all the writers under consideration felt themselves to be, and often called themselves, "Europeans," an identity which they opposed, in the sense of Edward Said's famous book, to "Orientals" or "Asians." The cultural, historical, and civilizational divide between those who felt themselves to be a part of "Europe" and those who were from what was understood to be Asia, was generally taken as a given, even among those most sympathetic to people from Asia. Except for Elena Blavatskaia, the writers discussed here felt themselves to be a part of the "civilizing mission" that would bring Asia into a more sophisticated, "civilized," and improved state, one which, it was typically understood, would value and enact orderliness, cleanliness, and hygiene, women's rights as then understood, the development of technology, and often the abandonment of religious "fanaticism." Concomitantly, research had to be done in order to understand the past, catalogue the geography, humanity, flora and fauna of new regions, and generally map and assimilate new knowledge and data both into the Russian empire and into the overall European scientific project. At the same time, as Daniel Brower and Edward Lazzerini point out, there is always an "other" looking back, creating a two-way appraisal, and no less important, Russians themselves have long been Orientalized by Western Europeans, as well as by themselves.[101] And indeed, "to describe the natives was to depict Russia, and it was not necessarily a flattering picture."[102] Added to this distinction was the class distinction; these writers were all educated, most were members of the nobility; hence at times Russian peasants seemed to them nearly as distant as any "natives" they encountered. While the women addressed here left disparate accounts about a broad range of places from Central Asia to India to China, their work helps indicate the kind of imperial consciousness they inscribed in their writings, artwork, and daily lives. Secure in their own identity as representatives of a civilizing and scientific class, their view of the Russian empire was usually an endorsement of Russian practices and participation in them. Anglo-India often loomed as rival, comparator, and sometimes threat, but these Russians usually felt, however mistakenly, that they were more humane, more accepting of difference, and more aware of the negative consequences of empire than their chief rivals.

Russia's Peripheries

This study owes much to those who laid the groundwork in situating the Russian empire and the construction of self-modelling that could encompass both its European and Asiatic identities, such as Mark Bassin, Richard Wortman, Vera Tolz, and Andreas Kappeler.[103] Scholars who have addressed Russian literature of empire in regard to the Caucasus and Trans-Caucasia, such as Susan Layton, Harsha Ram, Peter Scotto, Natan Eidel'man, Iurii Lotman, and more recently, not only Russian literature, such as Rebecca Gould and Leah Feldman, have helped to explore and explain the complexity of Russia's literary identity and its non-Russian interlocutors.[104] Alexander Etkind has examined the concept of Russia's internal colonization, while David Schimmelpenninck van der Oye, Susanna Lim, and Edyta Bojanowska have explored Russia's engagement with its identity vis-à-vis the Far East.[105] Russia-focused historians of Central Asia, such as Alexander Morrison with his *Russian Rule in Samarkand, 1868–1910, The Russian Conquest of Central Asia*, as well as numerous articles on the history of Russians in Central Asia in the nineteenth century, have carefully reframed and differentiated Russia's own colonial role in Central Asia from that of England's role in the advancement into India and Afghanistan.[106] Jeff Sahadeo's many articles, as well as his *Russian Colonial Society in Tashkent, 1865–1923* provide both historical perspective and a great deal of cultural context having to do with Russians' lives and practices in Central Asia.[107] Adeeb Khalid and Daniel Brower have provided important analysis of Turkestan, while Svetlana Gorshenina has written insightfully on art and art collectors, and Jennifer Keating on the aesthetics of landscape in Russian Central Asia.[108] Commentators such as Tolz,

Hermann Kreutzmann, and Eleonora Shafranskaia, as well as Nicholas Breyfogle and Nathaniel Knight, have noted how instrumental the role of government officials, military officers, and scientists were in creating mechanisms of the collection and dissemination of knowledge about Russia in Asia, such as organizations, publications, expeditions, exhibitions, and the commission of reports.[109]

Conceptualizing the status of Turkestan and other "peripheries" is a special topic of its own; Alberto Masoero's "Territorial Colonization in Late Imperial Russia: Stages in the Development of a Concept" indicates the complexity of terminology by the Russian state when describing its "peripheries," with a hesitation to name various regions as "colonies," at least in some contexts, lest they be understood as places that might develop their own separate political systems.[110] A great deal of nuance has been added to the discussion of individual ethnic groups in Central Asia by such scholars as Charles Steinwedel with his *Threads of Empire: Loyalty and the Tsarist Authority in Bashkiria, 1552–1917* or Virginia Martin's *Law and Custom in the Steppe: The Kazakhs of the Middle Horde and Russian Colonialism in the Nineteenth Century.*[111] Russian expansion and colonization to the east was closely intertwined with the building of the Trans-Siberian Railway. Steven Marks's *Road to Power*, Christan Wolmar's *To the Edge of the World*, as well as work by Claudia Weiss and Anindita Banerjee, have examined the power relations and imperial goals inherent in the massive project, which was heavily emphasized by the Russians at the 1900 Paris World Exhibition and was enhanced and advertised there by its representation in a moving panorama, a special category of display and entertainment that mixed art, illusion, and reality.[112] Technologies of photography, telegraphy, the railway, and highly regular steamship travel across the Caspian also played a huge role in the kinds of travel that took place and writing that could be produced in connection to Russia's eastern peripheries.

Composition of the Chapters

In order to look at multiple knowledge spheres and social conventions that constitute the practices that define a "woman's empire," I focused on three main areas. First, that of the role of the Russian woman in her "domestic" domain, whether fulfilling the role of an official representative of the empire or recording the effect of the Russian conquest and the newly Russian-controlled towns of Samarkand and Tashkent, as well as the experiences of Russians and non-Russians in those areas. Second, I look at Russian women's travel in the context of the "Great Game": Blavatskaia's travel in India, performing a constant critique of the Raj while spouting propaganda about Russia's own imperial policies, as well as Iuliia Golovnina's participation in a trophy-hunting contest thinly disguised as a zoological expedition, made against the backdrop of rival British hunter-explorers. Third, I examine writings from women who were scientists or scholars in their own right, along with one who accompanied her husband on a research trip by boat along the Amu-Darya and who participated in several Congresses of Naturalists and Physicians. These women received varying amounts of official recognition for their work, operating in some contexts as "honorary men," and perceived themselves as participants in exploration and civilization, assisting in re-inscribing territory in European terms.

Part One: Writing from Within

The first two chapters focus on writing "from within" the imperial endeavour. The first chapter addresses Varvara Dukhovskaia's (1854–1931) several memoirs, which are known for the fact that they come from someone highly placed in Russian society: a member of the prominent Golitsyn family, well off, and married to a highly regarded general and governor-general who served in the Caucasus, the Far East, and Turkestan.[113] Clearly not motivated by a desire to put down roots in any of the colonized areas to which her husband was posted, Dukhovskaia wrote in order to defend her sense of self-worth and to undercut the contradiction between her high status and the restrictions of her gender. By writing, she affirmed her importance in the world and the rightness of her viewpoints. While addressing Dukhovskaia's own sense of imperial consciousness, the memoirs also reveal many of the methods by which the empire was reinforced by its officials (and their family members, who often served as *de facto* government representatives, required to hold receptions, head charities, and the like), and importantly, how its psychological costs might be measured. Having begun her career in publishing by emphasizing her intrepid journey amid war, disease, and danger travelling from the Turkish border to Erzerum to join her husband and, having joined him there, closely assisting him in the governing of the city, Dukhovskaia seemed to want to retain that level of notoriety and importance in her later life but had to resort primarily to continued memoirs emphasizing her status and knowledge of events.

The second chapter of Part One focuses on Elena Apreleva's (1846–1923) Central Asian sketches, written under a male pseudonym. This was a wide-ranging set of sketches, published in popular journals, written from the point of view of a male narrator who, over the course of the stories, moved to Central Asia and became at home there, raising a family with attendant Russian and local servants. The stories, however, de-centre the writing self, and often even Russians, from the narrative. As published after her death, a collection of Apreleva's stories edited by her sons includes most of her best stories but tends to leave out the most disparate, non-Russian-focused narratives. Over multiple stories, the narrator chronicles aspects of Russian Turkestani domestic life, depicting a broad array of topics such as the tribulations of resettled peasants, the resentments of Russians tasked to carry out a "civilizing mission" far from home, the corruption of bureaucrats, and not least of all, the narratives of the local people as Russians took over their home. In some cases, this meant an end to slavery or religious persecution – in others, it meant a profound displacement of identity and loss of an independent way of life. Apreleva, under the guise of her typically male narrator, also shows the mindset of various Russian figures, including women, successful and unsuccessful bureaucrats, doctors, and military officers, and not infrequently touches on dark topics such as suicide and violence. A final piece, written from her own point of view and under her real name, chronicles a harrowing train trip back to European Russia in 1906 amid evident social collapse.

Part Two: Theosophy, Hunting, and Constructing the Nation in the Shadow of the Great Game

Russia's rivalry with England and the Russian sense of itself as an empire was always in the background in the later nineteenth century. The discourse of Russian imperialism often included a sense that Russia was itself akin to Asia and therefore that Russians had a special relationship to their "East" that countries such as England or France did not.[114] Part of this was a response, of course, to the Orientalization of Russia by Europe, but there was a growing sense as the nineteenth century went on that Russia should see its proximity to the East as an advantage. The first chapter of Part Two focuses on two of Elena Blavatskaia's (1831–91) travel narratives in India, *From the Caves and Jungles of Hindostan* and *The Durbar at Lahore*, and how they formulated both Russian imperial identity and Blavatskaia's own stake in this identity as a proponent of Russia's similarity to "the East," as well as Russia's superiority to England in the realm of empire and as a statement against racism, misogyny, and what Mary Pratt has called disembodied "imperial eyes."[115] Like many British women, whom she generally made a point of disparaging at every opportunity, Blavatskaia decried such things as sati, infanticide, child marriage, and oppressive marriage practices, but she did so as a Theosophist, a Russian patriot, and an Anglophobe. Her defence of

Russian imperial practices, although not in regard to the treatment of women, in part seemed to excuse Russia's own advances into Central Asia, which were occurring as she wrote and which she wholeheartedly supported. Likewise, like many reformers, both Indian and not, she denigrated the Moghul time period in India, calling the Moghuls the "dregs of Islam from Central Asia": "Hindostan was actually settled by Moslems, but not at all by enlightened Saracens. With the exception of the kings, direct descendants of Mohammed through the caliphs of Baghdad, the rest of the Mogul population, the people and the army, were the dregs of Islam ("otreb'em islama") from Central Asia."[116] In this regard, Blavatskaia blames many of the ills of Indian society on the previous invasion of India by the Muslims of Central Asia, Russia's then-current foe. The concept of a great but fallen "Aryan" civilization was certainly part of thinking at the time; Blavatskaia follows contemporaneous German Orientalists in dividing Indian history "into two halves (each with a further line down the middle): the period of 'free, independent India' and the period of 'foreign domination.'"[117] This was also typical of Hindu nationalist thinking, which relegated the Islamic period to a place essentially outside Indian history.[118] Blavatskaia combines travel narrative with political and Theosophical discourse, performing the role of a Russian patriot moving through British-controlled, exotic space.

The second chapter of Part Two focuses on Russian-controlled territory close to the British sphere of influence and concerns a far more obscure, but doubtless more straightforwardly written, woman's account. Iuliia Golovnina's (exact dates unknown) 1902 *In the Pamirs: Notes of a Woman Traveler* is also greatly informed by Russia's rivalry with England. Golovnina describes a zoological expedition that was, in effect, a part of the great trophy-hunting rivalry between Russia and England, and during the course of which she compares herself to Mrs. St. George Littledale, a British woman who was by all accounts the first foreign woman to travel in the Pamirs and whose husband was, according to Lord Curzon, "the first Englishman who has ever shot a male specimen of this famous and inaccessible animal [Ovis Polii]," while his wife was "the first, and so far the last, English lady who ever saw the Pamirs."[119] As is clear from Golovnina's account, there was essentially a race among "European" women to reach far parts of the globe, as well as a hunting rivalry among men.[120] Golovnina's expedition included a second woman as well, who served as the photographer of the trip, making it more unusual than many such expeditions, even if they were not necessarily actually the second and third "European" women to be in the remote Pamirs, given that some Russian officers' wives had preceded them. Golovnina's landscape descriptions engage multiple aspects of travel literature, using panoptic, sublime, and picturesque modalities to describe the landscape, and she includes ethnographic descriptions and a discussion of the politics of Russian control of Turkestan.

Part Three: Imperial Knowledge: Women Scientists, Archaeologists, and Ethnographers

Several women took part in scientific or exploratory expeditions to Central Asia, Mongolia, Tibet, and China, with their associated discursive practices, such as the collection of specimens; the recording and documenting of zoological, botanical, and meteorological information; the description and depiction of landscapes; the coordination and funding of these activities by government and various scientific societies; the publication of the results; and the display of materials at exhibitions. They were by far the most "official" women proponents of imperial expansion and control and of the appropriation of scientific and cultural knowledge, and they worked on the front lines – literally, in a sense, during Ol'ga Fedchenko's military expeditions, and figuratively during Aleksandra Potanina's government-sponsored expeditions. This was very much a sphere dominated by men, and one that took place in a national and international scholarly context, but a number of women participated in these expeditions, generally as spouses first and foremost, but once the project was underway, their role often expanded into that of full-fledged (if typically unpaid and often officially unrecognized) expedition participant.[121] In this regard, I analyse the writing and work of an ethnographer, Aleksandra Potanina (1843–93); a botanist, Ol'ga Fedchenko (1845–1921); an archaeologist, Praskov'ia Uvarova (1840–1924); and a spouse participating on a river expedition along the Amu-Darya, Anna Rossikova (exact dates unknown). Three of them participated in expeditions in Central Asia; the fourth, Potanina, in Mongolia, Tibet, and China. While these were generally enthusiastic participants in the project, their very bodily existence in space was different from that of their male counterparts, their view of their roles in these expeditions varied from person to person, and their range of emotional reactions to their travel and projects was typically quite broad. Many of these texts participated in the conventions of travel writing and the writing of ethnography, presenting complex intersectional constructions of the writing subject.

A guide indicating relevant information about each featured writer can be found in the Guide to Writers.

Writer	Professional status	Focus of journey	Territory discussed	Travel companion(s)
Elena Apreleva (1846–1923), *Sredne-aziatskie ocherki*, 1890s–1906	Professional writer	Some travel described, observations of local life (quasi-fictional)	Central Asia	Lived with husband, implied narrator has family
Elena Blavatsky (1831–91), *From the Caves & Jungles, The Durbar at Lahore* (1880s)	Theosophist, writer, propagandist	To develop theosophy in India	India, both physical and spiritual	Olcott and other local and "European" Theosophists, servant
Varvara Dukhovskaia (1854–1931) *Diary of a Russian Lady, Turkestanskie vospominaniia, Moi vospominaniia*, Erzerum article	Memoirist, official's wife	Accompanying husband on job postings	Extensive, primarily Caucasus, Far Eastern Russia, Central Asia, also Europe and U.S.	Husband
Ol'ga Fedchenko (1845–1921), edited *Journey to Turkestan*, published own illustrations, other botanical works	Botanist, artist	Scientific expeditions with husband to Turkestan under Kaufman	Central Asia	Husband, other scientists, military convoy in some cases
Iuliia Golovnina (dates unknown, approximately 1860–1940), *Na Pamirakh*, 1902	Fellow traveler, cashier of expedition	Research trip/hunting trip	Pamirs, journey through Caucasus and Central Asia	Husband, four other Russian nobles, military, servants
Aleksandra Potanina (1843–93), *Iz puteshestvii po Vostochnoi Sibiri, Mongolii, Tibetu i Kitaiu*	Traveler, ethnographer/folklorist, illustrator	Scientific expeditions with husband	Mongolia, Buriatia, China, Tibet	Husband and colleagues
Anna Rossikova (dates unknown, approx. 1860–1930), two articles on Amu-Darya, 1899	Traveler, travel writer	River journey on Amu-Darya accompanying husband	Central Asia	Husband
Praskov'ia Uvarova (1840–1924), "Poezdka v Tashkent i Samarkand," 1891	President of Imperial Moscow Archaeological Society, invited guest to Turkestan Exhibition of 1890	Tashkent, Samarkand (via Caucasus)	Central Asia	Family members, other dignitaries, Russian officials

Figure 0.5. Guide to Writers: A Woman's Empire

PART ONE

Women and Empire: Imperial Domesticity and Its Discontents

Chapter One

Reinforcing the State at the Imperial Periphery: The Governor-General's Wife

Varvara Fedorovna Dukhovskaia was a noblewoman from a prominent family who wrote several accounts of her life as the wife of a highly placed general and official of the tsarist government, allowing her readers the opportunity to vicariously experience the perspective of wealthy and highly placed administrators of the Russian empire. Well educated and well travelled, fluent in several languages, Dukhovskaia (1854–1931) was in many ways clever and perspicacious, but she was also very much a woman of her time, firmly ensconced in a privileged status that recognized few others as equals. Her writing career started successfully with a two-part article called "From the Diary of a Russian Woman in Erzerum," which chronicled her daring trip in March 1878 over snowy, treacherous mountain passes to reach her husband, Sergei Dukhovskoi, the governor of that city under Russian occupation during the Russo-Turkish War of 1877–8, and her stay there with him until the end of the Russian occupation later that year.[1] After the Caucasus, the Dukhovskois lived in Moscow, then in the Russian Far East, and finally Turkestan, with General Dukhovskoi rising ever higher in rank. After her article about Erzerum, which was republished, she wrote *Iz moikh vospominanii* (*From My Reminiscences*), published in 1900, as well as a continuation, *Turkestanskie vospominaniia* (*Turkestan Reminiscences*), published in 1913.[2] In 1917 she published an English-language version of her memoirs in their entirety, *Diary of a Russian Lady: Reminiscences of Barbara Doukhovskoy (née Princesse Galitzine)*.[3] The English version of her memoirs is something of an amalgam of the other three accounts, but with significant edits; it also contains new and expanded material that is not in any of the Russian versions.

Dukhovskaia's article about Erzerum was an up-to-the-minute and lively "behind the scenes" look at Russian rule in the city. It addressed not only the military operations but the ongoing typhoid outbreak in the area,

Figure 1.1. Varvara Dukhovskaia in 1900. Courtesy of Wikimedia Commons.

which killed thousands, including many members of the military; the eruptions of hostilities between Turks, Kurds, and Armenians; and also the daily life of Dukhovskaia and her husband, including Dukhovskaia's terror, as a newlywed, of losing her husband to either battle or disease. That she deals with this fear by insisting on joining him at every posting, despite attempts to prevent her, as a woman, from doing anything danger-ous or socially questionable, is part of the interest of the narrative, which was published alongside such items as memoirs and a political article by the famous ethnographer Arnol'd Zisserman.[4] One can catch a sense of the flavour of Dukhovskaia's approach as well as of her self-importance in the following quotation from her English-language memoirs:

> March 17th. – My arrival caused the greatest excitement among the Chris-tian inhabitants of Erzeroum. They are all singing my praises for hav-ing come out here by those shocking roads, and they say that I certainly deserve a medal as a reward for my bravery.
>
> Was it curiosity to see a European woman, or was it a desire to show devotedness to the Russians? Perhaps both reasons together made visitors overflow our drawing-room. All the big wigs of the town came to pay their respects to me.[5]

Dukhovskaia's article was certainly timely, with the first part appear-ing in August 1878, while the Russians still held Erzerum; the second part, appearing in November, included description of the September handover of the city to the Turks. Given her own bravery in travelling to Erzerum, through snow and treacherous roads, a typhoid epidemic, and social unrest, and how closely she worked together with her hus-band in administering the occupied city, with its many competing reli-gions, ethnicities, and political factions, Dukhovskaia experienced great appreciation for her personal qualities and ability to work and serve with her husband. Arguably in her further writing, she hoped to regain this pinnacle of positive notoriety both for her conduct and her writing, for which she was even invited to the Pushkin Celebration of 1880.[6]

Dukhovskaia, who was a member of the highest nobility in Russia, a princess Golitsyna, found every detail of her life to be important, mean-ingful, and worth recording. In part, this comes from her upbringing – a quasi-only child, spoiled by her own account, popular, wilful, sur-rounded by luxury and with extremely elevated social connections. She could not but see herself as important, her views and experiences of interest to others; she also experienced early success and satisfaction in her writing and was encouraged by it. Caught up in her husband's career trajectory and its demands both on her and on him, she needed a counterweight of her own, a project that partook of the highly valued Russian occupation, writing. Strenuously declaring her allegiance to her husband and to the Russian imperial project, this avowed subjection to him and, likely, her own inner rebelliousness led her at times to undercut her own message; she not infrequently admitted to resentment, depression, loneliness, and homesickness.

Indeed, the tension between Dukhovskaia's pride in her position and her frustration at being parted from family, friends, and the extensive cultural life available to a high-born Russian is evident throughout Varvara Dukhovskaia's multiple memoirs. It is certainly clear from the very beginning of Dukhovskaia's longest, 599-page memoir, *Iz moikh vospominanii*, that her life was shaped by the narrative, and the practice, of empire.[7] Dukhovskaia grew up in Kharkhiv and on her family estate, Dolzhik (present-day Ukraine).[8] She paints the portrait of a loyal, mischievous child of members of prominent Russian noble families. Brought up with the usual governesses of upper-class families, she learned French and English and was taken to St. Petersburg for several social seasons; she was acquainted with the tsar and many other members of the royal family. She also went abroad, travelling in France, Germany, England, and Italy. In 1876, at twenty-two, she married Sergei Mikhailovich Dukhovskoi (1838–1901), a highly regarded military officer who had already achieved the rank of general at thirty-six, likely in part due to his extensive service in the Caucasus.

Dukhovskaia's narrative of her life together with her husband reflects the history of Russian imperial development in the nineteenth century – she met her future husband in the Caucasus and travelled with him to postings in Tiflis, Kars, Erzerum, Moscow, Khabarovsk, and finally Tashkent, with intermittent trips to the capital and to her home estate. From the very beginning of her marriage she played a role in representing Russian government, both out of desire and out of necessity. Dukhovskoi attained ever-higher military ranks, was appointed governor-general of the Pri-Amur province, and finally governor-general of Turkestan. Her memoirs have been utilized as sources by multiple scholars.[9]

Dukhovskaia and her husband were nearly always situated not in the northern or western territories of the empire, where Russian cultural superiority could not be claimed, but rather in the Caucasus, Far East, and Central Asia, where it was assumed. Dukhovskaia always seems to feel sure of her civilizing mission, her cosmopolitan status. And indeed, with her multilingual education and extensive opportunities to travel the world, as well as through broad swaths of the Russian empire, she was certainly cosmopolitan. The cover of her first book featured a map showing in red the places she had travelled (see Figure 1.2).

Figure 1.2. Cover of Dukhovskaia's *Iz moikh vospominanii* (*From My Reminiscences*). (Golike and Vil'borg, St. Petersburg, 1900). Courtesy of Google Books.

Dukhovskaia establishes from the beginning of her narrative *Iz moikh vospominanii* that she intended to be not merely a spectator or detached spouse but a keen observer and participant in the official life of her husband. Despite an introduction by Konstantin Sliuchevskii, the poet and lifelong friend of her husband, in which he makes the not-unusual claim (for women writers) that Dukhovskaia never intended to publish her diaries, it is evident throughout her accounts that she was quite focused on publishing, and of course had done so already by 1878; Sliuchevskii himself admired the article, whose title included the word "diary" in it.

In an article on Varvara Dukhovskaia, Fritjof Schenk writes that aside from the value of using women's accounts as a chance to glean important insights about the life of the Russian ruling elite, women memoirists' accounts are valuable because women were allowed a greater emotional range than male memoirists.[10] Sara Mills reminds us that one must always beware of autobiographically oriented texts, be they memoirs or travel writing, since we cannot accept the writer's "self" as a coherent or reliably depicted entity in the first place, especially given differences of context and time period.[11] Nonetheless, there is much to be learned from Dukhovskaia's self-representation and what she chooses to focus on. While generally toeing the Russian official party line, she certainly allowed herself some dissent and some declarations of personal independence. When Dukhovskaia was in the Amur region during her husband's stint as governor-general there in the mid-1890s, Schenk notes, she was treated as a representative of the empress herself, and both there and afterwards in Tashkent as a kind of "first lady."[12] In terms of emotions, one detects along with Dukhovskaia's intense patriotic pride her sadness, loneliness, and the frustration of living life at the opposite end of the continent, far from the Russian capital and the Western European countries that she felt at home in. Indeed, it is remarkable to note how much of Dukhovskaia's writing is about her own frequent melancholy, especially when parted from her husband.

Writing for Dukhovskaia was a way to establish her identity, perspective, and authority. Especially when writing of events of historical prominence – the tsar's coronation, the taking and governing of Erzerum, the Andijan uprising – Dukhovskaia's perspective of someone close to the action, or married to the man in charge, lends her viewpoint a kind of insider's authenticity and authority.[13] Surrounded by privilege, she chooses to emphasize the drawbacks of her station, in many cases, or simultaneously take credit for her high status – the enumeration of bouquets received, for example – while avoiding participating in person. By describing her life both as a private person and as the wife of a prominent government official, Dukhovskaia asserts her own importance and asserts that by their nature, her accounts are valuable. Like royalty or a celebrity, even minor details of her life are treated as noteworthy because of whom they concern.

One aspect of Dukhovskaia's life that was never discussed in her memoirs, however, was the fact that the Dukhovskois did not have any children, nor are there any allusions to such things as miscarriages or apparent infertility (admittedly, such topics were typically taboo). Although it is made clear multiple times to the reader that she had no children, such as at moments when her "children" are alluded to by unaware others or when gifts are given to her presuming that she had children, she never addresses the topic directly, although some hints to her certainty that she would remain childless are evident. She describes, for example, a Chinese general in Khabarovsk who had been invited to dinner: "When drinking my health he congratulated me, through his interpreter, at the forthcoming birth of a son. He said he could read it in my eyes. Foolish man!"[14] One imagines that Dukhovskaia's childlessness, given social expectations of the time, might have played a role both in her frequent depression and in her sense of loneliness, especially when her husband was absent for long stretches. It means, however, that she had, or could portray, a fairly single-minded focus on her husband and his career, and that she had time to write; as Schenk rightly points out, she ends each memoir either when her husband dies (the English version, which came out in 1917), or when he is assigned to Tashkent (the Russian version, which came out in 1900; its sequel, *Turkestanskie vospominaniia*, was published in 1913 and also ends with the death of Dukhovskaia's husband). According to some sources she lived another thirty years after he died, but in her texts no allusion is made to her life after his death.[15] Interestingly, none of the four accounts (her two memoirs in Russian, her article on Erzerum, and her English-language memoir) is identical, even when discussing the same time periods; they tend to be distinct from each other in many ways, with the English version being quite different in tone and detail from its Russian forebears, as it was apparently oriented towards a wider, non-Russian audience, and as Schenk points out, might have been intended to act as a kind of anti-revolutionary gesture since it was published in 1917.[16] It leaves out some of the details that a Russian audience would relate to but a foreign audience might find to be too obscure, such as a comparison of the broad, quiet Euphrates River to "our sleepy Little Russian riverlets."[17] There are numerous allusions to Russian writers and literary texts salted through her Russian accounts – at one point, she discusses meeting her "Onegin" in Moscow – her mother tells her to react the same way Tatiana did in Pushkin's novel, with aplomb and without revealing any emotion – but these literary allusions are largely absent in the English-language version.[18] The English version also seems to leave out details that might show Dukhovskaia's husband in a less than perfect light; the English-language description of his visiting a religious school in Russian-controlled Turkish territory, for example, leaves out a sentence in which Dukhovskoi scolds the school officials for not teaching the students in Russian.[19]

A New *Journey to Arzrum?*[20]

It is apparent why readers found Dukhovskaia's article interesting: she begins with her treacherous journey in March 1878 (Erzerum had been taken in February), partially on foot and partially in an improvised side saddle, crossing snow-covered mountains between Aleksándropol', on the border with Turkey and Erzerum. She was warned not to risk her life at every turn. She had waited for months in Aleksandropol', and despite receiving frequent telegrams from her husband, she was no longer willing to stay there alone: one catalyst for her decision to leave was the sight of a dead Cossack officer's clothing being burned in front of her window.[21] Her risky feat was greatly lauded by those around her in Erzerum, including Turkish officials. In her article, she describes the epidemic of typhoid that was killing many acquaintances, the unrest occurring among various ethnic groups, and the numerous gender, linguistic, and religious conflicts that challenged Russian rule. There are frequent mentions of how happy the local Christians (mostly Armenians and Greeks) are at the Russian control of the area, while the Muslims grudgingly accept it. According to Dukhovskaia, after being under Turkish rule, none of the women will appear in public, no matter what their religion, and so Dukhovskaia, appearing both in public and uncovered, causes shock and the appearance of crowds everywhere she goes. The article ends just after her departure in September when the city is officially returned to the Turks, which was part of the agreement in ending the war. The article describes the tensions of the Russian administration trying to keep order, project calm, get the telegraph in working order, and assert their own rights to control the area. Dukhovskaia portrays herself as an active participant, taking part in a mixture of social and diplomatic events, such as church services, dinners, dances, and outings, often on horseback. She also describes episodes of war and violence, alarm over the prevalence of disease, and unrest and concern over retaliation among the local inhabitants, including moments when she feared for her life. The jockeying for power or fair treatment, as the case may be, among local residents, who are a combination of Turks, Kurds, Greeks, and Armenians, along with Russians and some Europeans (numerous foreigners served the Turks as doctors, for example), is vividly told by Dukhovskaia and indicates that administrators of Muslim areas in particular had a difficult balancing act to carry out. In her longer account, *Iz moikh vospominanii*, Dukhovskaia describes the local opposition to the Russians in vivid, gruesome, and arguably patriotic detail: Turkish women beat the wounded Russian soldiers on the day of the storming of Erzerum, one cut the throats of the wounded to avenge her husband, while Kurds desecrated the dead bodies of Russians in their villages.[22] Meanwhile, the Armenians fear the Turks and count on the Russians for protection against them. Dukhovskaia encounters not just ethnic others but Russian religious others; she participates as godmother in the baptism of a Molokan soldier who had sworn to adopt Orthodoxy after surviving a battle and also stays in a Molokan village in Georgia on her way back to Tiflis.[23]

Doubtless, Dukhovskaia's emphasis on her gender was of great interest to her readers; it colours almost every episode she relates, mostly because of the location of her narrative. Dukhovskaia's gender affects what she can do, whom she can see, whom she can meet, and who can travel to meet her. A description of the visit of some high-ranking Turkish women must have been eye-opening to readers; Dukhovskaia had to assure the women that they would meet no men on their way into the house. The women bring along an enslaved Black woman who had been purchased from a harem in Istanbul and openly discuss prices of enslaved people. Dukhovskaia has difficulty in turning away their recommendations that she buy a slave herself and is further shocked by their complete lack of interest about anything happening in the world beyond their own four walls.[24]

Dukhovskaia emphasizes frequently in her narrative that because local women were mostly forbidden (and, at times, overtly threatened) from attending social occasions, she and the French consul's wife, Madame Gilbert, were the only women even at very large social occasions. In her account in English, she describes with some pride the shock waves she created when, attired in a specially designed military-style riding habit, she rides out on her own, calling herself "a young giaour" and noting that Christians were just as bothered as Muslims by the shockingly independent behaviour of the young, married woman.[25] This information is imparted somewhat differently in the 1878 article: in it, Moussa-Pasha, the Turkish pasha returning to take control of Erzerum, praises her for her boldness and tells her that he has inspired lazy Turkish officers and soldiers by telling them of her bravery. He also describes another Turkish leader, Izmail-Pasha, who complained of Dukhovskaia's wanton ways, riding out uncovered in public, which he had claimed to Moussa-Pasha was causing dissension among Armenian and Muslim women and was creating "revolution" in their families.[26] In any case, the descriptions of Erzerum are vivid, the Russians were eager for a behind-the-scenes look at how things were handled there, and Dukhovskaia focuses in detail on the historic goings-on and on her own intrepid behaviour.

The East as a Career[27]

Sergei Dukhovskoi, Dukhovskaia's husband, was from a humbler background than his wife. He was the grandson of a priest and the son of a teacher who later became a government official, but his family was successful; his father left him two houses on the Malaia Italianskaia in St. Petersburg.[28] He graduated from the Cadet Corps, entered the Life Guard Mounted Grenadiers Regiment in 1855, and was enrolled in the Nikolaevskii Engineering Academy, graduating in 1862. He rose steadily through the ranks and spent several years in the Northern Caucasus, undertaking the "cleansing" ("ochishchenie") of local people in what is now Abkhazia, "cleansing" then being a term of art in the military; Dukhovskoi's own account of his time in Erzerum uses the term several times.[29] Many Cossacks were resettled into the property formerly held by the Circassians, something Dukhovskoi also helped to carry out. (The deportation of Circassians to Turkey in 1864 is now recognized as a form of genocide by the Circassians themselves.[30]) His official biography straightforwardly refers to "the obliteration of auls" and "the cleansing of local people (tuzemtsov)."[31] He continued to be promoted and served the Russian army in Kuban and then Tiflis and became a major-general in 1873. He participated in the Russo-Turkish War; was governor of Erzerum, about which Dukhovskaia published her article; and then in 1879 was stationed in Moscow as chief of staff of the Moscow Military District, where he was involved in the coronation ceremonies for Alexander III in 1883. He was appointed Pri-Amur governor-general in 1893 and commanded the Russian navy in the Far East. An 1893 article in *Niva*, announcing his appointment to governor-general of the Pri-Amur, noted: "Our Eastern periphery, at the very height of its cultural and economic development, by will of the Tsar has been given to the care and leadership of an enlightened government statesman, who is the newly appointed Pri-Amur governor-general ... Lt. General Dukhovskoi."[32] He participated in the coronation festivities for Tsar Nicholas II in 1896, and in 1898 was appointed governor-general of Turkestan after the Andijan uprising caused authorities to look for new leadership in Central Asia.[33] It is notable how much time Dukhovskoi spent outside of Russia proper, and further notable that he spent much of his life either engaged in war with subject peoples or dealing with them in administrative terms. Military service in the Caucasus, Far East, or Central Asia was, of course, an excellent way to further one's career, a point emphasized by the counter-example of Tolstoy's fictional Vronsky, who refused his appointment to Tashkent, thereby stalling his career. As Hans Rogger stated, "Central Asia was Russia's India and Algeria, the place where it was possible to build an empire and one's fortune."[34]

Imperial Roles

During her sojourn in Erzerum, when Dukhovskaia and her husband functioned together to represent the Russian government a great deal of the time, she embraced her role as the governor's wife, but she later made greater distinctions between what was required of her and what could be avoided. In the 1917 *Diary* version of her memoirs, she writes at some length about her hatred for society visits and society rules, and her determination to avoid them whenever possible. Such sentiments are alluded to in *Iz moikh vospominanii*, but in her English-language *Diary*, she openly declares that other society women are merely empty-headed mechanical dolls with a penchant for ugly gossip:

> Nothing is more horrible than these "At-Home" days; it is such a nuisance to have to be nice to people whom in the bottom of your heart you despise, and who devote their ample leisure to passing criticisms of no tender character on their friends behind their backs. All these Grandes Dames of the so-called Best World are more like mechanical dolls moving on wires, than living, feeling women. Their lives are framed uniformly on a fixed set of rules, and their gossip is perfectly intolerable to me. They talk either platitudes about chiffons, or make remarks about the weather; they murmer [*sic*] mechanically hospitable phrases, and then tear their guests to pieces and mock the weak points of the very people whose hands they had just pressed.
>
> … People wonder how I manage to kill my time, hiding myself from the world in a monastic seclusion. I am being talked about. "Mrs. This" and "Mrs. That" disapprove of my manner of life which gives rise to comment, but I am hopeless, and they have quite given up trying to reform me.[35]

On the other side of the coin, she claimed she had given her word not to stand in the way of her husband's career as he accepted a position in the Far East, although she did complain about her husband joining the English Club and returning very late from dinners there. She declares, however, that it was "service alone" ("odna sluzhba") that caused him to be absent, and hence she had no right to be angry with him.[36] L.A. Vostrikov and Z.V. Vostokov, who wrote a book on Khabarovsk and Khabarovsk residents and who claim to have used various printed and historical sources (without, however, citing any except for some newspaper articles), assert that it was really Dukhovskaia who controlled their relationship and who was instrumental, using her many connections, in having him promoted to a position in Moscow so she could leave the Caucasus.[37]

There was clearly quite a duality at work in Dukhovskaia's sense of herself as enacter of Russian imperial policy: Dukhovskaia could proudly quote her husband's entire title in full and provide detailed descriptions of the many honours and preparations devoted to the couple's travel, such as their arrival in Vladivostok. She often emphasizes the special attention paid to herself in her official capacity, but these moments of embracing officialdom stand in contrast to her avowed hatred of being in the spotlight, which she developed after her Erzerum days. In the late 1890s, as the couple travelled by train across Central Asia to Tashkent, there were numerous stops where local dignitaries greeted them at the station, bands played music for them, and they were invited to dinners and receptions. Frequently pleading a headache so as to avoid these various ceremonies, dinners, and receptions, Dukhovskaia nonetheless peeped from behind the curtains of her train car to see what was happening and kept close track of gifts given to her despite her absence. It is not necessarily easy to determine how she intended the reader to understand her own reticence – but it is clear that the reader is meant to get a good idea of all of the pomp and circumstance that her husband's position, whatever it was at the moment, elicited, and that she took great pride in it. As Schenk points out, Dukhovskaia went from being someone who only watched scenes of great pomp and display, in the sense of Wortman's "scenarios of power," such as the coronation of Alexander III, as a privileged insider, to one who herself became a part of the empire-instantiating spectacle, something she had effectively also practised in her early days in Erzerum, when her travel feat and her presence in the city impressed so many.

Dukhovskaia describes at length the final ceremonial joining of the railroad line between Vladivostok and Khabarovsk, which happened in 1897. After an unsuccessful attempt, which was supposed to be succeeded by a special dinner, followed by a ball – at four in the morning, it was discovered that the train had gone off the rails the day before, so the journey couldn't be completed – the women in ball gowns went home "angry and hungry" ("zlye i golodnye") and the task of joining the rails was left to be attempted again the next day.[38] This time it was successful and, near a station specifically christened "Dukhovskaia," the governor-general drove in the bolt to connect the two ends. Dukhovskaia writes in one of her most lyrically imperialist passages (absent in the English translation), "A touching picture ensued: the distant depths of the taiga, in the unpierceably dark night, and the completion, in these circumstances, of a mighty event, a train route from the Great Ocean to the Amur, a distance of 760 versts."[39] The description of this event does not specifically indicate whether Dukhovskaia was personally present, but there are no details indicating her own personal point of view, which usually prevailed when she did participate. As they later departed Khabarovsk for St. Petersburg, by train, Dukhovskaia noted with pride the silver plaque on the saloon car that proclaimed Dukhovskoi's role in opening up the new train route.[40]

It seems clear that Dukhovskaia suffered from depression, and according to her narrative of her early youth, she had long been prone to bouts of melancholy. She writes about her unhappiness when the couple's household goods were greatly delayed from arriving in Khabarovsk, when she sought morphine from the doctor: "The ennui gnaws at me, I am becoming extremely thin, I am completely sleepless and asked [Dr.] Pokrovsky for some morphine, but Anastasia Konstantinovna found out about it and so terrified the doctor that he took away the ampoule."[41] Anastasia Konstantinovna, the wife of an officer attached to her husband, had accompanied the Dukhovskois from Moscow all the way to Khabarovsk. This episode, probably due to its sensitive nature, is omitted from the English translation.

When Dukhovskaia did enjoy participating in events, they often consisted of her own performances. Advocating for and performing music was one way Dukhovskaia participated in gendered "civilizing mission" pursuits. She and her husband promoted music, the arts, and education in Khabarovsk. According to the authors of *Khabarovsk i Khabarovchane* (*Khabarovsk and Khabarovsk Residents*), on 24 January 1894, the newspaper *Priamurskie vedomosti* (*Priamur News*), which Dukhovskoi had started, reported: "We have long not seen such a confluence of the intelligent public, thirsting for aesthetic impressions, as at the latest evening of the Khabarovsk musical circle." The authors note that "the concert took place in an over-filled hall, there were many encores, and the president of the musical association, V. F. Dukhovskaia, attired in a Russian sarafan and with a kokoshnik on her head, demonstrated exceptional artistry in playing the mandolin, 'an instrument unknown in the periphery,' as the newspaper explained. 'Svetit mesiats' and 'Korobeinik' brought the public to ecstasy."[42] During a visit by delegates from the emir of Bukhara in Tashkent, she played the concertina for a Benevolent Society event, with listeners demanding, by her later account in English, five encores, earning the sum of 1,300 roubles for the charity.[43] She was ready as well to do what was necessary to keep up good diplomatic relations: "The Bokharian deputies were present at the concert and I wore in their honour the heavy golden necklace presented to me by the Emir. It is fortunate that I had to play instead of singing, because for the great weight of the necklace I could not have drawn one single note out of my throat."[44] The recognition of Dukhovskaia's musical achievements was nonetheless quite compromised by her position, as she herself recognizes: "All the same I had too good sense not to understand that my success was due especially to the position I held, much more than to my talent; it was only green paper laurels that I got, and I should have liked to win real ones and play in other surroundings, with veritable artists and amongst a less partial audience."[45] She makes this even clearer in Russian, calling the setting dilettantish.[46]

Another public endeavour Dukhovskaia enjoyed was providing her writing for charity; she participated in a volume issued for the benefit of sufferers of leprosy in Tashkent, *Turkestanskii literaturynyi sbornik v polzu prokazhennykh* (*Turkestani Literary Collection to Benefit Lepers*), published by the Turkestan Red Cross, contributing "Otryvok iz moikh vospominanii. Cherez Velikii Okean. Iz San-Frantsisko v Iaponiu" ("Excerpt from My Reminiscences. Through the Pacific Ocean from San Francisco to Japan").[47] In addition, she gave the proceeds of her *Iz moikh vospominanii* to the "use of the needy female students who have completed Tashkent Gymnasium."[48]

Scenarios of Power, Micro-politics of Empire

Dukhovskaia was generally more tolerant of the public role that required her to participate in grand public spectacles, such as the unveiling of the Pushkin monument in Moscow in 1880. Dukhovskaia observed the unveiling from a friend's balcony and says she was invited to a dinner in honour of writers, but declined; her husband attended in her stead. She did hear and admire Turgenev's speech.[49] Dukhovskaia relates that during a visit by Alexander III to Moscow, General Skobelev, hero of the Russo-Turkish War and commander of the bloody storming of Geok-Tepe fortress, much to the delight of Dukhovskaia's mother and another lady, kissed Dukhovskaia's hand.[50] Dukhovskaia left this element out of her English-language *Diary*, perhaps because Skobelev was seen far less favourably – or was simply little known – outside of Russia. Dukhovskaia was particularly enamoured of the elaborate coronation festivities and ceremonies for Alexander III in Moscow in 1883. At the coronation, Dukhovskoi, as the chief of staff of the Moscow military district, played a role in hosting members of the royal family and was a member of the "Moskovskie vlasti" ("Moscow authorities") who watched from a prominent viewing platform.[51]

As Richard Wortman notes, Alexander III set a different tone from his milder father, Alexander II, who had been assassinated by the People's Will, focusing on a display of power and "reaffirming conquest as a motif of imperial presentation."[52]

The heavy military presence was in addition to numerous dignitaries representing Russia's newly won territories. Dukhovskaia describes a city completely transformed for the coronation: triumphal arches had been built, as well as large tribunes for viewing the ceremony; houses were decorated with carpets and flowers. During the triumphal entry of the tsar into the city with ceremonial cannon fire and pealing bells, the tsaritsa and her daughters rode in a golden coach, the tsar and tsarevich behind it, along with officers of the guards. At the coronation in the Kremlin, the people were as colourful in their costumes as any of the troops or decorations, Dukhovskaia declared. In the evening there were fountains and vari-coloured lights set in all the belfries and towers. As Dukhovskaia describes it, the spectacle combined military might, riches, exotic foreigners, religious pageantry, and of course royal pomp and circumstance:

The large square was covered all over with red cloth. Ministers of the State and officers in full uniform began to assemble. The tribune on the opposite side was occupied by foreign Royalties and representatives of the different Oriental countries in gala costumes studded all over with precious stones. The Khan of Khiva was glittering like the sun. The Grand Duke Waldemar, accompanied by a numerous suite, came out of the palace and proceeded to the Cathedral of [the] Assumption where the Tzars [sic] are crowned, followed by all the members of the Imperial Family, the ladies of the Court wearing the national dress of the richest style, the Court officials resplendent in their gorgeous uniforms, the Ambassadors of foreign countries with their spouses, the personages of the first two classes and all the authorities of the town with my husband amongst them. The bewildering variety of the many different uniforms, both military and diplomatic, was striking. Our troops standing in long rows, with the standard of every regiment, were an imposing sight ... At the end of the ceremony there was a clamour of joy[ous] bells and the military bands began to play our National Anthem. It was a thrilling moment and my excitement was intense.[53]

A huge, very similar ceremony took place ten years later, in 1893, when Dukhovskaia and her husband arrived in Vladivostok upon his assumption of the governor-generalship of the Amur region. The ceremonies marking the arrival of the governor-general seemed to be clearly cast in the same mold as those of the coronation. When the Dukhovskois arrived in Vladivostok after a long voyage via the United States, Japan, and many other ports of call, from their ship they saw that the city was hung full of flags, and the troops were arrayed on shore. There were rugs placed on the pier and landing area, the head of the city presented bread and salt to General Dukhovskoi on a "wondrous silver platter," deputations from the Chinese and Korean societies of the city also bestowed bread and salt on silver platters, and Dukhovskaia received "marvellous" ("velikolepnyie") bouquets with greetings in large letters on attached ribbons.[54] Perhaps learned from the tsar's coronation, Dukhovskaia's sense of what would make the best spectacle was adept. By her request, she says, instead of riding in a carriage, they walked to the home of the governor, between two rows of troops, while the people massed around them. They were watched with binoculars through windows, she wrote; the people shouted "ura," military music played, and her husband bowed to the people. While they walked they were photographed six times. A girl from the local girls' school gave her a bouquet, and the rest of the girls curtseyed. They went to the church and participated in a service, then continued on foot to the governor's home. The priests came to the home and prayed with them, her husband went to see the admiral – greeted by cannon salutes – and there was a huge illumination in honour of their arrival that same evening.[55]

The similarities of Dukhovskaia's absolutely front-and-centre experience as a spectator of a "scenario of power" in Moscow and her own starring role in the later one in Vladivostok, at the opposite end of the empire, are quite striking. In Vladivostok, it was the Dukhovskois who played the role of the "majesties." The aim (despite Dukhovskaia's complaints about the lengthiness of some of these ceremonial events) seemed to be to prevent any daylight from coming between these displays of Russian power in different parts of the empire; arguably, the model for the behaviour of the honorees comes from what Dukhovskaia had experienced in the Moscow ceremony, when the tsar and tsaritsa and their party walked from the Kremlin palace to the Uspenskii cathedral between rows of soldiers to the coronation. The use of rugs, flags, cannon salutes, fireworks, the rows of soldiers, the foreign or subject people who greet them, the religious ceremonies – all were designed to send the same message of acceptance, and even welcome, of Russian imperial power; the repetition of the conventions of the ancient Moscow ceremony were instrumental in asserting the legitimacy of the new governor-general. There is an important aspect of empire-building that Dukhovskaia's narratives bring into focus, a kind of micro-politics of empire which occasionally is closely allied with macro-level pomp and circumstance. Dukhovskaia especially makes note, for example, of the shouts of "ura" on the streets, a topic that was much discussed by Russian and foreign journalists in 1883 in Moscow.[56] And both at the coronation and in Vladivostok, non-Russian subjects of the empire participated alongside ethnic Russians.

One might argue that Dukhovskaia and her ilk "core the periphery," meaning that rhetorical and bureaucratic methods typically used to represent the centre appear even at the very edges of the empire, where non-Russian ways and people potentially threaten the identity of the empire and the centrality of its Russian ruling class, as well as how the centre tended to account for and assimilate the periphery. Rhetorically, Russia had long depended on the idea that its greatness was a product of its size and breadth, setting up a paradox – how can something in a sense so empty of people, of history (as it was thought), of significance, be so crucial to Russian imperial identity? Certainly, as Richard Wortman reminds us, various social and government rituals played a vital role in enforcing the definition of the state and its relative parts. In major events in the centre, the imperial holdings of the periphery were evoked and represented, while on the edges, there was a replication in a minor key of the pomp and circumstance of the centre, reminding the local people that they were subject to Russian rule and asserting the essential uniformity of institutional power. Mechanisms and rituals of travel were an important part of this function; as we have seen, the Dukhovskois' arrival into Vladivostok by boat was carefully staged and managed, as was the later joining of the rails between Vladivostok and Khabarovsk.

As Jeff Sahadeo points out in his book *Russian Colonial Society in Tashkent*, in which Dukhovskaia's memoirs are cited several times, the arrival of the governor-general of Turkestan into Tashkent was a particularly momentous occasion, in which "the pomp of the ceremony reflected the arduousness of the journey itself," unifying "Russians from different social and regional backgrounds" and offering "a sense of uniqueness and self-importance, as pioneers working to foster a new civilization in distant Asian lands."[57] Sahadeo includes a photo of such an event, complete with triumphal arch, in his book.[58] Among other things, he notes, "Ceremonies that celebrated military prowess assuaged fears of uprisings against imperial power and bound the community under the supervision of its leader."[59]

Although Dukhovskaia lavishes great specificity of detail on their 1893 arrival ceremony in Vladivostok, she follows this description with admissions that seem to undercut it. After the ceremony, Dukhovskaia cannot sleep that night, awakes in tears, feels she is in exile or closed up in a gilded cage.[60] In the Russian version of her memoirs, she mentions that the ship carrying their household goods and servants is delayed and that a sailor who is serving them until their own servants arrive is from the ship on which they came to Vladivostok. When the sailor replies to her as a sailor, replying "est'" ("aye-aye") she feels nauseated, apparently reminded not only of her occasional seasickness on the long journey by ship but also of the transition from appreciative traveller to homesick governor-general's wife. Obliged to go to a dinner for sixty at which a Japanese admiral makes an interminable speech in Japanese; she has to stare at her plate so as not to burst out laughing. She and her husband are toasted, then serenaded, by a choir. She refuses, however, to go to a ball on the Japanese cruiser and another on the cruiser Kornilov. She hates, she says, to make herself the focal point and wishes she had a "shapka-nevidimka" in order to disappear; this last remark again is given only in the Russian version.[61] This duality appears again at the beginning of her *Turkestanskie vospominaniia*, which begin in 1897 when her husband is called to St. Petersburg. She hopes that a promotion means they will spend some time in the capital, but instead "my husband was suddenly named to a high and responsible post, that of Governor-General of Turkestan ... once again we must go past thirty lands (trideviat' zemel'), to the other end of the wide Russian Empire."[62] However, she approves of Turkestan's significance and historic pedigree: "In one of the most ancient books, the *Zend-Avesta* (two hundred years before Christ), it is said that Turkestan is one of the oldest cradles of humanity. This region is twice the size of France. Compared to Siberia it is thickly settled: in all of Pri-Amur there are one million inhabitants, but in Turkestan eight million; in Khabarovsk together with the troops there are 14,000 inhabitants, but in Tashkent 100,000."[63] Dukhovskaia mixes a Russian fairytale term, "trideviat' zemel'," for a kind of magical "land beyond" with ancient Oriental knowledge from the *Zend-Avesta* and contemporaneous statistics about population, indicating the complexity of categorizing how she viewed Turkestan and her own far-flung travels. She lauds the fairytale, *Thousand and One Nights* quality of this land (the name of Scheherezade's tales comes up occasionally in her account, as it does in many others'), its ancientness as recognized by non-Western authorities, and its meaning to the empire: twice of the size of France, Russia's civilizational model, and containing a large population, putting it ahead of other territories headed by governors-general.[64] Dukhovskaia, again perhaps contradictorily, mentions two articles written about her in the local paper *Turkestanskie vedomosti*; one was an article about her arrival in Tashkent for the first time, while another mentioned that she was holding receptions for visitors. While claiming disinterest in her own notoriety, she also draws attention to the articles written about herself that emphasize her own official role.[65]

After their arrival in Vladivostok in 1893, the couple departed a few weeks later for the trip north to Khabarovsk. This was a public departure; a crowd and a special train were assembled, huge quantities of bouquets were given, and at each stop there were triumphal arches, bread and salt, musical tributes, and bouquets. As Sahadeo points out, the experience of these ceremonies was not all positive; a prominent feature of the ceremonial receptions was the reception of petitions handed in by local residents, many of them Russians. This travel was extremely elegant; a yacht the couple was to take to Khabarovsk along the Sungacha river was "gaily tricked out with flags, with my husband's standard floating on the overdeck. The yacht was apparently quite new, all white and gold, with steam-heating and electricity ... I have a charming cabin with real windows and bed, not a hard shelf, but quite a wide, springy bed, and blue silk tapestries on the walls; ... The cookery on board is excellent."[66] There were numerous stops along the way, during which the Dukhovskois received bread and salt, a wild kid goat, and an enormous sturgeon. Clearly, every movement of the couple was intended to *be* an event, to show their power and status and consequently that of the Russian state. Even when Dukhovskaia travelled alone without her husband, however, she was expected to be received by various delegations and given bouquets and other gifts, although she frequently pleaded illness to avoid such official appearances. The telegraph proved very useful (though not infallible) in this regard: "Declining the honours the authorities of Blagoveshchensk wished to bestow on me, I telegraphed to General Arseniev, the governor of the town, that I could receive no one on board, having decided to play the invalid, and was disagreeably surprised to see that a great crowd awaited me on the quay. Mrs. Arseniev forced my cabin door open and transmitted to me three big bouquets tied with broad ribbons, sent by her husband, the chief of the Cossack regiment quartered at Blagoveshchensk, and the Prefect of the Police."[67] In the somewhat different account from *Iz moikh vospominanii*, Dukhovskaia is far more charitable (perhaps somewhat sarcastically so) in her description of the governor's wife and describes the thoughtfulness of the police prefect; she says that although she tele-graphed that she was ill, nonetheless the wife of the governor "was so kind, that she visited me on the ship. The agent of the steamship society and the commander of the Cossack regiment brought me bouquets, the latter with a broad ataman ribbon, on the end of which was sewn my monogram in silver ... The police prefect, having discovered that the ship offered yellow, muddy Amur river water, brought me a whole bar-rel of fresh filtered water and six lemons he had grown himself; these are a great rarity and in all of Blagoveshchensk one cannot find lemons for sale."[68] The tension between the "kindness" of the governor's wife visiting her despite her telegram seems evident when one compares the later English version, in which the governor's wife "forced open" her cabin door; the limits of Dukhovskaia's power to control her surround-ings were evident. The components of these spectacles and official stops and visits, with their great focus on military presentation, the partici-pation of townspeople, the local elites, schoolchildren, religious rites, decorations, gifts, and fireworks, created a specific identity for both the officials and their subject peoples. The ingredients for these ceremonies were not completely immutable; some governors, Sahadeo points out, focused more on Orthodox religious rites than others. Overall, how-ever, Sahadeo notes, local officials wished to put forward "a tableau of well-ordered, peaceful colonial society."[69] The ceremonies emphasized the power of the military and official elites, the ability of the Russians to control their subjects, and the satisfaction of the people with their gov-ernment. Dukhovskaia's perspective shows that she was also required to carry out her part of the scenario; with her general antipathy towards Russian society women, she appeared to find this an unpleasant bur-den. She was far more welcoming of the police prefect's gift of clean water and lemons.

When Dukhovskoi was appointed to the post of governor-general of Turkestan, in 1898, headquartered in Tashkent, the couple began to travel extensively by rail, which was made possible by the fact that the railway had by then been extended to Tashkent; they travelled in a style befitting their station: "A special train was waiting on the quay. All the cars were painted white. I have my private car provided with every possible comfort and luxury. At one end is the sitting-room containing sofas, armchairs, a large writing-table, shelves, etc. The furniture is cov-ered with red silk brocade to match the window curtains. At the other end a suite consisting of a bedroom with a bed with splendid springs, a bath and a dining-room."[70] As with boat travel, crowds, music, recep-tions, proffered bouquets, and bread and salt were the norm for the Dukhovskois. Despite her complaints about hot weather, insects, dust, and fatigue, the private car had its advantages. When Dukhovskaia was compelled to travel from St. Petersburg to Kissingen to see her husband in 1900 without a private car, the trip was quite unpleasant for her, as she experienced close quarters with numerous members of the public on the way.[71]

Dukhovskaia to all appearances was often more comfortable with men than women; she describes her enjoyment at outpacing a group of visitors, including a claimant to the Spanish throne, during a bicycle ride in Tashkent: "I organized a bicycle outing with the visiting officers, and completely tortured my cavaliers, who were not used to motion in such hellish heat; they barely were able to keep up and in their hearts probably cursed me."[72]

Dukhovskaia and the Great Game

Part of Dukhovskaia's sense of importance related to her role in the rivalry between England and Russia. References to the "Great Game" are sprinkled throughout her narrative but are more typical in her account of her husband's postings in the Far East and in Turkestan. Perhaps the most obvious is one that occurs late in her *Diary*:

> The greater part of the soil of Turkestan, as that of India, would have presented long ere this a veritable earthly paradise if it were not for the want of water. The Government and the inhabitants are doing everything in their power to overcome this difficulty. They profit by the proximity of every river, and if there is no river, they dig artesian wells.
>
> The English, in general, are very much interested in everything concerning Turkestan. I read an article about my husband which came out in the *Daily Chronicle*. I quote the following from the London newspaper: – "Every English officer, who understands the problem of Oriental politics, must know of what great importance is the centralisation of Russian powers in Asia. For the moment sixty thousand men are united under the command of General Doukhovskoy, one of the most able officers of the Russian army."[73]

In the version from *Turkestanskie vospominaniia*, embedded (as it is in the *Diary*) in a longer discussion of European travellers and British officers passing through Tashkent, Dukhovskaia includes the mention of General Kuropatkin, which she elides from the later English-language version.[74] In quoting from a British paper about the importance to the British of Russian troops in Turkestan, headed by her husband, Dukhovskaia points to Turkestan as a centre of Russian power and importance. In this same section of the text, she recounts the visit to Tashkent of Sven Hedin, "the renowned Swedish Pamir and Thibet explorer." She is more proprietary about him in Russian, saying that he had visited her in particular ("byl u menia s vizitom") and that "he fluently speaks dozens of languages, among them Russian."[75] Also visiting Tashkent were a British colonel, MacSwinee, who was on his way to India, as was a British traveller, Herbert Powell, who was trying to find the shortest route between England and India (a goal in which the Russian-built railroad played an important role). Dukhovskaia notes:

> For the present the English make this journey, via Brindisi and the Suez Canal, in three weeks' time, but as soon as the Russian and British railroad join, the trip will take but eight days. Only five hundred miles are wanting for the line to be completed, but political combinations are hindering the work. Mr. Powell had passed one month in Moscow to study the Russian language, so difficult for strangers. Nevertheless, many English officers serving in India speak our language, and it is a great pity that the same cannot be said of the Russian officers who serve in Turkestan.[76]

Dukhovskaia writes here as an authority on Russian officers' lack of linguistic preparation. In *Turkestanskie vospominaniia*, Dukhovskaia calls the impediment to completion of the railway "soobrazheniia vysshei politiki," or "the reasoning of politics at the highest level."[77] Besides the above-mentioned British visitors and Sven Hedin, Dukhovskaia names another Swede, an academic, and his wife, as well as a Frenchman travelling to Tibet and Wilson, a British man studying methods of harvesting in Turkestan, taking pride, it seems, in their presence at her house. She describes a dinner held for the visitors, along with a performance of bacha dancers, typically young boys dressed as girls, but here, Dukhovskaia notes with some condescension, the dancers were relatively old and inappropriate for the role.[78] In all, this encounter was emblematic both of Russian status – foreign visitors had to travel with Russian permission, and Russian military men were familiar with the lay of the land – and also the transnational status of those of high social standing from European countries as well as Russia, who often met with members of the Russian military leadership. Performances of dancers were not presented only for the "European" upper-class visitors and residents, but they were certainly *de rigueur* and commented on by most travellers.[79] Russian travel rules for "unknown travelers," less exalted than Sven Hedin and the other academic visitors, were stricter, however; Dukhovskaia writes in a description that is absent from the *Diary*: "For various political reasons, the travels of unknown foreigners in some areas of Turkestan are undesirable, and therefore tourists must request permission to pass through. The English embassy in St. Petersburg from time to time makes trouble about permission to travel through the restricted areas for this or that Englishman. Out of consideration to a more or less well-known traveler, one or two officers are attached to accompany him, precisely as Russian officers in India are always accompanied by an escort for their personal safety. One good turn deserves another."[80] Of course, Dukhovskaia here ignores the distinction between tourists or non-military visitors who wish to pass through Turkestan as opposed to Russian officers who wish to visit India, or perhaps assumes any traveller is likely to be a spy. Dukhovskaia gives a detailed description of the exiled emir of Afghanistan, who she says repaid the Russians for his lengthy protected stay in Central Asia by playing into the hands of the English.[81]

A frequent motif is visits and gifts from the emir of Bukhara, or by his representatives; both the emir and the Russians took care to show mutual respect and support in their symbiotic relationship, and Dukhovskaia was expected to be a full participant in this mutual arrangement, accepting gifts and performing music for the Bukharan delegation. Upon stopping near the emir's residence on his way to Tashkent in 1897, Dukhovskaia's husband remarked publicly that just as he was visiting the heart of Islam, Bukhara, in the name of the tsar, the emir was at the same time in the heart of Russia – in Moscow.[82] The Dukhovskois' servants in Tashkent were cosmopolitan, consisting of Poles, Germans, Tatars, Sarts, and Orenburg Cossacks; the butler had a Bukharan star, an honour bestowed by the emir.[83] Dukhovskaia describes the governor-general's residence in Tashkent as a kind of international oasis with a beautiful garden, a small zoo and spacious, elegant rooms. Praskov'ia Uvarova, visiting in 1890 when it was inhabited by Aleksandr Vrevsky, was quite complimentary. Departing for St. Petersburg, Dukhovskaia notes that there was a huge sendoff for her at the train station, with a sotnia of Cossacks and a "mass of honorable natives in rich costumes, astride their steeds. Such solemnity is necessary for the prestige of the powers that be in the eyes of the little-cultured local population."[84] As noted by Sahadeo, deputations of local people were customary at official occasions.

Threats to Empire

Despite, or perhaps because of, the fact that the Dukhovskois were so close to the aims of the empire, the sense that the Russian hold on power was not inevitable was something they experienced personally.

When Dukhovskaia and her husband travelled abroad during the siege of Kars, for example, she describes in *Iz moikh vospominanii* that it was unpleasant to be abroad, that people were cursing the Russians.[85] They were present in St. Petersburg in 1880 when there was an attempt on the tsar's life; during the second, successful attempt in 1881, they were in Moscow. Dukhovskaia described the uneasy feelings of the ruling elite at the time as well as the unwarranted attacks on the innocent; she describes how in one case a crowd attacked a young woman with glasses and short hair – styles adopted by the "nihilist" or emancipated women in Russia – calling her a "specialist" (spetsialistka), although clearly the crowd meant "socialist" (sotsialistka).[86] Dukhovskaia made disapproving note as well of the persecution of Jews.[87] She found it shameful, for example, that the famous actress Sarah Bernhardt had had stones thrown at her in Odesa by anti-Semites. To address this in Moscow, the head of the police met Bernhardt at the station.[88] The Dukhovskois went to Bernhardt's performances in Moscow and then in Paris in 1900.[89]

Danger increasingly became a part of the couple's life as Dukhovskoi rose in prominence; he had received death threats in the United States en route to Khabarovsk to take the post of governor-general of the Amur region and had to continue his travel to San Francisco incognito.[90] Later, as the couple travelled in 1898 by train between Samarkand and Tashkent in the wake of the Andijan uprising, which occurred in mid-May, Dukhovskaia noted that "the whole way is guarded by patrols to prevent the damage frequently caused to the line by hostile natives." In the Russian version, Dukhovskaia is somewhat less critical, noting, "The whole distance to Tashkent patrols are guarding the railroad bed, since here there are often repeated instances of the damaging of the railway by natives."[91] In fact, throughout Dukhovskaia's narrative, which describes the life of the highly privileged, well-connected ruling class of the Russian empire, there are frequent references to uprisings, discontent, and actual and potential terrorist attacks. While attending the coronation of Alexander III, whose father had been killed by terrorist bombs, Dukhovskaia describes being very hungry, but since no one in the crowd was allowed to carry anything for fear of concealed explosives, she had nothing to eat; even a lady nearby who had brought an orange with her was prevented from eating it by a guard.[92] Men with top hats, Dukhovskaia notes, were considered especially suspect since they might conceal something under their hats.[93] A number of times she mentions well-known terrorists and political operatives by name, such as Sofiia Perovskaia; the threats they posed were clearly well known to her.[94]

Of all the places they went, Tashkent, no doubt due to the recent rebellion in Andijan, seemed to create the most anxiety: "Our life had many dark moments. There had been a great excitement these last few days; bad news had arrived, a new rebellion was apprehended. We stood on a volcano that might explode at any moment; the only thing to ask ourselves was when will it begin to pour out its flames. Anonymous letters, splashed with blood, announced to my husband that on the night of the 30th July, a holy war would break out."[95] Interestingly, her Russian account mentions the letters but says they were sent to various government agencies; she describes it as a "smutnoe vremia," a time of troubles, that was happening "again" – presumably meaning again after the assassination of the tsar and its aftermath.[96] In the Russian account, Dukhovskaia explicitly compares the Russian occupation of Turkestan with the British occupation of India. She notes that while it is "not the most comfortable situation" it is still better that there are 124,000 local residents of Tashkent and 15,000 troops, compared to "one white soldier" for every 3,000 natives in India.[97] She notes as well that the Sarts, local town dwellers, were not allowed to carry guns. Written just after a grand celebration of the twenty-third anniversary of the Russian control of Tashkent, with a parade of troops, wreath-laying, and a grand dinner, this description indicates that Russian power was not unquestioned. Indeed, when travel writer/explorer Iuliia Golovnina, discussed in chapter four, arrived in Tashkent on 30 May 1898 on her way to a scientific expedition in the Pamir Mountains, she noted that her host, Nikolai Ivanovich Korol'kov, the military governor of Ferghana Province, could not immediately join his guests due to the current uprising in Andijan. Golovnina describes the arrival of the new Governor-General Dukhovskoi in Tashkent in June, echoing similar civilizing sentiments to Dukhovskaia: "the atmosphere is majestic and full of the most varied expectations. In at least one wish almost everyone concurs: that an energetic and powerful authority would be established in the region, which would awaken into activity this rich country, would cause all the branches of our government to work productively, and along with this, would lift up Russian authority in the eyes of the local people."[98] On Golovnina's return from the Pamir Mountains in August, she describes a parade taking place in Novyi Margelan, in the Ferghana valley, in honour of the governor-general (Dukhovskoi, although she does not name him); she notes that he refuses bread and salt proffered at the railway station by the local deputation, saying that he will agree to take it only after the Sarts have proven they are not taking part in disturbances. Golovnina provides a footnote that says "New Margelan was a stronghold of the uprising" ("gnezdo vozstaniia").[99] Golovnina's husband attended a ball in honour of the governor-general in order to thank him and General Ionov for their support of their expedition to the Pamir Mountains. At that time, Dukhovskaia herself was absent from Tashkent, having left on 9 August.[100]

Another commentator, an official in the office of the governor-general, G.P. Fedorov, also stressed the importance and change-making consequences of the Andijan uprising, leading Dukhovskoi to depart from St. Petersburg sooner than he intended, as well as to harsh punishments for the participants.[101] Fedorov commented quite negatively on Dukhovskoi, who he claims spoke rudely to him upon their first meeting and declared that Dukhovskoi's frail health prevented him from carrying out his job: "Dukhovskoi was appointed to us as an already completely sick person. His hands trembled to such an extent that he had to pick up a glass of water with both hands. He was not capable of any serious mental work."[102] He was slightly kinder to Dukhovskaia herself, describing her as reclusive (which he said gave rise to rumours he considered unfounded) but as admirably not someone who tried to interfere with her husband's duties, and who was understandably not enamoured of Tashkent society. He was quite critical of her writing, which he compared to the "diaries of boarding school girls, devoid of interest, talent or literary qualities of any kind."

> With him came his wife, still a rather young and attractive woman, but almost no one ever saw her, because she led an isolated style of life and almost never left her boudoir, where she remained in the company of her companion, a quite young woman, and rarely showed herself even at breakfast or dinner. In Tashkent, of course, such a lifestyle evoked many rumors, but I think that these rumors had the character of empty gossip. It seems to me that she simply didn't care for society in general, and Tashkent society could only strengthen her unsociability. I retained a good impression of her only for the reason that she didn't interfere in business. For the deep provinces this is a great service from the point of view of the wife of the commander of the region. Apparently she greatly loved music and had pretensions of being called a writer. There is a thick book of her travels published on her behalf. The book was published by a printing house with excellent connections. In regard to its interior qualities I can only wish that she didn't write any more and didn't waste money on publishing works that remind one of the diaries of boarding school girls, devoid of interest, talent or literary qualities of any kind.[103]

As Fedorov avers, the duties of the governor-general's wife in Tashkent were burdensome to Dukhovskaia, although she did pride herself on the attentions of the grand duke (Grand Duke Nikolai Konstanti-novich, who lived in exile in Tashkent),[104] a member of the royal family; further, her writing work no doubt at least partly explains her keeping to herself:

I held a reception once a week; between two and five about a hundred per-sons would pass through our saloons. The day I held my first reception, the large drawing-room was crowded with guests. I had to take up the subject of politics and be amiable to everyone. I was so tired with having had to talk all the time that my tongue, having refused to obey me, I said good- bye instead of good afternoon to a belated visitor. The Grand-Duke was amongst our guests and gained my sympathy at once ... Every day I grow more and more home-sick. I often was in tears, not taking inter-est in anything. The awful climate was injurious to my health ... I work hard at my book and give much time to my English concertina ... The life that I had to lead was entirely out of my line. I hate state receptions, state manners; grandeurs weigh heavily upon me, and etiquette to the laws of which I must submit. I have got a court like a little queen, everyone is charming to me, but I, ungrateful being, should have liked warm friend-ship far better than respectful homage.[105]

The Russian version of this passage in *Turkestanskie vospominaniia* indi-cates that Dukhovskaia shared a telegram with the grand duke that she had received from his mother, Alexandra Iosifovna, inquiring about her son's health. He had been banished to Central Asia because he had stolen some diamonds from an icon belonging to his mother but also because of a scandalous affair with American courtesan Fanny Lear, and presumably also because of his liberal ideas.[106] Dukhovskaia describes a visit to his palace the next day, which had many valuable objects worthy of a museum; in the Russian version, she describes the huge number of portraits of the royal family, something she leaves out of the English version.[107]

Dukhovskaia mentions the grand duke's presence at her first arrival to Tashkent in a passage that is mostly absent in the *Diary* and differs from it in a number of details, but seems to capture both her artistic sense and enjoyment of high status:

At half-past eleven in the morning our train approached Tashkent. In gray provincial life the arrival and departure of the chief official of the region is a huge event and entertainment. We had barely arrived at the station when our cars were surrounded by a crowd of curiosity-seekers. Bows – flowers, greetings – flowers, handshakes – flowers. Flowers, flowers, flowers, without end! Amongst the others stood the Grand Duke with an especially luxurious bouquet; the flowers were tied up with a ribbon of sand color, the emblem of the Hungry Steppe. With difficulty we moved through the well-dressed, merry crowd and came out onto the entrance porch. How unaccustomed I was to such celebrations, and truthfully, how little I care for them, but nonetheless the picture that opened in front of us was truly magnificent. The whole large square in front of the train station presented a whole sea, overflowing with all colors of the rainbow: there were local people in holiday khalats of all possible colors and shades; their turbans showed white like foam on waves. In the distance, like miraculous decorations, green splendid trees, and all of this was lit with blinding beams, pouring down as if not from the sun, but from the whole azure sky, such a sky as one can see only in Egypt or in southern Italy. There was not the least movement of wind, it was intolerably hot, but for all that, how brightly and in what high relief were all the colors and contours! An effective contrast among that orgy of colors were the identically uniformed, tightly-ranked troops.[108]

Like her description of the joining of the railroad in the wilderness, this passage is a highly successful one on Dukhovskaia's part. One can very nearly visualize the scene of tightly ranked soldiers creating a barrier to hold back the boisterous and brightly dressed crowd, while the comparison of the light to Egypt and Italy not only gives notice to the reader that Dukhovskaia is a widely travelled cosmopolitan Russian, but that her treatment of the event in primarily visual terms restricts her role to that of spectator, not someone taking part in the ceremony or connected to the picturesque sea of people. The phrase "gray provincial life" certainly seems to sum up her view of the necessity of living in Tashkent.

Towards the end of *Turkestanskie vospominaniia*, Dukhovskaia describes the racially tinged worries going on in the Russian empire in a clear allusion to the Yellow Peril: "A many-century sleeping 'Yellow Dragon' had awoken. Suddenly all China had been stirred up by the 'Boxer' rebellion. Foreign diplomats saw themselves cut off from the whole world, and set down amidst a hostile, wild crowd. All the civilized world had become troubled. Newspapers were full of descriptions of Chinese cruelty. The German ambassador was treacherously killed in Peking; they cut out his tongue, put out his eyes and buried him in the earth up to his head. Europeans had boiling water poured on them and were torn from limb to limb."[109] In the Far East the Chinese attacked the Manchurian railway, Dukhovskaia declared, noting that her husband had wanted to keep the railway construction on Russian territory.

The Dukhovskois and Russian Imperial Policy

Counter to Fedorov's accusations that Dukhovskoi was not fit for any work, Dukhovskoi was credited with writing an important, albeit draconian, report on the Andijan uprising containing recommendations about what the Russian imperial policy towards Muslims should be. Hisao Komatsu writes, for example, that although the uprising was "suppressed immediately," "an unexpected Muslim revolt in the most advanced cotton cultivation area had a serious impact on the Russian authorities who until then were confident of their colonial rule in Turkistan," and cites Dukhovskoi's 1899 report, *Islam in Turkestan*, advising the tsar "to draw up a state strategy against Islam, 'which had been hostile to Russian civilization with no exception.'"[110] Komatsu indicates that Dukhovskoi's ideas for how to treat Muslims were not carried out due to Russia's defeat by the Japanese, but were ultimately prophetic in nature: "When we consider the harsh experiences of the Muslim peoples in the Soviet Union, the Dukhovskoi report seems to have been an omen."[111] Adeeb Khalid also points to Dukhovskoi's rather anti-Islamic views, which were at least at the time not regarded well by those above him; Dukhovskoi "attacked not just Kaufman's policies, but also the very notion of tolerance that had underwritten Russian policies toward Islam since the time of Catherine II." However, the report "met a cold reception in St. Petersburg, where both the ministries of War and the Interior disagreed with his 'extremism,' and the project was consigned to oblivion."[112] Dukhovskaia seemed to hold not dissimilar views to her husband's. In Kazan', Dukhovskaia writes in her English-language memoir, "Sergei went to see the Governor of the city, having to discuss different questions concerning the Mussulmans, who compose the ninth part of the population of Russia … The task of administering equal justice to Muslims and Christians is a difficult one."[113] In her *Turkestanskie vospominaniia*, Dukhovskaia did not include the latter, diplomatic sentence, which somewhat leavens a lengthy description in both texts of how impossible it was for the Russians to administer correct policy to ungrateful Muslims, who are "clever diplomatists from birth."[114] Dukhovskaia contrasts the Muslims unfavourably with the Buddhist nomad Buriats, with whom Dukhovskoi met in Trans-Baikal to discuss their unhappiness with their recently changed position in the empire. Dukhovskaia remarks in *Turkestanskie vospominaniia*, "With such people one could still discuss and come to an agreement. It's a completely different matter with Muslims."[115]

Dukhovskaia does not criticize the Russian treatment of subject peoples, whom she considers are being civilized by Russian rule – but nevertheless it is striking that, according to his official biography, many of her husband's assignments in the early 1860s were expressed in such phrases as "the destruction of *auls* on both sides of the river."[116] Just as in Tolstoy's "After the Ball," which links Russian imperial policy – the flogging of a Tatar deserter – with the apparently "unrelated" world of the ball, with their paired rituals of music, movement, and dedication to the rules – "все по закону " ("everything according to the rules," a refrain in the story) – the destruction of that which does not comport with the goals of the Russian empire is inextricably linked to the far more genteel rituals of power in society life.[117] Dukhovskaia remarked with satisfaction, for example, that a "children's feast" had been put on "especially to attract the little natives; we wanted to tame these little savages and show them that the Russians were not so terrible as they are made to believe. The whole population, except a small part of civilized natives, bring up their children inculcating in them the fear of the Russians ... It is to be hoped that the little Sarts returned to their homes carrying sentiments of friendship to the Russians in their small hearts."[118]

The pièce de résistance for the Dukhovskois in representing Turkestan, and Russia, to the world was certainly their presence at the Russian Pavilion at the 1900 Paris Exposition, which relied to a surprisingly large extent on the possessions, good offices, and even personnel, sumptuously attired, of the emir of Bukhara. In that complex presentation for public consumption, ritual and empire were closely linked. The 1900 Paris Universal Exhibition, for which the Dukhovskois served as official government representatives, epitomized Russia's representation of itself as an imperial power composed of multiple nationalities and rich with natural resources and the latest technology, with a pavilion combining a fully realized Kremlin giving way to several exhibits on Russia's peripheries: a Central Asian market scene with huge panneau paintings and a real fountain, decorated with Bukharan treasures, along with exhibits depicting the spoils of Siberia and the Caucasus and a state-of-the-art panoramic "train journey" from Moscow to Peking.[119] Dukhovskaia was fully aware of her own role in the Russian effort, noting in her English-language memoirs that there were "four Bokharians and a Turkoman, sent to the Exhibition to look after the rich objects exposed by the Emir [of Bukhara], and to serve also as a vivid decoration in the Asiatic section ... These decorative personages, when passing through St. Petersburg, attracted much curiosity by their magnificent costumes, it is not astonishing therefore that they produced a great sensation in Paris."[120] When she and her husband arrived in Paris, a crowd expected something grand: "eager spectators wait[ed] to see the arrival of the exotic personages whom the Orientals had come to meet, expecting to see no less a person than a Rajah. People stood on chairs to get a peep at us, and great was their disappointment, when simple mortals clad in European dress, stepped out of the train."[121] The constant tension between what was expected of Dukhovskaia and what she actually embodied seems to be well illustrated by these observations. Beautiful and arresting clothing was misleading; it was the plain personages who actually held the power.

Representing imperial Russia and Turkestan at the Exhibition was one of the last official acts of the Dukhovskois. Soon thereafter, Dukhovskoi applied for leave and returned to St. Petersburg; he died the following year. Not surprisingly, Dukhovskaia keeps much of the focus on herself in her two accounts of the end of Dukhovskoi's life; she is delighted to finally no longer be moving from place to place, to be living in St. Petersburg – it is a dream fulfilled. However, as her husband became increasingly ill, Dukhovskaia realized that this achievement of her goals came at a high price, saying that "the sword of Damocles constantly hung over me" – the knowledge that her husband's life was ebbing.[122] A nightmare she had had on the train on the way to Tashkent, after receiving a telegram about her husband's ill health, she felt, had come true: "I clearly saw myself by the entrance to the cathedral, surrounded by a mass of troops; an officer came out of the cathedral and loudly announced to the soldiers: 'General Dukhovskoi has died.' I woke up with a painfully beating heart and all in tears."[123] The departure from Tashkent, too, prefigures Dukhovskoi's death; she remarks in both versions that as she is saying "Do svidaniia" ("until we meet again"), she is thinking to herself "Proshaite" ("farewell") (she translates these as *"au revoir"* and *"adieu"* in the English version).[124] This is both an indication that she wishes to leave Tashkent behind permanently but also that she realizes that a return is unlikely not so much due to her wish to remain in St. Petersburg as because her husband is so ill; in the Russian version she says that the doctors have given her husband an ultimatum, and that due to his malaria he must depart Tashkent. In the English version this is toned down to say simply that the doctors advise rest and change.

Dukhovskaia indicates in both accounts that her good luck had finally come to an end. True to form, she notes that the tsar (Nicholas II) attended a service for her husband and said some words of comfort to her, while Grand Duke Mikhail Nikolaevich, whom she had met while in the Caucasus, also treated her with great empathy; she ends as she began, emphasizing her social status. However, despite these kindnesses, "I saw nothing and heard nothing," she writes.[125] Her real life, it seems, was at an end because she had tied it so closely to her husband's; she has no desire to describe her life without him. Her English-language memoir, published in 1917, some sixteen years after his death, ends exactly as her 1913 *Turkestanskie vospominaniia* had ended, itself published over a decade after his death, with no mention of any events beyond his funeral. Having begun her writing career by proclaiming her bravery in taking a dangerous journey to join him in Erzerum, she does not wish to acknowledge the journey she took after he was gone, preferring to style her written persona as the wife and companion of her husband and to emphasize his status (as well as hers) in the Russian empire.

Chapter Two

Turkestan through Russian Eyes: Elena Apreleva's *Central Asian Sketches*

Not a horse, not a camel, that ship of the desert, which we, dwellers of Europe, expect to see on the horizon of an Asiatic landscape, not a single four-legged animal except for a tailless dog and a yellow kitten ... Boring, dull, horrible! ... Even the sun does not please us. On the contrary, one is frightened by this burning, merciless sun, under whose scorching rays not even a blade of grass grows.

Elena Apreleva, eight years older than Varvara Dukhovskaia and an established writer, editor, and playwright, thus presented Central Asia's impression on newly arrived Russians in her story "Uzun-Ada," which opens a collection of her Central Asian stories published by her sons. In the story she establishes the shocking experience of a Russian, having left the "familiar" Caucasus, encountering Central Asia for the first time, unprepared either by past experience or by past reading for the Dantesque vision that awaits. "Abandon all hope!" – Apreleva's (male) narrator specifically cites Dante in the first line, playing on the name of the city, "Uzun-Ada," establishing its location on the "Asiatic shore of the Caspian" as the steamship returns to Baku.[1] The snows of Russia are far away, the narrator remarks to his Russian readers, as are the mountains of the Caucasus and familiar Mingrelians, Imeretians, and Georgians. This is an entirely new territory. Unlike Dukhovskaia's approach to her memoirs, which emphasized her high status, Apreleva's approach to her short story writing, while still employing the perspective of a member of the Russian nobility, entails a far more ordinary observer of life in Central Asia, while any figure who might in some manner represent Apreleva herself is difficult to discern. Apreleva guards her identity, writing very often from a man's subject position, but frequently representing a couple, one assumes a married couple. This means that narrative situations are diffused and de-personalized,

Figure 2.1. Ilya Repin, "Elena Apreleva-Ardov." Courtesy of Wikimedia Commons.

especially since the narrator is never explicitly described. The outlook is observational; narrators typically exist as witnesses, to relate what they experience, with their identities (usually) as Russians a kind of guarantee of the veracity and reliability of the perspective presented. Some stories are in third person, leaving out a specifically Russian perspective, and at least one is told in the first person: a young official, Dragutin, tells of his difficulties in establishing his career. Women of her class were rarely unaccompanied, meaning that a plural narrator was common among women writers in foreign places, and "we" had the flexibility to ultimately encompass almost any group.

Apreleva provides a view of Russian-controlled Central Asia in which Russians are generally benevolent, ready to learn, and focused on bringing law and order to an oppressive society. Religious persecution and slavery must be ended, or already have. Ideally, women should be able to live freely, with a Russian woman's life taken to be the example of such freedom. Stories bear witness to corruption and prejudice, the costs of conquest and the often-challenging distance from Turkestan to Russia proper. Quite differently from Dukhovskaia, for whom all but the highest-ranking Central Asian dwellers existed primarily as a kind of picturesque crowd welcoming her to her husband's latest posting or serving as a potential group of enemies threatening Russian rule, Apreleva focuses on individuals, who have names, histories, and offer much more than a picturesque or threatening backdrop.

Elena Ivanovna Apreleva (1846–1923), née Blaramberg, who wrote under the pseudonym E. Ardov, was a prose writer, editor, memoirist, playwright, and children's writer. Quite a different figure from any of the others discussed in this project, she was a writer first and foremost. Although certainly personally imbricated into the imperial project, being the daughter of a naturalized Russian officer who served in the Caucasus and Persia, and the wife of a government official who served in Central Asia, Apreleva's views as interpreted through her literary texts were for the most part comparatively subtle, especially compared to her literary predecessor, Nikolai Karazin, and his bold, over-the-top characters. She spent seventeen years in Russian Turkestan, from 1889 to 1906, publishing her first Central Asian story in 1896 in *Russkie vedomosti*.[2] Apreleva was the daughter of a Greek mother and a Russified Belgian father, Lt. General Ivan Fedorovich Blaramberg (1800–78), a topographer and himself a prolific memoirist.[3] The family moved from Orenburg to St. Petersburg in 1854. In her early twenties she began contributing to "historical and educational journals," "edited a section of the children's magazine *Family and School*," and then studied in Geneva.[4] Through her brother, Pavel Blaramberg, a composer and journalist, she met the writer Ivan Turgenev, his companion Pauline Viardot, and Viardot's daughter Pauline. As was typical of Turgenev, who often helped young writers and artists, he introduced Apreleva (then Blaramberg) in turn to many of his literary contacts and interceded with them to help her, encouraging them to publish the work of the young writer, and helped create her pseudonym, "Ardov," from the letters in Viardot's name.[5] In an 1877 letter to the publisher of *Vestnik Evropy*, Turgenev praised the young woman's writing: "Her novel is worth publishing because she has that certain *je ne sais quoi*, as the French say; it is written passionately and honestly, and not without talent."[6] Apreleva did not hesitate to take on difficult topics. Mary Zirin notes, for example, that in Apreleva's 1877 novel *Bez vina vinovaty* (*Guilty without Guilt*), a character details marital rape in her diary, prompting the narrator to include "a passionate interpolation on the need for sex education for girls."[7]

Apreleva replaced her brother for a time at *Russkie vedomosti* as an editor while he was ill. She was one of several models who posed for Ilya Repin's famous painting, "Tsarevna Sof'ia" of 1879.[8] She became the third wife of Petr Vasilievich Aprelev before heading to Ukraine, the Caucasus, and then Central Asia with him in the late 1880s, and while in Central Asia, where she lived starting from 1889, she published a series of stories in *Russkie vedomosti*. After her death, a collection of her stories relating to Central Asia was published in Shanghai by her sons in 1935 under the name of *Sredne-aziatskie ocherki*, or *Central Asian Sketches*, which is what she titled them in a listing of her work.[9] In their introduction to their mother's *Central Asian Sketches*, her sons claim that her first Central Asian sketch was published in 1893, but according to her own bibliography the first was "Sail',"" published in 1896.[10]

Apreleva wrote for an audience that was likely twofold: first, local Russians who were experiencing life in Turkestan as transplants, and second, Russians in Russia proper who were not familiar with the vocabulary, weather, food, social life, and other elements of life in Russia's Central Asian territory. As a current ad for Apreleva's novel *Bez viny vinovaty* (*Guilty without Guilt*) notes, Apreleva's work had contemporaneous success but was not republished and hence is little known to current readers.[11] As published, some stories include glosses of Central Asian words and terms, others either incorporate an explanation into the story itself or leave the terms unexplained. There is a multi-page glossary of "Uzbek and Tadzhik (ancient Persian) words" in the 1935 collection. The stories as placed into the collection are numbered and seem to be chronological; they start with "Uzun-Ada," in which a Russian couple or group arrives in Central Asia after crossing the Caspian Sea, describing the intimidating severity of the climate and the newness of the experience, hence providing both a description of the experience to those uninitiated and a reminder of shared past experience to those who were already living in Central Asia. While the collection consists of the artistically most solid tales, the sons' collection leaves out stories that focused primarily or only on Central Asians, such as "In the Mountain Ravine," "Ishan," "Child of Nomads," and three that are particularly critical of Russians, such as "The Marriage of Captain Narkizov," "Notes of a Little Man," and "The General of Reseda."

Mary Zirin notes of Apreleva that she brought "an agreeable, light talent" to Russian literature, compares her favourably to Chekhov, and says she "deserves to be better remembered."[12] Perhaps of the greatest interest to current readers is her complex negotiation of the meaning of the Russian conquest of Central Asia over multiple stories and its significance to the various groups of people who live there: first the Russians, of course, both "old Turkestantsy" and those who had come more recently; upper-class Russians and peasants or servants; local nomadic and settled groups, who are Muslims; Jews; and finally Persians, many of whom had previously been slaves. Military life and its hardships; women's lives (both those of the settled and nomadic women and those of the Russian women); the changes wrought by Russian occupation, both good and bad; and the landscape of the region all receive significant attention in Apreleva's stories. The distance of Central Asia from "European Russia" is felt in many different ways by different characters, and the action takes place not only in Samarkand and Tashkent but also in more remote locations. All told, Apreleva's geography of Central Asia is varied and highly psychological; one's attitude towards being a resident there greatly determines one's outlook. It is clear that her sons chose the best stories for the collection. All the sketches that could be obtained are discussed here, except for three, as well as a memoir of Apreleva's return trip to Moscow in 1906, written under her own name.[13]

Apreleva's views of Russian power in Central Asia, while not all cut from the same cloth, are present in "Uzun-Ada" (1898), in which the narrator praises the Russian victory over the final Central Asian territories added to the empire, but also registers concern about the true nature of the territory, which might be either the "skazochnoe zhilishche" ("fairytale abode") of Eastern potentates or the frightening, secretive desert.[14] The genre of Apreleva's stories is unusual. On the one hand, the stories are set up as fiction, even if the most common narrator, who figures in most of the stories, seems to be essentially the same person throughout – or represents the same couple or group. This narrator never describes himself or his family overtly, although various details become evident to the reader as the stories accumulate. The primary narrator seems to be a nobleman who has come to be part of the ruling Russian power structure in Central Asia, and not a military man, although he interacts with numerous military men. And indeed, Apreleva's husband was a state official and not in the military. No name is ever given to the narrator, and if the stories are written about Apreleva's own family (the two boys match her two sons), then she is virtually absent, the wife of the narrator being mentioned only once, and given no name. Through the course of the stories, the narrator and his wife/family/companions gradually educate themselves about Central Asian matters, appearing in the latter stories as already knowledgeable about the area. In the published collection, breaking the illusion of fiction are a number of photographs (unattributed) said to depict characters mentioned in the stories – the wealthy merchant Solimka, Ulanka the Sart boy, the Jews at the Samarkand bazaar, three brothers – as well as a yurt in Gurimar, a village "in the foothills of the Tian-Shan" from which some of her stories were datelined when published in *Russkie vedomosti*.[15] The photographs are not located with proximity to the stories they allude to, but they are titled and clearly refer to persons/characters named in the stories.[16]

Apreleva places her narratives in time periods before, during, and after Russian conquest, and before and after the building of the railroad between Samarkand and Tashkent. She introduces many locally used words, such as ulak (a game played on horseback), tamasha (performance, gathering), tiubeteika (skullcap), and so on, either translated in footnotes or glossed in the text; in "Child of Nomads" alone (admittedly, an outlier) she glosses forty-eight words. Apreleva places emphasis on Central Asian ethnic and cultural diversity, with figures who are Persians, Jews, city residents, nomads, Russians, and others, and some of her stories focus almost exclusively on non-Russian views and experiences, such as "Ishan" about an Islamic religious leader and "In a Mountain Ravine" about a woman unhappy about her husband's plans to add a second wife. In her story "Ulanka the Sart Boy," Ulanka is very resentful of the infidel Russians and sees the Russian lottery tickets sold for charity as a form of dishonest trickery. Another story describes a merchant who, in his meteoric rise to power, is able to break a number of religious rules, such as the prohibition against alcohol, but runs afoul of his Muslim brethren when he effectively steals another man's wife. A story about three brothers indicates that the most pious of them is actually a great hypocrite, while a story about a wandering musician shows him to be truly a man of faith, who plays his music to comfort those in need and takes nothing for himself.

The treatment of women is an important topic for Apreleva, and her focus is split among the treatment of local women who suffer under oppressive marriage rules or requirements for proper behaviour, and that of Russian women who face their own challenges. Young Russian women who recently arrived in Central Asia are shown to be particularly vulnerable, while the narrowly circumscribed lives of women who are under their husband's control, in a harem or merely in a tightly controlled Islamic marriage, are shown in stark detail. Russian society women, however, unlike their peasant or servant counterparts, are shown to be devious and manipulative. The Russian conquest itself plays an important role in numerous stories; there are few that do not touch on the subject.

For Apreleva, it is evident that Russian rule over Central Asia implies responsibility towards those being ruled and a calling to account of Russian government organs. Russian rule, Apreleva implies, can only be justified if it truly improves the lives of Central Asians, if it brings them "civilization" and improves the lives of women and oppressed minorities, such as Persians and Jews. The British and India are not explicitly mentioned in the *Central Asian Sketches*. There is some mention of Indian tea and a "plague from India" that prevents a doctor from leaving his distant outpost, a place not named but clearly on some kind of travel route to India, but it is left to the reader to mentally compare the Russians' record in Central Asia with that of the English in India, if the reader is so inclined.

Apreleva's Central Asia

Detailing first impressions of Central Asia, "Uzun-Ada" (first published 1898, and chosen by her sons as the first story in their edited collection), emphasizes the severe, deadly beauty of the area – the beautiful blue sky, the burning sun, the absence of plants, and the vast stretches of sand, which necessitate wooden walkways in Uzun-Ada, where the railway commences on the shore of the Caspian. The story literally evokes hell, citing Dante's *Inferno* in a play on the name of the town, which includes the Russian word "ad," or hell.[17] Persian workers are said to take the place of pack animals, carrying heavy loads from the ship to the train. The narrator speculates on the various reasons Russians come to the area, describing an official "thrown here by fate," as well as seekers of adventures, since Russia "throws" such seekers into its Central Asian possessions, "na dalekoi okraine," on the distant periphery, evoking Karazin's *Na dalekhikh okrainakh* (and doubtless also Saltykov-Shchedrin's "Tashkenters").[18] Most do not succeed in becoming accustomed to Turkestan, while the "spider Armenian," the "money-grubber," is a necessary evil in order to keep life going in Central Asia.[19] Indeed, non-Russians appear on the scene right from the beginning – Bukharans, Armenians, Jews, and the local Sarts, all described as completely foreign to Russians; Bukharans in fact are drinking champagne and eating sausage (against the rules of Islam), to the shock of the narrator.[20] The railway joins them all together, however, and is also described as the civilizing technology par excellence, the conveyance and structure that most establishes the pre-eminence of Russian power and provides justification for its rule.

Conjuring the Russian troops who had taken the territory as if in a dream, Apreleva's narrator provides a lengthy description of a Russian soldier, separated from his fellows, who dies in the desert, grasping his copper cross. Without naming Vereshchagin or his painting "Zabytyi" ("The Forgotten [Soldier])" (depicted in the introduction), Apreleva provides a cinematic ekphrasis of it, describing what happened to the soldier and how he fell behind, lay down, and could no longer get up, staring at the sky and asking for God's forgiveness as birds of prey circled. The narrator goes beyond the time frame of the painting, imagining the soldier's bones being covered by the sands, noting how much Russian blood has been exacted by this desert. The train whistle jolts the narrator out of his revery and everyone – the previously mentioned Bukharans, Moscow merchants, and now also "ladies with children, obviously, local dwellers" and even a Teke (from a Turkmen group) joins those boarding the train.[21]

"Registan," from the same year (1898), also introduces an unknown place to readers, while also describing the experience of newly arrived Russians in the region. The tale combines a description of the famous Registan in Samarkand, the location of three madrassas and premier landmark, with the Russian celebration of Christmas in the region, complete in this case with snow, which reminds the narrator of Russia, although the appearance of camels and donkeys amid the snow breaks the illusion.[22] Holding in his imagination both the northern Russian snows and the Central Asian surroundings, and indicating that not long ago he had made the passage across the Caspian described in "Uzun-Ada," the narrator portrays himself as a Russian who is trying to find the familiar in the foreign. The narrator contrasts the daytime Registan, site of the Samarkand bazaar, its beautiful arches filled with "movement, colors, and the unique life of the East" – with the Registan at night, when "All are asleep. We [the Russian visitors] stand before the majestic monuments of a past culture, foreign to it, but not indifferent to its beauty, to its grandeur."[23]

The narrator notes that the three madrassas of the Registan were built in three different centuries, reminding the viewers (and readers) of "the power of the great Timur and his magnificent descendants."[24] But, the narrator warns, in fifty to one hundred years there will be little left of the "fantastic world of Scheherezade."[25] When two guards come by and break the spell of this evocation of past Mongol power, "obviously not understanding why we, 'the Russian tiuria,' [glossed as 'gospodin' in the glossary in the back of *Central Asian Sketches*] took into our heads to walk around the bazaar at night," the narrator and his companion(s) go back to the Russian city.[26] The passage of time – from the past Timurid age to the future after, one presumes, lengthy Russian rule of the area – is emphasized by Apreleva.

While the "Registan" story, named for the most famous Samarkand landmark, depicts the narrator in great part as a tourist, Apreleva's 1899 story "Golodnaia Step'" ("Hungry Steppe"), named for the desolate region through which it was necessary to travel between Samarkand and Tashkent, presents a narrator who is far more accustomed to the difficulties of life in Central Asia and indicates the dissatisfactions of many of the rank-and-file Russians who felt compelled in one way or another to relocate to Turkestan. Set three years before the railroad had been completed between Samarkand and Tashkent (1895, one infers), the narrative describes fly-ridden posting stations along the route, with nearly undrinkable water and few amenities.[27] The story sets up a discussion among Russian travellers of whether the Russian control of Central Asia is a good thing – the various interlocutors, all waiting at a station for horses, have different opinions, but many believe it is better for the Central Asians than for the Russians. Finally, the narrator, who has a government order for horses and so has precedence over the others (despite their accompanying wives and small children), continues his journey with both a sick driver and a badly-off lead horse of the troika.[28] At night, one can see the stars glinting off the many bones by the side of the road; by day, one sees the same bones and also carcasses. The lead horse collapses upon arrival at the next station, an event which has been foreshadowed by the eagles that had begun to follow and circle the carriage on the last part of the journey, sensing impending death. The Hungry Steppe, then, is literally hungry, waiting for its next victim(s), the horse and possibly also the ailing iamshchik (driver).[29] In their conversations, the Russian travellers focus on all the stereotypical things they had expected to find in the "rich Orient" – beautiful rugs, elegance, delicious fruit, fountains, melons and peaches, turquoise, obedient slaves – and what they had found instead – poverty, rags, and a rejection of Russians as "kafir" – infidels, unbelievers, "lower than a dog."[30] A number of the less well-off Russians indicate that they hate their lives and would never be in Central Asia except for the advancement opportunities service there afforded. One man says it is a "katorzhnaia strana, katorzhnaia zhizn'" ("a country of hard labour, a life of hard labour").[31] Patriotism goes only so far.

The stationmaster is indifferent both to the poor quality of the horses ("there are no others") and the sickness of the driver.[32] As they approach the second station and the birds of prey are circling ever lower, the story hearkens back to the first story in the collection that contains the narrative description of the circumstances of Vereshchagin's painting "Zabytyi."[33] After the horse collapses, the drivers rush to see what is happening, whereas the stationmaster goes indifferently into the station, followed solemnly by the narrator. Another traveller, Ol'ga Lobri, made the trip using postal horses in 1895, and described it in similar terms to Apreleva.[34]

Far more critical of the Russian role even than "Hungry Steppe" are such stories as "Turkestanets" ("Turkestani") and "General ot Rezedy" ("The General of Reseda" – not in the collection), which specifically take on the topic of Russian corruption. "The General of Reseda," published in 1906, is set in Tashkent. Reseda, or mignonette, is a fragrant plant often grown for its scent; perhaps germane to Apreleva's purposes, it is difficult to transplant and must grow where it is seeded. Apreleva tells the story of a sixty-five-year-old general who can't stand his wife but loves to garden, especially to cultivate roses but also reseda and many other plants, at his dacha in Tashkent. He spends a lot of time with his attractive neighbour, Magdalina Adamova, who has a young son, and with his underling, Tushkanchikov, who serves as a kind of assistant. On the day of his wife's nameday (she is elsewhere), he has an unpleasant day at first, dealing with the payment for a school that must be rebuilt. Magdalina's husband was in charge of handling the problem, and he visits and proposes to the general that he rebuild the school (damaged by water) on credit. The general is gradually convinced of this while the husband takes up the general's own idea of having the townspeople weave nets to protect their fruit trees from birds. Tushkanchikov has his doubts about these cozy agreements but must assent. The general, in a better mood, finishes his day at the attractive neighbour's, whose husband has conveniently departed again. The main thrust of Apreleva's story here seems to be to point to the comparatively loose morals of the general and the way in which he and his neighbour's husband collude to spend government money on credit (all while the general plays up to the man's wife). The underling, who has worked his way up in the world, is left powerless to stop the privileged from having their way.

"Turkestanets," which also addresses Russian corruption, was first published in 1899, in the same edition of *Russkie vedomosti* as Apreleva's stories "Gurimar" and "Tri brata" ("Three Brothers").[35] As Jeff Sahadeo points out: "'Turkestanis' first entered written discourse as those who conquered or supported the conquest of Central Asia. An anniversary of a military victory over Turkmen tribes on July 15, 1870, was a 'memorable day for all Turkestanis,' according to *Turkestanskiia Viedomosti*. In early years, representations of Turkestanis delineated complementary tasks of conquest and civilization. A gendered element emerged in these tasks through portrayals of the first governor-general and his wife. As Kaufman led his troops to battle, Iulia Mavrikievna fon Kaufmana headed the principal public organization in Russian Tashkent, the Turkestan Charitable Society."[36]

The titular character of "Turkestanets," German Mavrikievich Zotikov (who shares a patronymic with the above-mentioned wife of von Kaufman) had come to Central Asia twenty-five years before to try his hand at success.[37] Luck smiled on him. "I became acquainted with him when he had already risen to a high rank," the narrator, a younger colleague, declares. A consummate courtier, Zotikov was able to interact with his superiors with grace and good humour, and "no one had such a store of piquant anecdotes," or could tell them so good-naturedly and amusingly. "Yes, German Mavrikievich Zotikov was doubtless and in all respects a pleasant person."[38] He was a friend and comrade to the narrator, who describes his home office and its indications of Russians made wealthy by conquest:

> in his capacious office, decorated with Turkoman rugs, ottomans, velvet cylindrical pillows, gilt platters, chasework pitchers, saddlecloths embroidered with Bukharan gold, swords in a variegated frame, whips with turquoise trimmings. Here, in this beautiful office, where everything reminded one of the long and productive activity of the owner, where every object eloquently testified that the work of an administrator was met with the proper valuation from the side of the local population and the emir, our kind neighbor, German Mavrikievich, concealed in a coat, smelling pleasantly of the delicate fragrance of fresh linen and English scent, with the warmest smile on his rosy lips, dispensed selected superb Benedictine and no less superb cigars.[39]

After a change in the power structure, Zotikov is unsure of his prospects. As the narrator and Zotikov sit together, he says he is thinking of retiring. As the narrator protests against his retirement plans, Zotikov remarks: "We are old, this structure has become old that we have built, stone by stone … the sowers of Russian culture, perhaps in vain … There are new bosses … new trends … Thought up there in St. Petersburg … In an office, you know, at a writing table … They want to administer on a legal basis – the Law!"[40] German Mavrikievich "snorts" at this revelation: "They are there in St. Petersburg … no, you must live here!" suddenly growing angry and raising his voice, he continued … "Here, in Central Asia … from the day of its conquest … Then you can talk … I see how they, the Petersburg brass, will impose the law, equality before the law among the khalatniks [Asiatics] … To referee the raising of power … But our prestige! What will happen to our prestige?"[41] German Mavrikievich goes on to argue that the "khalatnik" blossoms, is richer, because of the Russians. The powers that be, he says, limit the powers of the local Russian rulers and make them servants. The narrator says uncertainly that "we cannot deny the fact that there was a misuse of power … For example, unfair taxes, extortion under the pretext of meeting the brass, the fictitious undertaking of public works, money that was allocated and was not used for the purpose for which it was allocated, assistance in the seizure of land and many other things, that should not go unpunished."[42] Zotikov retorts that it was important to keep Russian failures and corruption from the public eye: "'But why do you think that these things went unpunished!?' – he [Zotikov] haughtily asked, underlining every word. – 'The misuse was punished … There were punishments, just without noise, without scandal, on the quiet.'"[43] The narrator tries again to protest "meekly"; instead of replying, Zotikov looks at the gilded surface of a platter hanging on the wall, once brought to him by the people of the N. uezd (county) when he was in charge of it:

> – "They brought it willingly" – he said as if to himself. – "That means they were content … It means, they valued us … And such rabble-rousers the N-tsy were. Complaints … accusations … insubordination … I had a lot of trouble with them, while they assembled proper rulers of the administrative unit … Responsible people. Everything was in order with them … There was no extortion and complete loyalty to us … And what! … They were unsatisfied … People made money under them … Under me they stole … That is to say the "hakim" turned a blind eye to it, because he always needed money, but the administrative government could, when necessary, get a thousand, and two thousand, as many thousands as you want … They tried to elect their own … These, you see, promised all kinds of benefits …"
>
> "Producing income is the responsibility of the administrative government," – I noted.

German Mavrikievich shrugged his shoulders and quietly continued.

– "Dancing to the tune of the khalatniks is not my way. Those scoundrels, those troublemakers, should be compelled to sit quietly, not stir things up, it's not right!"

…

– "The general (thus German Mavrikievich called the new head of the oblast') – is a new person … He doesn't know the conditions of local life … He doubtless and urgently will undertake that device, that here on the periphery has been worked out by the path of experience: power and prestige! … Prestige and power! … In this is the whole secret of our peaceful governing of the region … All are satisfied, the population is getting wealthier … Some Islamka or other, Sadyk, Rassul, Umurbaev … Now all the renowned Sarts, sparkling in their velvet khalats at official balls and dinners … After all these are our previous servants, those who sold for five kopeks onions, melons and flatbreads … To whom do they owe their good position? … To us, to the old Turkestantsy, … And not to the judge, the control or to inspections," – he concluded ironically.[44]

Both interlocutors express the thought that the new general will come to understand how things have been done, and they are not wrong: "Already in a few weeks it became known to all that the general greatly values the opinion of German Mavrikievich; and a little bit later, every cloud of worry disappeared from the benign face of Zotikov, and with his previous pleasant smile he offered selected folk his Benedictine and sprinkled most piquant anecdotes. He did not mention retirement again."[45] At the end of the tale, all exclaim that Zotikov has gotten around the general, and all will continue as previously; no one, it is said, will go against "power and prestige, prestige and power."[46] The interpretation of this story is a bit tricky; the local people appear only as "khalatniks," Orientalized grateful or resentful people over whom the Russians rule, as former "servants" or low-class locals turned prosperous local leaders, such as Solimka, or simply as a metonymy of all the colourful local plates, swords, and other items adorning the walls of Zotikov's office. Khalatnik, as Sahadeo points out, is a derogatory term for a local person.[47] The narrator rather meekly brings up the ills that happen under Russian rule – extortion, bribery, misuse of funds – while the portrait painted of Zotikov is that of a perfect courtier, who always knows what to say and whom to flatter. Any reader of Russian literature recognizes this successful kind of chinovnik, almost a Stiva Oblonsky, who has everyone eating out of his hand because of his charming manner and ability to relate to everyone at every social level. Would-be reformers founder on the shoals of such embedded, wily courtiers. At the same time, there seems to be some sense of implicit approval of what he says, that many Central Asians have become wealthier under the Russians, that some of the "barbarism" has been tamed. Whom does the nervous narrator represent? He brings up the sins and the ills of Russian rule that Zotikov prefers not even to acknowledge. He seems quite unlikely to use the insulting term "khalatnik" or claim that gifts brought to a superior are a certain indicator of contentment and gratitude. Apreleva represents here at least three kinds of thinking about Russian rule in Central Asia, that of the Petersburg authorities, that of "old Turkestantsy" like Zotikov, and that of the timid narrator who is critical of Russian failings and corruption, yet who fails to voice particularly strong opposition, apparently approving some of what the Russians have done. While the story clearly condemns Russian corruption, it also acknowledges that Petersburg authorities have a bureaucratic, distant approach that does not really translate to reality on the ground.

In particular, "khalatnik" is a charged term that Apreleva uses to characterize the superior attitude Zotikov takes towards the local people. It is used elsewhere in her collection only in one other story, "Ulanka the Sart Boy," in a passage ventriloquizing the attitudes of high-ranking Russian women selling lottery tickets. It is not a word Apreleva employs straightforwardly, but rather uses to indicate a discriminatory view of a Russian. Zotikov, like other courtier-like bureaucrats who love the status quo, as in other works of Russian literature, are destined to win out even over their superiors. Jeff Sahadeo and other commentators note that such administrators as G.P. Fedorov were long serving, watching superiors come and go; Fedorov was in Tashkent from 1870 to 1906; in his memoirs *Moia sluzhba v Turkestanskom krae*, he commented on numerous governors-general and other officials as they ascended to the highest positions each in their turn; while they came and went, he remained.[48]

Consequences of Colonization

In what is doubtless the saddest tale in Apreleva's Central Asian repertoire, a doctor battles against entropic forces of Russian colonial inertia, unable to create a change in his enervating surroundings. "Dr. Kallinik" was first published in 1900. In this story, told in the third person, a young doctor moves to Tashkent and is admired, even loved. Upon being transferred to a remote military post in the steppe, his friends tell him not to become a drunkard. At his new post, the weather is bad, one gets mail only two times per month, and there is little "society." Upon arrival, he wants to make improvements to the infirmary, but his boss is not enthusiastic. He organizes a chorus.[49] He writes letters and asks others to write to him. He cannot stand the place where he is posted, with its endless card games, vodka drinking, and fever. The answers to his letters become rarer, and months go by without his receiving any letters from his correspondents.[50] He starts a garden, a positive step in terms of the Russian goals of "greening" Central Asia,[51] but feels increasingly hopeless:

> The doctor returned to his little house, carrying in his heart an impression of the deathly scorching desert and wanly returned to his work. Boredom, loneliness, and fever every day wore down his youthful strength more and more. No one had any books. Even a doctor had no means to subscribe to books. The inexpensive monthly journal and the little newspaper, which came twice a month, couldn't satisfy him; furthermore, the echoes of that world, which existed beyond the limits of the burning sands and unwelcoming sea, that divided him from his former vibrant life, were carried ever further away.[52]

Russia, or even Russian society in Central Asia, becomes, in effect, a mirage, a place that no longer exists. In his third year he begins to drink a little. A family of Cossacks arrives; each of their three children has malaria and dies one by one. Then the husband, an alcoholic, also dies; meanwhile, the doctor has come to be acquainted with the wife. He proposes to her and she refuses on the grounds that she is uneducated and therefore not fit to marry him.[53] She agrees to come to live with him but refuses to learn to read and write or to marry him. He stops writing letters, stops leading the choir, no longer subscribes to the newspaper. Then his common-law wife dies of malaria and he drinks more. He asks for a transfer, but plague is expected from India, doctors must remain in border areas to combat it, so the transfer is refused. A former Tashkent colleague comes to visit. The visitor, an older doctor, says that Doctor Kallinik has changed, gotten older, refuses to be familiar with him. He goes to find him where he is sitting in the graveyard – a telling detail. He tells him a vacancy will open, that Tashkent has better weather, the railroad is available, there is more society. But the doctor doesn't want to leave. A young doctor, he says, should be the one to be stationed near the railroad, to enjoy a better climate and more society – and he, Kallinik, should be left in the "devil's hole."[54] Sending a young doctor to such a place would be the end of him, Dr. Kallinik says, it would be a sin to send a young man to his post. A year later, Dr. Kallinik slits his throat while shaving. While the story starts out in a seemingly innocuous fashion, describing the doctor's arrival in Tashkent, the structural problems of the Russian presence in Central Asia are made evident in the story, as well as the sacrifices imposed. Other than in the main towns, life is asphyxiatingly dull, and any attempt to improve things eventually fails due to the nearly frozen bureaucracy (he is not permitted to improve the infirmary) or simple entropy (the chorus). Mail is too slow and subscriptions too expensive. The Cossack widow has such an engrained view of herself as illiterate and unworthy that she refuses to learn to read and write or even to marry the doctor. No one is able to break out of the mould, or wishes to, and the doctor also refuses the thought of another poor soul coming to suffer as he has been suffering, wishing to spare another that burden – but he is unable to continue living himself. This bleak story seems to show that Central Asian provincial life mirrors Russian provincial life, that the Russians have replicated their own problems on top of the ones they so readily diagnose among Central Asians, as we saw in "Turkestanets": women's difficult lives, the cruel laws punishing even minor crimes, the corruption, the poverty. Having made gains in terms of local problems, the Russians unintentionally add their own layers of problems. Rejecting many of the ways of the locals, which they consider barbaric, they bring their own barbarism of bureaucracy, reduction of relationships to money, and vices such as drinking and gambling. A highly colonial relationship of Russians to local people results in their loss of status and self-respect.

Captain Flor Lavrovich Narkizov appears often in Apreleva's stories. The main establishing story of Narkizov is "Kapitan Narkizov," originally published in 1899. Like many of Apreleva's stories, it is a frame tale, set during a beautiful moonlit night in Samarkand with the Registan in the background. Narkizov says to the narrator and his companion that despite the beauty of the night, people can do evil in such surroundings.[55] Narkizov, established in a previous story, "Solimka," as a kind of expert on local life and the relations between the local Samarkand residents and the Russians, gazes at some nearby trees. His story takes place when Russian officers, himself among them, were carousing under those same trees fifteen years before. Narkizov, having become extremely drunk that evening, avowed his hatred for the young officer Milyi (nicknamed "Milochka"). The other officers dressed Milochka as a local woman, and he not only looked the feminine part, but began dancing "like a bacha" and was "flexible, agile, shapely."[56] Milochka, thus attired, was both effeminate and "native," which seemed to be a combination that triggered Narkizov's insecurities. The other officers applaud and laugh. Narkizov, likely reacting with horror to his own feelings and desires and certainly also out of sorts because he has lost very badly at cards, declares the behaviour of Milochka "disgusting."

When Milochka approaches him, quoting a line from Lermontov's "Demon" that includes the words "love me," offering champagne with one hand and attempting to hug him with the other, Narkizov says that "rage seized me," and he loudly declared to all to all that Milochka was "sullying the uniform."[57] He then slapped him with all his strength in the face, but immediately regretted it, while Milochka declared that he would kill Narkizov and tried to do so right away, nearly succeeding. A duel is set.

At the duel, Narkizov shoots in the air, as he promised Milochka's mother he would, while Milochka aims for Narkizov's heart but hits him in the shoulder.[58] Narkizov goes to the hospital to recover from his wound, Milochka to Tashkent. Narkizov later gets a letter from Milochka's mother, declaring that her son had been wounded in battle and received a St. George's cross, and his wife nursed him back to health. Thus, Narkizov muses to his listeners, he is alone in the world while Milochka has honour, decorations, and a wife.[59] Ending the tale, Narkizov states that he gave up drinking and cards after that episode, and on such moonlit aromatic nights, the light and fragrance create a melancholy mood by reminding him of Milochka and his "beastly" act towards him.

The homophobia disguising a possible attraction to Milochka only seems underlined by Narkizov's melancholia when he recalls the conditions under which he cruelly overreacted to the lighthearted crossing of gender (and arguably, in some sense also racial or ethnic) boundaries by the young officer. The recognition that the territory where the soldiers were carousing was once as yet unsullied by the Russian advance into Central Asia indicates an association with the Milochka episode: what was foreign and strange, what crossed boundaries in an uncomfortable way, was shown no mercy, was forcibly taken, and the strangeness and threat of boundary crossing expelled or repressed. The drinking and gambling at cards, a constant theme in Apreleva's stories, is associated with the conqueror's recognition that the work of empire is destructive not only to the local people, but to one's fellow soldiers, betraying a savagery on the part of the Russians.

Earlier in the collection, Narkizov tells the story of a local man, Solimka, who rose from nothing to become wealthy, the kind of person Zotikov had pointed to as benefiting from Russian rule. Narkizov indicates that in the past, apparently in the early days of the Russian occupation, it took a very long time for things to come from Russia, by camel caravan, and asks rhetorically "What could you buy in this Asia?"[60] There was too much money, too much carousing, too little oversight, Narkizov notes. The narrator of "Solimka," for whom feminine endings are used at least twice, her companion(s) and Narkizov go to a large European-style house with columns, Solimka's house, planning to attend an auction of Solimka's possessions. Solimka is said to be pictured in a photograph in the book.[61] The group looks at the house, which has tasteful, Russian furnishings. The visitors/narrator ask where Solimka was educated, noting his many inkwells. "But why do you think he had some kind of education?" the captain asks sarcastically, telling them his only literacy skill was in signing his own name.[62] Narkizov reminisces about the parties that used to take place at the house and says the inkwells were displayed out of pride, to allow Solimka to be like the Russian tiuria, or officers. He was a savage ("dikar'"), Narkizov says, and became suddenly wealthy.[63] He could do anything, began to drink beer and champagne, got richer, obtained a first and then a second wife, and had excellent relations with the Russian rulers. They began to call him Solim Urumbaevich.[64] He shakes hands with the hakim, the governor graces his tamashas with his presence. He learns to use a knife and fork, drinks with the Russians. He has reached the zenith of earthly blessings, Narkizov says: respect, wealth, and health.[65] All Turkestan would come to know him, it would seem. But, Narkizov warns, "cherchez la femme" – The beautiful wife of a relative attracts him. Solimka was a liberal on the woman question, which is "fatal in the Muslim world," Narkizov declares.[66]

Solimka tried to buy the other man's wife, and when he refused, essentially stole her, giving her husband a large sum of money.[67] About half a year later, the man stabbed Solimka in the stomach in a public place, killing him. As the captain told the story, standing in Solimka's house, the dead man's seven-year-old son suddenly appeared. Narkizov tells him that his father had wished to travel to Moscow, Petersburg, London – he tells the son to go ahead and drink and play cards – "but don't touch other men's wives."[68]

Here Apreleva seems to focus on the pitfalls of Solimka's move into Russian territory – he became more and more like Russians, more and more respected, but as he began to think he could break the rules of his own culture, he discovered he could not. There are limits to assimilation. Inkwells did not bring true literacy, and a European lifestyle would not make him no longer a Muslim. Drinking alcohol might be overlooked, but taking another man's wife would not. Money might work as a currency among the Russians, but the stealing of another man's wife could not be recompensed with money. Certainly this story is about hubris, but it is also apparently about a fundamental divide between Europe and Asia, as it appears in Apreleva's stories: while in Russian society money could be used to solve virtually every problem, and every relationship could potentially be reduced to its baldest monetary terms, among the Muslim community it could not. By the same token, Apreleva also begins what will be a frequent theme in her stories: poor local men who become good at trading and earn fortunes, monetary power, and elevated status they would not have had had the Russians not begun to control Central Asia.

"Ulanka-Sartenok" or "Ulanka the Sart Child," which also focuses on the theme of money and navigating between local and Russian mores, was first published in 1899. It tells the story of Ulanka, a child whose father and uncle work for Russians, but whose grandmother instils in him a hatred for Russians as overlords and infidels (kafir).[69] This thinking prevails until he meets the son of the Russian "tiuria" for whom his uncle works as a dzhigit (a kind of all-around assistant in this context), Boria.[70] Ulanka and Boria (who shares the name of one of Apreleva's sons) become friends and work out their differences on such issues as the correctness of eating pork. Ulanka explains to Boria that he wants to grow up and do something that will make money, such as becoming a merchant, whereas Boria thinks that being a dzhigit would be the most exciting possible occupation. Ulanka responds that dzhigits are paid very little.[71] Ulanka learns Russian, and for a time assists Russian shoppers in the bazaar, for which he earns tips; he also makes faces and criticizes the Russians behind their backs. He becomes partial to gambling at dice and cards. Boria and Ulanka discuss Solimka, the subject of Apreleva's above-mentioned story. Ulanka condemns his stupidity and his crime of wife stealing.[72] Gradually, it becomes clear that only the grandmother of the household continues to hate and despise the Russians. The men believe working for them is the best way to get ahead, and Ulanka's father lists the horse, cow, property, and other things he has gained since working for the Russians. The young women of the household dream of being free to uncover their faces.[73] The young men and boys want to work for the Russians. Only the grandmother continues to dream of a future Central Asia returned to its former state and "cleansed" of all the infidels, the kafirs, something Ulanka had also once dreamed of.

Ulanka's friends tell him about a lottery being held by the Russians, with all kinds of wonderful prizes, such as a horse and cart, a cow and calf, other animals, silk garments, samovars, and the like, all of which can be had by purchasing cheap lottery tickets.[74] He is put off by the Russian girls and women who are dressed up, faces uncovered, selling tickets, but he buys tickets anyway, and despite winning nothing at first, continues to buy tickets. He nets only a pincushion and a child's necklace, becoming completely disgusted at the whole affair as he watches the town drunk take home the horse and a Russian soldier and his wife take home the cow and calf.[75] Things are unfair, he believes, and he has spent all his money for nothing. He falls asleep, dreaming of the prizes and of renewed conflict with Russians. His grandmother comes to him with a cooling drink and reassures him that Allah will send him riches. He tells her he will no longer be friends with the Russians but will remain with his own people, and he will become strong and rich.[76]

This story seems to explore the vexed identity politics of the local people who need to get along with the Russians to get ahead, but who lose their identity and deeply held beliefs in the process. Values that did not depend upon money – even the Russian boy Boria has decided that it would be more exciting to be a dzhigit with a horse than to work at a "regular" job – have now been converted into things whose status depends upon money. Through the estrangement of Ulanka's perspective the charity lottery comes across as strange, unfair, and vaguely immoral. It does not assure that the "deserving" get the best prizes, although of course his participation and disappointment serves, one imagines, to make Ulanka less naïve about the world. Ulanka is said to be pictured in a photograph on page 185 of *Central Asian Sketches*.

Another story of clashing values, including those involving money, and the only one that addresses art, "Brodiachii muzykant" ("Wandering musician"), was first published in 1900, and besides being included in the *Central Asian Sketches* of 1935 also appeared in *Detskii otdykh* in 1904.[77] Here the issue is poverty and selflessness that end up being contrasted to Russian values, which look problematic by comparison; Islamic values are seen favourably. An extremely poor man, Mir-Raim, is an orphan who becomes a sheep herder, and when already an adult, is left a two-stringed instrument called a changaus, which he begins to play only after he has survived a lengthy illness during a kind of plague (probably cholera) that killed huge numbers of his compatriots. On his deathbed, he dreams about Allah, dressed in brilliant white, who brings him spirits or demons and tells him to chase them away with his music for the benefit of those who are suffering from sadness or illness.[78] After this he is rejuvenated and begins to chase away the spirits from those who are sick, disabled, and grieving, something he has done, at the time of the story, for thirty years. Unlike the stories set in towns, this story is set in Gurimar, in the foothills of the Tian-Shan, in a ravine that affords some respite from the heat and where families live in yurts. The narrator's cook, Hamid, has told Mir-Raim's story to the narrator, who is the father of a family that includes a wife and two sons (replicating the structure of Apreleva's family).[79] Hamid announces that Mir-Raim has arrived, and the locals all run down the hill to help bring the old man up the mountain, dressed in a white chalma with a long white beard. Mir-Raim asks permission to sing for the narrator in case there is any worry in his soul. He takes the instrument, with everyone arranged around him in a half circle, and begins to sing. He praises the narrator, his wife, and sons, and sings of a battle fought by his dog Alapar with a storm. The listeners are enthralled, and the younger son puts his hand on his knees, which pleases the bard, who now tells a much merrier story of birds learning to fly out of the nest.[80] He holds everyone under the power of his music, which is "wild, strange for the European ear not used to it, at times lulling and tender, and poetic, and so harmonious."[81] The audience is rapt, but after a time the old man becomes tired. The narrator's young sons give him money, with Hamid declaring that Mir-Raim keeps none for himself but will give it to someone else; admirers feed and clothe him.[82]

In this story, Apreleva foregrounds a very non-Russian perspective. In the "Ulanka" story, Ulanka's grandmother had prayed over him, asking Allah to take care of him, upon which he slept without nightmares. In "Wandering Musician," Mir-Raim's dream of the prophet is an important moment. Reminiscent of the charge to the prophet in Pushkin's poem, in Mir-Raim's dream the musician is given a charge from on high, in this case to comfort people and drive away their evil spirits. The music Mir-Raim produces for his audience with his singing and playing, for all that it is "non-European," wild, and foreign, is enticing, tender, poetic, and harmonizes with the blue sky, the forested mountains, and the weathered faces of the listeners, whom the narrator calls "half-nomadic."[83] It certainly evokes Russian literature's history of creating a kind of Asiatic sublime, an evocation of idealized and overwhelming Eurasian features that combine to transport the reader to a higher realm.[84] Indeed, the giving of money afterward almost seemed intended to break the spell, to re-establish Russian (and financial) superiority over Mir-Raim's God-given gift that has transported all of his listeners and inverted, however briefly, the power hierarchy. Although the narrator asserts that Hamid's Russian is broken, this is to an extent a compensating mechanism for the fact that Hamid tells the narrator something important of which he himself is completely ignorant but that everyone non-Russian around him knows well – the story of Mir-Raim and the news of his imminent arrival. This gulf of ignorance hints at other gulfs that surely must be there, other vast reservoirs of Russian ignorance. It also raises the question about the relative status of different kinds of art – and the acknowledgment that art's scope must be far greater than often assumed, while the focus on wealth is clearly misplaced by all who espouse it.

Gender Trouble

One of the most interesting problems presented by Apreleva's writing is that of the status of the narrator and how the narrator relates to issues of gender and the problems that women, both Russian and non-Russian, face in her stories. In the story "Aishe," first published in 1898, Sofiia Nikitichna, a young Russian widow of about thirty, explains to the newcomer narrator (and hence also to the readers) what a "tamasha" is – any kind of entertainment, gathering, holiday, or even a long walk.[85] The perspective of the story is that of one Russian telling a newcomer Russian couple about life in Central Asia "shortly after our move here."[86] "Tamasha" or "tomasha," in the case of Golovnina, is used by Blavatskaia and Golovnina besides Apreleva, and had long before also appeared in Karazin's work, as Shafranskaia has noted.[87] Sofiia Nikitichna describes a "tamasha" she had been to before her husband's death, given by a rich Sart on occasion of the marriage of his youngest son. Arriving at the party, she and her husband are invited into the garden, where there is a large tent set up with food and (notable under the circumstances) alcoholic beverages.[88] The Russian governor, a guest of honour, is in attendance. Western music is played, as well as local music, complete with bacha dancing boys.[89] All of this is described in detail, but, Sofiia Nikitichna declares, this scene is simply all very familiar, there's nothing new to experience, since Russians frequently intermingle with local people and it is ordinary. Sofiia Nikitchna declares that she was interested in another world, the world of women, hidden from everyone.[90] She asks the groom's handsome, dandyish older brother to acquaint her with his wife. As he leads Sofiia Nikitchna further and further back into the recesses of the private quarters of the compound, she attracts attention with her uncovered face and feels she is being silently censured.[91] They go to one courtyard, then another, then a third, full of women and children. She meets an attractive young woman of about twenty-five, dressed in golden silk, with a neckline and sleeves decorated with lace – "a Russian innovation in the costume of a Sartianka, which isn't much different from men's clothing."[92] To the surprise of Sofiia Nikitichna, the young woman speaks Russian, and declares that she has lived among Russians.[93] Her name is Aishe. After passing her husband's first wife's ordinary room, Aishe leads her guest towards her own room, on the way passing the fourteen-year-old bride.[94]

Aishe's room is luxurious, with a French bed, a parquet floor, silk furniture, costly draperies, expensive wallpaper – a major contrast, Sofiia Nikitichna notes, to the far more spartan room of the first wife.[95] She remarks to Aishe that her room is a gilded cage – "but a cage just the same," Aishe responds.[96] Aishe indicates a bricked-up window, preventing her from seeing out to the street, and preventing anyone outside from seeing in. Sofiia Nikitichna discovers that Aishe is a Tatar, married for the second time. Her first husband was also a Tatar, an official who served as a translator.

> We lived in the Russian town. I was in society, at gatherings. I was at almost every evening party. Who didn't know Madame Tankacheeva! I went out, danced, went to the theater. Of course, I dressed like all the fashionable women. My husband did not grudge me anything. But he died … I lost everything …[97]
>
> …
>
> … Maulian-bek convinced me to marry him. He, you know, used to visit us when my husband was alive. After all he is handsome, yes? Of course, I liked him … But he gave me his word that, after marriage, he would move to the Russian town with me and live in the Russian way. He promised … he promised everything … and yet …" Aishe with indignation indicated the bricked up window. – "It wasn't closed off when he brought me here, but on the next day he gave the order to have it bricked up.[98]

Aishe declares that it won't be long before her circumstances change. As the narrator is leaving, Aishe identifies a particular waltz that the orchestra is playing, and, the narrator notes, "How much bitterness, how much regret about what she had lost could be heard in her voice."[99] She does not say "farewell," but "until we meet again."

Sofiia Nikitichna relates that it has been three years and she has not heard anything about Aishe, comparing her to a "fly in a web" who mistakenly failed to believe the bricked-up window.[100] Though he might use knives and forks, how likely was it that Aishe's husband, a "crafty, jealous and powerful Muslim husband," would be "a liberal on the woman's question?" Sofiia Nikitichna asks her listeners rhetorically.[101] On the one hand, an inhabitant of a harem speaks in her own voice; on the other, she is an inhabitant who speaks Russian and would prefer to live life in the Russian fashion. Women who feel differently do not speak in the story. The height and beacon of women's freedom appears to be life in Russian society, at least for those who are "liberal on the woman question." Those who do not know a different life, or approve of it, are seen as either hateful and cruel (the first wife and mother-in-law), as naïve and powerless (the young bride) or as absorbed in everyday matters. The bride is depicted as a lamb being led to the slaughter, but Apreleva gives her no voice in the narrative. In a sly move on Apreleva's part, Sofiia Nikitichna is herself a young widow but is not forced to remarry just to maintain her standard of living, as it is implied that Aishe was obliged to do and, of course, continues to live an independent life in Samarkand. Apreleva thus invites a comparison between the two women, both young widows. Having journeyed into the depths of the harem, Sofiia Nikitichna journeys back out again – the prerogative of a "free" Russian woman. However, Apreleva also indicates that the young Tatar woman should have realized that being the second wife would make her subordinate to the first; she neglected, the narrator says, to take the first wife's status and wishes – and indeed, local Muslim practices – into account.[102] It is a classic "foreigner goes into a harem" story, except that it is a woman who enters the harem (this also occurs in other women's travel stories, as well as in such stories as Karazin's "Doktorsha" ["Doctor's Wife"]) and the twist (although perhaps not so unusual, as one can see in Rossikova's account in chapter five) is that the inner sanctum is Russian.[103] More unusual is that Aishe, the woman in the harem, herself narrates a fairly large portion of the story. "Aishe" addresses different levels of female status among different ethnic groups, the role of the Russian language and culture, the power of Muslim patriarchy, and the limits of Russian laws and customs. Muslim women's utter lack of power – at least those who live in the city – is emphasized.

Apreleva approaches the topic of a man marrying a second wife quite differently in her story "In the Mountain Ravine," published in 1900 and datelined Tashkent (not in the collection).[104] It is a story that essentially stays within the purview of an Uzbek family and is told in the third person. A poor family lives in a yurt in the ravine. The only mention of Russians is to say that the father, Mukhamadi, works for a Russian "tiuria" during the day; this has led to slightly more prosperity for the family, and as a result of this wealth Mukhamadi is now thinking of taking a second wife. The wife, Mastiura, is bothered both by the idea that her husband will take a second wife and even more, that the one he intends to marry is her own sister, recently widowed and with an eleven-year-old son. Mastiura vows to run back home to her father, taking her children with her. Much of the story is taken up with describing the family's daily lives, feeding and milking the cow, pasturing the animals, baking bread, repairing their clothing, and the like, as well as describing the typical Central Asian setting with special weather conditions, animals, bird cries, and the like. Numerous glossed Uzbek words are used; the approach tends towards the ethnographic.

Mastiura's sister, Fatma, comes to visit. At first angry, Mastiura calms down when she discovers that Fatma does not care to marry her husband. Her son does not want it, and her father will not force her to accept. Fatma is noticeably better dressed than her sister, and the narrative describes her son taking a gift to a rich man in the village from her father. It seems apparent that Fatma hopes to marry a richer man than Mukhamadi. Fatma further declares that she does not want to be the cause of her sister losing favour with her husband, nor does she approve of his doing so when her sister has had three sons, even if two of them had died. At night, Mastiura suddenly awakes and begins to fear that he will marry someone else – someone who is a stranger to her. Her mother-in-law says a prayer over her and she falls asleep again. The story ends. An important component of this story is Mastiura's fourteen-year-old daughter, who is about get married herself – to a rich older man. The daughter is content with this, although she clearly has little interest in her husband – she mainly looks forward to the wedding feast and hopes that she will receive silver earrings and a new silk shirt. Apreleva seems to be focusing on the endlessly repeating cycle of women who are married to men they do not love, and whose main sense of family comes from their children and the older women in the family. Their daily work together is the most concrete part of their identity, their relationship with each other more powerful than any marriage.

Apreleva addresses another unhappy marriage in her story "Kerbalai i Zogra," from 1899, which takes place in Gurimar and is narrated by Apreleva's typical narrator, who is the father of a family.[105] Kerbalai is a Persian who serves the family as a gardener; he had once been a slave, along with his father, and was freed after the Russians took over. Zogra is his much younger wife, who seems to be having an affair with a young dzhigit, Yakubka. When she goes out to meet him, Kerbalai strikes him with a farming implement and beats Zogra as well.[106] She is distraught until she learns that Yakubka did not die in the attack. Apreleva draws attention to many viewpoints in the story: the hard life of Kerbalai as enslaved person, orphan, and longtime servant; the judgmental but concerned Russian peasant nanny, who expresses dismay at how Zogra, and women in general, are treated; as well as the view of the Russian head of a family and of the local servants, who have their own insights into the situation. Apreleva draws attention to the change that occurs when Kerbalai, having been caught and tied up and told he cannot stay in the household, is no longer a servant and is now dealing "man to man," so to speak, with the narrator. He drops all pretense of respect and humility so often noted by the narrator in previous interactions, his voice changes, he insults the narrator and looks at him with hatred.[107] Indeed, the narrator becomes angry and strikes him with his walking stick, but then thinks better of any further blows, saying that a Russian should not strike an old man.[108] Zogra has a number of opportunities to speak herself in the narrative, during which she decries her husband, who has whipped her, and says she wants a divorce.[109] Among the household, support of the two breaks down along gender lines, with the Russian nanny completely supporting Zogra and the cook, Hamid, supporting Kerbalai. The nanny has already stated that Zogra was "in prison" – married off when she was fourteen, and Kerbalai almost forty, and that he keeps her like a dog on a leash.[110] Khadzhi the one-eyed servant, having declared that another person would have killed Yakubka outright for his actions, triumphantly announces (after some time has passed) that Kerbalai now has a son and that he and Zogra are happy.[111] The narrator notes that Khadzhi, too, has a pretty young wife. The story raises the question of whether such young men as Yakubka are valuable for impregnating young women, as long as they do not get the upper hand. Russian ways, and Russian treatment of women, at least among the upper class, are clearly seen as superior. The Russian nanny remarks, when describing the fact that the men are all on Kerbalai's side, and that he himself won't eat, drink, or otherwise react: "In a word – Asia ('Aziia')."[112]

Russian women, too, can be victimized as a result of marriage or courtship (they can also be victimizers), which Apreleva shows in her stories "Pereselenka" ("The Transplant") and "Na rybalke" ("Gone Fishing").[113] In the first, a young peasant woman comes to Samarkand at a time when many families came to the region hoping for a better life. As Apreleva's narrator says: "True, the first transplants, unexpectedly and unsuspectingly arriving in the winter in a thickly populated region around Samarkand, where every bit of cultivated land is being used, worked over, they presented themselves as castoffs, unneeded even in their native land, and an incomprehensible sight for the locals. But among these first transplants I recall one family remarkable in its way. By the way not the whole family, but its head, the seventy-year-old Trofim, and his daughter Frosia."[114] The emphasis in the story is on Frosia's powerlessness as a woman, a daughter, and a peasant, unable to make her own decisions. She sends her earnings to her Russian peasant family, while the noble family that employs her buys her clothes to wear. Women are treated poorly by the Russian peasants, it is made clear; her sister Raisa hated life at home and escaped to a nearby nunnery, something Frosia also claims she wants and plans to do.[115] The story explores the pitfalls of poorly educated peasants moving to Samarkand and starting over. Although the family is warned that the village they are intending to move to has a reputation for cheating newcomers, they don't listen and get cheated.[116] The employers of Frosia love and appreciate her excellent qualities, and reluctantly allow her to move away with her family to the village where they know she will be unhappy. In fact, they discover that her loving father Trofim died along the way to the village, which is 200 versts from Samarkand.[117] In the village, Frosia is married off to a drunkard, with whom she has a child. She leaves her husband; the noble family, hearing about this, tries to find her, but they are unable to do so, so they can only think of her fondly and guard her memory.[118] As with "Kerbalai and Zogra," the nanny plays a large role in the story, here as protector and champion of Frosia. One wonders if she is ultimately a stand-in for Apreleva's own views, although the narrator of the story, who is the father of the family, also makes his similar views clear. Apreleva also uses the story to showcase peasant speech, the nanny's and Frosia and her family's.

"Na rybalke," or "Gone Fishing," also addresses the fate of a naïve young Russian woman, the uneducated sixteen-year-old daughter of an official, Fisochka, with whom many men are in love. In the early days of the conquest, Russian women are greatly sought after and the company commander asks for her hand.[119] Instead (it is discovered later) she leaves town with a scoundrel of undetermined background, a dancer and gambler. The narrator later encounters her by accident, after the driver of a cart begs him for help for a dying woman he is conveying.[120] She gives birth to a child and dies. The narrator brings the baby to Fisochka's father; as the story takes place twenty years after the event, he does not know what became of the child. Notably, among the men discussing the story, one of whom is Narkizov, there is no condemnation of Fisa's behaviour, only empathy.

On the opposite side of this equation are Russian society women who are themselves the manipulators. In two stories, one of which follows the character of Captain Narkizov, whose presence in several stories seems to serve to show the many ways in which the Russian conquest can exact a cost on the Russians themselves, women manipulate their admirers and leave them crushed and betrayed. In "The Marriage of Captain Narkizov" (1902, not in the collection), a beautiful but impoverished society woman, Ketevan' Martynovna, convinces the bachelor Narkizov, sixteen years her senior, that she cares for him and has only pretended to be attracted to the handsome young officer von Vigand. The narrator of the story is suspicious, knows of her attachment to von Vigand and considers her somewhat less than respectable. Ketevan' tells her parents that Narkizov has proposed, although he has not; her parents are delighted, and he falls prey to her protestations of love. Before the wedding takes place, the narrator glimpses her with von Vigand at

Samarkand's Gur-Emir mausoleum – he reports this to the captain, but he refuses to entertain any doubt. It turns out that she is already pregnant; the newlyweds remain married but live separately; Narkizov is very bitter at being misled but keeps up the proprieties. She dies in childbirth and the child dies shortly after. Narkizov comes across as a paragon of the civilized, gentlemanly Russian military man, at least after the Milochka episode. Naïve to a fault, he suffers the consequences of his ill-fated marriage in martyr-like fashion. He admits what really happened only, apparently, with the narrator. It is certainly clear to the reader that, faced with pregnancy, Ketevan' needed to marry someone and chose him. Von Vigand had no responsibility and yet earned society's approbation for his show of sorrow after she died. Underlying this story is a critique of superficial Russian society and its desire to reward romance above moral rectitude. Flor Lavrovich Narkizov's name associates him with the natural, floral world, perhaps indicating that he belongs in Central Asia even if happiness eludes him there; clearly, the flower imagery also underlines his role as a civilizer and greener of Central Asia. Meanwhile, women's narrow choices in marriage are brought out by the story, as well as the role that money plays in many of the characters' choices.

Society women and marriage also figure in "Zametki malen'kogo cheloveka," 1905 ("Notes of a Little Man," a title recalling Gogol', also not in the collected stories). Dragutin, a young man who is from a good family, tells the story from the first person. With his parents gone, he has become a bureaucrat of low rank and is asked to help a local general's family, after it becomes known that his father was a general and he speaks French. He is put to work by a general's wife and her thirty-five-year-old unmarried niece, Zizi, creating tickets for a charity lottery. At first treated as a servant, he gradually becomes more and more a part of the family, particularly assisting Zizi in her charity work in Tashkent. She is seven years older than him, but he begins thinking about marrying her and how it might benefit him. Before he can propose he discovers that another suitor has already proposed and that the general's family is moving to St. Petersburg. Although quite commonly literary texts treat women who feel obliged to improve their position by marriage, Apreleva looks at the potential for marriage that would raise someone's status from a man's point of view – and the compromises that would have to be made by him. Seen from a male point of view, these compromises look unappealing, but at the end of the story, Dragutin is basically assured that he will probably have another chance to rise through the ranks as a result of marriage. The fact that he owes the tailor for several suits, with the general's family having left town, may perhaps mean that he will settle for less when he gets another chance.

Navigating Russian Responsibility

The sense that life is difficult for many Russians is brought out often by Apreleva, and a topic that weaves through many of Apreleva's stories is the cost of Russian conquest, both to Russians themselves and to the people of Russian Turkestan. "Ne podvodi" ("Don't Let Me Down") was first published in 1901.[121] It tells of Galenchuk, a sergeant, who neither drinks nor gambles and stays aloof from his troops, who fear him and dislike him, and his friend Mitiukhin, the orderly of Captain Narkizov. The two often get together and drink tea; in his spare time Galenchuk reads and writes poetry. Both reminisce about home and their wives – Galenchuk gets approving reports about his wife from his parents and has a son whom he has yet to meet (the men have been gone for six years), while Mitiukhin hears that his wife is not faithful to him. Both complain about Central Asia, particularly the weather, and the soldier's life. To them, "Russia" is an entirely separate country.[122] As his posting in Central Asia is drawing to a close, Galenchuk goes to the bazaar to buy his wife a gift.[123] He shows the ring and beads to his friend and confides that his soldiers are angry at him. Mitiukhin tells him to pay no attention. Not long before, Galenchuk's soldiers had beaten a local man, who claimed they had stolen from him. Galenchuk has punished them for the beating and they are angry. Galenchuk leaves his friend and sits for a while on a bench on the main boulevard.[124] He thinks of home and what his family must be doing there, and he feels apprehension on heading back to the barracks. In the evening, after he sits down to read and write, his men come up and kill him. It is announced the next day that he has cut his own throat with a razor, which was found in his hand.[125] The doctor examining the body realizes that, although Galenchuk's face is covered with red spots of blood, the razor has absolutely no such spots – obviously, it wasn't what killed him, nor did he kill himself.[126] Nevertheless, the doctor and other officers declare that he has committed suicide. The officers sit down to drink to his memory.

This story, much like the story about Dr. Kallinik, shows how difficult life is for those who feel themselves to bear some responsibility for Russian life in Central Asia and hints that suicide (even if it is not committed in this case) occurs with some regularity. Galenchuk, like Narkizov, is a teetotaler, which makes him an outsider to his own men. A soldier, Galenchuk says, is always on view and must always control himself.[127] He is the visible representative of the Russian government, of the "civilization" that the Russians are so confident of bringing to Central Asia.[128] Angry that he demands that they be respectful to a local man, his men kill him, something he clearly realizes they are going to do, since he is so afraid of returning to the barracks.[129] In the cases of Dr. Kallinik and Galenchuk, the proper administration of the region extracts a huge toll on those who are conscientious in carrying out their duties.

A somewhat different perspective on the conquest comes in the story "Ditia kochevnikov," or "Child of Nomads," Apreleva's 1905 story, datelined Gurimar, which was published again in 1909 and in 1915, though not included in *Central Asian Sketches* (see footnote 2). It follows a nomad family near Samarkand who live hand to mouth. Told in the third person, it uses forty-eight terms glossed with footnotes, such as tiubeteika (skullcap), teng (Bukharan coin), and bai (rich person). The story is set just before the arrival of the Russians to the area. Marefa, a baby girl, is born in the yurt occupied by her family. Her grandfather and brother Iusuf herd the goats of a richer man, while her father is a day labourer. The father of the family, Yakub, decides to join the troops of Murad-bek, who is planning to prevent the Russians from taking Samarkand. The departure of the father leaves the family even more destitute, and because they are waiting for him, they don't move their yurt to the greener pasturage as they usually do at that time of year. As time goes on, they hear little about him and receive only a tiny amount of money from him. There are rumours that the Russians have arrived. The family is hungry and sick; Marefa has a fever, and the mother takes her outside to be cool in the shade. The Russian soldiers are nearby, they hear, so they quickly take their animals and belongings and head for the mountains. In the hubbub each adult thought the other had Marefa, and they don't realize until later that she has been left lying on the ground. She quietly awaits her mother; meanwhile, the "whiteshirt" Russian soldiers ride up to her and one of them, Fedot, takes charge of the girl, carefully washing her and her clothing, finding milk for the "dika-rochka," all with the approval of his captain.[130] Yakub comes back to the site to try to find her, and finds the cloth that had protected her from the sun – but she is not there. From his perspective, the cloth khalat was very valuable, so because it was not taken he did not think a human had taken his daughter, but rather a wolf.

The Russian soldiers try to find the family but cannot, as the nomads had fled beyond the boundaries of Bukhara into the Hissarsky moun-tains. Marefa, meanwhile, becomes the pet of the unit. She regains her health and is adopted by the Russian captain and his family, who have a daughter of similar age. Five years pass; she is now called "Mari-sha" and is very much part of the family, although she feels closest to Fedot, who had originally found her and now serves his captain in the household. She had a "typically Uzbek face, round, somewhat flat, with prominent cheekbones and thick lips."[131] She dreams of her mother and remembers all that happened to her. Early one morning, an Uzbek man calls her name – it is her father. In the last five years, the nomads had been returning to the area, including Marefa's family. At the bazaar, Yakub hears of a girl named "Marefa" who speaks Russian but is clearly from a local family originally. Yakub asserts his rights; although the captain, Egor Semenovich, attempts to pay a generous bride price for Marefa, and her father is tempted by the money (the narrator calls him "greedy"), he refuses to allow her to stay. Although extremely sad, the Russian family relinquishes Marefa to her father. A week later, Fedot goes to look for her, but the family is gone without a trace.

In this story, Apreleva begins with Marefa's family's story, but the girl is never really developed much as a character, she is more important as a pawn in adjudicating, in a sense, which side is most civilized. Yakub, though his family is extremely poor and relies for food in part on his own father and his nine-year-old son, joins the anti-Russian forces, even though this further impoverishes his family. The Russian soldiers who find Marefa are kind and treat Marefa as their own. The captain considers her his daughter despite knowing he might have to give her up. Yakub wants her back because his "fanaticism" does not allow him to imagine his Muslim daughter living with infidels. While the confusion over the children that allowed Marefa to be abandoned is made understandable, the narrator clearly shows the Russian soldiers would not have harmed the family. The panic that caused her to be left was actually unfounded, from the perspective of the story. The default view of the event seems to be that Marefa should have remained with the Russian family, that only her father's "fanaticism" made him decline the money he was "greedy" for. Nonetheless, the very fact that fear of the Russians led to the family's disruption and loss of their daughter – who continues to dream of her mother – is a significant aspect of the story, while the fact that the narrative begins in Marefa's nomad encampment, rather than from the perspective of Russian characters, is notable.

Apreleva's 1899 story, "Dzhugut-khana," or "Jewish Quarter," on the other hand, emphasizes the good the Russians have done, despite widespread anti-Semitism.[132] The narrator, part of a pair or group, goes to visit a rich Jewish merchant in Samarkand, Moshe Borukhov, in the Jewish quarter for Passover. The narrator remarks at how similar the food is to other local food – pilaf, lamb, dolmas, Bukharan sweets – everything is similar except for the matzo.[133] An old man, the patriarch of the family, drinks to the Russian tsar as his grandson translates his whispered words to the Russians. He explains that before the Russians came he used to be chased by a whip for being Jewish, that Jews were

Figure 2.2. "Marefa's meeting with the soldier," by N.N. Gerardov. In Apreleva, *Dva Mira: Razskazy dlia detei sredniago vozrasta*, s deviatiu illiustratsiami khudozhnika N.N. Gerardova (Two Worlds: Stories for School-Aged Children, with nine illustrations by N.N. Gerardov), 1909, second edition, Petrograd, 1915. Courtesy of Lib.ru.

oppressed and treated cruelly, but when the "White Tsar" began to control Central Asia, Jews were treated fairly and not persecuted for their religion.[134] They begin to multiply and could carry on their business in normal fashion, next to Sarts in the bazaar. (On page 161 of *Central Asian Sketches*, there is a photo of a Jewish shop at the bazaar in Samarkand). The old man lays his fragile, shaking hands on the Russians in blessing, and smiles at them.[135] After the feast the Russians return to the dzhigits who have been holding their horses. The narrator asks one of the dzhigits about Moshe Borukhov, who proclaims him the richest man in all of Samarkand. "'And is he a good person?' I remarked in the form of a question. The Sart was silent. 'He is a yid,' (dzhugut), he hissed finally, through his teeth, and in his voice one could hear unexpressed contempt."[136]

While clearly this story paints Russians in a good light, as bringers of equality to Central Asia, it points as well to the anti-Semitism that is endemic to the area, suggesting, perhaps, that Central Asians simply cannot be left to their own devices, they must be ruled by the Russians. It also continues the theme that under Russian rule, Central Asians have benefited from a law-based society and have been able to become wealthy and influential, even if they came from modest origins or a persecuted religion. Apreleva's narrator of course also foregrounds the fact that even the richest man in Samarkand, if he is Jewish, can suffer from unchanging anti-Semitic views; Moshe's sudden turn from cheerful to serious as he exits his inner sanctum, as well as the dhzigit's remark, seems to be evidence of this.

"Tri Brata" ("Three Brothers"), from 1899, is set in Gurimar.[137] Of the titular brothers, the eldest, Umur-Khodzha, is an oppressive and tight-fisted leader and smuggler; the second, Sha-Niaz-Khodzha, prays five times a day, has been to Mecca, and is also rich; and the third, much younger brother, Isliam-Khodzha, is primarily a hunter and known for being kind to the Russian children in Gurimar, bringing them birds' nests and other treasures. This story seems designed to show how cruel and unfair the local leaders can be to their own people – Umur-Khodzha's goats damage a lot of property, but he does not pay a fine; rather, the poorest people in the village pay fines for the damage. It also shows how hypocritical a religious Muslim can be, in this case the middle brother, who may pray five times a day and appear distant from any business dealings, but who is just as rich as his older brother, who protects him from paying any fines for his wayward goats. The youngest brother, who earns his living honestly and is not rich, is loved and approved of by everyone. The Muslim servant of the narrator, Khadzhi, states that the eldest brother and middle brother are con artists, but the third brother is a very good man.[138] This very short story is meant to illustrate the internal politics of the region but also certainly indicates both the responsibility of the Russians for creating or allowing to persist an underclass of ill-treated locals and serves to indicate that observers such as the narrator's servant are fully aware of these inequities. There is also an implicit questioning of any local who is rich.

End of Empire

"From Tashkent to Moscow," published in 1906, datelined St. Petersburg, and signed "E. Ardov-Apreleva," is not part of the Central Asian sketches per se but is listed in Apreleva's own bibliography as *vospominaniia*, memoirs. Here, then, is an account by Apreleva herself, as herself. Apreleva did indeed leave Central Asia in 1906. The account is tightly meshed with contemporaneous events and circumstances. It is more overtly political than most of the fictional stories. The narrator, whose gender is revealed only by the signature at the end but who seems to be very familiar with the ladies' waiting rooms in train stations, travels extremely slowly and with much interruption and discomfort from Tashkent to Moscow and is still on the train when the text ends. There have been railway strikes and rumours of revolution, social norms are going by the wayside, and class distinctions are in peril. Soldiers, officers, and reservists are coming back to Russia Westward from the Russo-Japanese War, filling and overfilling the trains and the train stations. Railway personnel are few and far between, and the sanctity of the first-class train cars is threatened. Problems with the railway track beds near the river Syr-Darya are emphasized, as well as the officers' suffering and disillusionment at the front. Cursing and fights break out on the platforms and in the railway stations. One young Polish engineer behaves in a chivalrous manner to protect another officer; earlier on the train he had proposed a toast to the tsar's Manifesto of 17 October 1905, which promised basic civil rights to the population. The officers, despite their bravery, speak mostly of the horrors of war and the drunkenness and unreliability of their fellows. Drunkenness occurs throughout the narrative, and its open ubiquity seems to disturb the narrator more than anything else; Apreleva used drunkenness throughout her stories as a sign of Russian failure. As the unnamed traveller gets closer to Moscow, order seems to return and the last vignette concerns merry young Russian women teachers who are returning with a Yule tree for their young students. They care for their young charges, and the narrator feels that the "nightmare" of the previous trip has been dissipated by the earnest and committed young women. However, despite the cheerfulness of the last scene, it cannot undo the strong impression that Russia is in great disarray, its typical rules, decorum, and class system falling away. Equality is desired by those who have been kept down, and that means that the rules of the first-class carriage will no longer be held sacrosanct. It will have others brought into it, it will be invaded by soldiers, upper-class women will need to share space with lower-class men and women. Massive forces are being unleashed that will not be subject to Russian control. As the account ends, there continues to be peace and order in Moscow, but trains of disorderly soldiers and lower-class people are constantly approaching it, threatening to infiltrate its orderliness.

Although not technically part of the "Central Asian Sketches," the account of Apreleva's return to Moscow from Tashkent, written under the dual Ardov-Apreleva name, allows the reader to make better sense of the narrators of the Central Asian sketches, who while they are usually male, appear to have the same general outlook as the narrator of the memoirs. The interest in society and social mores is the same as that seen throughout the stories, but as a memoir telling of the author's own experience, it eschews Apreleva's otherwise fictionalized presentation, delivering a narrative understood to be completely factual. The question of whether disorders of the periphery can be left behind, or whether they in fact perhaps stem from Russia proper, or are intimately connected with them, is raised in the narrative. Is there ultimately a dividing line between Russia and Asia, the narrative asks?

Much like the Caucasus of Tolstoy's "The Wood-felling," in which a Russian veteran of the Caucasus, Captain Trosenko, a Kavkazets who has almost forgotten what Russia is like, equates Russia with the Caucasus, Central Asia too is intimately linked with Russia. Tolstoy's Trosenko wonders "And what is there for me in Russia?" – just as Apreleva's Turkestan exists in close relation to Russia itself, a copy that is neither authoritative nor identical with its model. As in Trosenko's imagination, both locations may ultimately become Asiatic:

> "And tell me, is it nice there in Russia?" said Trosenko, inquiring about Russia as though it were China or Japan. ...
>
> "For my part I shall never go there!" Trosenko continued without heeding the major's frowns. "I have lost the habit of speaking and walking in the Russian way. They'd ask, 'What curious creature is this coming here? Asia, that's what it is.' Am I right, Nicholas Fedorovich? Besides, what have I to go to Russia for?"[139]

For many of Apreleva's Russian characters, in fact, Russia becomes something similarly foreign and far away: Zotikov, the bureaucrat, has been in Turkestan for twenty-five years; Dragutin, the young man trying to better his station, does not imagine himself following his employer back to St. Petersburg; the gardening general is firmly planted in Tashkent; and Narkizov, who goes to Russia for his unlucky honeymoon with his faithless bride, is forced to return to Central Asia for lack of money. Of the two officer friends who left their wives in Russia, they speak of it as of a foreign country. These are Russians who have become firmly ensconced in Turkestan; even the unhappy travellers described in "Hungry Steppe" are resigned to their fate.

By the end of the set of Central Asian stories as edited by Apreleva's sons, there is a noticeable change in tone from the first story, "Uzunada," which focuses on the strangeness of Central Asia upon first arrival and the heroic cost of blood needed to control it. Vereshchagin's shadow is there from the beginning, at first apparently as a marker of Russian sacrifice, but later as a question of the cost of battle and the consequences of Russian rule. Increasingly, Apreleva's local residents become individualized, as do at least some of her Russians, and direct comparisons of Central Asia to Russia become rare; Turkestan becomes its own entity. The edited collection ends on the bleakest note of all, when Dr. Kallinik becomes hopelessly estranged, even from Tashkent, and loses all ability to imagine his life becoming better. Perhaps, editing the collection from emigration in Shanghai, this served as an allegory of Apreleva's sons' own sentiment towards a Russia that felt to them lost forever since they hoped that the collection would serve not only as "the best wreath on our mother's grave" but also an addition to the "attempt to preserve in its entirety our Russian soul and our great Russian language."[140]

The edited collection, while it definitely contains Apreleva's best stories, leaves out some of her more ethnographically oriented stories and creates a more "domesticated" view of her work. It is clear that she wished to portray Central Asians who were living their own lives separately from the Russians, with their own values, as much as she wished to portray Russians in intersection with Central Asians. She says as much in the foreword to the collection, which she wrote in 1923 in exile in Belgrade, preserving one of the few oblique references to the British in India, a colonized subcontinent so often called "the jewel in the crown" of the British empire:

> Seventeen years in the Turkestan region gave the author the opportunity to become familiar both with the nature of the area and with the Russian population, both military and civilian, and also with the local people, their customs and habits.

I offer to the attention of the reader these "Central-Asian sketches," –
the author imagines that these sketches depict what are pictures of a now
bygone, marvelous region, in the not too distant but irretrievably departed
past, fairly considered the pearl in the crown of the Russian empire.[141]

Imperial Turkestan here is already irretrievably lost, the "pearl in the
crown" of a country now superseded by the Soviet Union. While written
contemporaneously with Russian imperial control of the region, the stories have become artefacts, as the sons note, and are published, among
other things, as an attempt to preserve Russian culture and language
and as a record of Russian power and its discontents in Turkestan.

PART TWO

Theosophy, Hunting, and Constructing the Nation in the Shadow of the Great Game

Chapter Three

Propagandist of Russian Imperialism: Madame Blavatsky in India

From Apreleva's closely observed sketches of Central Asian life, which require the reader to interpret the Russian imperial role in Central Asia, we turn in Part Two to two far more outspoken writers who place Russian imperial efforts into the context of the Great Game rivalry with the British, Elena Blavatskaia and Iuliia Golovnina. Chapter three addresses the former, the famous Madame Blavatsky, and her quasi-travel-writing narrative texts written about India. In these texts, while India and the British control of the country are Blavatskaia's main focus alongside her thoughts, observations, and proclamations about numerous topics, the issue of Russian imperialism in the Caucasus and Central Asia is never far from the surface. Blavatskaia often uses British examples in order to promulgate Russian counterexamples, typically defending the Russian empire as a "better" one and serving as a Russian propagandist. She also makes much use of a critique that was widespread both among Indians and the British that the period of Moghul domination (a group that had originated in Central Asia) had ultimately led to most of the ills of the country. It led as well, it was thought, to a great fall in culture and the building up of women's inequality and the development of a strict caste system, thus providing reasons why Russian control of Central Asia (with continued Russian expansion then currently underway) would be beneficial for the world. Unlike most of the writers considered here, many of whom travelled only due to their relationship with their husbands, Blavatskaia operated completely independently and made her own living.

A powerful force both in person and in her writings, Elena Petrovna Blavatskaia (née Gan [Hahn]), 1831–91 left a complex legacy that continues to resonate to this day. Blavatskaia, who in the English-languge context typically went by a form of the masculine version of her surname, Blavatsky, or by her initials HPB, is easily the most

Figure 3.1. Helena Petrovna Blavatskaia, 1877. Courtesy of Wikimedia Commons.

prominent figure discussed in this book. Born into a noble family in Yekaterinoslav, the daughter of famed writer Elena Gan and granddaughter of Elena Fadeeva, who was a well-known and avid botanist, she spent a peripatetic youth as the daughter of a military officer. Her mother died when she was quite young, and she spent a great deal of time with her grandparents, the Fadeevs. A much-younger cousin (by eighteen years) was Sergei Witte, who became prime minister of Russia. He related in his memoirs how she was married at a young age in 1849 to the vice-governor of Erivan, Nikifor Blavatsky, but soon left the marriage, although she later returned at least briefly.[1] A great deal of her biography is contested, since she claimed at times contradictory or arguably fantastical things. Most agree that she spent time in Constantinople, Greece, Cairo, Paris, and England, and then Canada, India, and the United States, and back to Russia in 1858. She also claimed to have spent seven years in Tibet, one of the most problematic claims she made.[2] No one disagrees that she arrived in the United States, to New York, in 1873, nor that she founded the Theosophical Society, with Col. Henry Olcott, in 1875. One might call her a performance artist avant la lettre, but one can also think of her in terms of media history, since she excelled in performing her life and ideas both in person and via various kinds of media.[3] Notoriety was her métier. As Maria Carlson notes, "She has been called a genius and a charlatan as though the two were mutually exclusive; Mme Blavatsky was clearly both."[4]

Blavatskaia's Theosophy grew out of her interest in, and background in, the occult, a term that has numerous meanings, but is, as Maria Carlson describes it, "a system, a body of knowledge with both a practical and theoretical dimension … a manner of perceiving reality" that allows the human consciousness to go beyond the self.[5] The then highly popular spiritualism, the "most prominent, most recent expression of an occult tradition,"[6] was incorporated into Blavatskaia's conception of the occult, in which ideas about magic and the supernatural could be understood simply "as natural powers that science did not yet acknowledge."[7] Blavatskaia's great-grandfather, Pavel Dolgorukii, had been a Freemason and had left a large library with occult books, which she was free to explore as a youngster.[8] Many followers of Christianity in the nineteenth century were increasingly frustrated by what they perceived as its opposition to science; in contrast, Theosophy could accommodate Darwin's theory of evolution, with a "God who created the world slowly through natural processes," while retaining a focus on humans' spiritual evolution.[9] Further, as Carlson points out, occult systems such as alchemy, astrology, and so on, typically require study and a period of apprenticeship, a need for initiation; the occult is thus "esoteric, i.e., intended for a small group and concealed from the uninitiated."[10] As Carlson notes, "Theosophy offered access to the divine not through faith, but through the study of a higher knowledge, through the 'secret science.' To the modern European mind, whose loss of faith threatened it with fragmentation and alienation, this was a seductive offer indeed."[11] Blavatskaia also innovated within the occult tradition in another way, as Mark Bevir points out, making India the source of the ancient wisdom rather than Egypt.[12] This meant claiming that Buddhism was founded on Vedic works and that Indian civilization had given rise to that in Egypt.[13] The Tibetan "masters" that Blavatskaia claimed guided her, first only through spiritual connection but eventually through increasingly material ways, such as with letters and telegrams,[14] were thus, as Bevir points out, not necessarily anything supernatural, they were "part of the natural order. They are highly spiritual beings near the end of their evolutionary cycle who have chosen to remain around to help the less advanced."[15]

The idea that Eastern or Near Eastern cultures were, or had been, the foundations of wisdom and culture, rivalling or displacing Western ideas of antiquity, was a prominent one in the nineteenth century. As Suzanne Marchand notes, "'Orientalism' certainly contributed to European empire-building, but it also helped to destroy a narrow Christian-classical canon."[16] As Raymond Schwab noted, once the *Avesta* was translated by Abraham Anquetil-Duperron, a "universe in writing" became available, and its realization "reached dizzying heights owing to the exploration in Central Asia of the languages that multiplied after Babel."[17]

It is possible to read two sets of Elena Petrovna Blavatskaia's collected travel letters, published in Russian newspapers in the 1880s, through many different lenses.[18] Titled *From the Caves and Jungles of Hindostan: Letters to My Homeland* and *The Durbar in Lahore*, they are signed "Radda-Bai," or "Sister Success." A third text about India, also signed Radda-Bai, called "Mysterious Tribes: Three Months in the 'Blue Hills' of Madras," was published in *Russkii vestnik* from December 1884 to April 1885, but will not be addressed here because it is significantly different from the other two, being much more ethnographically focused.[19] Of these by far her most famous account, *Caves and Jungles of Hindostan*, first and foremost depicts a journey to India made at the invitation of Arya Samaj, a Hindu reform movement started by Dayananda Sarasvati, in order to consult with practitioners of various kinds of spiritual practices, primarily Hindus and Buddhists, and to found new chapters of the United States–based Theosophical Society, founded by Blavatskaia herself along with American Colonel Henry Steel Olcott. *The Durbar in Lahore* is a more typical travel narrative, primarily describing the 1880 durbar, or public reception, that took place to welcome the new viceroy of India, Lord Ripon. Both sets of letters can certainly be read as a condemnation of the British rule of India and veer between the author's primary view that India should be independent and her sometimes-expressed view that India would be better off being ruled by the Russian empire, which often comes via "quotation" of a local person.[20]

Great Game–inspired tensions between India and Russia are a frequent topic for Blavatskaia, as is spying in both directions. British racism towards Indians is frequently a target of the letters, which also condemn patriarchy in its many guises. *Caves and Jungles of Hindostan* argues vociferously that ancient Indians did not oppress women, but that such oppression was brought about by later rulers, Persian but especially Muslim ones, and by the ascendance of Brahmins as a caste, who reinterpreted ancient texts in a way that promoted practices like sati (ritual immolation of widows), betrothal, and marriage at extremely young ages, and exacerbated the pronounced stratification of castes. A noblewoman herself, Blavatskaia decries social stratification, especially as it is enforced by the British. As a number of scholars have pointed out, "caste organization became projected [by the British] not only as hierarchical, but increasingly also as discriminatory and stultifyingly ritualized."[21] Missionaries were frustrated by Indian resistance to Christian conversion and blamed it on the caste system, while others equated caste with slavery and used it to justify missionary work and the civilizing mission.[22] Another Blavatskaian point, which is that Brahmin scholars interpreted sacred texts so as to increase the status of Brahmins as a whole, is substantiated by more recent scholarship.[23]

Caves and Jungles of Hindostan is certainly also a travel narrative, despite its relative distance from factual reliability. It describes the trajectory of Blavatskaia's group as they followed, at least in Blavatskaia's telling, a particular itinerary across the landscape, describing people, places, transportation, foods, animals, and other details of the journey of a group of travellers. According to Blavatskaia, this group consisted of white "Europeans" (Blavatskaia, who was a naturalized American, Col. Olcott, an American, and two British citizens, Miss Rosa Bates and Edward Wimbridge) travelling with their local fellow Theosophists, servants, and guides, who hailed from different regions, castes, and religions. In fact, it is not clear that such a large group actually ever travelled together, but Blavatskaia's purpose in describing the interactions among them is frequently political. Writing in Russian, a language unknown to her fellow Theosophists and friends from the subcontinent, Blavataskaia created her own narrative reality for her readers, secure at least at the time in the knowledge that the others did not know what she was saying, although they knew she was writing letters for Russian publications. She states in *The Durbar in Lahore*, however, that she knew the British were reading translated versions of her *Caves and Jungles* letters to the *Moscow Herald* as early as 1880.[24]

The Theosophical Society's own and the travellers' mixture of cultures and castes is a frequent topic of *Caves and Jungles*, as is its tendency to describe shock in British observers, who, according to Blavatskaia, could not conceive of whites treating Indians as full equals. Blavatskaia contrasts the successful visits of individual (typically high-caste) Indians to England proper, where they were well received, with their execrable treatment by the British in their own country, asserting that those British citizens who had never been to India did not realize how poorly the local inhabitants were treated by the British.[25]

The "Plums and Spices" of Blavatskaia's Account

Inarguably, *Caves and Jungles* is also in no small part a work of fiction and also draws to some extent from Constance Gordon-Cumming's travel book *From the Hebrides to the Himalayas*, with some passages more or less plagiarized, while others are attributed.[26] It may also include plagiarism from travel guides, although Blavatskaia claims her reliance on other sources did not go that far:

> It is like my *Russian Letters* from India, where while describing a fictitious journey or tour through India with Thornton's *Gazeteer* as my guide, I yet give there true facts and true personages only bringing in together within three or four months time, facts and events scattered all throughout years as some of Master's phenomena. Is it a crime that? Because Scott thought so. Why, if having been in Calcutta and Allahabad I have to write upon their antiquities – *which I have seen myself* – why shouldn't I resort to *Asiatic Researches* and even Thornton's *Gazeteer* for historical facts and details I could never remember myself. Is it considered a literary theft to refer to Encyclopaedias and guide books? I do not copy or plagiarise, I simply take them as my guides, *safer than my memory.*[27]

In some cases, she cites guidebooks but quotes and documents them appropriately, such as Edward Eastwick's *A handbook for India* of 1859.[28] In her claim above, it should be noted, Blavatskaia is also relying on her claim to have previously been in the Himalayas and Tibet, as well as elsewhere in the subcontinent, in a sojourn that has never been factually documented, in which she met her Tibetan "Masters" with whom she studied and could communicate in mediumistic fashion.[29] Hence, what she had "seen for herself" was partly true and partly what she had "seen" during this earlier "trip."

Henry Steel Olcott, the co-founder of the Theosophical Society, who also wrote his own account of his time in India with Blavatskaia, in the second volume of his memoirs, *Old Diary Leaves*, by then had had the opportunity to read the first, partial translation of her letters to Russia.[30]

He points to multiple episodes that, while undoubtedly interesting and surprising in and of themselves, were heavily, perhaps nearly unrecognizably, embroidered by Blavatskaia:

> Shortly after our settlement in Girgaum [in Bombay] occurred an incident which H. P. B. has embalmed as a permanent record, in her delightful *Caves and Jungles of Hindustan*. When I give the simple, sober facts, the reader can see how the glow of her splendid imagination has transformed them beyond recognition, and out of a commonplace incident created a picturesque and awesome romance … if the reader will turn to *The Caves and Jungles of Hindustan* (p. 176, "A Witch's Den") [Johnston edition], he will see what H. P. B. made out of them. Instead of a wretched hovel in the densest quarter of Bombay, with an audience of coolies, we are led on elephants, by torchlight, through a dense forest, "Two thousand feet above the Vindhya ridge"; … we reach the "den" of the *Kangarin* – "the 'Pythia' of Hindustan,' who 'leads a holy life' and is a prophetess." … and so on through twenty pages of as picturesque writing as can be found in our language … What she did in this instance, she did throughout the book – a minimum of fact was, in each case, made to cover a great area of fancy; as the small lamp in the engine head – light is by parabolic reflectors made to shine over the line like a sort of sun on wheels.[31]

The translator of the edition Olcott refers to, Vera Johnston (also Blavatskaia's niece), noted that Blavatskaia called her letters a "romance of travel":

> "You must remember," said Mme. Blavatsky, "that I never meant this for a scientific work. My letters to the *Russian Messenger*, under the general title: 'From the Caves and Jungles of Hindostan,' were written in leisure moments, more for amusement than with any serious design.
>
> "Broadly speaking, the facts and incidents are true; but I have freely availed myself of an author's privilege to group, colour, and dramatize them, whenever this seemed necessary to the full artistic effect; though, as I say, much of the book is exactly true, I would rather claim kindly judgment for it, as a romance of travel, than incur the critical risks that haunt an avowedly serious work."[32]

From the Caves and Jungles of Hindostan also promotes Blavatskaia's ideas, some of them then widely agreed upon by scholars, about how the Slavs are likely closely related descendants of the ancient Aryans, that Greek heroes and gods are derived from those of ancient India, and that Russian in particular is closely related to Sanskrit. Blavatskaia followed German Orientalists in dividing Indian history "into two halves (each with a further line down the middle): the period of 'free, independent India' and the period of 'foreign domination.'"[33] Blavatskaia was not immune to the racialization of various ethnic groups, as one can see when she uses such terms as "pure-blooded Aryans," but for Blavatskaia, the fallen ideal state of gender equality that needed to be restored took precedence over any racial categories. That the study of religion and culture was itself racialized had strong effects on the representation of India and Central Asia; Vera Tolz notes that V.V. Bartol'd observed in 1914: "The exaggerated perception of the cultural achievements of the Aryans and the barbarism of the Turks could not avoid having an impact on the understanding of Russia's scholarly tasks in Turkestan."[34] Western Orientalists, especially those who never travelled to India, such as Max Müller, receive a great deal of criticism from Blavatskaia, while a few Western figures, mostly Englishmen such as James Tod or Rous Peter[s], who she believed devoted themselves to truly understanding India, are praised.[35] Blavatskaia, in concert with many others, viewed the subcontinent as having fallen into ruin and disrepair after the Persian, Muslim, and English conquests.[36] Nonetheless, as Srinivas Aravamudan points out, "Theosophy was a cosmopolitan alternative when compared with the parochial nature of the Raj," and Blavatskaia's focus is as much on contemporary leaders, life, and people as it is on the impressive and majestic ruins she often defends as superior to later, Moghul-era edifices.[37] As Peter van der Veer points out, "spiritualism, and Theosophy in particular, played a significant role in the development of radical, anti-colonial politics both in Britain and India."[38] Further, Blavatskaia focuses on and celebrates local knowledge and expertise, frequently (and not always fairly) denigrating that of Westerners. Behind the very founding of the Theosophical Society was her communication with her masters, some of whom were Egyptian but others of whom she had supposedly met in Tibet, and who taught and inspired her, at times dictated to her.[39] Blavatskaia compared the communication of the masters' "thought-waves" to the waiting pupil ("chela") who transfers them to paper to the electrically powered telegraph, which can transmit perfectly or, if there is a fluctuation in electricity, with mistakes.[40]

There is by now a lengthy bibliography of research on Westerners, such as Blavatskaia, Olcott, Sinnett, Annie Besant, and the like, who developed their own religious ideas and worked with local reformers in the subcontinent.[41] Although this bibliography very much informs my account, my focus in this chapter is on Blavatskaia as a Russian-language writer and pro-Russian propagandist, addressing her audience in Russia and on the Great Game context of her writing. She was quite capable of writing in English, and indeed wrote voluminous correspondence as well as other texts in English, such as *Isis Unveiled*, but the letters from India were intended for her Russian readers, and in collected form were subtitled "letters to the motherland." They were published serially, and then in collected fashion, in two separate volumes published as supplements to *Russkii vestnik* in 1883 and 1886.[42] As previously noted, a portion of the letters was translated into English by her niece, Vera Johnston, in 1892.[43] A second, complete English translation was published in 1975 by the Theosophical Society, translated and introduced by Boris de Zirkoff, who also acknowledges the often-fanciful nature of Blavatskaia's accounts of her sojourn in India.[44] Importantly, Blavatskaia's writing was her source of income.[45] In an undated letter to Katkov, written from Paris after she had left India, she tells him her friends are telling her not to publish in his journal, *Russkii vestnik*, but that since he had published her *Caves and Jungles of Hindostan* when no one yet knew her, she wanted to offer him a new piece – but she wanted to get a contract that would assure her payment by the line and would protect her against his leaving out parts of her work. She tells him she knows he has published her letters as a separate edition and they are "going like hotcakes." She reminds him of her uncle's admiration of him and of her sister's six children and their need for money from her writing.[46]

In *Caves and Jungles*, the main perspective in the narrative is certainly Blavatskaia's own. Blavatskaia's main "character," and main perspective, is that of her travelling and Theosophical self, as well as her fiercely, patriotically Russian self. Blavatskaia plays the role of an interpreter and travel guide and places much emphasis on her interlocutors. The other main characters are Col. Olcott, her "chum" and co-founder of the Theosophical Society, as well as the Britishers Miss Bates and Mr. Wimbridge.[47] Her Indian companions are harder to pin down, and some are fictional. Decidedly non-fictional were Moolji Thackersey, a textile magnate and convert to theosophy also mentioned by Olcott, and a friend of his going back to 1870, as well as Babula, a linguistically talented servant of fifteen.[48]

Others included Narayana, a mysterious travelling companion, and the Thakur, or Gulab Lal Singh, the latter of whom can be described as "a fictionalized character in the narratives published in the volume *From the Caves and Jungles of Hindostan*. The character broadly corresponds to Helena Blavatsky's spiritual Master."[49] Not only that, but as K. Paul Johnson points out, his presence sometimes serves as a way to give the Indians a voice against the British: "Miss B – is clearly providing an opportunity for Radda-Bai to demonstrate to her Russian readers the hatred felt by Indians toward the British. Not only does Gulab-Singh exhibit an attitude which is both threatening and derisive, but he also asserts that a successful uprising will occur the moment his brotherhood decides to allow it. Such a portrayal of the Theosophical Mahatmas was quite different from that conveyed to Anglo-Indians like A. P. Sinnett!"[50] Although Blavatskaia is mostly, although not always, complimentary about her close associate Olcott, she disparages the Englishwoman Miss Bates without mercy; Olcott himself writes that he had advised against allowing Miss Bates to come to India to begin with and then had to undertake the unpleasant duty of expelling her from the Theosophical Society; the parting of ways of Miss Bates and Edward Wimbridge from Blavatskaia and Olcott was even chronicled in the newspapers.[51] Olcott does corroborate the reasoning behind allowing Miss Bates on the trip that Blavatskaia also frequently references in her letters: with two English citizens accompanying them, the Theosophists hoped to keep British suspicions at bay as to the aims of the Theosophical Society and to prevent them from interfering with their undertakings. Certainly, it is also true that Miss B. served as a useful literary foil for Blavatskaia. Olcott, as already noted, wrote his own account, based on his diaries, after Blavatskaia's letters had already been translated into English and after she herself had passed from the scene; while sympathetic to Blavatskaia and impressed by her many gifts, he was eager to correct the record as needed, but acknowledged "the plums and spices that H. P. B. put into her charming Indian wonder-book, to make it interesting to the Russian public, in whose language it was originally written."[52] The quality of Blavatskaia's writing was indeed appreciated in Russia. Vsevolod Soloviev, though later a detractor of Blavatskaia, writes that he had admired her *Caves and Jungles of Hindostan*, "which had been read with so much interest in Russia."[53] He wrote that she was "a writer who impressed one with her literary talent, enormous memory and facility of quickly grasping the most varied topics and write about absolutely anything, write interestingly and appealingly, if often unclearly and in all directions."[54] Maria Carlson describes Blavatskaia as an accomplished and imaginative writer, noting that the "literary merit of *Iz peshcher i debrei Indostana* is undeniable. Like her personality, Mme Blavatsky's style is lively and untraditional ... Readers seeking exotica, entertainment, and sensation loved her work; it was popular."[55] Sergei Witte, in his memoirs, describes meeting Katkov in Moscow, who told him about his cousin's famous *From the Caves and Jungles of Hindostan*. Katkov noted that he did not know her personally but that he bowed before her talent, considering her a completely remarkable person, and "he was quite surprised when I told him that in my opinion one could not take Blavatskaia seriously, although she had a preternatural talent."[56] Esper Ukhtomskii, who travelled with the Tsarevich Nicholas in 1890–1, met with Olcott in Madras and praised Blavatskaia in the second volume of his book about the trip:

> Blavatskaia provoked a storm of denunciations of charlatanism, and was practically forced by the suspiciousness of the English to leave forever her wonder-filled and much beloved peninsula; but her art called her to itself with unselfish sympathy and the devotion of the local people, their vague thirst is united under the flag of this strange *northern* woman of a people who are radically foreign to that of Albion; – her constant travels around the country so as to become closer to the wise men and in an attempt to be admitted to various treasuries of the secrets of the Brahmins and the Jains, – all of this taken together created for her an exceptional position, such as no one since ancient times anywhere ever occupied … For India of the present and the future E. P. Blavatskaia did not die and will not die.[57]

From the Caves and Jungles of Hindostan is designed from the beginning to appeal to the Russian reader; Blavatskaia makes frequent reference to cultural touchstones that her readers will appreciate. Her anti-British and pro-Russian stance seems perfectly in accord with her real views, but doubtless also appealed to Russians' sense of national pride, an important topic in Katkov's publications. As Andreas Renner points out, "*Moskovskie Vedomosti* was successful because it was nationalist."[58] Blavatskaia's account constructs, I would argue, a sense of solidarity between the disrespected and Orientalized residents of the subcontinent and Russia's own resentment at European condescension, and continually draws contrasts with how the Russian empire treats its own "subject peoples." In an 1880 letter to the editor of *The Pioneer* in Allahabad, Blavatskaia takes umbrage at an article that stated that "an ambitious Indian lad, full of half-developed power, is in a more hopeless position than an Armenian under St. Petersburg, or an Algerian under Paris," noting that the Russian military actually boasts many Armenians, Georgians, Tatars, and at the highest ranks.[59] Arriving in Bombay, Blavatskaia says: "there is as much difference between *officially* explored India and (what we may be permitted to call) *underground* India, as there is between the Russia of the novels of Dumas-père and the real *Russian* Russia."[60] She rankles at the British assumption that any Russian is a spy, noting that their reply to her objections is "kovarstvo Rossii davno voshlo v poslovitsu," or "the wiliness of Russians has long become proverbial."[61] As if anticipating Tolstoy's future "Letter to a Hindu," Blavatskaia points out that there are only 60,000 British and 245 million Indians in India.[62]

In her second letter/chapter, Blavatskaia indicates that she and her group are staying in bungalows in the Indian part of town, "We were living *in* India, unlike the English who are merely *surrounded* by India at a proper distance." Living among the Hindus, she writes, is inaccessible to the English because of their native prejudice and the "innate haughtiness of the Anglo-Saxon race."[63] Indeed, Blavatskaia often casts Englishwomen as the villains of the story, especially Miss B., but also others whom she portrays as rejecting would-be Indian visitors, marching off at the sight of a mixed group dining together, or rejecting Blavatskaia herself because she refuses to pay calls.[64] On the one hand, as Éadaoin Agnew points out, colonial wives were sometimes criticized by critics as "prudish memsahibs totally disconnected from the historical and political situation," but that "private lives in India were part of a public and imperial narrative," so that actions taken by Anglo-Indian women played a role in the construction of the imperial operation of British power, and Blavatskaia (constructing her own counter-narrative) reacted strongly to the social power of British women.[65]

Blavatskaia acknowledges (unlike Dukhovskaia), then firmly banishes racial prejudice from permissibility early in her third letter: "Gone are the days when, proud of our white skin … we could look down on Hindus and other dark people with a feeling of contempt well-suited to our own magnificence."[66] About to attend a performance of the famous epic Ramayana, she points to the ancient derivations of the Sita-Rama story in which Europe was given as a prize and quotes Pushkin's "Ruslan and Liudmila's" "[дела] давно минувших дней/Преданьях старины глубокой" ("deeds of long forgotten days/traditions of a distant era") to attest to the ancientness of the tale.[67] With only four "Europeans" in attendance, the performance is an exclusive experience, and one on which Blavatskaia lavishes attention for her readers, painting vivid, exoticized pictures for them. The women look like a "bed of flowers" in their colourful clothing, Parsee (Parsi) women look like Georgian woman, and there is a veritable "sea" of turbans – it is easier to count the stars than to distinguish the number of different turbans, she writes. Further, the ambassador accompanying them wore diamonds in his turban and a necklace that would have "driven a Parisian woman out of her mind."[68] The foreign audience members themselves were garlanded with jasmine and sprinkled with rose water, "like idols." Making clear to her readers that she and her compatriots were not just disembodied viewers, she describes the "hullabaloo" ("perepolokh") that ensued when, having been at the performance for several hours and having become quite overheated, they decided to leave.[69] The whole performance stopped, and the main character came to the front of the stage to make a speech in English thanking them for attending. The fourth wall was broken for Blavatskaia and her companions, just as she hoped to do for her readers, as she included in every letter various levels of anticipation of her readers' recognition and reactions, desires, and readiness for education.

Besides comparisons from the Caucasus and Transcaucasus (Parsi women look like Georgian women), she uses Russian literature, myth, and history to place these new sights, ideas, and figures into context – quoting Pushkin, as we have seen, mentioning Afanasy Nikitin in her second letter to remind readers that he, too, had reported that Indian women were naked, comparing a local leader to the Russian folk hero Ilya Muromets in chapter five and the length of men's hair to that of Zaporozhian Cossacks. A lock of hair is said to be like a "kudel'ka," a word "used by Russian servant girls of former days,"[70] witchcraft is cited as something that occurs in Russia, and mediumship is called "klikushestvo" among the Russian people.[71]

Blavatskaia also does not skimp on the kind of amazing adventures her readers might enjoy hearing about. One of the most poetic descriptions in the letters apparently describes something almost completely imagined, or rather imagined with the not inconsiderable help of Constance Gordon-Cumming, the sister of the famous hunter R. Gordon-Cumming, and author of *From the Hebrides to the Himalayas*. As Olcott's quotation above explained, Blavatskaia describes a complex and far-flung journey to go see a witch or holy woman (Kangalin, in Blavatskaia's texts, Kangarin in Olcott's), whereas Olcott says they did see such a woman, but in their neighbourhood in Bombay, walking there on foot and staying an hour and a half.[72] In the version created for her readers, however, Blavatskaia creates a quite poetic and compelling vision of night travel by elephants, lit by starlight and flashing fireflies:

There is something indescribably fascinating, almost solemn, in these night-journeys in India. Everything is quiet and silent; everything sleeps, both below us and above us. Only the heavy and regular thud of the massive tread of the elephants breaks the stillness of the night ... Heavens! What teeming life, what stores of vital force are hidden under every leaf, under the smallest blade of grass in these tropical forests! Myriads of stars shine in the dark blue of the sky, and myriads of fireflies gleam with their phosphorescent sparks, like pale reflections of far-off stars, twinkling at us from the dark green bushes, as if showing us our way and lighting it for us.[73]

For this passage, however, she is much in debt to Gordon-Cumming, who describes a similar night journey, though enabled by bearers and not elephants:

> There is something very strange – almost solemn – in such a night march; when the deep stillness is only broken by the measured tread of the bear-ers, and the deep-toned "Khaberdar," "take care!" which, uttered by the leader, is chorused by all at every difficult bit in the road. Then, too, strange voices resound through the forest; insects of every sort awaken, and by turns you hear sounds of chirping, and drumming, and whirring; some harsh, some shrill. Sometimes they seem all to join in chorus, as if to suggest something of the exuberant animal life which lies hidden under the green leaves. Then pale phosphorescent lights glimmer in the dark-ness, and mark the track of the fire-flies.[74]

For Blavatskaia, the correlation of the fireflies with the stars (stars are not mentioned in Gordon-Cumming) seems to be a crucial component of the scene. In concert with Theosophy, it seems, the whole external world is full of various lights and beings, with the human travellers alone able to partake of the exalted experience; the stars above mirror the fireflies below. At this juncture, as alluded to above, Blavatskaia compares "demoniacs" to peasants in Tikhvinsk who burned the witch Agrafena alive, and, for further "colour," claims that the colonel, during the nighttime ride, is thinking of night sallies against the Confederates in the Civil War, a war in which he did indeed serve.[75] According to Blavatskaia's account, the witch uses almost as a prop the skull of an ancient sivatherium, which was a type of prehistoric giraffe, another engrossing embellishment by Blavatskaia, who also injects the whole fantastic scene with various reality-enforcing details, such as noting the number of minutes "by our watch" that the Kangalin danced in a frenzy, mentioning a grain of rice stuck in W.'s (Wimbridge's) throat, as well as describing Miss B.'s false teeth being aired "in the light of the stars."[76] On the less-realistic side, she says that Narayana, one of the quasi-imaginary Hindus accompanying her group, fell onto the giant skull and upset it, knocking the "witch" off her perch.

After describing the elaborate observation of the possessed Kangalin, Blavatskaia portrays herself and her group as being on an extended trip. She describes Sikhism, Hyderabad, and a number of buildings there, before noting that it was too hot to go to Hyderabad, so they went to the caves of Bagh instead.[77] Before turning to those caves, Blavatskaia discusses whether Scythians are related to Rajputs (a clan group from northern India) and describes as well her disdain for the oppressive treatment of women in India, especially the practice of child marriage. She disputes the interpretation of Sanskrit texts on the harsh treatment of widows, stating that Horace Wilson, the noted Sanskritist, had claimed that the Vedas did not require widows to self-immolate. Wilson did in fact argue that the Vedas did not mention such a practice and that only much later texts did.[78] Blavatskaia also gives rare approval to the British:

> If the English ever did any good in India, it is undoubtedly that they succeeded in suppressing, if not uprooting altogether, the terrible custom of *infanticide*. The killing of little girls was practiced almost universally throughout this country, but especially in central India, and this practice was prevalent among the tribes of Jadeja, once so powerful in Sind, and now reduced to petty brigandage ... in ancient days this brutal custom – to dispose of daughters because of fear of having to arrange a marriage for them – was unknown to the Aryans. The ancient Brahmanical literature shows that in the days of pure-blooded Aryans, woman enjoyed the same rights as man. Her voice was listened to in state councils; she was free in choice of her husband and was at liberty to stay single if she so chose. Many a woman's name plays a prominent part in the chronicles of the ancient Aryan land and has come down to posterity as that of eminent poets, astronomers, philosophers, and even sages and lawgivers. But with the invasion of the Persians in the VIIth century of our era, and later of the fanatical brigand-like Moslems, all this changed. Woman became a slave and the Brahmanas took this opportunity of placing additional shackles on her.[79]

Blavatskaia gives the British credit for doing away with widow burning, although unlike most of the British, she also states that the Hindus' powerful desire to control women comes from resentment against British rule: "Powerless against British law, they revenge themselves on the innocent and unhappy women."[80] Blavatskaia recognizes, unlike some British women writers, that colonialism has much to do with the oppression of women, as it interacts with local patriarchal mores.[81] Mark Bevir argues that the Theosophists, in their attempt to both respect Indian culture and confer rights on women, too easily believed that women had once been equals and notes that female Theosophists "constantly grappled with practical issues such as what rights women should have in India," while the domestic space could constitute a "domain of native sovereignty within colonial society ... free from imperial interference."[82] Another feature that sets Blavatskaia apart from many travel writers is her focus on the material, from bodies to transportation methods to the actions of servants. In a dramatic episode Blavatskaia describes what occurs at the caves at Bagh, a famous place where temples are carved into rock (and about which Olcott is silent). Blavatskaia claims to enter secret cell-like rooms that progress back into the rock, but then faints due to the lack of oxygen and is carried out by the others, after which she becomes an "interesting invalid" for a time and is carried in a folding chair.[83] In those rooms there are "spiders big as crabs" which the Hindus decline to kill, angering Miss B. [Bates], who is further angered when Moolji Thackersey says he would prefer to transmigrate into a spider than into an Englishman.[84] Whether dealing with real or fictional individuals, Blavatskaia emphasizes the physicality and embodiedness of both travellers and people encountered, as well as the work done by servants.[85] She acknowledges the weight of her body: "However trying archeaological explorations may be for a person of my weight," she remarks in English, and more specifically in Russian: "Как не тяжелы археологические разследования при пяти пудах бреннаго тела" (however difficult archaeological explorations are for someone whose mortal body weighs five poods [180 lbs]."[86] She expresses a great fondness for this exploration, even if she sometimes has to be dragged or carried and often rides in a palanquin, in a cart, or on an animal. She typically almost always acknowledges this human or animal transport and notes also that tents are set up by workers, meals are cooked by servants, and it is also servants who crank the indoor fans – elements that are often not acknowledged by travellers, or simply "appear" or happen.

A succeeding stop on the itinerary is Madan-Mahal in Jabalpur, which Blavatskaia claims is a house built on a huge boulder that wobbles at the least touch, but which at least according to contemporary sources is a fort built on a non-mobile rock outcropping. Blavatskaia uses this mention of a wobbly rock as a segue to discuss the idea that "Indians can sit on anything unsteady" and to move to a discussion of the "fakir's avenue" that they visited in Jabalpur, where they saw "fakirs in impossible postures" standing for hours on one hand or one leg.[87] They visit a pagoda courtyard where neither Europeans nor Muslims were allowed; upon leaving the courtyard they rejoined their Hindu friends: "All three of them had long before released themselves from the iron claws of caste and openly ate and drank with us, and for this offence were 'ostracized' and despised more than even Europeans. Their presence in the pagoda would have polluted its holiness forever, whereas the pollution brought on by us would be only temporary; it would evaporate in the stench of cow-dung burnt after we had left."[88] The British, as always with Blavatskaia, come in for frequent criticism. As Blavatskaia describes it in multiple letters of her account, towns were divided into "black" and "white" portions, much as in Central Asia there were Russian and Asian parts of town. The "white" town in Allahabad, she writes, contains broad boulevards, trees, squirrels, and bungalows; it is like a park 32 miles in circumference, in which villas are half a mile apart from each other, and in which the British try to create an artificial London, remaining tightly laced in corsets and wearing formal evening wear in 120 degree weather.[89] In keeping with her argument about the racist British occupiers that she and presumably her Russian audience despise, Blavatskaia gives a spirited account of her group's mixture of "Europeans" and Hindus dining together in the train station's Refreshment Rooms (English in the original) as they waited for a train to Allahabad. According to her, this scandalized the British passengers and culminated in the discovery that they were under surveillance.

> Our appearance caused an evident sensation. Our party which included four Hindus occupied the end of a table at which were seated some fifty first class passengers who all stared at us with undisguised astonishment and contempt. Europeans on equal footing with Hindus! ... Hindus dining with Europeans! ... The subdued whispers grew into exclamations, and one important-looking lady, unable to stand it, got up and walked away. Were it not for the impressive presence of some unquestionably familiar types, such as W. and Miss B, both English and the Colonel who was being mistaken by everyone for an English officer, a scandal would have been unavoidable. Two Englishmen came up to the Thakur and after shaking hands with him – another rare occurrence – took him aside as if to talk business, but actually to satisfy their curiosity; they happened to be acquainted with him ... Here we learned for the first time that we were under police surveillance. The Thakur, pointing out to us a captain of very rosy complexion, with a long blonde moustache and wearing a white summer uniform, quietly whispered to me: "Beware of him!" ... He was an agent of the secret police from the political department and had followed us from Bombay ... We learned afterward that all the servants in the hotel were *in duty bound* to spy. The custom in India is to have your servants accompany you even to a dinner; so a Hindu stood behind each of us, while behind the Thakur were his four shield-bearers and two servants. The enemy was thus completely cut off by this army of naked-legged defenders, and the hotel spies had very little chance of overhearing our conversation.[90]

Olcott never mentions this incident (and in any case the Thakur was fictional), which may only have been intended for Blavatskaia's Russian readers so as to *épater les bourgeois*, but he confirms the fact that the party was surveilled by spies, although he places this at Agra, near the Taj Mahal: "At Saharanpore the Arya Samajists welcomed us most cordially and brought us gifts of fruits and sweets.[91] The only drawback to our pleasure was the presence of the Police spy and his servant, who watched our movements, intercepted our notes, read our telegrams, and made us feel as if we had stumbled within reach of the Russian Third Section by mistake."[92] The moustached spy in particular is also mentioned by Olcott: "Some English officials attended and our Police spy with his moustache shaved – apparently for purposes of disguise – graced the scene."[93] In Olcott's account, Blavatskaia later scolded the spy in no uncertain terms:

> Days and nights of torrid discomfort carried us at last to Bombay, but before H. P. B. would look after her bags and parcels, she marched off to our adhesive spy, and then and there, on the platform, gave him a piece of her mind. In sarcasm she complimented him upon the great results he must have reaped from his expensive trip in first-class carriages, and bade him present her best compliments and thanks to the authorities with a demand for his promotion! The poor man blushed and stammered, and – we walked away leaving him there. Then, instead of going to the house for the bath and breakfast of which we stood in so much need, we drove them [sic] to U.S. Consulate and demanded that the Consul should send a vigorous protest to the Chief of Police for his insulting treatment of inoffensive American citizens.[94]

According to Steven Prothero, Olcott was able to secure an interview with Sir Richard Temple, the governor of India, to persuade him to terminate the surveillance, which he did.[95]

Blavatskaia makes many references throughout her text to the fact that she was not welcomed into British intellectual and society circles in India and that critical newspaper articles circulated about her in the local press; there is plenty of documentation to attest to the existence of these articles.[96] She complains that the British viewed her as a spy. Indeed, it is apparent from her collected writings that she wrote numerous letters to the editor and that the doings of the Theosophical Society were at times chronicled in various Anglo-Indian publications.[97] In reality, the British may not have been far wrong about Blavatskaia being a spy; Blavatskaia, in a sense, "agitated among the natives against British rule" (as one commentator puts it), and she apparently offered her services as a spy to the Third Section (tsarist secret police) in 1872, well before she went to India.[98] She was not, however, accepted and so was at least not formally a spy. Olcott, on the other hand, was at least a kind of reporter for the US government and had made arrangements through the Secretary of State to report on potential US commercial interests in Asia.[99]

The Indian Rebellion of 1857

Apropos of her visit to Cawnpore (Kanpur) (Olcott also affirms they went there), Blavatskaia devotes a fair number of pages to the 1857 Indian Rebellion, or Sepoy Mutiny as it was called at the time. She notes, in a way that might recall Russian frustration at having their history told by foreigners: "What was the true cause of this bloody mutiny? Europe reads English accounts and imagines that it reads history. It never occurs to anyone to ask whether among the many accounts of the mutiny there is a single truthful and dispassionate one. No one asked the Hindus what truth there was in the accounts of their conquerors, which of the two belligerent sides was guilty of the greatest crimes and which committed the most bestial cruelties, the educated and humane Europeans or the wild natives driven to desperation."[100] Blavatskaia points out that while Nana-Sahib's actions of killing and disgracing the British were extremely violent (and enacted as vengeance for the destruction of his own family and privileges by the British), most British-leaning accounts leave out the violent and vicious reprisals that took place after the rebellion:

> This is the story of an English witness. But he does not relate how the next morning the people of Cawnpore were gathered together and *every tenth man* shot dead; he is silent about the fact that, having caught several hundred men (probably mostly innocent), they made them *lick the caked blood on the floors of the room*; silent also about the fact that this blood was licked by some five hundred men, prevented from getting up from the floor for 48 hours; that two-thirds of them died from vomiting and the other third were clubbed to death by the English; and finally, that not merely a few dozen mutineers were loaded into guns and fired off (which is confirmed from English sources), but that *several thousand men died that way*, is left unsaid.[101]

In fact, Vasilii Vereshchagin illustrated men being tied to cannons in his huge 1884 canvas, *Suppression of the Indian Revolt by the English*.[102] Blavatskaia does not mention this canvas, which post-dated the first series, but praises his depiction of moonlight in India in her fifth letter.[103] Historical accounts list these kinds of torture of the Indians as well as others unmentioned by Blavatskaia.[104] The upshot of her view places emphasis on the longstanding oppression of Indians by the British: "Great and terrible are the sins of Nana-Sahib, but who would dare to assert that his acts were not called forth by the bloody tears and the groans of the 200 million people in a country which was trampled under the foot of her conqueror, a people despised, starved to death by hundreds of thousands during the last long century?"[105] In fact, Blavatskaia might well have been referring as well to the recent, catastrophic "drought-famine" of 1876–8, in which the British rejected age-old systems of community grain storage for times of drought in favour of free-market prices and the selling of grain to London. They used the railroads for this purpose, which could have carried grain to places with shortages, but instead were used to remove grain from areas in great need to protect it from being seized by the starving.[106]

In Blavatskaia's account, the group then visits the special garden containing the well into which the British corpses were thrown and around which a memorial had been built, a memorial she finds "Jesuitical, full of secret hypocrisy," and which she claims has a sign saying "Hindus, pagans and Moslems [forbidden] to approach the garden enclosure," as well as, among other inscriptions, the quotation by Horace, "Hic niger est: hunc tu, Romane, caveto" – i.e., "That man is black (i.e., bad): Roman, beware of him!" This inscription is understood by the colonel, Blavatskaia says, to be an insult to dark-skinned people, on behalf of whose rights he had already fought in the Civil War.[107]

As if to counteract this unpleasant experience, and apropos of the caves they are visiting near Cawnpore, but also to deepen the idea that the English versions of the rebellion are untrustworthy, Blavatskaia's Thakur tells the story of Lakshmi-Bai, or Rani of Jhansi, a woman who was in fact a leading member of the rebellion in 1857, a cousin of Nana-Sahib, and a woman raised to have military skills.[108] Blavatskaia retells the story because, she avers, it has been covered up by the English:

> I will now try briefly to tell the history of this cave and the episode referred to by the Thakur, concerning the mutiny of 1857. The latter belongs to history, though the English tried to distort the accounts of it, as they have distorted and even *concealed* many other facts of this, to them, disgraceful epoch. Having learned these facts first from Gulab-Lal-Singh, we later heard some very interesting details concerning them from several old Hindus, some of whom had been eyewitnesses to the events; and on one occasion we heard about them from an Englishman, an old Anglo-Indian officer.[109]

Having told the story of the heroic woman warrior who, having broken her legs in battle, gives orders to be burned alive before the British could get to her, Blavatskaia remarks that the British did not know about the secret cave passages which the members of the rebellion used to spread their message far and wide, and the Thakur tells her to be silent about them.[110] She asks if she can tell her Russian readers, which he says she can:

> Not long ago, intending to describe this trip, I asked him: "Would you mind if I told my Russian readers about the underground tunnels of Jajmau?"
>
> "Certainly not," he said, "if you will trust your memory."
>
> "… But you said that the English do not even suspect their existence? What if they should read my article and make note of these facts? They avidly read all Russian papers and translate at once into English everything that in any way concerns India or even Asia in general."[111]

The Thakur believes that the British will be too arrogant to imagine there is anything important in their dominions that they don't know about. Essentially, then, Blavatskaia is indicating to her readers that through her letters they have learned things even British spies did not know. In a footnote, Blavatskaia declares that the Indian population knew about the events of the rebellion right away, due to these networks of caves and tunnels, but the British did not understand why or how the news spread so quickly among them.[112] The caves of Hindostan that comprise part of the title of Blavatskaia's narrative, then, are not merely caves but signifiers of Indian revolt against the British. One of Blavatskaia's associates, who became a fervent detractor and debunker of Blavatskaia's supernatural abilities, indeed claimed that the whole point of the Theosophical Society was intended to overthrow the British rule of India, as well as of Christianity in general.[113]

In Chapter XXVIII, Blavatskaia introduces Delhi: "И вот мы в Дельи – великом граде Могулов" ("And now we are in Delhi – the great city of the Moghuls").[114] In this letter, Blavatskaia emphasizes the magnificence of Delhi, but keeping in mind her mission to criticize the British, also emphasizes the fact that it is a set of marble ruins, and the site of the fall to the Moghuls that then ultimately, having weakened India and made it more "effeminate," led to British control of the country. The Thakur states, "with eyes glowing like burning coals and seemingly overcome by a heretofore repressed and therefore even more intense impulse of anger. 'Yes! … It was only the depravity and effeminacy of this accursed race, which opened wide the doors to the European conquerors! … It was the Moguls alone that ruined our India! If this generation of harems had not settled in our fatherland, we would not have had a single Englishman here now!'"[115]

Blavatskaia frames the visit to Delhi as a kind of visit to the under-world, to the great but forgotten past, now merely a "poem of the glorious past of numberless generations of heroes," but also, precisely as a text, an "epic poem":

> Along this valley, in an unbroken file seven miles wide and more than thirty miles long, are scattered on the banks of the Jumna the ruins of not only one, but of several ancient and modern towns. It is an entire epic poem in marble, a poem of the glorious past of numberless generations of heroes … At every step there are ruins; wherever one looks, one sees some tumbled-down wall, an overturned statue or a broken column … And over this marvellous and strange world of well-nigh living ruins, there reigns day and night a deadly silence. What a strange scene of devastation! When we found ourselves in it, we thought we had wandered into the fairy kingdom of the "Sleeping Beauty."[116]

Indeed, the whole of Delhi had seemed to be a city of mausoleums: "Whole cities of mausoleums and sarcophagi of precious marble – that is all that remains of what was once the most wealthy of Moslem empires! 'Those white monuments you see in the distance,' an unusually candid English judge said to me recently, 'positively produce in me a feeling of unaccountable fear and make me nervous, when I sit in the evening alone on my balcony … They seem like an army of the dead in their white shrouds, who have come to demand an account of the fate of their descendants.'"[117] Due to the sheer volume of sightseeing, she says, they all have "ruin indigestion" and the ruins chase them in their very dreams: "We began to have nightmares in the form of towers, palaces and temples; fleet-footed minarets chased us, and [the] black marble sarcophagi danced a dance of death around us."[118] Upon the Thakur then discoursing morosely, as quoted above, on the fact that the Moghuls weakened India and allowed it to be conquered later, Miss Bates is offended and claims the British always win their battles (and arguably would not have needed any help from the Moghuls). She in turn is reminded by the colonel that the Americans defeated the British twice, both in the Revolutionary War and in the War of 1812. Then follows a discussion of everyone's desire to be rid of Miss Bates, who is there mainly to protect against British suspicions; it also serves to make the case that Britons do not deserve their power in India (of course, in Olcott's version, the split with Miss Bates occurs before the trip to Delhi).

Agra is the next stop on the tour, and much description is, unsurprisingly, devoted to the Taj Mahal. After describing all the beauty of the Taj Mahal and its remarkable interior work made of precious stones, portraying leaves and petals of flowers, Blavatskaia criticizes the fact that the British hold "a dancing hall for picnics" in a mosque near the Taj Mahal, praising "Gordon Cumming" for criticizing this impolitic decision.[119] Here Blavatskaia comes quite close to the text of Constance Gordon-Cumming: "Unfortunately our quarters were fully three miles distant, at an execrable and ruinous hotel. Had we but known in time, there are rooms to be had, as in a Dak bungalow, in one of the small mosques close to the Taj, where indeed one large room is, with most execrable taste, sometimes used as a ball-room. Imagine our feelings if the New Zealanders come and dance their war-dances in our mausoleums, or rather our very unromantic cemetery chapels!"[120] In de Zirkoff's translation, an "R." is added in front of "Gordon Cumming"; one assumes the translator thought it was Gordon-Cumming's more famous brother who had written these observations, but Blavatskaia is quite clear as to the author being his sister. Blavatskaia says, "Living quite close ('v dvukh shagakh') to the Taj Mahal, we visited it daily and used its shady, cool gardens as our drawing room. Sitting there we listened to local legends and breathed more freely than in the stuffy dak- bungalow, erected by the government in one of the ancient mausoleums and mosques, near the gates of the Taj."[121] Then she quotes the above "Gordon Cumming," criticizing the "dancing hall for picnics." Seizing on Constance Gordon-Cumming's words, Blavatskaia remarks: "Without making any comments of my own, I purposely quote one of their own countrymen, in order to show the English that is it not only the Russians, whom they generally suspect as spies, who notice and point out to the world their repulsive egotism and lack of consideration for the feelings of their conquered peoples. It is not the Russians but they, themselves, who arouse the just hatred of the Asiatic people by means of such dangerous behavior."[122] In fact, Blavatskaia also takes from Gordon-Cumming (this time without attributing it) a statement about how most people would prefer to be deaf rather than blind, given the choice, as well as evocations of Sadi, the thirteenth-century Persian poet, who bored his friends with his fulsome praise of his beloved. Embroidering on Gordon-Cumming's statement about deafness being preferable to blindness, and on her description of the "fairylike, snowy, palace-among-tombs, the Taj Mahal" which Gordon-Cumming calls "the loveliness of this fairy architecture,"[123] Blavatskaia extends the comparison of Sadi's inability to sufficiently express his love from Gordon-Cumming's admiration for the Taj Mahal to all of India, and adds in lameness in both legs, as well as the Paris Opera, to her version of the statements: "And he whose good fortune it has been to get but a glimpse of one of the fairy-like corners of India, that land of lace-like marble palaces and enchanted gardens, often reminding one of the most fantastic stage settings of the Paris Opera – impossible, one would think, in nature – would willingly add to deafness, lameness of both legs, rather than miss such sights."[124] Moving to another famous literary predecessor, Blavatskaia then describes the fortress of Agra, alluding to its caliph sitting contemplatively with a quotation from Pushkin's "Bakchisaraiiskii fontan" ("Fountain of Bakhchisarai"), "with eyes cast down and smoking his pipe."[125] The group visits a ruined palace and enters the zenana, or harem, where the seventeenth-century traveller Tavernier had seen a huge marble pool and many mirrors, elements that Gordon-Cumming also remarks upon, although she does not mention Tavernier.[126] Perhaps inevitably, a Russian visitor coming upon a harem in ruins cannot but think of Pushkin's famous narrative poem nor resist quoting from it: certainly Blavatskaia could not. Blavatskaia describes the scene in quite Pushkinian terms: "Все эти чудеса архитектуры, где люди жили, любили и страдали, все это ныне пусто, заброшено и словно заснуло непробудым сном." ("All these wonders of architecture, where once people lived, suffered and loved – all these are now empty, deserted and as if slumbering in an endless sleep.")[127] As Pushkin wrote in "The Fountain of Bakhchisarai":

Еще поныне дышит нега
В пустых покоях и садах;
Играют воды, рдеют розы,
И вьются виноградны лозы,
И злато блещет на стенах.
Я видел ветхие решетки,
За коими, в своей весне,
Янтарны разбирая четки,
Вздыхали жены в тишине.

Luxuriance to this day enthralls
Those vacant pleasances and halls;
The roses glow, the waters jingle,
The tendrils of the vine commingle,
And gold still glistens on the walls.
Frail lattice still shuts off each chamber
Where in the spring of years confined
Distraitly fingering beads of amber
The harem wives in silence pined.[128]

Blavatskaia compares the palace to a fairy-tale setting, although she has quite effectively already cast the palace under a Bakhchisarai-like spell, only awaiting rejuvenation in the imagination of a wandering poet – or Theosophist. Blavatskaia follows the general outlines of Gordon-Cumming's descriptions of the zenana, noting such things as walled-off areas where skeletons had been found, and the like, not precisely plagiarizing but describing the same elements in the same order. She then quotes her again, with attribution:

> Upon the sarcophagus are carved in Persian letters of gold the ninety-nine virtues of Allah. On three sides of the lower terrace of the mausoleum are colonnades with numerous arches, covered with inscriptions from the *Qur'an* and the more recent curses upon the unbelievers; all this is laid in black marble. Between every two columns there is a window of the usual Indian architectural style – a sort of stone lacework. As the sister of R. Gordon Cumming, the Scottish Nimrod of modern England, very justly said, this stone lacework finally begins to impress one as being something commonplace. "But if we could transport one of these windows," she goes on to say, "into some Christian cathedral, what a crowd would be pressing to see it, and what exclamations of delight and amazement would be heard from the experts! Here in India, however, such work is only the accomplishment of *despised niggers* (negrov) and our haughty Britisher will hardly even look at it!"
>
> This is the opinion of a patriotic English woman.[129]

In the original Russian the last statement is even stronger – "This is the opinion of an Englishwoman and – a patriot." Gordon-Cumming had written: "All round this court are arches and pillars, which serve as an immortal page, inlaid with verses of the Koran, in black marble. In every niche of those long arcades is a window of the usual lace-work carving in marble. Yet if we could transport but one such window to some English church how the people would flock to see it, and how the newspapers would laud the skill of the artist! But this is only the work of 'those wretched niggers,' so few Britons take the trouble even to look at it!"[130] At this point in the narrative, Blavatskaia dispatches Miss Bates by subjecting her to an attack of sunstroke, a danger to all the non-natives, but a departure not attested to by Olcott, who describes the group parting ways after a trip to Ceylon, whereas Ceylon does not figure in Blavatskaia's account.[131] There is an amusing interlude in which the colonel wishes to speak to Blavatskaia in her tent but is not allowed to enter after sunset since it is then considered a zenana, or harem.[132] This has occurred, they are informed, because they are now among the Rajputs, who are stricter about these things. At the same time, Olcott hears he will be given the opportunity to apprentice to become a Hindu ascetic, something Blavatskaia finds to be a ridiculous proposition, given the typical requirements of extreme asceticism (she describes the colonel as slightly plump) and celibacy (according to Blavatskaia, having been married, as Olcott had been, was disqualifying).[133]

Part Two begins here, having begun to be published in 1885. Blavatskaia is visiting Bhurtpore, once its own kingdom and now a small independent dominion. During this visit, a number of strange things happen; as they visit the Raja, they are shown to a special room and offered racy pictures to look at (something they do not welcome), the palace is dusty and dirty, the table contains a colony of red ants, and the Hindus are horrified to be offered alcoholic beverages. The letter now turns to a whole litany of topics, among which is the way in which people feel resentful of the behaviour of the British:

> Here the religious feelings of both Hindus and Rajputs are offended at every step. Their sacred *pipal* [fig], the refuge for pure spirits, falls daily under the axe of the English planter; the peacock, the bird consecrated to Krishna, is shot under the very nose of the natives, with equally cool indifference as if it were a crow. The English do not, and do not wish, to understand that every blow of the axe and every bullet leaves a mark in the heart of the devout Hindu, widening more with every hour that abyss of hatred in the soul of the defenceless native, which the English themselves have dug with their own hands.[134]

Blavatskaia quotes a pamphlet called "Our Conquerors, Who Are they?" which notes that it is with Sepoys, with Hindus themselves, that the British conquered India, and that they had also conquered other places with the help of Indian forces, whose loyalty to the British was frequently praised.[135] On the one hand, Blavatskaia expects a general uprising and describes certain protest movements, on the other hand, she notes: "It is difficult, when writing of the past, not to linger in the present, particularly when the matter concerns a people full of excellent qualities, with a heart as gentle as a baby's and the head of a sage, but as spoiled also as a baby, not by indulgence but by the cruel thrashing of an unbidden and unloved stepmother."[136] In the second letter of Part Two, the group goes to Digh, whose palace Blavatskaia says is second only to the Taj Mahal; Olcott also gives it high praise.[137] Here, after Blavatskaia remarked that some have tried to claim that it was not the Hindus who built the beautiful structures but the Muslims who came after them, Blavatskaia debunked this view by noting that depictions of humans are not made by Muslims and that the Muslims in India are not Saracens and Moors, but the "dregs of Islam" ("otreb'em islama") from Central Asia.[138] Here they encounter some Englishmen who despise Hindus and refer to their companions as servants, whereupon Blavatskaia bursts out with a proclamation that they are gentlemen, friends, and brothers. They appear to know who she is, saying that the newspapers are warning about a Russian lady ("*vy ta samaia russkaia ledi*" – "*you are that very [same] Russian lady*") who cares for the "black rabble" (chernaia svoloch', glossed as "black rable" [*sic*] in a footnote, although "svoloch'" typically means "bastard") and that there is "*no room for Russians in our British dominions.*" The colonel defends her and tells them she is actually an American, while Blavatskaia proclaims that she "was born a Russian and … shall die a Russian. I am a Russian in my *soul*, if not on my passport." Blavatskaia then notes that "in *our* Russian dominions, for example in Georgia and in the Caucasus, there is room for every foreigner, even for *scores of English paupers* who come to us without boots and leave with millions in their pockets." The Hindu companions are angry with the rude Britons, and Blavatskaia is angry that she might be putting them in danger because she is Russian.[139] "Russia and everything Russian are a constant nightmare for Anglo-India. The closer to the Himalayas, the more violently does the Russian 'house-demon' [домовой] choke every Britisher at night."[140] More disturbingly to her, Narayana tells her he wants to kill the man who has criticized her, and declares that there are not even two dozen Englishmen who respect Hindus. Babu[la], their assistant, says that is too many. By way of compensation, Moolji, Olcott's longtime friend, tells them of the story of the Collector Rous Peters (or Peter).[141] The story of Peter[s], "the Anglo-Indian who loved the Hindus," takes place in the third letter of the second volume, in which Blavatskaia recounts the story of a collector, a British official in charge of the local government, in Madurai, in southern India.[142] Collector Peter[s] was an archaeologist who admired ancient manuscripts and consulted with local Brahmins in order to understand them. At first he was known as an atheist, but gradually he came more and more under the sway of Hinduism as various miracles occurred that saved his life. As a 2015 article in *The Hindu* relates,

> Rous Peter, who took over as the third Collector in 1812, is held dear to the heart of Madurai. Historians recall that Rous Peter acquitted himself as the administrator of the temple with sincerity and respected the religious sentiments of people.

He is said to have begun his official work by going round the temple on horseback in the morning. His contributions to the Meenakshi temple and Sundararaja Perumal temple in Alagarkoil are celebrated in folk songs. According to a legend, Rous Peter was woken up from sleep by a three-year-old girl in his room and led by the hand outside, where it was raining heavily. When the Collector stopped and looked back, lightning struck his bungalow. The girl ran away in the direction of the temple. Goddess Meenakshi is believed to have appeared as a three-year-old child thrice … The third instance involves Rous Peter.

In another legend, Rous Peter had to run for his life when an elephant attacked him during a hunting expedition. He prayed to Goddess Meenakshi and killed the animal with a single shot.

The Collector donated a pair of gold stirrups, studded with rubies, to Goddess Meenakshi, who had saved his life.

Refusing to go back to England after superannuation, Rous Peter spent his last days in Madurai.[143]

Blavatskaia tells a far more complex story about Peter[s], not surprisingly, but the gist of it is the same; she declares that Peter[s] became a devout Hindu, after the goddess saved him, and he was deemed a "white saint," but the government declared him insane and tried to have him sent by psychiatrists to England for a cure, "but even here the 'goddess' did not betray her admirer. The doctors … gave him a clean bill of health."[144] According to his wishes, she says, he was buried within view of the temple. Discussing the spirit of pantheism, Blavatskaia notes:

It follows that the pantheists of India, in retaining their idols, sin merely by an overdose of religious, though badly applied, feeling. In addition, after the total destructiveness and non-creativeness of animal materialism in Europe, such pantheism appears as morally and spiritually refreshing, a blossoming oasis in the midst of a barren, sandy desert. Better to believe *at least in one of the qualities of divinity*, personifying and worshipping it under that particular guise … than to deny the *All* under the pretext that it cannot be proved by scientific methods, and to believe in nothing, as do our learned materialists and fashionable agnostics.[145]

Hence, Blavatskaia writes, Peter[s]' conversion is understandable and even sensible.

The group then returned to Digh; in the fourth letter, Blavatskaia describes a beautiful garden full of peacocks and parrots, with a central "kiosk" that created the effect of being surrounded by streams of water that sheltered inhabitants from fierce heat. Olcott poetically concurs:

The centre of the garden is marked with a domed marble water-kiosk, surrounded by a shallow tank from which rise 175 water jets, met by streams that fall from an equal number of nozzles projecting from the underside of the cornice of the structure, and when in play shroud the occupants from view by a translucent wall of water; which keeps the air within deliciously cool in the hottest day and sparkles in the sun-shine like a silver veil embroidered with gems. From this centre raised walks radiate in every direction and one strolls about under the cool shade of neem, tamarind, mango, babul, banyan, and pipul trees. No less than one hundred grand peacocks were strutting about on the day of our visit, swift parrots darted in emerald flashes through the air, striped squirrels flitted from tree to tree, and flocks of doves softly called to each other in the dense foliage, completing an ideally beautiful picture. The palace architecture is all Indian, the carvings in stone exquisite in design, and the angles as sharp as if but finished yesterday.[146]

Here they meet a guru, with whom Col. Olcott, according to Blavatskaia, wanted to study, despite his past marriage and children. He is told he still might be able to be considered a disciple, and he is given a special stone to wear. In the sixth letter, they go to Mathura, and on the way, monkeys jump into their conveyance and steal food, they encounter numerous sacred elephants alongside the monkeys, and Blavatskaia and the colonel visit temples.[147] At that point Blavatskaia goes into a lengthy discussion of the similarities between the Egyptians and the Greeks, claiming that every mountain, river, or god in ancient Greece or Rome has a prototype in India, citing the now commonly debunked theories of Edward Pococke. Blavatskaia provides some additional thoughts on bhats, a group of people whose frighteningly strict code of honour, she avers, allows them to be employed to transport valuable items, particularly money, and describes as well a visit to some singers of ancient songs. They also visit some burial mounds of warriors, guarded by both humans and stone figures, which Blavatskaia, ever the patriot, compares with regret to forgotten graves of soldiers in the Caucasus and Sevastopol.[148] A view of yogins spreading live coals from altars on their feet is "too disgusting even for the inquisitive Colonel. He could not stand it and turned away, saying that he preferred the tombs of the dead to the tortures of the living yogins."[149] Evidence of tombs where the wife had also immolated herself after her husband's death "spoiled the pleasure of the walk for me," Blavatskaia notes on the same page.

Blavatskaia's last letter ends with "to be continued," although in fact the series was never continued.

The Durbar in Lahore

Concurrently with her series *From the Caves and Jungles of Hindostan* being printed in *Moskovskie vedomosti*, Blavatskaia published a series of letters called "The Durbar in Lahore" in *Russkii vestnik*, also edited by Katkov. Initially said to be "From the Diary of a Russian woman," the letters were signed "Raddai-bai" at the end, the same way the letters *From the Caves and Jungles of Hindustan* were signed. "The Durbar in Lahore" is a much more tightly focused narrative than the *Caves and Jungles* letters, addressing the events surrounding the 15 November 1880 durbar, or grand reception, held to celebrate the accession of Lord Ripon, the new viceroy. These appeared in *Russkii vestnik* in 1881, in the months of May, June, and July, in volumes 153 and 154.[150] They later appeared for the first time in English in *The Theosophist* in 1960 and 1961.[151] The durbar was also documented by Olcott.[152]

Blavatskaia's "Durbar" letters start in Simla, the summer capital of the British rulers of India, a mountainous place Blavatskaia and her group visited relatively early on in their sojourn to India when they were still allied with the Arya Samaj, a Hindu reform group who had been instrumental in inviting them to India. From Simla, they travelled to Kalka and then to Amritsar, where they visited the Sikh centre surrounding the Golden Temple. In the Durbar letters, Blavatskaia is focused on politics throughout, never losing a chance to criticize the British for their racism, ignorance, and cruelty, nor their wrongful suspicion of her as a Russian spy. The year 1880 was essentially the height of the Great Game, with the British having just made incursions into Afghanistan, provoked by the Russians having first created a plan to invade India and then having made diplomatic overtures to Kabul, which precipitated the Second Anglo-Afghan War.[153]

First commenting favourably on the beauty of the Golden Temple and the surroundings, including the gardens, Blavataskaia then critiques the bazaar full of foreign wares which is effectively depriving the Indians of their own cottage industries:

The bazaar is overflowing here with wares from Central Asia and cheap imitation products from Manchester. The latter city is trying with all its might to kill the local craftsmen with its own imitations, which are cheap beyond the possibility of competition ... Little by little ancient handicraft is disappearing and will soon vanish altogether ... The Manchester machine will soon have destroyed even the memory of all these products of the patient Hindu, whose genius is willing to manifest itself for a few pennies a day, and from whom the British huckster's greed takes even these wretched pennies! Those 20 millions of the Afghan fiasco [fiasco in Roman letters – KH] have to be paid, don't you see! And if it does not come from taxes, the last buffalo, the last cow – nourisher of a whole family – will be sold, and if these cannot be obtained, then there is the jail![154]

Blavatskaia also connects the Second Anglo-Afghan War, which took place from 1878 to 1880, and its costs, to the problem of cheap wares and Indian losses. References to the Great Game, to Russian culture, and to the oppression by the British intersperse Blavatskaia's Durbar letters, as is typical for her, and she creates an "answer" from the Indians in quotations: "Now the last drops of juice are being squeezed out and absorbed forever by the fogs of Great Britain. Our Golconda diamonds have become glass; our sacred idols are displayed in the British Museum; and our countless treasures repose in the vaults of the Bank of England. Our famous Koh-i-Nor (mountain of radiance) – a diamond without its equal, which was removed by force and with bloodshed from the conquered Shah-Shuja by Ranjit-Singh, now sparkles on the crown of the Empress of India" (i.e., Queen Victoria).[155] Blavatskaia notes how native dwellings pile one on another, "crooked hovels supported on chicken legs press against each other" (a reference to Baba Yaga's hut), contrasting them to the British homes that are quite separate from each other and sheltered by dense foliage and built "after the Mutiny,"[156] while shops in the local town sell multitudes of items, including "the works of Annie Besant which treat of the mysteries of present-day physiology and are banned in England."[157]

Blavatskaia in her third letter digresses to break the fourth wall, telling her Russian readers that she must explain "more clearly the mutual relations between conqueror and vanquished, and give a sketch of the country itself" lest the description of "The Durbar in Lahore" "remain both obscure and inexplicable."[158] Blavatskaia states she cannot fathom the contempt for the Indians felt by the British, claiming that an Indian who travels to England experiences a journey in two parts: to Aden, he will be found to be a lesser being, but once past Aden he will be treated as a fellow human being and drawn into conversation. This also happens on the return trip, when he will start as an equal and then after Aden will become a member of a subject race. Blavatskaia describes drawing the brother of her British host into conversation, needling him over the deplorable way in which he was treating both a petitioner of noble birth and a gardener, treatment he attempts to defend, finally declaring that while the gardener may be a British subject, he is not English, and therefore does not have equal rights despite his nominal status as a citizen of the British Empire. Blavatskaia does not criticize only the British, however, pointing out that the extreme non-compatibility of the different castes and religions (whose divisions, Blavatskaia claims, made the Indians an easy target for their conquerers) had to be overcome by medicine, ice, and soda water, once spurned because it was not considered feasible to share such substances among castes and religions.[159]

The British, Blavatskaia notes, would be better off being more humane; the British government's reliance on absolute power is not only wrong but liable to be exposed by defeat or loss. Perhaps ironically at this juncture, Blavatskaia defends the East India Company, whose rule was ended with the rebellion in 1857. The East India Company officials, she states, at least lived among the Hindus, even intermarrying, and felt sympathy and solidarity with them in many cases, and did not "flaunt their white skins."[160] "It follows, then, that the British government, with the best of intentions, is ruining India," she declares.[161] "The waters of the Thames will sooner merge with the waters of the Ganges than will the Englishman in India look upon the Hindu as an equal, though the latter were a hundred times a Maharaja and his family descended from the days of Adam."[162] The Indians themselves, however, have their own challenges, she avers; someone may easily look upon his neighbour as a "foreigner" (bellati) because he is of a different caste or religion, while the divisions among both Muslims and Hindus are manifold.[163]

"With such a system, can India not only be a nursery for patriotism, as some writers imagine her, but in addition bring forth her own patriots in time?"[164] Even the British themselves do not really understand or acknowledge that they were able to put down the rebellion in 1857 because different castes and ethnic groups in India turned against each other, never having felt themselves to be part of the same people at any time.[165] That the British are the ones who relate the history of India, a frequent Blavatskaia hobbyhorse, compounds the problem. The British took over the country gradually, with each minor rajah being bested by them in turn: "With the passing of the ages, the code of the Laws of Manu became a dead letter, the country was covered with slime, like a pool of stagnant water, and was overcome by a senile sleep, awakening only spasmodically here and there, whenever occurred some momentary trouble, occasioned by one of its enemies."[166] In her fourth letter, Blavatskaia describes the group arriving at Lahore in time for the Durbar, passing by the leper colony on their way. The reception of the new viceroy was being prepared, and there was little room in the town, but the local Theosophist branches offered them a place to stay. This was much to the consternation of the authorities, she writes, although they then decided that the Theosophists were not actually laying the groundwork for a Russian invasion, so recently envisioned by General Kaufman, then the governor-general of Russian Turkestan.[167] "The Calcutta sages came to know us better, and became entirely convinced that we were not on intimate terms either with General Kaufman or the Afghans."[168] Blavatskaia describes Lahore and then describes at great length the extreme luxury of the clothing, the plethora of jewels, and the tents and mounts of the attendees of the durbar. Blavatskaia quotes the well-known phrase of Thomas Moore's *Lalla Rookh* several times ("the happy vale of Kashmir") while describing the opulent tents, gold embroidery, mirrors, candalabra, a phaeton made of silver, and lavishly bejeweled elephants and horses.[169] Moore, while familiar to Russian readers, did not provide the only inspiration to Blavatskaia, since numerous details from Gordon-Cumming's description of the 1869 Durbar in Umballa, at which Lord Mayo received the emir of Afghanistan, also appear in Blavatskaia's narrative. Pushkin had used quotations from Moore in his "Fountain of Bakhchisarai" and *Journey to Arzrum*. Moore's famous 1817 *Lalla Rookh* describes the travel of the eponymous young princess from Delhi to Kashmir as she goes to meet her husband-to-be, who unknown to her has posed as a poet and accompanied her through her journey. *Lalla Rookh* focuses lavish description on such topics as gardens, flowers, and beautiful colours, but it also contains a fairly rapturous description of Lalla Rookh's ride to and visit in Lahore, of which Blavatskaia may have been thinking since she quotes "vale of Kashmir" several times in her description. Moore writes:

> Seldom had the Eastern world seen a cavalcade so superb. From the gardens in the suburbs to the Imperial palace, it was one unbroken line of splendor. The gallant appearance of the Rajahs and Mogul lords, distinguished by those insignia of the Emperor's favor, the feathers of the egret of Cashmere in their turbans, and the small silver-rimm'd kettle-drums at the bows of their saddles; – the costly armor of their cavaliers, who vied, on this occasion, with the guards of the great Keder Khan, in the brightness of their silver battle-axes and the massiness of their maces of gold; – the glittering of the gilt pine-apple on the tops of the palankeens; – the embroidered trappings of the elephants, bearing on their backs small turrets, in the shape of little antique temples, within which the Ladies of Lalla Rookh lay as it were enshrined.[170]

Blavatskaia, perhaps with Moore in mind, not to mention Gordon-Cumming, is similarly flowery in describing the tents of those waiting to be in the procession to be received by the new viceroy, the Marquis of Ripon, describing "cushions the like of which were not seen even at the Paris exhibition" (which Paris exhibition is not mentioned, but there had been one in 1878). "In the room, in the space reserved for the throne under the canopy, are two circular easy chairs decorated with very rare and rather excessive inlays of pure gold, in those most fantastic designs for which "the happy vale" of Kashmir is so famous ... During the local durbar, the Maharaja himself, and with him the Viceroy, will occupy these thrones."[171] In the fifth letter, Blavatskaia describes the durbar itself and focuses much attention on the elephants:

> Before us was an enormous yard filled with variously bedecked "royal" elephants covered with caparisons of gold brocade embroidered with pearls and precious stones that reached to the ground; with rings of gold, studded with emeralds, in their flapping ears, and on the extremities of their trunks; with bunches of superb magnolias and ostrich plumes on their heads and at the base of their tails, these huge animals appeared to us, innocent Occidentals, the most original and wonderful spectacle in the world! ... Behind one female elephant of astounding size trotted her calf, carrying on his back a long ladder of pure silver, by means of which his master, the raja, climbed, to occupy the howdah on its gigantic mother's back.[172]

There were also bedecked camels, as well as bejeweled high-ranking human beings; the Maharajas, of whom Blavatskaia says, "I can never forgive their habit of piercing the most precious emeralds as though they were mere beads, and of mounting their almost priceless rubies in silver!"[173] The description of the animals, and details such as a smaller elephant carrying a silver ladder to be used to climb up on a larger elephant, the objection (in terms of European sensibility) to carving or piercing precious stones and to setting them in silver rather than gold, also appear in Gordon-Cumming's account.[174] Blavatskaia is always ready to mock the British: "Here are the rajas of Chamba and Suket arriving in their carriages, one after the other; also the Sardar of Kalsia and the Nawabs of Malerkotla, Logarh and Dujana, blazing with all the colors of the rainbow and resembling walking jewelry exhibits. All these effeminate petty kings spread around them the stupefying odor of musk, rose oil and amber ... From a distance it is easy to mistake their variegated figures, as they mount the staircase each paired with a British officer, for ladies at a fancy-dress ball, executing a stately polonaise with their partners."[175] Perhaps not surprisingly given Blavatskaia's criticism of the British, the viceroy, when he arrives, is "difficult to distinguish" and is a "rather corpulent, short man of about fifty" although he is also "a real gentleman."[176] After the viceroy's greetings to those waiting for him at the railway station, a procession of fifty-nine elephants heads to town, the viceroy at the head on the largest elephant. Breaking the fourth wall, Blavataskaia "apologize[s] in advance to those Anglo-Indian authorities who should happen to read these lines," remarking in a footnote: "There is no doubt, and it flatters me, that many among them actually read, in translation of course, my letters to the *Moscow Herald*. The *Bombay Gazette* recently quoted whole sentences, somewhat twisted, from 'The Caves and Jungles of Hindustan.' This paper, as well as the *Times of India*, which persecutes me *because of my nationality*, did me the honor of denouncing me to the public."[177] "Truth compels" Blavatskaia, despite this criticism, to say that while the Indians look handsome and magnificent in their costumes and in the howdah on the elephant, "just as ridiculous does a Britisher in uniform in three-cornered hat appear … From a distance one would fancy them to be monkeys in red Generals' uniforms."[178] Blavatskaia, "constantly forgetting my delicate position in India," upbraids a young man who wishes to punish the Maharaja of Kashmir (who left suddenly, abandoning his place in the procession), proclaiming that "Our administrators are too tender-hearted with these darkies" ("Nashe pravitel'stvo slishkom nezhnichaet s etimi chernomazymi").[179] Wondering why the reception of the viceroy was so muted, Blavatskaia discovers that an editorial had appeared, complaining of the expense of the durbars, which drained the treasury. Blavatskaia ventroloquizes the editorial as follows:

> Our rulers seek to produce the strongest possible impression on us natives, to overcome us with the greatness of the British nation. Do they take us for stupid asses? Do they really hope to captivate us with glass beads and shining brass buttons, as the Spaniards once captivated the redskin Indians in the days of their invasion of South America? We may be Indians, but we are not redskins … Away then, with tinsel and empty amusement! Their railways, their telegraphs, the splendid army discipline, these are the things that have inspired us with respect for the English nation, but never these stupid displays of pomp, this futile expenditure of capital from the ever- draining treasury of our country.[180]

In the sixth letter, Blavatskaia writes approvingly of the Shalimar Gardens, which also feature in *Lalla Rookh*, and corrects a Lahore newspaper that favourably compares the muscular British to the feeble Indians, noting that the British bodies are far better fed. Frequent famine under British rule was one of the reasons Tarak Nath Das, in 1908, appealed to Tolstoy for his support for an armed uprising against the British, resulting in a reply by Tolstoy that was famously reprinted by Mohandas Gandhi.[181] In her seventh letter, Blavatskaia also makes much of the speculation about Russian involvement in the sudden departure of the Maharaja of Kashmir, who to everyone's surprise, despite his apparent faux pas, was treated well by the viceroy and given expensive gifts. Russian interference is suspected, a "letter from St. Petersburg" is rumoured, while an attack by Kaufman and Skobelev is expected; as a Russian, Blavatskaia feels somehow guilty about the terrible impending fate of the Maharaja.[182] But like a good parlour joke, the reason for the abrupt departure is revealed as being merely the effect of a strong cathartic drug as prescribed by a doctor – which revelation leads to the near fainting of the "English ladies" and a sudden dropping of the subject.[183] "In this simple way, prosaically and unexpectedly, the formidable cloud that had hung suspended over the political horizon was dissolved, solving the mystery that had stirred the Anglo-Indian colony, the mystery of the 'Russian intrigue,' and the 'unprecedented' impertinence resulting from it, displayed by the Maharaja of Kashmir."[184] Or as Olcott told the story: "Her comments on the show and the bedizened participants kept me in continual laughter, and later on, in one of her incomparable letters to the *Russky Vyestnick*, she set all Russia laughing over the incident of the absence of the Maharajah of Kashmir from the parade; which was at first suspected to cover some political plot, but which turned out to be only a case of diarrhoea!"[185] Scatological humour aside, Blavatskaia had not escaped the woes of the body herself: shortly after the durbar, she came down with dengue fever and was nursed with great kindness and assiduousness by many local specialists, students, and theosophically minded compatriots. While her treatment was mainly focused on driving away the dengue by insulting it, the kindness of her supporters and a Bengali doctor helped her through it. Blavatskaia was ready to leave Allahabad (where she had relocated), remarking:

> How boring are the English, and how suspicious! In India, they positively fall from one hallucination into another. Having freed myself from their idée fixe regarding the "Russian intrigue" in Kashmir, I came upon another similar "cock and bull story" in Allahabad! They now doted on Merve ... this wretched Merve did not leave their tongues, and etiquette demanded that the English in India, having come together, must not speak about anything but politics and especially about the "evil of the day," as our papers now express it. And what better "evil" was there than Merve? ... I finally suggested the publication of a new Anglo-Indian political lexicon wherein the word "merve" would be substituted for "nerve" and "mervousness" for "nervousness." They were almost offended. I then took advantage of

the gracious invitation of the Maharaja of Benares to stay with him, and thus was rid at one stroke of both the dengue and Merve.[186]

In fact, the British were correct that the Russians planned an attack on Merv.[187]

Blavatskaia notes that the viceroy too came down with dengue, and was bedridden for seven weeks. She now describes him positively, finding him to be warm and caring and far better than his predecessor, Lord Lytton. She does not neglect to add a parting shot against the British, however: "After almost five months spent in the social circles of Simla and Allahabad, where the very air appears to be infected with 'politicophilism,' and the foliage of the trees in the avenues of the 'cantonments' whispers to the passing Briton of 'Russian designs,' I succeeded for the first time in resting and getting down to work."[188] While *Durbar* is far less fantastical than *Caves and Jungles*, and clearly sticks far more closely to the truth, it also reflects Blavatskaia's antipathy to the British and their prejudices and anti-Russian suspicions extremely clearly and lays out numerous concerns: that such displays of pomp drain the sources of funds of the people, that even minor disruptions are read in a politically suspicious way, that cheap, factory-made goods are supplanting locally made goods, while also transferring the wealth needed to buy them to England, and indeed India's very patrimony, such as her diamonds and precious stones, not to mention her grain stores, essential to the people's well-being, are being appropriated by the British. Blavatskaia sees things through a political lens: "But I suggest the reader slip behind me into the interior of the audience hall arranged in the tent, or, rather in two tents, as the exterior one merges into the interior or, as it is here called, the 'shamiyana.' Everything here is calculated to produce a political effect; everything is planned, and the actors, having learned well their parts, are ready. I will describe the effect produced on me, in addition to that produced on the native public."[189] As she claims, newspapers do in fact mention the Theosophists and their presence, and Blavatskaia extends her policy of directly addressing bodily infirmities and restrictions rather than suppressing them. Perhaps not surprisingly, however, *Durbar* did not get translated into English until the twentieth century, since it is far less fanciful and, ultimately, for the most part, Orientalist than *From the Caves and Jungles of Hindostan*, despite the opulent description. It does show that Blavatskaia might have written a more straightforward style of travelogue in her first letters but opted instead for the "plums and spices" of her "charming Indian wonder-book," as Olcott put it.

Blavatskaia also writes completely differently about the ethnic "other" than any other writer considered here except for Apreleva and

Potanina. While she clearly is not above ventriloquizing a favourable opinion of Russian imperial rule, those who are portrayed by her are given representation in terms of their thoughts, their ideas, their speech, their beliefs, and their abilities. They are virtually never reduced to their external appearance or to mere clothing or incomprehensible rituals, with the possible exception of the fakirs, whose statue-like poses are nonetheless stressed as being enabled by mental abilities at least as much as physical ones. While the fakirs' feats of immobility and asceticism are astonishing to Blavatskaia, she does not mock them or find them to be unclean, in fact she describes how their attendants assiduously care for them. Here, a contrast with Gordon-Cumming is instructive; describing an important place along the river in Hardwar (Haridwar), Gordon-Cumming states:

> These trees are surrounded by short, very broad pillars of divers heights, whereon loathsome, naked Fakeers, of varied degrees of sanctity, lie crouching or sprawling the livelong day, awaiting the offerings of the faithful. No beings could be imagined more villanously [*sic*] ill-favoured and repulsive than these revolting creatures, the very sight of whom always fills one with invincible disgust, and not always without good reason, for though some doubtless are earnest enough in their austerities, the sanctity of others is merely assumed as a veil enabling them the more easily to

> "Compound for sins they are inclined to,
> By damning those they have no mind to."[190]

As Blavatskaia writes about India, obviously she is not engaged in familiarizing the reader with new Russian possessions or even necessarily spheres of influence, as are the other writers, but under the surface there is a constant assurance that Russians are far more civilized than the British, that "natives" in the Russian empire can be respected and reach high ranks, and that Russians are simply not the same kind of racist snobs that the British frequently show themselves to be. Perhaps because as a Russian she herself is treated with suspicion by the British in India and therefore finds herself opposed to the authorities, Blavatskaia, in concert with other Theosophists and reformers, as well as many Orientalists, takes the part of the Indians, defends their way of life and the nobility of their ancient traditions, and declares that, had the Hindus not been subject to various invasions and to the deleterious power of high-caste interpreters of their sacred texts, that they would never have been defeated by the British and that women also would be equal to men as they had been in the distant past. Simultaneously, Blavatskaia also ultimately defends Russian control of Central Asia, first by attacking the "barbarous reign" of the Moghuls in India, who are held as the destroyers of a superior civilization, and then by frequently assuring readers that Russian imperial conduct towards its ethnic others is entirely positive and defensible. If the Russian empire takes control of Muslim Central Asia, she seems to assert *sub rosa*, then the area can be re-civilized, much as the culture and wisdom of ancient India ought to be re-established in the subcontinent. Throughout she insists on her complete equality with men and on Indians' complete equality with her and all other "Europeans," disdains the company of British women, and insists on her profoundly Russian viewpoint, using it to decry the British and to proclaim Russian superiority, affinity to Eastern culture and higher spiritual values.

Chapter Four

Hunting, Photography, and National Rivalry: *In the Pamirs*

Quite unlike Madame Blavatsky's travel around India, which consisted of a kaleidoscope of ideas, conversations, and historical sights, Iuliia Golovnina's 1898 trip to the Pamir Mountains, now in Tajikistan and then between Russian Turkestan and Afghanistan, was focused and factual. The expedition travelled to and from a specific area and had the goal of obtaining zoological specimens and taking measurements of height, temperature, and barometric pressure at key geographical points. Unlike Blavatskaia's tales of her spiritual superiors, all the relationships with the local people that Golovnina describes were those of employer and employee, "European" visitors interacting with guides or local officials, or simply those of curious and somewhat voyeuristic travellers. Nonetheless, towards the end of her narrative Golovnina breaks through some of the purely hierarchical nature of her relationship with local people hired to help with the expedition and describes them in familiar and solicitous terms. Golovnina, unlike Blavatskaia, does not advocate for the rights of local women, although she makes note of how they are treated and shows an interest in their way of life, particularly in the Pamir part of the journey, and implicitly compares their lives to those of Russian women. Golovnina overtly draws attention both to the challenges of travelling as a woman and to her concern about not being considered a hindrance to the expedition because of her gender.

In the late spring and summer of 1898, Golovnina, a middle-aged Russian noblewoman, travelled from Moscow by rail and boat through the Caucasus, across the Caspian Sea to Samarkand and then Tashkent, Kokand, Andijan, and Osh, whence she and her party set out southward into the Pamir Mountains, travelling by horse, camel, and donkey. Her book about the experience, *Na Pamirakh: Zapiski russkoi puteshestvennitsy* (*In the Pamirs: Notes of a Russian Woman*

Figure 4.1. "Our yurt and my traveling costume," *Na Pamirakh* (*In the Pamirs*), p. 59. Photo by Nadezhda Barteneva.

Traveler) was published in 1902.[1] Golovnina travelled with her husband, David Nikolaevich Golovnin, a professor at an engineering college and the organizer and head of the expedition, as well as a close friend, Nadezhda Petrovna Barteneva, who served as the trip's photographer, and other members who joined the group in Central Asia.[2] Golovnina served as the cashier for the expedition and included a detailed account of expenditures for the trip.[3] They collected specimens for the Moscow University Zoological Museum, focusing particularly on the *Ovis polii*, or Marco Polo sheep (technically, *Ovis ammon polii*), some of which remain in the museum's collection to this day.[4] Golovnina claims that she and Barteneva were the first Russian women to travel to the Pamirs, Teresa (Mrs. St. George) Littledale having been the first "woman-traveler," i.e., the first European woman traveller to go there, both in 1888 and 1890.[5] Perhaps if one restricts the definition to "woman-traveler," i.e., a woman there specifically to travel, Golovnina could claim the distinction of being the first Russian one, but at least one other European woman had already been all the way to Pamirskii Post, the most distant point of Golovnina's trip, and in fact had lived there: Sofiia Georgievna Skerskaia, the wife of Aleksandr Genrikhovich Skerskii, a captain who commanded Pamirskii Post, and who accompanied him and his military party there.[6] The Golovnins have, however, been called the "first Russian 'tourists'" in the Pamirs.[7] Robert Middleton and Huw Thomas also cite Mrs. Leslie Renton and Mrs. Edward Kivekes in addition to Ol'ga Fedchenko, Teresa Littledale, and Mrs. Skersky.[8]

Besides Golovnina's book-length account of the trip, there were also two other written accounts of the same scientific expedition: first, an eight-part article for the journal *Okhota i priroda* (*Hunting and Nature*), "Ocherki okhoty na Pamire" ("Sketches of hunting in the Pamirs"), written by Golovnina's husband, David Nikolaevich Golovnin, and a second, an article for the journal *Zemlevedenie* (Earth Science), "Iz nabliudenii na Pamire" ("From observations about the Pamirs") written by Mikhail Mikhailovich Voskoboinikov, a zoologist who was in charge of the trip in an official sense.[9] All three texts are accompanied by photographs taken by Nadezhda Barteneva, which are uncredited except in the book. Because together all the accounts give a more complete picture of Golovnina's book and of the trip she undertook, I discuss and contrast the work of all three chroniclers here. Also, because photography by women was not well documented at the time, I discuss an earlier traveller, Lidiia Poltorataskaia, who left an album of photographs she took herself as well as two accounts of travel in the Altai region close to Semipalatinsk, where her husband was the governor. In her second account, she discusses, at least briefly, her photographic work, which preceded Barteneva's by about twenty years.[10]

The Trip to the Pamirs: Transnational Destination

A contemporaneous reviewer notes that Golovnina kept a diary during the trip to record details, from which she created her narrative, and in fact most of the narrative proper is designated by date. Although diary-style entries of women's travel writing were sometimes a mere convention,[11] Golovnina herself mentions that she kept a diary[12] and discusses as well the time at the end of each day it took to clean guns, "bother with photography," and create notes.[13] She begins her account with her group's departure by train from Moscow; they travelled through the Caucasus, stopping in Tiflis; she then travelled by steamboat over the Caspian Sea and by train through Central Asia to the city of Andijan, which had experienced a large uprising the previous month, and from Andijan to Osh by phaeton. The railroad that joined Samarkand to Tashkent was still not quite completed and did not have regular service, but with their connections Golovnina's group was given a goods wagon to travel in.[14] That trips to places like the Pamirs were undertaken by a transnational group of wealthy people is very clear; the English Littledales, on their trip to the Pamirs via Tiflis, Georgia, had met with the director of the Natural History Museum, G.I. Radde, as did the Golovnins and Barteneva. The Briton George Curzon, who passed through Tiflis in 1888 on his way to Tashkent, indicates that his travelling party included Englishmen, Italians, and Dutch citizens, along with their guides.[15] What the travellers had in common was their education, high social standing, and keen interest in hunting the Marco Polo sheep, *Ovis polii* as a kind of national sport, an undertaking which would bring status to their countries even as they filled out specimen collections. Curzon called the animal "the most cherished object of the modern sportsman's ambition."[16]

The Pamirs also functioned as the border between the Russian and British spheres of interest; in fact, the border had been officially adjudicated by the time of Golovnina's visit by the joint Russian and British Pamir Boundary Commission.[17] As alluded to by Blavatskaia, the British had feared a Russian incursion into Afghanistan and India through the Pamirs. The Pamirs also served as a source of fascination in the quest to find the source of the Oxus River, as the Amu-Darya was known to the Greeks. John Wood, who accompanied Alexander Burnes on an 1836 mission to Afghanistan, wrote up an account of the "discovery" of Lake Sarikol, which he considered to be the source of the Oxus.[18] Golovnina was well aware of the politicized setting of her travel: "This deserted and difficult-to-reach country could never play a leading political role; however for the last quarter of a century, thanks to Russia's gradual movement deep into Asia, the interests of Russia and England have clashed precisely in the Pamirs."[19] In Central Asia, Barteneva, Golovnina and her husband were joined by a doctor, a student, and the zoologist Voskoboinikov, as well as by hired local guides and workers, a cook, and finally a military hunting team sent to accompany them. Jonathan Slaght notes that "hunting teams" were "Russian military units used as training platforms for elite soldiers" who gained knowledge of wildlife and the outdoors that benefited both those they accompanied and the Russian military itself, providing a highly trained resource.[20] Golovnina, in fact, mocks Curzon's lack of understanding of this term in her comments to her "Geographical Sketch of the Pamirs," which gives the history of discovery and travel in the region, as well as outlining the contest between the British and the Russians.[21] She also disdains the claim made by the anonymous author of *Russia's March towards India, by an Indian Officer* (1894) that Russia's goal in Central Asian expansion was to take India.[22]

The Golovnins had met Nikolai Ivanovich Korol'kov (1837–1906), the military governor of the Syr-Darya region, in Moscow. Hearing of Golovnin's interest in hunting in the Pamirs, Korol'kov invited them to come to Turkestan, where he had lived for many years. When they arrived in Tashkent, he had been called away due to the Andijan uprising (an absence to which he had alerted them to via telegram along the way), so they waited at his dacha until he returned. Golovnina highly approved of Korol'kov's dacha and its garden setting:

> Nikolai Ivanovich's dacha is in the city itself, on the edge of it; we were given a large wing for our exclusive use, beautifully situated and surrounded by green plants; in it we settled ourselves for an amount of time not yet known to us. This dacha is like a beloved child of Nikolai Ivanovich; each tree in it was planted by his hands 25 years ago. Now the dacha is one of the most beautiful places in the city, it has a wonderful collection of varied types of roses and rare plants, presenting no small interest to the botanist and gardener.[23]

Most trips taken to this sensitive region, on the border between Russian, Chinese, and Anglo-Indian spheres of influence, whether by Russians or Europeans, had to some extent a political subtext and had to have official approval; Curzon notes that foreigners who lacked the correct documents were turned back by Russian officials.[24] Information of many kinds was constantly being gathered, and permissions by rival governments to pass particular borders were not easily or readily given.

The Littledales, for example, had to get permission both to go to Central Asia and to travel there by train; in fact, a set of letters published in the London *Times* by Curzon, who had earlier been given permission to travel in Central Asia, had made Russian authorities reluctant to allow more such travellers when the Littledales applied.[25] Dukhovskaia also discussed these permissions in her memoirs.[26] In the context of the Great Game, each side kept a careful watch on the other, and opportunities to travel and hunt in the Pamirs, and to acquire specimens of *Ovis polii* and other mountain animals, played a role in the rivalry between the two countries. Curzon writes in his *Russians in Central Asia* that the Pamirs are the "sportsman's El Dorado" in his "Directions to Travellers" section.[27] Though they were certainly political rivals, because those who could afford to travel and hunt in such obscure and hard to reach areas of the world essentially were wealthy, well educated, and well travelled, in reality they had more in common with each other than not. There are numerous accounts of British and Russian representatives meeting cordially with each other and exchanging information about their travels, despite their countries' rivalry and, in the case of Ralph Cobbold, his strong criticism of Russian aggression.[28] The British officer Francis Younghusband met imperial officer and explorer Bronislaw Grombchevskii as well as Mikhail Ionov, who had orders to detain him and remove him from the Russian-controlled Pamirs. This did not prevent the two from dining together, with Ionov apologizing for having to carry out his orders and Younghusband warning Ionov that he would have to lodge an official complaint, which was later taken up by Petersburg.[29]

Curzon notes that "English is an extreme rarity in Transcaspia. French and German are not spoken except by Russian officers of the highest class"; hence he advised learning some Russian and engaging knowledgeable guides in order to travel in the area.[30] The various national writers and explorers also relied on each other for their factually based accounts. The Geographical Society in London, for example, relied on the accounts of travellers and explorers in multiple languages; Curzon alludes to the Russian accounts of the prominent zoologist Nikolai Severtsov on birds and *Ovis polii* sheep, for example, and to Russian historians, as well as to Russian maps.[31] In turn, both Golovnins were clearly familiar with Curzon's work and cited it in their texts. Furthermore, a striking photo of the head of an *Ovis polii* sheep from Curzon's publication found its way into Golovnina's book and one of Golovnin's articles, which will be discussed below.

The Golovnins' trip occurred at a moment when Turkestan was in turmoil and the Russian leadership in Turkestan had recently changed, with Sergei Dukhovskoi (the husband of Varvara Dukhovskaia) replacing Alexander Vrevskii as governor-general of Turkestan.[32] Golovnina's party visited the prison in Osh to have a look at the prisoners who had rebelled during the uprising in Andijan, and even took pictures of them; as Golovnina notes, the group was always "armed with cameras and tripods for them."[33] Golovnin, writing in his hunting articles, acknowledges to his readers that it is difficult to get to the Pamirs, as one must have much free time and an ability to prepare for a nomadic life. He notes jokingly that if any Englishmen had seen the large size of their group, they'd have feared the imminent occupation of India by the Russians but assures the reader that the group's goals were in fact completely peaceful and focused on acquiring zoological specimens.[34] This Great Game subtext is frequently encountered in both Golovnins' accounts. In his second article, while describing the Marco Polo sheep, or arkhar, as it was called locally, Golovnin gives the measurements of the largest specimen in England, at the Kensington Museum of Natural History, noting that its horns measured sixty-eight inches, while the largest one in Moscow, located at the University and obtained by Severtsov, measured "only" fifty-seven inches.[35] Golovnin notes that he has a personal specimen only one inch shorter, at fifty-six inches, which he took from a pile of horns near Pamirskii Post, a place the expedition visited.[36] "Arkhar" was also used to name a different but closely related species, *Ovis argali*, found particularly in the Altai region; a zoological guide from the period describes the imprecision of the term but notes that "*arkar* is the Turki name of O. polii."[37]

Golovnina describes the Andijan uprising, which had occurred in May 1898, only a month before her group's arrival, and describes as well the tale of Kurmanjan Datka, a woman ruler of the Alai region, who, wishing to avoid bloodshed, decided to align with the Russians even at great personal cost.[38] Golovnina claims that "rumors about disorders in India and news about the victories of the Turks over the Greeks" no doubt influenced the rebels, alluding apparently to the Greco-Turkish War of 1897.[39] Golovnina also criticizes the overly lax governing of Turkestan which allowed the uprising to happen, in her view, noting that "humanitarian behavior" is thought of as being weak in Central Asia and implying, by means of her critique, that strict measures ought to be taken.[40] Golovnina describes an encounter with the wives of Russian workers on the train in Kokand, who complain to her about their unhappiness at having decided to come to Central Asia, in the process having sold their land and all their worldly goods. Golovnina decides that their real complaint has to do with homesickness and not being accustomed to Central Asia: "they complain most of all about the expense and fevers."[41]

Still, even if she is dismissive about the complaint itself, she includes the detail that the women feel they have been misled, having listened to the khodoki, or walkers, who were peasant scouts designated to search out new land in Central Asia for peasant settlement.[42]

Genres of Travel

Golovnina's account, which extends to 244 printed pages, covers all aspects of the expedition from start to finish and includes a geographical essay that also addresses political topics, a guide to equipping the expedition that includes prices, and a bibliography of literature about the Pamirs. Expedition member Voskoboinikov's thirty-page article, published in the then recently founded geographical journal *Zemleve-denie*, focuses on the geography of a portion of the area visited, mainly near the lakes of Bol'shoi Kara-Kul', Rang-Kul', and Shor-Kul', describing the makeup of the soil, the detection of permanent ice in the soil, the flow of rivers, and an investigation into the small number of fauna in that specific part of the Pamirs. In his article, Voskoboinikov acknowledges that he participated in an expedition but names only one of the other members of it; in several cases he uses the same photographs that later appeared in Golovnina's book; those that did not also appear in Golovnina's book were probably also taken by Nadezhda Barteneva. Voskoboinikov intends to avoid repetition, remarking: "I will not expound upon a description of all the places we visited, the majority of which have already been visited and described by many travelers. I will indicate only a few points, which present the greatest geographical interest, by their character as well as because of several facts that I was able to observe and which, as far as I know, have not been published."[43] Barteneva is not credited in Golovnin's or Voskoboinikov's articles, but Golovnina says in her foreword that Barteneva undertook "all the photographic work of the expedition."[44] Several notices about and reviews of Golovnina's book call the photographs zincographs, a type of photogravure created with zinc plates.[45] David Nikolaevich Golovnin's seven-part article for *Priroda i okhota*, along with an additional, eighth article on hunting birds, which appeared from February to September 1901, is also illustrated by many of the same photographs that appeared in Golovnina's book. The first five parts of the article, "Ocherki okhoty na Pamirakh" ("Essays on hunting in the Pamirs") with various subheadings, focus mainly on the hunting group's attempts to take specimens of the *Ovis polii*, a sheep with large, curving horns that lives very high in the Pamir Mountains and was first described by Polo in his travels.[46] Parts six and seven discuss the hunting of a type of mountain goat, the kiik (*Capra sibirica*, Siberian ibex), and other animals. Golovnin's article, quite lively in its own way, provides a contrast to Voskoboinikov's dry and pessimistic article focusing mostly on the paucity of flora and fauna in the area. Whereas the scientist found few living creatures to make note of, Golovnin, who climbed high into the mountains both on horseback and on foot in search of the mountain sheep (and did not restrict his comments only to the areas treated by the scientist), describes a whole menagerie of animals in the Pamirs: marmots, rabbits, various birds, mountain goats, plants like lavender and highly aromatic wildflowers, and insects like bumblebees and butterflies. The Pamir Boundary Commission report, completed only two years before the Golovnin trip, also found numerous animals, fish, and plants in the region.[47] In what amounted to an eighth section of his article, "Okhota na Pamirakh po peru" ("Hunting for birds in the Pamirs"), Golovnin discusses the large variety of birds found during the trip and mentions Voskoboinikov's findings of only immature fish in Lake Rang-Kul.[48]

Reinforcing the idea that scientific and travel writing (along with, in this case, writing about hunting) were not fully differentiated at the time, it is notable that the genres of the three examples are far more similar than one might expect. The scientist Voskoboinikov, for example, at times trades heavily on emotion. He notes, for example, that the extreme slowness of the process of erosion creates a picture of decay, underscoring "the dreariness of the pictures here, the apparent lack of life, which so strikes the traveler in these parts of the Pamirs … Add to that the almost complete lack of signs of organic life and you will arrive at the typical landscape of the central part of the Pamirs."[49] Voskoboinikov likewise noted that the area near Karakul Lake was full of desolation; the many horns and skulls lying at every step indicate that the *Ovis polii* are present, he notes, but it is so hard to see them that "their presence does not at all destroy the sense of the deserted character of the country."[50] Golovnina, describing the same area, evokes Dante: "Unbidden comes to mind a comparison with the entrance to Dante's hell, before which everything is empty and hopeless all around; the impression of this strengthens in the profusion of the skulls and bones of fallen horses we encounter, having perished, probably, in the winter at the time of storms, the characteristic picture of the Pamir surrounded us, the 'roof of the world.'"[51] All three chroniclers clearly (and, in fact, explicitly since Voskoboinikov specifically mentions what travellers experience) think of the landscape as something to be experienced and adjudicated by a "European" visitor. Golovnin at one point recounts some animal behaviour, goats jumping downhill to land on their horns, that the local inhabitants have described to him, but since not a single

"European-naturalist" has seen this behaviour, Golovnin does not deem it reliable.[52] For Golovnina aesthetics prevail for the most part, although she also closely describes the weather, providing temperature measurements. For Golovnin, hunting comes first and foremost, but from his perspective failure in hunting can be just as informative and engaging as success, especially when going after such high-status and elusive prey. Among British hunting accounts, colourful descriptions of failure in hunting were not uncommon, as Harriet Ritvo attests: "In this unremitting spotlight, the protagonists often presented themselves with modest, and even whimsical understatement. They insistently exposed their failures and frustrations – a litany of bad luck ('whenever anything large appears I always seem to have dust shot in my gun') and bad judgment (on the part of a 'dreadfully annoyed' sportsman who had spared a wild boar, thinking it was a donkey) ... Rather than undermining the stature of the hero, such rhetoric implicitly enhanced it. Abjuring braggadocio and hysteria, the hunter used his tone to display the manly British qualities of coolness, restraint, and humor."[53] All three chroniclers carefully engage their predecessors and interlocutors, aware that they are not the first to describe what they see and experience, although they remain among a very privileged few "Europeans" to have had the experience. Lurking in the background was always the spectre of other European hunters, visitors, and commentators, especially the British, with whose control of India they also implicitly and explicitly compare Russian rule over Central Asia.

Besides fuzziness of genre in the three accounts, there is also in some sense a fuzziness in roles, perhaps not surprising for the time period and the role of scientist/observer/traveller/hunter that prevailed. Voskoboinikov, though a zoologist, at times seems to be unaware of which species he is seeing evidence of, whereas Golovnin, an avid hunter, names almost every species he comes across. Although Voskoboinikov provides scientific names for some species, he also describes "little birds" and "a quantity of insects" without being more specific.[54] We know from Golovnina's account that he was in fact collecting specimens of insects during the trip, and both they and he mention the small fish and crabs he observed in the lakes. Vladimir Arseniev, who mapped out the territory along the Ussuri River in the Russian Far East in the early part of the twentieth century, also had extensive knowledge of flora and fauna of the area he visited and also collected specimens; the expectations for the activities and knowledge of travellers, hunters, geographers, military explorers, and topographers were overlapping, and precision of information, measurements, and scientific names of phenomena tended to come to the fore regardless of the specific intent of any given journey. The Western-centric scientific record was being built up through the work of many different participants. As Sara Mills points out, women travellers, like male ones, added to the kind of scientific knowledge that promoted the view that "European activities [were] essentially civilizing," and although the figure of the (female) naturalist might seem less "guilty," it nevertheless implied that the colonized region consisted of a repository of interesting items and a space in need of the importation of European order.[55]

The mixed nature of this kind of writing, which invariably touched on such subjects as zoology, cartography, ethnology, and the like, is also evidenced in such texts as General Gerard's Pamir Boundary Commission report, published in 1897, the year before the Golovnins' trip, which contains an extensive list, including several detailed drawings, of specimens obtained during the course of the adjudication of the boundary, with scientific names and detailed descriptions. These specimens included birds, fish, plants, insects, molluscs, and mammals, many of which were given to the Indian Museum in Calcutta.[56] Gerard also collected numerous mineralogical specimens. Colonel T.H. Holdich wrote a section of the report, "Narrative of Proceedings," which discussed British interactions with both the Russians and the "Kirghiz" (a term that could denote either Kazakhs or Kyrgyz) noting that the latter hunted the *Ovis polii* with dogs, leaving the useless heads in the field. The Russians also came in for ethnographic observation by the British officers: Holdich described the makeup of the commission and noted that the participating general, General Povalo-Shveikovskii, governor of the Ferghana Province, had a portrait of Nicholas II, the tsar, in his comfortable yurt, alongside many elements of local production: "They were comfortably quartered in Kirghiz akois, the General's residence being distinguished not only by outside decorations of Kirghiz embroidery, but hung inside with Bokhara silks, and well furnished with Central Asian carpets and divans. A portrait of the Emperor Nicolas II. occupied a place of honour on the walls of the akoi."[57] Holdich also described a Russian feast day that included the entirety of the commission and featured a game of ulak, a polo-like game, races for boys, Cossack dzhigitovka, a form of expert trick horseback riding (Holdich was particularly impressed that all the Cossacks were highly skilled horsemen and not merely a select few of them), and a festive meal. Holdich noted that the Russians were "impress[ing] the native mind" by their careful etiquette and generous, ceremonial prize-giving. Another moment astonishing to Holdich was that the Cossacks gave a dinner for the Sepoys and orderlies, and "even the native servants" of the British camp.[58] While the commission on the English side included

Indian officers and other personnel, Holdich clearly made a distinction between them and the native servants, which the Russians did not. It is evident from the excellent photography included in the *Proceedings* that the undertaking was of the highest quality, far more "scientific" than anything produced during the Golovnin expedition. While in the Pamirs, the boundary commission group encountered Sven Hedin, the noted Swedish explorer who met with Dukhovskaia in Tashkent; a picture of him astride a local camel is included in the report. Gerard's group, too, was interested in the status of the *Ovis polii*, and a picture of a hunter (perhaps Ossetinski, who was cited as having successfully shot two of the sheep) with a "head and skin" of one is printed on page 61 of the *Proceedings*. It is clear that both the collecting of scientific specimens and the shooting of *Ovis polii* (counted among the former) were typical undertakings of any trip to the Pamirs; Younghusband also makes frequent allusions to *Ovis polii* hunting in his account.

Conventions of Writing

Golovnin's hunting notes, designed both for armchair reading and for practical use by future hunters, are far more upbeat than Voskoboinikov's more morose observations and acknowledge many more details of the overall trip, although, like Voskoboinikov, he is himself quite parsimonious with names. Golovnin declares in the first part of his article that he was collecting zoological specimens, especially the large mountain animals, for the zoological museum of Moscow University; he notes that the zoologist Voskoboinikov was actually in charge of the scientific part of the expedition.[59] Golovnin counts ten members of the hunting team, two Cossacks and the lieutenant, whose movements were coordinated with the expedition's. He names six participants in the expedition, among them "two ladies – my wife and Madame B." (photographer Barteneva), present along with the already-described military accompaniment of thirteen, four servants and three pack animal drivers, a total of "26 people and with them 35 horses, four camels and two donkeys."[60] The zoologist, the doctor, and the student made up the remaining three of the six main participants.

Golovnin makes it clear that hunting the intelligent and alert *Ovis polii* sheep is the main goal of the trip. It is extremely difficult; Golovnin makes no bones about how exhausting it is to climb a mountain at high altitude, holding a heavy gun. He gives credit to local "Kirghiz" (as common usage among Russians and other "Europeans" then designated both Kyrgyz and Kazakhs) guides (without, however, providing any names of individuals) and the military hunting team sent to accompany the group for their knowledge and expertise.[61] As Virginia Martin notes, before 1920 in Russia "all Kazakhs of the Great [Uli], Middle [Orta] and Little [Kishi] Hordes were referred to as 'Kirgiz,', while the Turkic, nomadic Kyrgyz peoples of present-day Kyrgyzstan were called 'Kara-Kirgiz' [black Kirgiz] or 'Dikokamennyi Kirgiz' [wild mountain Kirgiz]. Kazakh [Qazaq] was a self-appellation not recognized by the Russian imperial administration in the nineteenth century."[62] British travellers also referred to the people of this region of the Pamirs as "Kirg(h)iz."

Golovnina's much longer format book is designed to appeal to a broader audience than were the hunting articles; judging from reviews, it seems to have done so, although references to it in scholarship are relatively rare.[63] She emphasizes her gender in the title, calling it "Notes of a Russian Woman Traveler" (puteshestvennitsy), possibly in reference to Karamzin.[64] Even if Golovnin's hunting notes are of interest not only to hunters, Golovnina's focus is much more on the travellers' experiences, impressions, and practical details. She did not take part in the hunting expeditions; hence, reading the texts of each spouse creates a fuller picture of the overall activities of the group. Similarly, Golovnin did not spend much time at camp and therefore others' daily non-hunting activities were less known to him. One day, returning from a hunting expedition near Karakul Lake, he wrote, "We returned to the camp only in darkness, satisfied with our first success. Our fellow travelers were also happy with the day they had spent; some photographed, some hunted for wildfowl on the lake, some made observations and an excursion around the lake, where much that was interesting was located."[65]

The accounts are all written from the point of view of privileged, well-educated Russian members of the nobility, who are firmly in tune with the administration of the Russian government and confident of its rights to control Central Asia. There is a very settled hierarchy from the point of view of the Golovnins: the top military commanders in the region, as well as Grand Duke Nikolai Konstantinovich, who lived in exile in Tashkent, make up the highest level of society; the non-governmental Russian nobility, including the main six travellers, come next; then Lt. Masterkov, head of the hunting team; then his (apparently ethnic Russian) soldiers, as well as the Cossacks; followed by the non-Russian, settled, city dwellers who live in the towns (Sarts) from whose ranks are also taken their immediate servants on the trip; and then the nomadic people who are in isolated communities beyond the cities, many of whom serve as guides or support staff for the travellers.

Into the Pamirs: Entering the Hunting Great Game

On 24 June, the journey proper begins, with pack animals carrying the goods of the group. Golovnina hastens to say at the beginning that it is often thought that "ladies" ("damy") slow down travel, but that she and Nadezhda Barteneva were never the cause of late departures and any delays were caused by their fellow travellers.[66] Golovnina plays the role of the mistress of the expedition. She describes how one of the dzhigits sent to accompany them spent time singing and otherwise amusing them in the mode of a "ladies' *cavalier servant*" and notes that he was particularly taken with Nadezhda Barteneva's blonde hair.[67] The women opted (taking the advice of experienced travellers) to ride astride and not side saddle, and had also equipped themselves with Circassian outfits consisting of trousers underneath skirts so that they could ride astride the horse but upon dismounting, look appropriately "feminine."[68] This seems to have been a common method, one that Karazin describes in his story "Doktorsha," for example.[69] Skerskaia is described as having worn men's clothing to ride, as did Poltoratskaia.[70] This attempt to look "feminine" and socially presentable as a woman, as Golovnina describes it, was a constant struggle:

> Good heavens, what has happened to our costumes, relatively proper at the beginning? Due to the cold, over our worn cherkeski we must doll ourselves up in dresses that have nothing in common with a cherkeska: thus, for spending time in the yurt I put on my black wool sweater with modish wide sleeves; on my head I sport a silly Sart tiubeteika [embroidered pillbox hat], in which I must also sleep; huge men's hunting boots, crumbling with age and abundantly smeared with lard, which little helps the elegance of my costume ... the cold and the wild conditions definitively paralyze even the weakest attempts at elegance.[71]

While fully involved in all the trip preparations, Golovnina is also capable of portraying a kind of credulousness about her status in the world that seems almost hard to believe:

> Having stopped for a moment near a station and having each drunk a tumbler of cold kumys[72] (an absolutely nasty drink, besides which, also for some reason full of an abundance of horse hairs), we moved further in the company of our new dzhigit, who had replaced our "scarecrow," these dzhigits hand us off to each other, ahead of time notifying the next volost' of the arrival of "the important gentlefolk" ("bol'shikh gospod").

> Who gives the news of our movements and when, we don't know, but as we arrive at each overnight spot, we invariably as a result found yurts put up for us, kumys, mutton, where possible also milk, as well as almost always a few Kirghiz appeared as servant-volunteers.[73]

Golovnin, too, mentions "Kirghiz-volunteers" who "accompany us from one station to another."[74] After the midway point, these "volunteers" were no longer provided, since the group sacrificed their minders when they decided to go in a different, non-approved direction back to Margelan. At an early stop, Golovnina describes a meal or dastarkhan put on by the elders of the local volost', which included melons, flatbread, fruit drops, and halvah. She notes that "we attacked the melons greedily, not at all in keeping with our status as 'important gentlefolk.'"[75]

Ultimately, of course, it was the Russian government that fully supported and sponsored the party's travel; the military hunting team and accompanying local government personnel, as well as the prepared yurts and food, were part of that support. The party's safety had been personally guaranteed by Korol'kov and others. Hence no chances were taken in terms of providing for the group's security and well-being, while it was also clear that participating in the collection of specimens of *Ovis polii* sheep was essentially part of the construction of national pride. Curzon, in an extremely political book about the rivalry between Russia and England, had written about St. George Littledale, whose wife Teresa had preceded Golovnina and Barteneva to the Pamirs: "Mr. Littledale, a sportsman, who had with great difficulty obtained leave to go as far as Samarkand with a view of proceeding from there in quest of the *ovis poli* in the remote mountains of the Pamir. In this pursuit I record with pleasure the fact that the last-named gentleman was entirely successful, being the first Englishman who has ever shot a male specimen of this famous and inaccessible animal."[76] Curzon himself shot two *Ovis polii*, although smaller than others that had been taken, and was actually concerned that there was already too much hunting of the animals.[77] General Ionov, who controlled the troops in Andijan, assigned the women two Cossacks to guard them specifically; Golovnina describes them by name, appearance, and personality; ultimately they carried out many household chores, such as washing clothes, for the "ladies," a term Golovnina herself uses in quotation marks.[78] At a number of points in her text, Golovnina addresses hygiene and fashion; she criticizes the men for not wishing to keep themselves cleaner (they protest that she and Nadezhda Barteneva have their own tent for washing), and she laments her bronzed skin and the extreme dryness of the air, which she and Barteneva combat with lip balm and chocolate oil.[79] As a number of commentators have pointed out, women's participation in what were primarily seen as male pursuits led to a destabilization of the typical public/private dichotomy; hence Golovnina's concern about her appearance and whether it was sufficiently feminine, even while she embraced the ability to break out of typically female constraints.[80] Horseback riding, in particular, was often associated with women's freedom and licentiousness in literature, such as in Karazin's "Doktorsha" and *Na dalekikh okrainakh*, in Karolina Pavlova's *A Double Life*, in Lermontov's "Princess Mary," and in Turgenev's "First Love." Dukhovskaia too had revelled in her boldness of going out riding in Erzerum by herself. Golovnina thus openly referred to these conflicts of feminine identity.

Europeans, Tuzemtsy, Women: Golovnina's Cast of Characters

The Cossacks are the first underlings who are given much characterization by Golovnina, although the horse groom, Tashmet, the cook, Murza, and the caravan leader, Alim-bai, who was hired as a translator but moved to the position of caravan leader, all receive some characterization early on. All of the latter are Sarts, i.e., people from the settled cities. The Cossacks, whose first names only are given, Pyotr and Dmitrii, are described as sweet, mischievous boys, although both are in fact already married, and their friendship is described, perhaps unflatteringly to them, as similar to that of the two donkeys on the expedition, who are closely bonded. Sent ostensibly to specially protect the two women, the young Cossacks essentially are turned into household servants. They, along with Tashmet, are prized for their childlike and good-natured obedience. As Golovnina writes towards the end of her account:

> My fellow travelers this time were just Murza and Tashmet. The latter is unusually touching in the care he proffers in regard to me and N. P. [Barteneva]. Maintaining a watch on us, he takes care of us and it is as if he appears out of the earth just when we need some kind of help. He knows only a few words of Russian, so our explanations with him are mainly mimicry and imitating sounds, but his simple, completely childlike soul understands with great delicacy how he can be helpful. During the whole of the journey we could depend on Tashmet with complete faith, that everything he undertook would be done precisely and in and good conscience.[81]

Murza, the cook, is not quite such a favourite as Tashmet, but as the trip wears on, both his personality and his cooking come to be more greatly appreciated. In general, Golovnina's account is quite hierarchical at the beginning, sharply distinguishing between the gentry and the soldiers, the "Europeans" and the locals, but towards the end, when much of the party has broken up, she indicates a fondness for Tashmet and Murza, in particular, and they receive more characterization in the narrative while her dependence on them is made increasingly evident. Alim-bai, the head of the caravan, is seen as the least sympathetic of the three; he had previously been a man of means but had made a bad business deal and was reduced to working for others again. He appoints himself mullah of the Muslims in the group, Golovnina says, and criticizes them for insufficient prayer and incorrect smoking and eating practices, whereas Murza, though a Muslim, manages to cook pork on occasion for the group without undue concern, asking a soldier to help him cut the meat so as to avoid touching it, for example.[82] Tashmet, Murza, and Alim-bai (Figure 4.2) are all photographed individually in the book, with captions that indicate their names and roles.

Just as Tashmet's solicitousness in regard to the women travellers is noted, so too is Murza's distress from a lack of tobacco, remedied when a member of the party is sent to Pamirskii Post, the garrison, to buy more tobacco; its renewed availability reanimates Murza. Murza also discovers, towards the very end, a penchant for shooting a gun, not really in an attempt to hit anything, but for the sheer enjoyment of it. Alim-bai, too, has his positive qualities; he evinces a talent for difficult river crossings and saves one of the donkeys from drowning. It is Alim-bai who is entrusted with selling all the items used for the expedition after it is over.

As the book wraps up, Golovnina describes each of the three of them coming to her, her husband and Nadezhda Barteneva to give a thank you speech and in essence, indicate how each will use the money earned; Tashmet has opted to add a second wife to his household with his earnings, although mainly apparently to divert to a new bride the unpleasant querulousness of his first wife. Golovnina adds, in a footnote, that she wonders how it turned out, three years later as the book is going to press.[83] Murza comes to receive his pay in elegant new clothes, since during his absence on the trip his parents had betrothed him to a young woman.

Ethnography and Animal Husbandry

Not surprisingly, Golovnina ventures into the sphere of ethnography at times in her account. Comparing the nomad women to the Sarts, she finds the nomads to be more sympathetic and attractive and keen

Рис. 24. Караванъ баши Алимъ-Бай.

Figure 4.2. "Caravan Leader Alim-Bai," *Na Pamirakh*, p. 75. Photo by Nadezhda Barteneva.

to put together social events; the smallest news is reason to have a "tamasha," or celebration, she says.[84] As other travellers also note, it is the women, however, who do all the work, and for that reason women fetch a high bride price. Nomad women do not have to cover their faces and have a voice in the family household; divorce and remarriage are allowed. This is in both implicit and explicit contrast to the Sart women, whom she describes early on in her book and who are pictured in the third plate on page 16. She finds it notable that men must pay bride money, kalym, to the parents of the bride and that divorce is easy; however, women must stay covered in public and are consigned to childcare, sewing, and cooking.[85] In line with many other Russian women of the period, Golovnina supports freeing them from these strictures: "Our administration has already long acknowledged the necessity of changing the position of the Sart woman, and the first step toward this goal were several attempts to reveal their faces, but such a decisive rebuff occurred that the authorities did not insist to prevent the inescapable general uprising that would have taken place under the circumstances."[86] That these kinds of sentiments on the part of European or British women travellers are fraught with complexities has been pointed out in numerous places, as they could imply that Western women were not themselves subject to patriarchal restrictions and could certainly also be thought of as "maternalistic" or patronizing, recapitulating imperial superiority.[87] However, it is clear that Golovnina, and others as well, recognized that even under the same religion, practices involving women's status varied from group to group. These concerns and comments, shared by many Russian travellers, including Vasilii Vereshchagin, Anna Rossikova, Praskov'ia Uvarova, and others, also showed a concern with women's rights common in Russian society at the time.[88] Golovnina also pays attention to the animals involved in her trip, such as her horse, Ryzhok, and the camels and donkeys employed as pack animals. She notes with disapproval the "barbarous custom" of putting a stick through a camel's nostrils to control it, something she says the Emir of Bukhara had forbidden in his territories.[89]

Both Golovnins' accounts describe how Golovnina's name day is celebrated, which is quite revealing of the social hierarchy on the trip. Samarkand wine is produced by Lt. Masterkov, the leader of the hunting team, according to Golovnin. In honour of the occasion, the soldiers of the hunting team, as well as the two Cossacks, each got a silver rouble and a cup of vodka. The cook, Murza, apparently with great pride, created a concoction meant to resemble a chocolate dessert, made with sour yak's milk. Golovnin touches on this topic in the fourth section of his article, placing great emphasis on the extreme rarity of having wine on the menu and noting as well that if the group was able to eat half the "dessert," then their tastes had certainly changed during their trip. Both note here that the usual fare during the expedition is mutton and rice, although at the highest altitudes they reached, rice could not be cooked, since at high altitudes water boils at too low a temperature.[90]

Mentions of the local people who are not specifically employed by or guiding the group occur occasionally. In one extended section, the group goes to watch ulak, a game like polo but played with a goat carcass (a version of it is also called baiga); Apreleva also describes this game in her story "Sail'," as do the authors of the *Proceedings of the Boundary Commission*, and it is mentioned by many other travellers as well.[91] Except as guides and in part as local administrators of the area, the local inhabitants of the Pamir are little described. Golovnina does note the elegance of some of the elders who greet them along the way, as well as their penchant for blue glasses, which she thinks is for the sake of fashion.[92] She describes a local invitation to tea drinking in some detail; the Russians are invited because they had earlier made the acquaintance of the owner of the yurt that was situated at a later point in their journey, and they were served by the sister and two wives of the host.[93] Golovnina acknowledges the hostesses' proficiency in cooking and the tastiness of the food, and without commenting specifically on plural marriage, quotes the host as he declares that a good (Muslim) husband must create an atmosphere in which the younger wife obeys the elder one, a situation, Golovnina confirms, that he believes prevails in his household. Golovnina goes on to describe the large and somewhat awkward headgear of the women, while professing that the rest of their clothing seems perfectly practical. There is also a photograph, "Kirghiz women," showing the large white head coverings, which seems to show the hostesses.[94] On the one hand, Golovnina is clearly the outsider describing the "native" with some sense of superiority; on the other hand, the awkwardness and confining nature of her own "women's clothing" is brought out on several occasions. Further, early on she and Nadezhda Petrovna both had to exchange their poorly constructed women's boots for men's; the photographer buys some from a soldier, while Golovnina uses a spare pair of her husband's. Besides an apparent comparison to Russian women's clothing, implicit in the description of the women serving food in the yurt seems to be an acknowledgment of the fact that the Russian women were also accustomed to following sharply defined gender roles.

Hunting

Golovnin readily admits that usually only the local guides could even catch sight of the *Ovis polii* sheep, and on several occasions, the hunters, including Golovnin, give their weapons to them, unable, it seems, either to properly see the sheep or (this is never admitted) unable to climb and move fast enough at the great heights (14,000 feet) to go after the animals quickly and stealthily enough to be able to shoot them.[95] Golovnin advises the reader on how to do better, carefully analysing animal behaviour and methods of getting close to the sheep. Golovnina states quite straightforwardly in her account that only the guides are able to sight the prey and claims that for them, "our hunting is a holiday, since for their help with the work they get a whole sheep, which they eat down to the bones. Today they got, besides the sheep, 50 kopecks a person; they were in ecstasy."[96]

The genre of hunting literature was extremely popular at the time and was often combined with travel and exploration accounts. The thick journal *Priroda i okhota* had been founded in 1878 and covered a wide range of hunting topics, including articles about laws, meetings of hunting groups, specific hunts, and even poetry. In Golovnina's bibliography are multiple European accounts of combined travel and hunting books and articles, along with many in Russian; the hunting of animals, usually but not always for food, was also a regular feature of Vladimir Arseniev's accounts.[97] The Golovnins admired the Natural History Museum in Tiflis, which had the only stuffed specimen of a Caucasian zuber, or European bison. They stressed the skills of the curators, noting that the displays included multiple animals in each scene, while the scenes were "full of life and movement" and both walls and ceilings were painted as backdrops.[98]

In parts six and seven of his article for *Priroda i okhota*, Golovnin goes into great detail about hunting the kiik, or *Capra sibirica*, a large mountain goat with prominent horns, though a much smaller animal than the famed *Ovis polii*, and a picture of him with a slain kiik is in the book, with Golovnin wearing a British-style helmet (Figure 4.3).

On the lookout for two colours of kiik, Golovnin declares he has encountered one of the rarer white variety – but admits he himself actually never saw it, even though the "accompanying Kirghiz hunter tried to show it to me."[99] As always, the British collection of specimens is on Golovnin's mind: "The color of the fur of the Capra Skyn is much lighter than that of the Capra Sibirica, while it also has a clearly defined dark stripe along its back. I was able to see a goat with grayish color at the London Museum of Natural History with a notation saying that it had been obtained in the Hindu Kush, that is, on the southern border of the Pamirs."[100] Golovnin writes in one fell swoop about how marvellous it felt to shoot such a goat, – which he does not think of retrieving himself but "which I sent a Kirghiz" to go get.[101] Needless to say, the guides do all the work of carrying the

Рис. 29. Охотники съ убитымъ кіикомъ.

Figure 4.3. "Hunters with a slain kiik," *Na Pamirakh*, p. 89. Photo by Nadezhda Barteneva.

shot animals down the steep and icy mountains. Golovnina describes a young kiik with beautiful horns that took eight shots to bring down due to the trembling of her husband's hands as he wielded the gun. Shot through the shoulder and dragged over rocks by the hunting party's guides, neither the skeleton nor the skin were usable for display, she notes.[102]

Numerous elements were implicated in the role of hunting. As Harriet Ritvo remarks, wild animals in many ways stood in for imperial suppression of local people, and even more remarkably so when they were dead: "Rows of horns and hides, mounted heads and stuffed bodies, clearly alluded to the violent heroic underside of imperialism ... Each stuffed animal represented a bloody triumph in the field, an impression that might be enhanced by arrangements and backgrounds ... designed to suggest the animal's native territory."[103] "The most attractive specimens," Ritvo notes, "were those that were hardest to kill."[104] As Ritvo attests, hunting became more and more common in British imperial territories, especially Africa and India, eventually even developing into a kind of middle-class attainment, especially with the increasing availability of fast modes of travel, such as steamboats, railroads, and the like. The English-language literature about hunting was quite large, and like Golovnin's articles, could at times be self-effacing in exposing the hunter's mistakes and failures.[105] Although in the British imperial context much of the finding of game was done, as in the Golovnin expedition, by local experts, and often centred on surrounding or surprising game or lying in wait for animals at watering holes, the most popular British written accounts tended to focus on a kind of individual combat against (ideally) a fierce animal, with much emphasis on the hunter's bravery and cool temperament.[106] As is also evident in the Golovnin expedition, over time hunters "turned to modes of accumulation based on connoisseurship rather than simple arithmetic," such as going only after particular, rare species, or focusing on collecting trophies of animals from a particular region.[107] Also similar to Golovnin's aspirations, there came to be an interest in attaining only the most aesthetic specimens, or at any rate, the largest and most perfect horns. As Ritvo points out, the techniques of accurate measurement of specimens brought to bear such "administrative virtues" as "rationality, precision, and truthfulness, while collecting a worthwhile trophy involved the exercise of force."[108]

Given that the Zoological Museum was to receive the specimens, there was a focus on the size and beauty of the specimens, even if, upon reading Golovnin's accounts of the hunting, it was clear that choosing the best specimens from a huge distance was actually not realistic. At one point, Golovnin asks for a specific goat specimen obtained by the hunting team, since the museum did not yet have such a specimen in its collection.[109] Describing one kill made by a local "Kirghiz" guide, Golovnin notes: "To remove the skin from the sheep, gut it, divide it into parts, wash each one in the stream and then load it onto horses took no longer than a quarter of an hour. And all of this was done with an ordinary, small, dirt-cheap Kirghiz knife with a blade length of only three inches. The skin was removed artistically – the knife served only to make the first cut in the stomach and the legs, and then the throat, so as to separate the head, the rest was done by hand."[110] This specimen, Golovnin writes, with some apparent disappointment, was a juvenile male. The next day, when his hunting group encounters a group of sheep, but none of the sheep are struck with bullets, he notes that none of that group had big horns anyway.[111] At another stop on another day, the hunters show him two very small sheep who do not even have horns. Later he regrets that they did not preserve the skeletons and hides for comparison with domestic sheep.[112] Golovnina mentions one subordinate member of the hunting team by his full name, Mustriakov, describing him as "a specialist and great artist in the removal of skins and preparing them for stuffing."[113]

Harriet Ritvo notes that the art of skinning and preserving hides and bones, as well as the art of stuffing and mounting specimens, was a complex one. "To present an effective symbol of the hunter's heroic appropriation, a trophy needed to evoke the aspect of the animal that had provoked and justified the killing ... The nobler the slain animal, the more difficult it was to reproduce its living fire. Sportsmen were advised to note carefully the appearance of their victims before and just after they killed them, lest 'the taxidermist at home may be led to a wrong conclusion.'"[114] Indeed, she notes of the display windows of *Field* magazine in London, which covered big game hunting and displayed the finest taxidermy in its windows: "These trophies represented the highest ideals of the magazine and its readers. Their physical perfection reflected a great deal of technical ingenuity and careful craftsmanship."[115] Arguably, the display of stuffed animals in their lifelike settings, such as in Tiflis, at zoological museums and such places as the Biological Museum in Stockholm, founded in 1893 and containing dioramas depicting stuffed animals and birds with highly acclaimed background paintings, can be related to the penchant for panoramas with their combinations of real objects and painted backgrounds.[116]

Documenting the Trip

Photography, almost exclusively by Barteneva, plays a variable role in the work of all three authors. Golovnina is the only one who acknowledges the identity of the photographer, although the conventions of photographic credits were clearly not well developed at the time; a three-page book review of *Na Pamirakh* in *Priroda i okhota*, for example, mentions the photographs but not who took them.[117] The possibility of copyrighting photographs in Russia did not occur until 1911.[118] Confusingly, one of the most striking photographs in the book, depicting the head of an *Ovis polii* sheep on top of a trunk, was not taken by Barteneva, although it is also not attributed. It was used by Curzon in his revised and reprinted article from *The Geographical Journal* of July, August, and September 1896 (two years earlier than the Golovnin expedition), and he also used what is clearly a photograph of the same head from a different angle in *The Geographical Journal* in the first version of his article printed in the *Journal* in the same year.[119] Golovnin, in his third article for *Okhota i priroda*, also used the same photo of the sheep head.[120] As Curzon himself hunted during his trip to the Pamirs in 1894, one would infer that the photos were taken by a member of his party. Golovnina does not indicate that that particular photograph (which is also used in cutout form elsewhere in the book) is not by Barteneva; it is certainly possible that it was considered to be sufficiently well known that it need not be differentiated from the others.[121] Barteneva's photographs certainly attest to the veracity of the descriptions of the barren hills, icy lakes, and snow-capped mountains, but they also record "tourist" sights on the way to the Pamirs, depict some of the lesser-known items described, such as the travel trunks (iakhtans, shown on page 36), and piles of teresken fodder (page 104), along with the expedition's employees (see Figure 4.2) and the people encountered along the way, including prisoners from the Andijan uprising. The photographs also show the travellers themselves and some of their more important or risky undertakings, such as river crossings (Figure 4.6). As depicted in Figure 4.3, Golovnin appears in Great White Hunter-style poses with some of the animals he has shot. Golovnina herself also appears, in a picture depicting "our yurt and my travel outfit" (Figure 4.1).[122] There is nothing in the narratives about the process of photography, unfortunately, only the description of how difficult it was to wrestle the boxes with the plates onto the trains and the note that towards the end of the trip Barteneva had used all of her plates and that some were lost along the way; there was also a reference to the "bother" of photography ("voznia s fotografiei").[123] Given the rarity of women travellers' visits to the Pamirs, this minimal description of Barteneva's photography seems particularly frustrating, although perhaps also an indication that photography (despite the heaviness and inconvenience of the plates used in this case) had become fairly commonplace, not eliciting much discussion. In fact, twenty years before there was at least one woman precursor of Barteneva, Lidiia Konstantinovna Poltoratskaia (1833–?), the wife of the Semipalatinsk military governor, Vladimir Aleksandrovich Poltoratskii, who took high-quality pictures of people and landscapes of the Altai during travels with her husband and published her own album, *Al'bom tipov i vidov Zapadnoi Sibiri, sniatykh L. K. Poltoratskoi* (*Album of Types and Views of Western Siberia, taken by L. K. Poltoratskaia*) in 1879, as well as two accounts of her travels, the 1871 "Poezdka po Kitaiskoi granitse ot Altaia do Tarbagataia" ("Journey along the Chinese Border from Altai to Tarbagatai") and the 1879 "Bremenskaia ekspeditsiia v Semipalatinskoi oblasti" ("The Brehm Expedition in the Semipalatinsk Region"), which was published in the same *Priroda i okhota* journal in which Golovnin published.[124] Poltoratskaia was awarded a silver medal at the Moscow Anthropological Exhibition of 1879 and another by the

Russian Geographical Society and was made a member of the newly established Photography Department of the Russian Technical Society.[125] Like Golovnina and Barteneva, Poltoratskaia dressed in men's clothes to ride, stating that riding side saddle was completely impossible.[126] Poltoratskaia was also unusual in that she and her husband also travelled with their children, about whom they often worried when the going was difficult.

In her accounts Poltoratskaia gives some details about the process of photography, which according to scholars, was more difficult before the 1880s, requiring wet solutions.[127] Poltoratskaia describes the difficulty of needing a tent set up, the interference of wet weather, and the ease with which one could ruin a glass plate.[128] In her second article, she describes accompanying German naturalists, including Alfred Brehm, who hunted and collected specimens similarly to the Golovnin expedition, in the Altai region bordering China. She writes movingly of the "Kirghiz" who were being displaced by Russian settlers while bureaucrats who were supposed to protect their rights got lost in a morass of paperwork (including her own husband, who wished to protect them, she says).[129] Poltoratskaia describes the memorable reaction of some visiting "Kirghiz" from a group who had not yet agreed to be subjects of the Russian empire (nepodannye). She records their remarks upon seeing her camera, doubtless similar to a theodolite used by topographers: "They were terribly worried, seeing the tripod and the machine on it. 'Russians come – they take pictures of the land with a machine – and the land becomes Russian.' About 12 years before some Kirghiz had attacked a party of our topographers who were measuring distance where Zaisan Post is now, and only thanks to the interference of Dzhan-Sultan were they not killed but only badly beaten."[130] The displaced people clearly understood that the process of documenting the land meant that the Russians were establishing control over it, as Poltoratskaia's very example indicates, in which measurement had been followed by the building of the post. Poltoratskaia had to calm them down: "To finally reassure our guests, I proposed to take a picture of their group. I had to seat our own people with them so as to convince them that my machine would not harm them or be dangerous to them. The group [photo] came out well and they were very surprised and entertained when I showed them the plate, that they could recognize each other on it."[131]

Although no additional information could be found about Barteneva at this juncture, Peter Palmquist notes that women photographers were not particularly rare at the time; there were at least 850 women photographers, ranging from professionals to amateurs, in pre-1900

Figure 4.4. "Kirghiz Hunters with Golden Eagles," Lidiia Poltoratskaia. "Altaĭskiĭ al'bom." (Altai album) List No. 32. Poltoratskaia, L.K. *Kirgizskie Okhotniki s Berkutami.*, 1870. [place of publication not identified: publisher not identified, to 1879], World Digital Library. https://www.loc.gov/item/2018683642/.

California, while photography was considered a socially acceptable occupation for women there.[132] Further, the 1900 Universal Exposition in Paris featured a "prestigious exhibition" called "Ambassadors of Progress," with 142 photographs by "twenty-nine female practitioners from all over the USA, including California and Oregon."[133] A prominent member of Russian photographic societies, W.I. Sreznewski, arranged for the exhibit to be shown in Russia as well, where it made a positive impression.[134]

As a number of commentators have pointed out, photography went hand in hand with the development of the railroad in order to expand the nation and conquer distances. In relation to North America, Simone Natale points out, the railway and photography were technologies implicated in nation-building, and both became "symbolic protagonists of the western frontier."[135]

Figure 4.5. "Cliffs on the Banks of Lake Rang-Kul," *Na Pamirakh*, p. 122. Photo by Nadezhda Barteneva.

The railway certainly also played a large role in Russia's eastern expansion. In a sense, on the Golovnin trip, photography extended the reach of the railway, continuing its role in recording the trip even as travel continued on foot and horseback. Aside from a few relatively close-up photographs of people, however, once the railway had been left behind, Barteneva's photos mostly show large landscapes with people either absent or only a small part of the enormous whole; during the railway portion of the trip, her photos are much more tightly focused on people, buildings, street scenes, and the like. There was clearly a shift from a kind of documentary, more tourist-style photography to a kind of aesthetics of travel and landscape as the party moved into the Pamirs, at least in terms of the kinds of photographs selected for the publications.

A major landmark of the trip was the arrival of the party at Pamirskii Post, a remote Russian military installation full of bored soldiers, according to Golovnina's description, as well as a place presenting the now-unaccustomed opportunity to walk on wooden floors and sleep in a bed. As Robert Middleton points out, the fortification, built in 1893, included "a reception area with a small pharmacy, an officers' wing with offices and a common canteen, together with huts for half a company, a kitchen, a bakery and a sauna."[136] There, "real life" again intruded; the higher-ups there were awaiting, in almost Gogolian style, a "general-inspector," in anticipation of whom they were having the installation cleaned and repaired; the awaited official, however, upon arrival turned out to be a veterinarian instead. There was also discussion of a British spy whom the officials of the garrison had apprehended previously, as well as other British spies or would-be spies. General Gerard, the British commissioner negotiating the Pamir boundaries with the Russians in the mid-1890s, was criticized by Golovnina for having been among the commanders whose men were absolutely freezing in the harsh winter, while Russian soldiers were properly dressed. The British officers were also said to be condescending towards their men:[137]

> According to the same [artillery] colonel, the position of the Sepoy soldiers who accompanied the English representative Gerard at the time of the work on the boundary commission was quite sad; in the severe winter cold, at a time when our soldiers were dressed in sheepskin jackets, long sheepskin coats, fur hats and felt boots, those unfortunates were rigged out in short paper-thin trousers, with feet dressed in sandals and wrapped up in woollen strips. One felt sorry to look at them: they were absolutely freezing; their rations were beggarly. One might also recall that right alongside, before the soldiers' very eyes, their leadership traveled with all possible comfort and luxury. The English officers and generals treated their soldiers haughtily and with extreme cruelty.[138]

Gerard, for his part, called Pamirskii Post "a mere field work" and a "fort" in quotation marks.[139] Nonetheless, Gerard (as well as his fellow author of the Boundary Commission volume, Col. Holdich) was at many points complimentary of his Russian hosts, who treated him with hospitality, were cheerful, brave, and efficient and often volunteered to toast to Queen Victoria.[140]

Travelling in such a forbidding, harsh, and unknown landscape had seemed to require many accompanying guides and protectors. However, once Golovnina's group got to Pamirskii Post, the point at which, in order to stay on established routes in Russian territory, the group had to head back towards their point of origin, they expressed a desire to go back a different way, along the river Pshart. Everyone at Pamirskii Post, including some local guides, told them they could not and should not go along the river Pshart, which lay to the west, that it was too far and the paths through the passes too narrow and dangerous. Golovnina's group continued despite the warnings and ultimately discovered that much of what they had been warned about was true, if perhaps not immediately as dire as first described. The group eventually did have to abandon their travel along the Pshart.

Instrumental vs. Aesthetic Landscapes

Emily Laskin, in an analysis of N.I. Grodekov's 1879 travel narrative, *Cherez Afganistan* (*Through Afghanistan*), indicates that in Grodekov's account the landscape is engaged in an instrumental rather than an aesthetic way, as a material object.[141] It is an obstacle, or it is described in terms of use value, for example as a supplier of fodder for animals. There is some of this approach in Golovnina's account, and quite a bit of it in Golovnin's hunting article, but Golovnina often does approach the landscape as an artistic object, which I have also discussed elsewhere.[142] Probably most striking about Golovnina as a writer is her occasional, rather perceptive, painterly descriptions of the landscapes. Whether describing delicate colours and shapes, giving a sense of the desolation of some of the landscapes, especially those with piles of horns and skulls, or likening the smooth ground to parquet or a valley to a theatre, Golovnina proves herself a sensitive observer and one attuned to the aesthetic expectations of her audience. The discourses of the sublime and the picturesque in travel writing, of course, have their own history; Golovnina's treatment of landscape is variable, and she often incorporates the non-visual, stating actual temperatures and describing the effects of the altitude, sun, wind, and cold on her face, arms, and hands. "The significant height (about 9,000 feet) already makes itself felt: one gets short of breath, one gets tired quickly while walking, there is a light flowing of the blood in the nose. Despite the damp, the air has the ability to terribly dry the skin; one's face begins to peel, the hands, besides their bronze color, which they had turned, somehow shriveled up, the palms and ends of the fingers became rough. M-skii assures us that this is just a toy compared to what awaits beyond the Alai, and that there especially our nose and lips will suffer."[143] Golovnina also emphasizes the deception of visual perception in her account:

> At about 8 a.m. we left in the direction of Bar-Dabe (White mountain) which lies in the same direction as the Alai valley, at the foot of the Zaalai ridge. We were so spoiled now by the variety of mountain roads, that this trip seemed to us to be dull, and therefore also long; the whole time, spread out before our eyes, was an even, green valley with a snowy ridge

showing white in the distance. The deceptive impression of the distance also was annoying: to our unaccustomed eyes it seemed that the width of the valley was completely negligible, about 4–5 versts, and that momentarily we would be at Bar–Dabe, but time passed, and the goal of our trip was still just as far as it had been earlier.[144]

On occasion Golovnina utilizes an aestheticizing approach that is certainly a taming, a domestication, an appropriation of the landscape. She writes, for example, about Lake Rang-Kul:

After the deadly, ennui-inducing monotony of the Pamir mountains this valley exerted an enchanting impression. The lake spread out for a distance of about five versts; pulled close to one of its shores were mountains of a general Pamir character, rounded and bare of plants, but on the other side stretched a wide even band of land, which was covered in a mass of grass that was good for fodder, and beyond this band immediately rose cliffs, almost vertical, lilac, sharply divided against a blue sky by their crenelated peaks. These cliffs, judging by their appearance, had been created once as a whole, single wall, divided (probably by water) as a resulting in four separate parts with deep crevices among them; these cliffs are punctuated with furrows and caves. When in the evening behind their crests the full moon showed itself, it lit up the whole width of this sleeping lake with our camp thrown up on its shore; the picture appeared unreal and recalled a theater set for a fairytale ball.[145]

On another occasion, she focuses on the incredible dreariness of the scenery and the company, the unpleasantness of the hot weather, the unnerving quantity of sheep skulls and horns, and the sharp stones on the ground as she rides along with the scientist Voskoboinikov:

We went 18 versts along the very dullest bumpy places; all around was clay with small stones and gravel, some places there were clumps of teresken [a plant]; a small pass, a descent into the larger basin, hundreds of rolling arkhars' horns; there is no water anywhere; the sun bakes mercilessly, it is boring, and it is time to eat something, nor would it be bad to rest. We got off our horses and lay down to rest on the sharp stones; our breakfast was a cold piece of fried kiik (the remainder was taken with the hunters) and black sukhari; we dreamed of a cup of tea, but had to satisfy ourselves with a swallow of water, which I always carry in a bottle by the saddle. There is absolutely nowhere to hide from the sun, and lying on the sharp stones is worse than sitting in the saddle.

"Let's go," I said to M. M. after a quarter of an hour. "Let's go," he sadly answered me. My horse Ryzhok is also sad and sleepily shook his head, and we continued on.[146]

This passage, however, was closely followed by an enticing, picturesque view that revivified Golovnina: "From above the river seemed like a blue ribbon, its banks grown over with thick grass, a view with which the Pamir so rarely spoils one. We came to life; the path runs along far from the river, and again we trotted along from little hill to little hill, along sand and rocks, but our hearts already felt merrier: from afar glinted the blue ribbon of the Murghab."[147] The overwhelming sublime could also be in evidence; Golovnina took an opportunity at one point to describe her utter defeat by the landscape, admitting that she was "horrified to the point of nausea" by a steep, narrow path she traversed on horseback and while extremely afraid to be on horseback, was even more afraid to be on foot.[148]

Golovnin, in his own descriptions, could be quite clinical and "instrumental;" he describes the Pamirs in the first part of his multi-part article as follows: "Thanks to its altitude, the climate of the Pamirs is extremely severe and the earth is nearly devoid of plants. Neither trees nor bushes exist on it. In places in the valleys, usually along the banks of the few mountain streams here, or near the lakes, one encounters oases of alpine meadow plants, fairly luxuriously spread out, but the greatest surface area of the hills and cliffs is simply bare rock."[149] However, he at times also exuded strong aesthetic appreciation; unlike Golovnina, as a man he could be completely alone in the landscape, with undisputed right to exist there:

Having stopped, I lay down in the grass and decided to wait for the hunters here, who would definitely have to pass by me. From here one could admire as much as one wished the miraculous picture of the high mountain landscape. Before me extended a wide valley, spread with a magical carpet of flowers of the alpine meadow; on each side are gentle hills, also partly covered with grass, in places obstructed by rocky crushed stone; above the valley is a wide glacier, from below sending a thin little stream of crystalline clean water into the valley, from above covered with blinding white snow, untouched by anyone's foot.[150]

Golovnin went on to describe the aromatic quality of the plants and flowers, as well as the great variety of colours of the alpine flowers; at this moment the landscape functioned as an aesthetic object for his enjoyment alone, something Golovnina, who was never unaccompanied, did not experience.

The Self-Conscious Guide: Humour and the Conclusion of the Journey

Golovnina's book has a particular trajectory, starting out on a fairly serious note through much of the narrative, but softening and becoming somewhat more informal towards the end of the trip and the end of the account. Humour tended to be a rare commodity on the trip, at least in Golovnina's telling. The first really lighthearted episode in the narrative occurs when Golovnina describes the obvious enjoyment she and the others found in the unusual situation of having to cross the river Murghab on the back of a camel. To cross, a caravan driver rode a horse into the swift river, leading a camel with two of the members of the main party aboard – first Golovnina and her husband, then Nadezhda Barteneva and Voskoboinikov. This unusual method of travel was described with touches of humour by Golovnina, even though at first there was concern that the party might have to turn back if it could not cross the river. Golovnina mentions that Barteneva did not lose the opportunity of taking a picture of the crossing, which is included in the book (Figure 4.5). Most humourous of all is the verbal picture she presents of the two upper-class smokers, Voskoboinikov and Barteneva, who, forgetting their previous attempts to conserve their remaining cigarettes for the balance of the journey, hurriedly chain-smoked all they had left after the adrenaline-inducing crossing.[151]

In fact, after this point in the narrative, perhaps in part because the trip was coming to a close, Golovnina allowed her narrative to become more personal. The young Cossack assistants and the hunting team had declined (or were not allowed) to accompany the group on their unauthorized leg of the trip, so the group had become quite a bit smaller. Personal habits beyond smoking also become a subject of description:

> We don't always manage to leave early in the morning, because of the deep sleep taking hold of our cavaliers: during the time we cannot succeed in waking them up (something that requires no little amount of time), we cannot carry out in the yurt the necessary manipulations to pack our things, and therefore to pack up the baggage caravan. For awhile, the following device helped: one of us (odna iz nas), leaning over M. M., loudly said: "the kasha is ready" – that worked like magic, but only 2–3 times. After that N. P. and I conferred and she recommended the following very simple method: at 6 a.m., when she and I are already ready, the servant begins to pack up the yurt; the sky is opened over the sleeping one, then

Figure 4.6. "Crossing the river Murghab," *Na Pamirakh*, p. 181. Photo by Nadezhda Barteneva.

right away they take all the side felt pieces and there is only the slatted frame remaining. The first time M. M. opened his sleepy eyes, with shock he looked up and, when he guessed what was up, found that this method of waking people was very unpleasant, although quite effective.[152]

Golovnina also spends some time describing horse groom Tashmet in the latter part of the account, praising his uncanny ability to anticipate and prepare whatever they needed, and indicating that she was becoming more cognizant that this time in her life was about to end. As the group disperses – "dwindles," as she phrases it – there is definite regret expressed.[153] Having spent a page or so describing the "tourist donkeys," a pair of donkeys purchased for the trip but in the end allowed to simply wander on their own, entertaining the group with their antics, Golovnina describes their sale with evident regret. Both Golovnins' accounts indicate that this trip allowed them to escape a more ordinary life; she had stated at the beginning of her account that she was heading "somewhere far away, to Asia, leaving behind everything conventional (uslovnoe), gray and everyday."[154] While details about Golovnina's life after the trip are not known, other than some posts on a website (see footnote 1), Golovnin continued to travel; a note about him in a journal indicates that he was away travelling to the Sayan Mountains (see footnote 9), while a biographical article about him indicates that he became a specialist in refrigeration, working extensively in Central Asia and Baku, and establishing a journal about refrigeration in 1923.[155] According to posts quoted in footnote 1, said to be written by the Golovnins' relatives, he remarried but she continued to live with him and his new family.

Perhaps the most entitled, even shocking, measures taken by Golovnina's expedition occurred on the way back, when the group no longer had official guides but needed help finding resources during the return trip. If they could not find a local guide, they essentially kidnapped someone and forced him to guide them; after twenty versts, she reports, the "guide" would try to get out of this enforced "job" and go home, but would be "convinced" to go further; the more intelligent among them, she says, left in the middle of the night but missed out on their pay if they did so.[156] The "guides," Golovnina notes, were not really needed in order to show the way but to enable the group to find firewood and mutton along the way.

The return to Margelan meant a gradual return to "civilization," some of it relatively unwanted. The food was not all that good compared to what they had on the road, the European-style clothing the women had to resume wearing was uncomfortable, their skirts hampering their movement and their pockets now located in the wrong place.[157] Local common people appeared sober, clean, and well dressed, their houses and yards tidy, and hence led to comparisons quite unflattering to Russians and Russian peasants. Green trees and cultivation become ever more evident, a positive experience, according to Golovnina, but the mountains recede into the distance and become mere brown hills.[158] More typical Russian social life resumes, with dinners, balls, and social visits, which require the requisite clothing, even if an eager official reassures them their travelling clothes are perfectly appropriate attire in which to be received for dinner. As Golovnina and her party were visiting New Margelan, the new governor-general, Sergei Mikhailovich Dukhovskoi, was making a tour of Turkestan. Golovnina describes the troops and other members of the procession that paraded down the streets, as well as the city illuminations, that occurred on 19 August. This accords with an account of the trip by Vasilii Piankov, who described in reverent tones Dukhovskoi's official travels around Turkestan upon assuming the governorship, travels that began in Tashkent on 9 August 1898. On 20 August Golovnina's husband attended a ball in order to thank Dukhovskoi (he is not named by Golovnina but is named by Golovnin in his article) and General Ionov for their support (Varvara Dukhovskaia had previously departed Turkestan, as noted in chapter one). Piankov describes a number of elements that accord with Golovnina's account; the specific meeting with Golovnin is not mentioned, however.[159] Immediately after the ball, Golovnin went to the freight car where the others were waiting; at two in the morning the train departed Margelan. Once in Tashkent, staying again with N.I. Korol'kov, Golovnina was overjoyed to be back at the elegant and well-kept house, with attentive servants; she declares that, waking up in the same wing of the house where she had stayed before the trip to the Pamirs, it seemed as though she had dreamed the entire trip: "And it seemed to me miraculous, that I went to sleep then in that guest house, and what appeared to me was a long, fantastic dream of a trip to the Kirghiz with their yurts and camels, the Pamirs with their lakes, mountains and deserts, and now again I woke up here, in the guest house, in the garden."[160] They said goodbye to their servants, who gave parting speeches, and said farewell also to those who had helped them prepare for the trip, such as the Oshanins.[161] In the process, a local Russian noblewoman expressed her disappointment that they had not had any life-threatening adventures during the trip. "'But tell us, didn't something unusual happen? Didn't you fall into an abyss, didn't you nearly drown?' I had to acknowledge that, unfortunately, nothing of the sort happened – her interest in us then ceased immediately."[162] On the way back, having met the man in charge of the Imperial Murghab Estate, they stopped to visit it. As they left on their steamship in Krasnovodsk, Golovnina noted: "Behind us remained Asia with her bright colors and burning sun; our trip, the expected dangers – everything passed by and with every turn of the wheels we came closer to Europe. Our steamship acquaintances are interested in us, are asking all kinds of questions and trying to convince us that N. P. and I have achieved a great feat. This flatters our self-regard; but we must admit, that we got these laurels very cheaply. And from whatever perspective I view our trip, unfortunately there was no heroism; everything went terribly simply."[163] Golovnina, reviewing the trip on the final two pages of her account, acknowledges that all the local municipalities looked after them, setting up yurts, obtaining mutton and guides for them, and that the local leaders were responsible for their safety. Without these, she admits, they indeed would have been put into critical situations, not so much due to any hostility from other people but simply from the elements, since auls were only located in certain places not known to travellers, and to obtain mutton in some cases would have been virtually impossible. To have yurts already set up, she acknowledges, was a great convenience, since the pack train often didn't arrive until several hours later, and they would have had to wait outside in bad weather. The hunting team assigned to them by General Ionov, although in the end not really necessary, made them feel comfortable early in the trip when they otherwise might not have felt so safe. N.I. Korol'kov, Golovnina avers, was most responsible for all of these arrangements, and therefore she dedicates her book to him.

Further sections of her book include a "geographical sketch," putting forward the political history of the Pamirs and a list of its explorers beginning from BCE, supplemental notes, and a bibliography. In the geographical sketch, Golovnina acknowledges that to be in the Pamirs was to be on the dividing line of world powers, a highly politicized exercise, as disputes over the border had only recently been adjudicated, a topic that Golovnin also brings up early in the first section of his article. Golovnina's geographical sketch contains a description of the Pamir geography, topography, meteorology, and zoology, as well as a supplemental set of notes describing various practical details of the trip for anyone who might be planning to go. In fact, this supplemental section is praised by the reviewer N.V.T., almost certainly N.V. Turkin, the editor of *Priroda i okhota*, who indicates that it is vital information for those planning to go on similar trips.[164] Here Golovnina includes prices of buying yurts, renting and buying horses and camels, paying servants, and the like. A camel cost two roubles a day to rent, a pack horse cost one rouble. The Sart and other local servants employed did their jobs well. Golovnina describes the various provisions they bought, how much they cost, and where they bought them, the clothing, the saddles, the cookware and tableware, and the like. Not least, Golovnina discusses the necessity of having appropriate soap for washing clothes in cold water, something she had ordered in Moscow; one had to wash clothes along the way, and it was best to be prepared. When the group re-sold their items in Novyi Margelan, she notes that they received about half of what they had paid, and for some items, about a third. Counting the trip as beginning on 12 June in Tashkent and ending there on 23 August, and taking into account the money recovered in the resale, each of the four main participants paid 250 roubles; for the doctor and Count B., who left earlier, it was less. The book ends with a bibliography of books and articles about the Pamirs in Russian, English, French, and German; two of the items are the article by Voskoboinikov and the multi-part article by Golovnina's husband.

The trip seems remarkable most of all, perhaps, because it was made so matter of factly; the extra protections and conveniences afforded by Golovnina's group's high status smoothed out any sense of anxiety over safety or the ability to obtain food and shelter. The extent of the railway and the apparently firm control of the territory by the Russian government eased the travellers' way. In that sense it was quite modern travel, when danger or an encounter with the completely unknown was not really a factor; the adventure was to be found in the novelty of the area, as well as the novelty of the participation of two women travellers, of course the potential to gain internationally famous zoological specimens, and the complexity of getting to and travelling around the location, rather than in any hardships or dangers encountered. And woven into the account, as into other contemporary accounts, was the spectre of the Great Game: comparisons with the British, descriptions of British successes and failures, speculation about how the British were likely to receive various pieces of news, are constantly evoked. For the British, the "Great Game" was certainly about their status as the premier empire in the world, their unparalleled dominance in "civilization," whereas for the Russians, what was at stake was the ability to compete at some level with the British and of course, as always, their identity as Europeans.

Perhaps inevitably, the most complex pictures of others among these writings about the expedition are the ones in Golovnina's lengthy travelogue, at least in terms of the non-Russians with whom she had regular contact. The local hunting guides were not characterized by her, nor apparently did she have much sense of the caravan driver or kerekesh, although she knew the head of the caravan, Alim-Bai, the cook Murza, and the stable hand Tashmet reasonably well. However, the hierarchy of ranks and peoples for Golovnina is extremely obvious, the right of Russian dominion over "Kirghiz" and Cossacks alike is unquestioned. That she implies that she realizes that both she and the local Pamir women are obliged to wear impractical clothing is clear, however; she is also determined not be responsible for holding back the group because she is a "lady." The palpable sense of regret as the journey ends and "normal," far less interesting life resumes, as well as her rejection of having completed any feat of heroism, also seems indicative of a certain amount of self-consciousness. In turn, Golovnin's hunting articles focus primarily on the hunting itself, with far less interest in the human beings involved, and they generally take a completely instrumental and impersonal view of local hunting guides. Voskoboinikov also focuses little on other people, but includes some recognition of Lieutenant Masterkov, and credits the "stories" of the local guides who accompany the group, since they know of various details about the caves, such as one with an optical illusion, and had abundant local knowledge.[165]

One senses that the relative ease of travel is both a blessing and a curse; the smoothness of the journey allows Golovnina and her fellow travellers to feel safe, but deprives them of any sense of real anxiety and, in turn, of real adventure. While the amount of money that was required to undertake such a journey was doubtless quite large, and hence out of the reach of most, still her readers could certainly imagine themselves participating in such a trip, since she provided plenty of practical information and pricing and made it sound quite acceptable and even easy for women to participate, aside from a few moments of fear and nausea and some bronzed and wind-burned skin. Even the Pamirs, so recently almost unknown to Russians, now formed a part of a quite attainable travel itinerary.

Science in the Name of the Nation: Women Scientists, Archaeologists, and Ethnographers

In Pursuit of Imperial Knowledge: Ol'ga Fedchenko, Aleksandra Potanina, Praskov'ia Uvarova, and Anna Rossikova

The last section and chapter of this study turn to women who were scientific practitioners of empire, serving as botanists, ethnographers, archaeologists, research assistants, and editors. One of them, Ol'ga Fedchenko, was in the vanguard of official government scientific exploration in Central Asia, while also responsible for completing her husband's work and publishing it, thus cementing his reputation. Unlike Iuliia Golovnina, who travelled as a "civilian," more or less, despite her manifold assistance with the expedition, two of the four women addressed in this chapter travelled under completely different circumstances, Fedchenko as an official part of a military expedition at times literally under attack, and Aleksandra Potanina on a scientific expedition explicitly supported by the government. Of the two others, Praskov'ia Uvarova and Anna Rossikova, the former participated in a relatively tame journey to Tashkent but was invited to make the trip due to her status as an archaeologist; the other, although she was primarily accompanying her husband who was doing scientific research along the Amu-Darya River, was a member of the Russian Geographical Society. Another woman who in some ways also fits this category was Lidiia Poltoratskaia (1833–?), the wife of the Semipalatinsk governor who took photographs during her husband's yearly inspection trips to the Altai. These were published in an ethnographic album and displayed at the Moscow Anthropological Exhibition of 1879. Certainly one of the earliest Russian women photographers, she also published two written accounts.[1] While her trips were expeditions, they were taken comparatively close to her husband's home base and sphere of control as the military governor. Poltoratskaia is discussed in chapter four.

The four women addressed in this chapter were entirely or in part assistants to their husbands, but three of them also contributed their own work to their chosen field, whether in botany, ethnography, or archaeology. The fourth, Anna Rossikova, left travel accounts related to her husband's work as a zoologist and also participated in several Congresses of Naturalists and Physicians under the rubric of geography, ethnography, and anthropology, and was a member of the Caucasian section of the Russian Geographical Society.[2] These women took part in scientific or exploratory expeditions to Central Asia, Mongolia, Tibet, and China, and participated in associated discursive practices, such as the collection of specimens; the recording and documenting of zoological, botanical, and meteorological information; the description and depiction of landscapes; the coordination and funding of these activities by government and various scientific societies; the publication of the results; and the display of materials at exhibitions. Of the women discussed in this study, they were by far the most "official" women proponents of imperial expansion and control and of the appropriation of scientific and cultural knowledge. The women may have begun as spouses, but once the project was underway, their role often expanded into that of full-fledged expedition participant, even if they were neither paid for their work nor officially recognized.[3] While they were generally enthusiastic participants in the project, their very bodily existence in space was different from that of their male counterparts, their view of their roles in these expeditions varied from person to person, and their range of emotional reactions to their travel and projects was typically quite broad. Many of their texts participated in the conventions of travel writing and the writing of ethnography, presenting complex intersectional constructions of the writing subject.

The women discussed in this chapter are presented in the order of their dates of travel, starting with Ol'ga Fedchenko, who first travelled to Turkestan in 1868; then Aleksandra Potanina, who first travelled to Mongolia in 1876; Praskov'ia Uvarova, who travelled to Tashkent in 1890; and Anna Rossikova, who travelled along the Amu-Darya River in 1898, the same year Golovnina travelled to the Pamirs and Dukhovskaia's husband Sergei Dukhovskoi was appointed to the Turkestan governor-generalship. Both Fedchenko and Potanina had associations, through their families, with revolutionary or Siberian separatist causes.

Ol'ga Fedchenko

Ol'ga Aleksandrovna Fedchenko, née Armfel'd (1845–1921), was a noted botanist and an artist who participated in several expeditions in Central Asia (Figure 5.1). Her non-academic writing is extremely scarce, although besides botanical work and editing an important compendium on Turkestan, she published a number of her artworks, both in scholarly contexts and as a separate volume of artistic views. Born into a large, wealthy, and well-educated noble family that was

Figure 5.1. Ol'ga Fedchenko. From A.P. Bogdanov, *Materialy dlia istorii nauchnoi i prikladnoi deiatel'nosti v Rossii po zoologii i soprikasaiushchimsia s neiiu otrasliami znania, preimushstvenno za poslednee tridtsatiletie* (1850–1887) (Materials for the History of Scientific and Applied Activity in Russia in Zoology and Adjoining Branches of Knowledge, Primarily in the Last Thirty Years), T. 1, M., 1888, fifth table (unpaginated).

acquainted with the Tolstoys, Ol'ga Fedchenko's father was a professor. Her sister Natalia Armfel'd was a Narodnik and a revolutionary and was sent to Siberia; she served as a model for Tolstoy's revolutionary Maria Pavlovna Shchetina in *Voskresenie*.[4] Fedchenko's younger brother was also a revolutionary.[5] A botanist and founding member in 1864 of the OLEAE, or *Obshchestvo liubitelei estestvoznaniia, antropologii i etnografii* (the Society of Lovers of Natural Science, Anthropology and Ethnography), she married a co-founder of the society, A.P. Fedchenko (1844–73), a man of modest means from Siberia and a scholar interested in botany, entomology, and anthropology, in 1867.[6] She travelled with her husband on a set of trips to Turkestan commissioned by the first governor-general of Turkestan, Konstantin Petrovich von Kaufman, who had become acquainted with the new society in 1867 and asked its president, G.E. Shchurovskii, to find someone to expand the knowledge of the newly Russian-controlled areas in Turkestan.[7] These officially sanctioned trips took place from 1868, immediately after the conquest of Samarkand, to 1871.[8] Ol'ga Fedchenko was understood, by Kaufman as by others, to be an integral part of the research endeavour.[9] Ol'ga Fedchenko took primary charge of the plant samples and helped with the work of the Turkestan expeditions in multiple ways, for example, by handling compass measurements when it was considered that it would be less noticeable to the "Kokand dzhigits" who were watching the Russian expedition closely if she took them rather than her husband, and serving as a visual recorder with her drawings since there was no photographer along.[10] In fact, one scholar believes she was the first Russian artist after Vereshchagin to depict Turkestan, and also among the first to produce lithographs depicting Central Asia.[11] She was often called a "pioneer," both as a woman and as a botanist, and earned an international reputation.[12] Hence she played a significant role in assimilating Russian Turkestan into the Russian imaginary. As another woman botanist, O.E. Knorring, who eulogized her, observed, Central Asia was literally understood as a region to be "conquered by science": "In the person of the departed Ol'ga Aleksandrovna Fedchenko we lost one of the pioneers of Russian science, a participant in that glorious epoch when this science had the opportunity to study new regions unknown to it. Almost simultaneously with the appearance of the Russian administration in Turkestan began its conquest by science, a period of the work of Severts[o]v, I. V. Mushketov, A. P. Fedchenko and other no less famous names."[13]

Fedchenko was acknowledged to be an accomplished artist; her work was displayed at the 1872 Polytechnic Exhibition in Moscow, which was initiated by the OLEAE and had a special section on Turkestan, for which she helped prepare the exhibit and write the catalogue. It was one of the most visited of the exhibition, especially given the interest in Turkestan as a colony, and its striking entrance was a façade of the Shir Dor Madrasa in Samarkand.[14] As a result of the expedition,

Ol'ga Fedchenko received a gold medal from the OLEAE for her herbarium and her artwork.[15] After her husband died unexpectedly during a research trip to Switzerland the following year, she and the OLEAE obtained funding from Kaufman to complete the publication of the results of the expeditions, *Puteshestvie v Turkestan of A. P. Fedchenko*, which ultimately came to twenty-four volumes. She was effectively the chief editor and organizer of the project, though unacknowledged officially. Her husband had projected the publication to include only four volumes; under her editorship it became much larger, and she provided illustrations as well as being solely responsible for the third part of the botanical volume, after one of the primary botanists involved did not complete his work.[16] Besides her artwork and the accounts of others, there is little to document her travels from her own personal perspective, as she did not keep a diary or leave memoirs, and few of her letters have come to light.[17] According to Ol'ga Val'kova, it is difficult to tell the extent to which Ol'ga Fedchenko herself wrote *Puteshestvie v Turkestan*; she certainly edited what her husband had already written, and possibly what others had written, and was someone who had participated in all of the expeditions, so she might have written up parts of the travel accounts herself. She did write up parts of the botanical sections. Her name appeared only on the signed illustrations, but the volumes themselves would not have emerged without her work and her lobbying for monetary support.[18] As Val'kova points out, the volumes made her husband's reputation.[19] She did compose one travel account herself, an article in German about her husband called "A. Fedtschenko's Reisen in Turkestan 1868–71," in which much of the writing is extremely cryptic; even the several brushes with armed and angry locals (the expedition was accompanied by military escort) are related with extreme brevity. However, there is a brief passage where Fedchenko endorses an engagement with the sublime:

> On the twentieth of July the view opened up to the south, from the peak of the Isfairam Pass, of the huge snowy mountains, called the Trans-Alai chain by A. Fedchenko. This delightful view was truly astonishing … Any possible description of this view can only give a weak impression. This unending, 60-verst long steppe with the river Kizil-su in the middle and the giant snow-capped chain in the background, in which some peaks reach up to 25,000 feet, was the most beautiful that Fedchenko had ever seen during his whole trip to Turkestan. An illustration of this view, as well as several others of the most interesting views can be found in "The Journey to Turkestan of A. P. Fedchenko" (Russian), soon to be published.[20]

Figure 5.2. "The Alai and the Zaalai Mountains in July 1871." "Alai i Zaalaiskie góry v iule 1871 goda," by Ol'ga Fedchenko, in A.P. Fedchenko, *Puteshestvie v Turkestan* (Journey to Turkestan), vol. 1, part II, *V Kokanskom khanstve*, St. Petersburg, Moscow, 1875, between pp. 140 and 141.

In her description of the view, Ol'ga Fedchenko also showed a certain flair for advertisement, enticing the reader with a description of mountains that had actually only been recently named, in the Western context, by A.P. Fedchenko himself. Notably, of course, she also wrote herself completely out of the narrative, presenting these experiences and aesthetic reactions as her husband's alone. Showing the "European" bias typical for the time, a Russian traveller and commentator, I.V. Mushketov, claimed that

> until Fedchenko the Alai was completely *terra incognita*; except for a few reports communicated, as we will see below, by pundits, sent by Englishmen, one can say that no one had any idea of them, since not one educated European before Fedchenko had seen the Alai range. To Fedchenko belongs the honor of the discovery of the Alai and its colossal peaks, and as well as that, the honor of the first initiative of scholarly study of the Pamirs after Wood; in this regard the journey of A. P. Fedchenko to the Alai is the same kind of epoch in the history of the study of the Pamirs as was the famous trip by Wood in 1838 to Lake Sary-Kul.

Mushketov even quotes Fedchenko himself, proclaiming that a trip through "Karamuk, Alai" to Kokand by Abdul-Medzhid in 1863 was not "scientific" since, "except for the name, he doesn't report anything, and according to his account it is impossible to accurately determine his path, as Fr. Wolker tried to do on a published map of Central Asia."[21] Curzon, however, in his Geographical Society article "The Pamirs and the Source of the Oxus," says that an Abdul Mejid, a mulla, made the "first recorded passage of the Pamirs from south to north," although it was a somewhat different route from Wood's. Curzon names numerous non-European travellers, many of whom were in the employ of the British government, who preceded Fedchenko.[22]

Wherever Fedchenko stood in the line of travellers to the area, the illustrations Ol'ga Fedchenko mentions, such as the one depicted above, were made by Ol'ga Fedchenko herself, and illustrated several of the volumes of *Puteshestvie v Turkestan*; some were also published in a separate volume.[23] They were also used with permission in such books as Mushketov's *Turkestan*, and without permission by others, among them Marie de Ujfialvy-Bourdon.[24]

Fedchenko also wrote to her son years later about the view described above in a letter, saying, "In my opinion there is no better view in the world."[25] It is unclear whether Ol'ga Fedchenko had seen any of Vasilii Vereshchagin's depictions of Turkestan at the time that she created her own artwork. He first went to Turkestan in 1867, the year before the Fedchenkos, and he published some sketches in French journals in 1868 and exhibited some of his paintings in St. Petersburg in 1869.[26] While his large canvases are formally quite different from Fedchenko's more delicate, more distantly viewed vistas, they are not necessarily so dissimilar from some of his pen and ink drawings, such as "Khodzhent. Vid so storony Syr-Dar'i" ("Khodzhent. View from the Syr-Darya side") and "Ulitsa v Khodzhente" ("Street in Khodzhent") both from 1868.[27] Fedchenko's work tends to be quite delicate and detailed; her drawing of the Registan, for example, renders the buildings in very detailed style, with small figures of people, animals, and tents in front of the ruins. Some of her pictures of ruins, such as that of the mosque of Bibi-Khanym and the tomb complex of Shakh-Zinda, show very few or no human figures. Her "Interior of Gur Emir (Tomb of Timur)" is completely devoid of people, and compellingly austere. Her landscapes are subtly shaded and beautifully differentiate different planes. Her art instructor was A.K. Savrasov, a Peredvizhnik who also taught Isaak Levitan and encouraged him in landscape painting. One can see, especially in Fedchenko's "Mogila sviatogo v Urgute" ("Tomb of a saint in Urgut") beautifully drawn trees that somewhat echo Savrasov's style.[28] Savrasov created most of the lithographs of her drawings.[29] For her "Vid Zaalaiskikh gor s perevala

Figure 5.3. "View of the Zaalai Mountains from the Isfairam Pass." Ol'ga Fedchenko, *Puteshestvie v Turkestan*, vol. 1, Part II, p. 137 (Note: Fedchenko created her own lithograph for this image.)

Isfairam" ("View of the Zaalai mountains from the Isfairam pass"), however, she created her own lithograph (Figure 5.3).[30]

Fedchenko's expeditions and publishing project were underwritten by the government, and the members of OLEAE saw both the project and the Turkestan section of the Polytechnic Exhibition as being of political importance and closely associated with Russia's rivalry with England, with one commentator even declaring that Aleksei Fedchenko, who had died in 1873, "fell like a brave warrior on the battlefield."[31] An important condition of Fedchenko's Turkestan publication was that it be written in Russian, which presented an important investment of translation work, since work submitted in German necessitated translation.[32] In fact, the OLEAE had been founded in 1868 as an organization that declared from the beginning that it would do its work in Russian, thus predating Baron Rozen's call for Russian Orientology scholarship to be published in Russian by almost two decades.[33] For the expedition itself, the tsar awarded A.P. Fedchenko the order of St. Vasilii, fourth class, while Ol'ga Fedchenko received a gold bracelet with diamonds and rubies.[34]

In a biographical sketch for which Fedchenko apparently provided the template herself, she describes her continued work on *Puteshestvie v Turkestan* after her husband's death by saying that he wanted it to be "an important contribution to Russian scientific literature and serve as a textbook for further study of Turkestan, but one which could also be used not only by specialists but by any educated person."[35] Ol'ga Fedchenko also carried out other work expressive of the Great Game, such as translating Col. Henry Yule's essay "Geography of the Valley of the Oxus" into Russian.[36] In general, she helped facilitate knowledge in her field by translating in multiple languages and also used translation as a means to support herself.[37]

While Ol'ga Fedchenko herself did not leave much by way of her own writing, accounts of her written by others revealed much about the ways in which women scholars and travellers, especially in the early, relatively dangerous days of the newly conquered lands in Turkestan, were understood. Commentator and colleague Dmitrii L'vovich Ivanov, then in the military, a scholar and political exile who participated in two expeditions with the Fedchenkos and assisted with the Turkestan Exhibition, painted a vivid picture of what Fedchenko had to withstand, even casting her in his diary as a heroine, "the female botanist" ("botanika") while casting a certain Captain Grebenkin, who spoke Tajik and considered himself a scholar of the region, as a villain.[38] Ivanov sets the scene, indicating that things were still very raw in Samarkand in 1869 when he met the Fedchenkos, with many visitors descending on what was essentially a garrison; he even evokes Saltykov-Shchedrin's "Tashkentsy" as being among the newly arrived. Under these circumstances, he notes: "The arrival of the Fedchenko spouses, of course, evoked much conversation: the fact that the [newly arrived] scientist was a woman traveler was huge news for the area."[39] Having travelled back to Moscow for a period, the Fedchenkos arrived late the following year to the military-sponsored 1870 expedition to the Zarafshan glacier and Iskender-Kul (lake), which was already in progress. As Ivanov describes it: "The arrival of the Fedchenko family created a sensation in the military unit. Everyone was taken aback at the appearance of a woman, who 'would bring shyness into the environment of military men and would herself be shy.' … However, the Fedchenkos arrived into the unit so simply, quietly made themselves at home in their tent and did not in the least disturb the life of the expedition."[40] Grebenkin was critical of

Ol'ga Fedchenko's participation in the expedition, while Ivanov was delighted with her:

> Grebenkin especially stressed the "huge height" (ogromnyi rost) of O. A., her weight and the difficulty of finding a saddle horse for her, predicting that she would be a complete failure as a rider and so on.[41]
>
> Soon in my expedition diary appeared a note that was fully positive toward O. A. as a traveler (puteshestvennitsy). Thus for 6. VI it says: "The botanika (the pseudonym for O. A. in my diary) turned out to be a champ (okazalas' molodtsom): she rode bravely, quickly, and carried herself simply."[42]

Ivanov notes that the riding was particularly difficult on that day, with very narrow paths. This was not Ol'ga Fedchenko's first success in winning over her critics:

> But even earlier, on the fourth day after the Fedchenkos arrived, sympathy for them overrode the skeptics: a company of several persons went to the tent of the scientists: there O. A. met them cordially, served tea with fresh lemons (then an unusual rarity in Turkestan) and also fresh Moscow sushki. This lemon and sushki finally triumphed over the skepticism and already in conversations one could hear of approval of wives who take care of their husbands, with an example of this being a chest for cigarettes for A. P., in which O. A. created partitions so that the cigarettes would not scatter about.[43]

Perhaps not surprisingly, most of those who wrote about figures such as Fedchenko and Aleksandra Potanina, who travelled in Mongolia and China, found ways to stress their womanliness, as if to counteract their scientifically oriented minds; both Fedchenko and Potanina were said to be hospitable hosts who cared for the well-being of their guests, whether in their own apartments or out in the field. Any idea that they were demanding, weak, or a detriment to the expedition was denied, just as Golovnina had felt it necessary to proclaim her own preparedness for travel. Even when Potanina was effectively dying, she went along on her final expedition until her heart ailment overcame her.

Ivanov worked with both Fedchenkos to prepare the Turkestan pavilion at the Polytechnic Exhibition, submitting sketches which were used to create the façade to Ol'ga Fedchenko for approval.[44] Reviewer V. Iversen described the 1872 Polytechnic Exhibit in Moscow, giving a detailed look at raw and finished products, plants, animals, hunting and farming implements, crafts, and the like. He described skeletons, skulls, and photographs of "typical representatives" of "Tajiks, Kirghiz,

Uzbeks, Sarts and others," as well as full-sized mannequins of various "typical" figures such as "a Sart, an Indian from Tashkent, an Afghan, a Persian, a Tashkent Jew, a girl and woman Sart in street costumes with covered faces; a Kirghiz woman in a very luxurious, sewn gold costume in the first year after marriage, loaded camels with a woman sitting on one of them, a farmer astride a bull, ... further on was a representation of a bazaar with two rows of stores and various commercial businesses."[45] A reviewer for *Vsemirnaia illiustratsiia* noted that the Turkestan section was "built with the means of the Turkestan governor-general and on his initiative." Both reviewers indicated that the represented row of shops included not only mannequins representing a barber and many other figures but also featured a real live person sewing silk.[46] Ol'ga Fedchenko showed her own artwork, helped prepare the catalogue and helped create exhibits, especially the botanical ones. Iversen made note of the extensive herbarium in the Turkestan section, which covered seven different types of Turkestan environments. Two sketches of the interior of the Turkestan pavilion printed in *Vsemirnaia illiustratsia* were created by Nikolai Karazin, who was also an artist (one is Figure 5.4); the publication also printed a depiction of the façade.[47]

Ol'ga Fedchenko's husband died in Switzerland in 1873 when their son was less than a year old, while preparing for a return visit to the Pamirs. A German scientist, Georg Lohde, who had met both Fedchenkos, wrote of the loss to science created by Fedchenko's death and praised Ol'ga Fedchenko: "His wife, who had already accompanied him during his first trip and through her outstanding drawing talent was a help to him that is not to be undervalued, wanted to assist him scientifically as well and therefore in the previous winter had studied botany and the use of microscopes."[48] After his death, she published her husband's work, became secretary of the Moscow Society for Natural Science, and was elected by the Russian Geographical Society as a "cooperating member" in 1877. In the 1890s she resumed participation in botanical expeditions, going to the southwestern Urals, the Crimea, and the Caucasus. Her son Boris Aleksandrovich Fedchenko too became a botanist, and they travelled together on expeditions, including to Turkestan in 1897 and to the Pamirs in 1901; they also published together.[49] The twenty-four-volume set of *Puteshestvie v Turkestan* was finally completed in 1902, when Fedchenko was able to publish the complete list of 1,527 plants gathered in Turkestan from 1869 to 1871.[50] Her *Flora Pamira*, in four parts, published from 1903 to 1905, became a classic.[51] In her later years Ol'ga Fedchenko lived mostly in St. Petersburg and worked for the Imperial Botanic Garden, of which she was elected an honorary member in 1912.[52] Although Ol'ga Fedchenko is

Figure 5.4. Nikolai Karazin, "Moscow Polytechnic Exhibition – Turkestan Department, Main Room." From *Vsemirnaia illiustratsiia* (World Illustrated), 1872, vol. VIII, No. 194, p. 180. Engraved by K. Veierman.

remembered primarily as a botanist, she was one of the first to assimilate the region of Turkestan into the Russian empire through publishing the work of the Fedchenkos' expeditions, creating her own highly praised artwork and her continued botanical work.

Aleksandra Potanina

Figure 5.5. Portrait of Aleksandra Potanina. Frontispiece to *Iz puteshestvii po Vostochnoi Sibiri, Mongolii, Tibetu i Kitaiu* (From Travels in Eastern Siberia, Mongolia, Tibet and China), Moskva: Izd. Geogr. otdeleniia Imp. Obshchestva liubitelei estestvoznaniia, antropologii i etnografii. Courtesy National Electronic Library, Russia.

Aleksandra Potanina (1843–93) is the only member of the raznochintsy discussed in this study. She travelled with her husband, Grigorii Niko-laevich Potanin (1835–1920) to Siberia, Mongolia, Tibet, and China and published her own research, primarily on ethnography, although it has been argued that she saw herself mainly as her husband's research assistant.[53] She also sketched and made representations of ethnographic everyday items, some of which are reproduced in the main collec-tion of her work, published after her death in 1895, *Iz puteshestvii po Vostochnoi Sibiri, Mongolii, Tibetu i Kitaiu; sbornik statei* (*From Travels in Eastern Siberia, Mongolia, Tibet and China*).[54] Born Aleksandra Lavrskaia into a priest's family in Nizhnyi Novgorod, she was educated at home and then served as a teacher at a girl's school. On an 1872 visit to her younger brother, Konstantin, a newspaper editor who had been exiled to Nikol'sk, she met Potanin, also an exile. Potanin, whose botanical work as a Cossack officer had attracted the notice and patronage of P.P. Semenov-Tian-Shanskii, was recommended by Semenov to attend the university in St. Petersburg, where he studied mathematics and phys-ics and was expelled after participating in student demonstrations.[55] He was imprisoned in the Petropavlovskaia fortress for several months and then exiled to Omsk. In 1865 he was arrested again for advocating Siberian separatist causes, for which he was sentenced to hard labour and then exiled to several places, including Nikol'sk. During this time, he continued to work as an ethnographer and participated in several expeditions. A year after meeting, the Potanins were married, and in 1874 after a petition from the Russian Geographical Society, Potanin received amnesty from the government. The Potanins first went to Nizhnyi Novgorod and then to St. Petersburg when he was allowed to return to "the capitals."[56]

With her husband, Potanina went on four major expeditions: to Mongolia from 1876 to 1878, to Mongolia   second time from 1879 to 1880, to China and Tibet from 1884 to 1886, and once again to China and Tibet from 1892 to 1893. She died during the course of the fourth trip, in China, at the age of fifty. Potanina's contributions to these travels were many: she collected meteorological data and botanical and zoological specimens and helped preserve them, she kept dia-ries, she talked to many local women about their lives and recorded the details she learned, and she provided well-regarded drawings of ethnographic elements, such as everyday items like women's jewelry or horse tack, as well as drawings of people and landscapes. She was not paid or acknowledged for her work, nor even listed as a member of the expeditions in which she took part, although in a Geographical Society report, Semenov-Tian-Shanskii noted among the participants of the first expedition Potanin, Pozdneev, Rafailov, Berezovskoi, "and finally the spouse of G. N. Potanin, his active colleague, accompanying him beginning from this first Mongolian expedition, and in all the subsequent ones, with uncommon courage and self-sacrifice."[57] Scott Bailey, who wrote on both Potanins, points out that Potanina was in a sense limited to "acceptable" topics for women, such as daily life and interiors, as opposed to her husband's focus on space and land.[58] Ol'ga Val'kova points out that while we do not know how Ol'ga Fedchenko regarded being the only woman on her expeditions (Ivanov suggests she had a good store of equanimity, not to mention bravery), Potanina was afraid of being the only woman on hers, a sentiment she expressed several times in letters; she was concerned about how her participation would be received by the other members of the expedition.[59]

Potanina wrote her own ethnographically oriented articles, which appeared in such venues as *Vostochnoe obozrenie*, *Russkoe bogatstvo*, *Russkie vedomosti*, and *Detskii sbornik*.[60] In the "biographical sketch" introduction to a collection of her articles assembled in her honour after her death, published by the OLEAE (the organization founded by the Fedchenkos), *Iz puteshestvii po Vostochnoi Sibiri, Mongolii, Tibetu i Kitaiu*, the compilers emphasized not only her well-admired work but also the fact that she mentored and inspired women students and gave an apparently unprecedented (for a woman) lecture on ethnography at the university of Irkutsk.[61] She was, as the compilers noted in 1895, a "woman of the 60s," who was concerned about the common people and their lack of education; her brother Konstantin met Lev Tolstoi in connection with their common concern about land issues.[62] Biographers also note her admission to the Russian Geographical Society (one of the few women to be a member in those years), and her gold medal awarded by the same society.[63]

Potanina wrote articles on the Buriats, in whom she had a particular interest, including their methods of milk production, on the Uriankhai (Tuvans), on the Mongols and the Shirongols, who are a Mongolic people, on Chinese women and on Chinese theatre, as well as travel descriptions of excursions in Tibet, Utai (Wutai), and China.[64] She wrote a well-known children's story based on the life of a Buriat scholar, Dorzhi Banzarov.[65] In her writings, she made efforts to acknowledge the barriers to her understanding, such as general lack of language (she knew some Mongolian and a few Chinese words, and indicates that although her expeditions had translators, they were not always either very good or very conscientious). In general she acknowledged her extremely incomplete knowledge of local cultures, and her limited ability as a traveller, a foreigner, and a woman to gain insight into the ways of local people, except that in some cases, as a woman she was able to gain entrée into women's quarters and women's society. She writes with great empathy especially about the poor and about servants and children, and describes with great concern the practice of foot-binding, which according to her observation rendered women and girls weakened and vulnerable to attack, as well as causing a great deal of pain during childhood.[66] Although this criticism can in some ways be compared to the common practice of Russian women writing critically about the plight of Central Asian women, Potanina of course writes as a visiting foreigner in Chinese-controlled territory, not as a part of a colonizing force; however, as a "European" she certainly feels entitled to pass judgment on Chinese society, as well as on other Europeans, such as missionaries, in China. Potanina does not hesitate to give her opinion or call other Europeans to account on the same issue: "Belgian Catholic missionaries, preaching Christianity, demand that Chinese women abjure this practice; the French missionaries have not resolved to go against fashion, and in their missions girls are subjected to this deformity. I cannot call this fashion anything else: thanks to it, all Chinese women are bent over while they walk and help themselves by balancing with their arms, but if they have to walk quickly, then, without being embarrassed, they use crutches. It is awful to watch a pregnant Chinese woman walking along the street or road where there is a lot of traffic."[67] She also noted in her essay on Chinese women the great number of unwanted girls killed in infancy or abandoned; missionaries created shelters in which unwanted girls could be brought up, educated, and provided with a dowry, making them ultimately marriageable, although she indicates that she is aware of the disadvantages of patriarchal family life for women. She even broaches the topic of suicide: "Family life for a Chinese woman is often very difficult, and therefore suicide among Chinese women is quite frequent."[68] In some cases Potanina's stories focus on herself as narrator and participant, such as one about an exiled Cherkes named Akhmet ("Akhmet") whom she tried to help return to the Caucasus, as well as one about a chipmunk-like animal she had as a pet in China ("Kitaiskii zverok," "Little Chinese animal.").[69] She also wrote a first-person account about a trip taken almost entirely by palanquin, "Tysiacha sto verst v nosil'kakh" ("1,100 versts in a Palanquin").[70]

A particularly notable piece by Potanina, mentioned by many commentators, such as Sergei Ol'denburg, the famous Orientalist, who wrote a reminiscence about her, was the aforementioned "Dordzhi, the Buriat Boy" ("Dordzhi, Buriatskii mal'chik"). In general, Potanina's work on the Buriats was highly praised.[71] In the story Potanina described the youth of a Buriat boy named Dordzhi, based on the real-life figure Dordzhi Banzarov (1822–55), a Buriat philologist and ethnographer who studied at Kazan' University and worked under the governor-general of Eastern Siberia, Nikolai Muravev-Amurskii.[72] In "Dordzhi," writing for children from a feminine first-person perspective, and addressing "you, Russian children," Potanina writes about how far away Buriatia is, close to Lake Baikal, and describes in great detail the appearance of Dordzhi, a boy from fifty years ago, how happy he is and his life in his village. Drawing on the far dryer, more ethnographical observations of her work on the Buriats as expressed in her essay of the same title, which was placed first in the memorial edition of her collected works, in "Dordzhi" Potanina brings to life a boy, his family, his village, and a whole way of life in a manner that strives to make it familiar and accessible to a young Russian reader. In a way that seems remarkable for the daughter of an Orthodox priest, she explains to her young readers that Buddhists are not idol worshippers but revere Buddha's example in the way that Christians revere the example of Christ's life, and create and display statues of Buddha in order to recall this example. The joys of the Buriat way of life are depicted enthusiastically by Potanina; the family is happy and loving. There is a detailed description of the boy's dwelling and its furnishings. In the summer the whole family, along with farm workers, goes to the summer fields and puts up yurts; there they spend several months harvesting, eating from a common pot, and singing and playing games in the evenings. After the family returns to their winter quarters, the narrator breaks in again to note that "at the time of our story, that is about 50 years ago," Buriat leaders, called taisha, thought that Buriats in Russian territory, under Russian laws, should know Russian and "become closer" ("sblizhat'sia") with Russians.[73] The taisha of the Selenga Buriats, which is to say Dordzhi's taisha, commands that several Buriat boys be sent to Russian schools, where they would learn Russian subjects and the Mongolian language. One of these was in Kiakhta, "on the very border between Russia and Mongolia" and not far away from Dordzhi's village (ulus). It is decided that Dordzhi should go. The lure of travel and discovering the larger world is a motif in the story, a topic that seems to echo details from Potanina's own life, in which she heard, as a girl, stories of the travels or religious pilgrimages of others.[74]

Father and son complete a several-day journey south, to the border of Russia and Mongolia, with Potanina movingly describing Dordzhi's first impressions of Russian ways and a school shopping trip with his father to the Chinese part of the city. The boy is at first quite unhappy at the school, feeling tormented by the Russian boys, and attempts to run away. He doesn't get far and must stay overnight in the woods, during which he thinks better of his situation and realizes that some of the Russian schoolmates are kind. The story ends with a brief coda about how Dordzhi continued with his studies and became a scholar and someone who, had he lived longer, would have made a mark for his people.

Despite the tendentious nature of the story, with its at first condescending Russians who then learn to respect the Buriat students, and its wise and multiculturally oriented Buriats, the tale is striking in its level of detail about the everyday life of Dordzhi's family and Potanina's striving to create a non-estranged, non-othered set of protagonists.

> Once on a July morning of 18**, into one of the further buildings of the ulus already described, entered a Buriat woman with a large pail of just-drawn milk. A pace after her a little boy dragged another small pail, which served him as a container. The mother was in a black velvet cap, under which on her chest was suspended a whole set of silver jewelry. Two braids were arrayed on her shoulders. She was dressed in a dark blue rather worn-out khalat and a velvet vest. The boy was without a cap, his hair was cut straight in front, but in the back was plaited into a braid; he also wore a long khalat and home- made boots. The swarthy color of his face and the narrow, as if always laughing, eyes did not prevent him from being handsome. He was called Dórdzhi. And it is about him that I want to tell you.[75]

Potanina goes on to explain that the family sleeps together in one room and does not use the kind of Western furniture that Russians are accustomed to, but they feel perfectly content with their lives and are, in essence, to be admired.

Potanina even worked into the story information about the heritage of shamanism that pre-existed the Buriats' turn to Buddhism, something that she described in some detail both in her essay on the Buriats and in others dealing with Mongolians or Shirongols. In the story, it is noted that one boy at the school was well versed in ancient Buriat fighting techniques and teaches them to the other Buriat boys. Dordzhi and his family require that he be asked to change neither his religion nor his style of clothing in order to attend the school, and he is not asked to change either one. Ol'denburg remarked:

> Involuntarily one now recalls her story "Dordzhi, the Buriat boy," and the ethnographic essay "Buriats." Especially now, when a breaking apart of all Buriat life is being prepared and has in part been completed, one deeply regrets that the authoritative and decisive voice of Aleksandra Viktorovna cannot resonate in defense of the independent development of the Buriats,

to whom she always related with warm sympathy and of whose ability to independently, without compromising valued national features, become attached to Russian culture she was deeply convinced. For Aleksandra Viktorovna it was clear that it was necessary not for the Buriats to become Russian, but to learn to value Russian culture, applying its adoption into their national uniqueness.[76]

The Potanins' trips were often dangerous and problematic. Potanina's biographers, V.M. Zarin and E.A. Zarina, and V.A. Obruchev, the geologist and traveller (and later science fiction writer) who met her and accompanied Potanin on his fourth expedition, remark that Grigorii Potanin was, as the Zarins put it, a "trusting and completely unpractical person" who was not adept at planning the details of the complex trips he undertook.[77] Multiple times, he went against the recommendations of local people and insisted on taking steep, difficult paths that took a great toll on man and animal alike. Camels and horses fell off steep paths, mules fell into the water and the collections packed on them had to be dried, yaks bunched together and crushed the items packed on them.[78] The Potanins often found themselves travelling as snow began to fall, causing frostbite and other ills. In a rather dry depiction of the Potanins' second trip, Semenov notes that for a mountain crossing that typically required ten days, the Potanins took twenty-five because of snow and the use of camels, stating flatly that "the local people do not travel by this road by camel," and use only horses.[79] Food was often in short supply, and several times, the travellers raided the grain stores of field mice, which they dug out of their burrows.[80] On the second expedition, they began to wonder if they might need to slaughter some of their horses for food and had to buy local grain to make up for their lack of wheat.[81] N.M. Iadrintsev, a friend of the Potanins, noted that Potanina's "knowledge of life and perspicacity were qualities that supplemented the lack of practicality of [Potanin], weighed down by science and always knowing little of reality."[82]

Being a man of few means to begin with, and relying mainly on the Geographical Society for funds, Potanin's trips, although lengthy, were far less luxurious than that of the Golovnins, and likely the Fedchenkos.[83] The Potanins travelled mostly on foreign territory and hence lacked the ability to wield the machinery of the Russian government. I.I. Popov, a member of the Eastern Siberian section of the Russian Geographical Society, and future revolutionary, wrote that Potanina's presence improved Potanin's expeditions:

Before Potanin, and even during his time, the expeditions of Przhvalskii, Pevtsov and others were more similar to military detachments than to scholarly expeditions. The locals reacted to them with fear and caution. But there was nothing for them to fear from an expedition in which a woman took part, where there was no military convoy; it was clear to them that such an expedition followed scientific goals, and not military ones. Thanks to such relations to the local people, Potanin could quietly pass among the aggressive Tanguts, hold conversations with fanatical Tibetans, and passed through areas where no European foot had ever trod and each time brought out rich material for scholarly work. ... before [Potanina] doors were open that no man had never been able to penetrate, she paid attention to and noticed those sides of life that easily escaped from men and worked hand in hand with her husband, supplementing his work.[84]

Obruchev, describing his final meeting with Potanina at the Russian embassy in Beijing, notes that she was exhausted from overland travel to Beijing and suffering from a heart ailment. The doctor wanted her to stay in Beijing and not travel; Obruchev makes it clear that Potanin was not really looking after his wife and notes that they ought at least to have travelled more slowly and comfortably. There was great pressure, however, both to continue expeditions and not to lag behind the work of others; when Potanin was sent to Tibet and China, it was because Przhvalskii had travelled via a different route and Potanin's expedition would supplement Przhvalskii's findings.[85]

Potanina's views of her role in terms of Russian national status are present in her writing and sometimes are made unambiguously evident. She states very clearly at the beginning of her essay on the Uriankhai (Tuvans), "Iz stranstviia po Uriankhaiskoi zemle" ("From Travels along the Uriankhai Lands") that Russians should know the territory adjacent to their newly expanded empire:

> Our sketch represents an attempt to acquaint the reader with a new country. It usually happens that, thanks to tempting descriptions and interesting travels, we are made more closely acquainted with various wild corners of Africa, America or India, while countries that lie on the edges of our Russia and near her remain almost completely unknown. The Uriankhai country is remarkable because it constitutes our border for a distance of almost 1,000 versts, and furthermore it is a rare Russian reader who knows even its name. This country takes up the southern slope of the Saiansk mountains, bordering from the south the Siberian gubernii of Irkutsk and Yenisei.[86]

Potanina described visiting two Uriankhai shamanesses in this essay and clearly indicates her self-consciousness about desiring and evoking a spectacle for foreign visitors and of expecting women to provide this spectacle: "In the Uriankhai land there are many shamans, men and women, in fact more women than men."[87] The first shamaness they meet does not perform for them, although another, much poorer shamaness does, but only under duress since she fears the Russian visitors, Potanina says. She enters into an altered state, falling into convulsions during the process. Potanina remarks: "This kamlan'e (performing as a shaman) left me with the most unpleasant impression. It made us feel guilty that we arranged for ourselves a spectacle, costing a poor woman, obviously, much spiritual and bodily strain, the more so because in her kamlan'e there was nothing poetic."[88] A third shamaness, much younger, prettier, and better off, according to Potanina, also performs for them, a performance that is described at length.[89] Potanina questions her own role as spectator, gazing on a spectacle put on by someone less fortunate who was performing or being presented for the view of visiting foreigners. Potanina indicates numerous problems with the expedition in this essay; poor planning leads to the death of some of their animals, they become short on food, members of their expedition are overdue in Omsk, and local officials are angry that their animals are eating the overwintering fodder needed by the local people. In fact, the whole trip had to be curtailed until the following year, when it was ultimately cancelled. Heading north back to Russia, Potanina and her husband sleep out in the open, without tents; she describes becoming exhausted, getting sick, and the frostbite on faces and one participant's feet. At the end of the essay, however, Potanina continues to uphold her role in the "improvement" of the Uriankhai, optimistically describing her contention that the Uriankhai are becoming accustomed to the Russians:

> now already their relations with the Russians have become completely peaceful, and we notice the quick successes of our rapprochement (sblizhenie), a peaceful rapprochement, naturally worked out by life itself on the foundation of mutual relations and services. Last year one of our teachers visited the Uriankhai land from the Minusinskii okrug, with the sole goal of helping the Uriankhai population which was suffering from an epidemic of smallpox, with a vaccination of smallpox. He was received as is the best guest, he was brought from one ulus to the next. Only the lack of lymph and the end of vacation prevented him from returning.[90] Such peaceful and beneficial relationships, one might think, among the "wild and cruel," as it was previously thought, Uriankhai people, will raise our meaning as a people standing before them on the road to the benefits of life and civilization.[91]

Potanina, if optimistic about the "civilizing mission" in which she was herself participating, was certainly not naïve about the wishes of those she encountered. In her essay "O kitaiskoi zhenshchine" ("On Chinese Women") originally published in *Russkoe bogatstvo* in 1887, she chronicled, for example, a kind of "photo diplomacy" among upper-class Chinese who hosted her party in Sinin in the spring of 1885.[92] A high-ranking Chinese lady, having discovered that the photographer was taking pictures of the local heads of government, including her husband, wanted the group's photographer to take a picture of her as well and invited Potanina to her house in order to prevail upon her to arrange for the photograph.[93] In her description of the visit, Potanina makes it quite clear that the woman's pushy ways are not to her liking, perhaps revealing Potanina's desire not to recognize the upper-class Chinese woman as her social equal. During the same visit, Potanina is shocked when the servants immediately seat themselves at the table after the meal and eat the leftovers.[94]

Photography, its monetization, and its role in tourism were also a major consideration in her essay "Utai" (present-day Wutai, a chain of mountains and a designation for five important Buddhist monasteries in China).[95] A.I. Skassi, a geographer and the group's photographer (he also participated in one of the Fedchenkos' expeditions), was engaged in photographing the monasteries in Wutai and invited Potanina along; they took a mule to carry the camera equipment, as well as a guide and a Chinese servant, Ten.[96] As Skassi took photos, Potanina sketched, but soon a large crowd of boys, lamas in training, surrounded them, followed by adults; she attempted to distract the boys with some pencil drawings, but the adults were more interested in "watching the strange procedure of photography," even if the boys were interested in the fact that when she put her sharpening knife into the pockets of her kudzy (trousers), it did not fall to the ground.[97] As they approached the Iun-chzhao-sy monastery and Skassi began taking pictures, at first the lamas disapproved, but then they allowed the photography. Potanina notes that the monks were selling pictures, statuettes, and other representations of the monasteries and the gods, just as "for example, a photo of the mosaic of the Mother of God in St. Sophia Cathedral in Kiev, which is sold by the monks at the entrance to the cathedral."[98] In general, Potanina seemed open to understanding parallels such as the selling of photos or representations of holy places, both Buddhist and Christian, and the correspondence between Christian and Buddhist religious iconography, rejecting the idea that statues of Buddha were any more problematic than representations of Christ.

As Popov mentioned, Potanina had multiple opportunities to become familiar with women's lives during her travels, and she did not shy away from comparing Buriat women to Russian peasant women. In her essay on the Buriats, Potanina describes household interiors with great specificity, something she utilized in her story about Dordzhi, and she wrote in very detailed fashion about all the milk products produced by the Buriats, which was the subject of her scholarly lecture at the university in Irkutsk. She also wrote about marriage customs, including the freedom of unmarried women, whose children out of wedlock are welcomed by her family of origin, who keep them when she is married. She notes that Buriat women were not hurriedly married off since they do as much work as men in the field, and quotes a scholar, Dubrova, who says that women are looked at as working livestock, "rabochii skot." Potanina quickly notes that one can say the same about Russian peasant women.[99] She further compares Buriat women with Russian peasant women when discussing the fact that the women share almost all the work of men but also take care of livestock. She notes, "But a Buriat woman has neither kitchen garden, nor the washing of dishes, nor the washing of laundry, nor the bathhouse, that is to say all of those trifling occupations that swallow the time of a Russian peasant woman; the Buriats don't even have the habit of washing dishes with milk in hot water."[100] Potanina biographers Zarin and Zarina write of Potanina that "Sharing the work of her husband (the gathering and preservation of collections, the keeping of meteorological observations, diaries and so on), she found time as well for literary-artistic activities. The work of Potanina appears as a marvelous supplement to the rather dry travel diaries of G. N. Potanin, and has a great deal of value independent of them."[101] Potanin himself expresses regret that he is unlikely to produce the kind of "travel sketches" that would have interest for a general public and would have included in such sketches more subjective impressions.[102] Potanin underscores, in effect, his own gendered writing: "[I] restricted myself to the presentation of only the facts of topography and ethnography, excluding from my trips both personal impressions as well as the stories of extraneous persons, with which could be depicted both the character the local natural surroundings as well as the way of life of the local population."[103] Potanin, like his wife, was also likely to compare non-Russians favourably to both nomads and to Russian peasants. He is extremely complimentary of the local Mongolian princes, especially by contrast to other nomad peoples "such as the Turkmen or even our Kirghiz," noting that the Mongolians are educated and "often speak several languages of the empire to which they belong, write in Mongolian and Tibetan, sometimes even study Sanskrit; many of them have lived for a year or more in Peking, the capital of their government, they compete with each other to build monasteries and temples … The life of the Mongolians proceeds quietly, their manners are mild, crime is rare, nothing is heard of any animalistic treatment of women or children."[104] The "animalistic treatment" here generally refers by implication to the nomads, but most readers would also have had Russian peasants in mind. Implicitly or explicitly comparing "natives" to Russian peasants, usually to the Russians' disadvantage, was done by many of the writers discussed here, such as Potanina, Uvarova, and Golovnina.

Although assuredly writing from a "European" point of view, describing the bodily ethnic "type" of various groups she encountered and understanding them as being less "civilized" than Russians, Potanina was rarely dehumanizing. She was noticeably more judgmental about the Chinese government in terms of its responsibility for the many structural disadvantages for the women under its jurisdiction than about how women were treated among any individual ethnic group either within China or in Russia. Rarely did a particular role, whether it be lama in training, shaman, lady of the household, or milk-product processer, hide from Potanina's view the person who embodied that role and her circumstances. Typically, Potanina addressed her own status as a woman and a foreigner with a fair degree of self-consciousness, and with an awareness that there was no possibility of any kind of "objective" observation or interaction. One can also see from the reproductions in the volume of her writings that she was a close observer of women's clothing and jewelry (Figure 5.6).

However, she was also very much a woman of her time and circumstance who believed both in bringing enlightenment to the "natives" and taking them to see art museums, while her "soul suffered at the ignorance and the poverty of the Russian narod," whom she rejoiced to see visiting the Hermitage in St. Petersburg: "'It made us very happy,' she writes, 'that there was a mass of common people at the Hermitage, boatmen, sailors, soldiers, women in head scarves, muzhiks, and children with them. Before, this sort of thing, it seems, did not happen.'"[105] According to her biographers, she preferred Russian painters over foreign ones, particularly prizing the work of Vereshchagin.[106] Despite her sense of the civilizing abilities of the Russians, however, she was a great critic of the Russian court system and how it treated the exiled, whom she tried to help; her story "Akhmet" touched on this topic.[107] Aleksandra Potanina died during a trip that began in 1892 and was intended to go as far as Eastern China and Tibet; she died in China, after a series of strokes left her increasingly debilitated. Her body was transported back to Russia and she was buried in Kiakhta, on the Russian side of the border between Russia and Mongolia. In 1955 a column topped by a bust

Табл. III.

Figure 5.6. Aleksandra Potanina, "Table III" (illustration of Tangut jewelry pieces). Plate from *Iz puteshestvii po Vostochnoi Sibiri, Mongolii, Tibetu i Kitaiu*, Moskva: Izd. Geogr. otdeleniia Imp. Obshchestva liubitelei estestvoznaniia, antropologii i etnografii, 1895, p. 301.

of Potanina by Buriat artist Aleksandr Timin was put up at Potanina's gravesite.[108] After her death, admirers raised money for a library to be created and named after her in Irkutsk.[109]

While beyond the scope of this study, another ethnographer, Maria Nalivkina, should be mentioned alongside Potanina. Together with her husband, Vladimir Nalivkin, she lived in an Uzbek village for six years, speaking the local language, dressing as the local people did and doing all the same work they did, essentially engaging in participant observation while raising her own family. Together the Nalivkins wrote an ethnographic study focusing on women in particular, considering themselves to be co-authors and clearly relying on Maria Nalivkina's ability to get to know the local women intimately in order to write the study, called *A Sketch of the Everyday Life of Women of the Sedentary Native Population of the Fergana Valley*, published in 1886.[110] As the editor, Marianne Kamp, points out, the Nalivkins may well have written in response to Fedchenko's *Puteshestvie v Turkestan* of 1875 and were likely inspired in their outlook by such figures as the Narodniks and Chernyshevsky; in fact, at times they speak directly to the reader in a Chernyshevskian style.[111]

Praskov'ia Uvarova

Praskov'ia Uvarova (1840–1924) came from a noble family similar to the Armfel'd family; she was born Princess Shcherbatova, was acquainted with Leo Tolstoy, and was said to be the model for Tolstoy's Kitty in *Anna Karenina*.[112] Aleksei Savrasov, Ol'ga Fedchenko's art instructor and lithographer, also instructed young Princess Shcherbatova in art. In 1859 she married well-known archaeologist A.S. Uvarov and assisted him with his archeological projects for many years. Only after his death was she able to join the Moscow Archaeological Society, since he opposed women members, and swiftly thereafter she was elected president of the society. It was as president that she went to Tashkent in 1890 as an invited guest (among other dignitaries) to participate in the celebrations marking the twenty-fifth anniversary of Russian rule in Turkestan (1865–90). Although she had spent much time in the Caucasus and visited excavations there on her way to Central Asia, by all accounts it was her first trip to Central Asia. Uvarova indicated without saying so directly (she was more direct in her personal memoirs) that she was travelling as a recognized archaeologist (she had by then been president of the Moscow Archaeological Society for five years) and a member of the inner circle of the nobility, as well as an invited guest of some reputation. In her two-part article "Poezdka v Tashkent i Samarkand," published in *Russkaia Mysl'* in 1891, Uvarova begins her narrative from her arrival in Baku.[113] Having crossed the Caspian and embarked on the train to Samarkand, she immediately places her trip

Figure 5.7. Praskov'ia Uvarova, 1870s. Courtesy of Wikimedia Commons.

in the context of the Russian conquest of Central Asia, losing no time in evoking the "famous storming of the late Skobelev" as she describes her quick detour to the Geok-Tepe fortress and the monument to the fallen Russian soldiers: "Peace be to their dust! … The further you move into the interior of these lands, the more you are surprised at the patience and fortitude of those to whom Russia owes the conquest of these far territories (etikh dalekikh okrain)."[114] Whether on purpose or not, Uvarova alludes in her comments to the title of Nikolai Karazin's most famous novel, his 1872 *Na dalekikh okrainakh,* or *In the Distant*

Confines/In Far Peripheries, which depicts Central Asia in great part as a place of terrifying danger and barbarity.[115] At the time she travelled, the railway did not continue from Samarkand to Tashkent, so the next leg of the journey was made by carriage and tarantas, through the Hungry Steppe, the same trip described by Apreleva in her story "Golodnaia Step'."[116] On the way, travelling at full speed through the night and then during the day, Uvarova took note of persistent mirages. She also took note of the fatalism of a dying horse awaiting its fate, vultures circling. Uvarova explicitly evokes the painting Apreleva had clearly alluded to in "Uzun-ada," saying that one:[117] "involuntarily recalls the painting of Vereshchagin, 'The Forgotten [Soldier]' ('Zabytyi'). It was very much criticized in its time, they found it necessary to remove it from the exhibition. Come to these steppes and judge for yourself, what to do in the case of a campaign with the backward and the weak, when the smallest mistake can expose you to the death of the whole unit, and imagine how it must have affected the heart of the soldier, the commander and simply the eye-witness, such as Vereshchagin, who painted such a picture."[118] The 1872 painting (printed in the introduction), which shows birds circling and perching on a soldier's body placed at the centre and front of the painting, gun flung to the side, certainly pulled no punches. Uvarova's evocation of it doubtless indicated to readers her knowledge of Vereshchagin and her assertion that judgmental readers should experience the area for themselves, although of course Vereshchagin was not merely an observer of the conquest of Turkestan but a participant. It was true that the painting was removed from the exhibit, but more than that, Vereshchagin burned it, along with "Surrounded! They're Pursuing" and "By the Fortress Wall. They Have Entered." Russian censorship forbade any reproduction of "The Forgotten [Soldier]" for twenty years.[119] Uvarova's comparison also showed the extent to which travellers to Central Asia were conditioned to see it through Vereshchagin's lens; the iconography he created was extremely powerful and was to last for many decades more, including through the twentieth century.[120]

After situating herself as a more or less typical educated Russian travelling to Central Asia with thoughts of Vereshchagin and Scheherezade (she references the *Thousand and One Nights* to describe Samarkand),[121] Uvarova turns to a more scholarly style of narration, framing the journey in the most historically oriented way possible, alluding to the Arab enlightenment of Central Asia from the eighth to ninth centuries and the reign of Ghengis Khan in the thirteenth century.[122] She notes that the Syr-Darya was called the Jaxartes and that Cyrus the Great died there in 560 BCE, fighting the Massagetae, a nomadic group. Approaching Tashkent, Uvarova appraises what she sees in aesthetic terms, comparing bronzed people bathing to figures in Egyptian art and declaring that the light and shadow of greenery along the road are not like Italy but rather like the work of the newest French school (meaning the Impressionists): "where everything is planned for effect, in bright colors; take away here the camels and horses from their bright spots, the colorful khalats and rugs – and from the paysage will remain only a gray expanse, saying nothing more to us."[123] At ten in the evening, Uvarova's party arrived in Tashkent at the home of Baron A.V. Vrevskii, the governor-general of Turkestan at the time. Uvarova describes the Russian and non-Russian parts of the city for her readers. The Russian part is difficult to navigate, she notes, due to the "mass of greenery," and has, in her view, only a few important buildings, such as the church, men's and women's gymnasia (schools), the new home of Grand Duke Nikolai Konstantinovich, and the governor-general's home, which, while "just as low and on one floor, as all the other city buildings, and like them, hidden from the side of the street and from all sides surrounded by a wide courtyard and garden, is well situated and planned out, with a mass of water, which is obligatory in this area."[124] The "main bait" ("glavnaia primanka"), however, she says, is the exhibition: "put on by the Russian governmental personnel of the area to show what Russia has done for the region after 25 years of its subjugation (pokorenie) and how it responded and cared for the well-being of the residents, their production and trade."[125] In a separate memoir, in which she also briefly describes this trip, *Byloe. Davno proshedshie schastlivye dni*, Uvarova declares that "we" were invited to the celebration of the twenty-fifth anniversary by the governor-general, Baron Vrevskii, who noted that Finance Minister Vyshegradskii, the director of the Finance Department Sergei Witte (Elena Blavatskaia's younger cousin), and the creator of the Trans-Caspian Railway Mikhail Annenkov would be attending "and recommended we go to Baku for their arrival and travel further with them, which we did."[126] Hence, Uvarova was no ordinary visitor, since Vyshegradskii was "the star guest" of the exhibition, as Daniel Brower puts it. Brower points out that Russia had joined in the fervour for exhibitions that had arisen in Europe and elsewhere; as has been noted above, the 1872 Polytechnic Exhibition in Moscow, participated in by the Fedchenkos, had been a major event there:

> The Russian Empire, with some delay, joined in the great exhibition endeavor ... In the 1880s, the new goal of the post-Kaufman generation of administrators was to place Turkestan in the marketplace. Every public celebration offered the opportunity to organize an exhibition. Special occasions were created if need be. The first fair [in Tashkent] in 1886 became the

> affair of the Turkestan branch of the Russian Society of Gardening [sado-
> vodstvo] … The second Tashkent fair, held in 1890, coincided with the
> twenty-fifth anniversary of the Russian conquest of the region. The event
> became in its own way a celebration of colonial achievements … The star
> guest was the Minister of Finance [Vyshegradskii – KH], who traveled
> from St. Petersburg (via the Trans-Caspian Railroad) to visit the fair along
> with his assistant Sergei Witte.[127]

According to her memoirs, Uvarova's own travelling party was fairly large, consisting of herself, two daughters, the fiancée of her eldest son, her younger son, her fiancé-son and his friend Orlov.[128] She also notes in her memoirs that in Tashkent they stayed in the home of Vrevskii and "thus, obviously, were in the center of all the activity, saw and heard everything and everyone and became acquainted with those who had traveled to the celebration."[129] In contrast to her article, her description of the celebrations is relatively cursory in her memoirs: "The appointed celebrations went just as they usually do: with a huge mass of people, with festive services, with speeches acknowledging what is owed to those responsible for the events being celebrated, with a parade and review of our glorious troops, among whom could be seen, and were especially honored, the remaining and living heroes who occupied the region."[130] In her article, Uvarova is extremely complimentary and far more detailed about the exhibition, noting who had been on the planning committee, how much money had been spent on building the exhibition (36,547 roubles), declaring it "completely successful and striking in its external elegance," and naming many of its sections, such as the agricultural-industrial, gardening, and handicrafts sections. The military section was placed at the beginning, she noted, and showed "a statue of a Russian soldier raising the flag of victory above the walls of the conquered city."[131] The exhibit guide, written by Nikolai Aleksandrovich Maev, the editor of *Turkestanskie Vedomosti*, also lists such items as the railroad pavilion (which had a model train), a beekeeping exhibit, a hunting and fishing exhibit, and several others.[132] Uvarova found the "best and most meaningful" exhibit to be the agricultural one, which included tobacco, viniculture, gardening, and the cultivation of cotton and silk. Uvarova noted that both Russians and local Tajiks demonstrated their methods and even machines they had designed themselves for the processing of silk, and also noted that the exhibition was popular with the "local inhabitants" ("mestnykh zhitelei"). Whether she meant by that term mainly Russians, or Russians and non-Russians, is not specified. However, a visiting French photographer, Paul Nadar, extensively photographed the exhibition, and his photographs indicate that clearly not only ethnic Russians visited the exhibition.[133] Inessa Kouteinikova notes that it was in fact Vrevskii, the governor-general, who had persuaded Paul Nadar to travel from Istanbul to Tashkent "to document the enormous leap that Russia's leading colony had performed in little more than twenty-five years. Nadar's photography was very present in Tashkent, and his arrival was announced in advertisement and on billboards, since the organizers hoped that his fame would help to turn the whole enterprise into a great success."[134] Vrevskii, Kouteinikova notes, was a "cultivated military officer with a good instinct for new trends" and had himself visited a number of universal exhibitions in Europe. "Vrevsky's basic idea was to bring together all ethnic and religious groups of the Russian Empire to celebrate its unity in diversity while at the same time ignoring all cultural differences, such as between Orthodox Christians and Muslims, between Sunni and Shia."[135] Besides the exhibit, Uvarova singled out Tashkent's museum and library, both founded by Kaufman, making note of the library's excellence but also noting that, under Cherniaev, it had been decimated.[136] Uvarova and her group also visited the Nikolskii village, the first Russian settlement, established twenty-five years before. While there, she detects some cracks in the Russian official façade: "they live, it seems, very well (bogato), but they are not all satisfied and only a small percentage of them actually practice agriculture; the larger number of them work in the city as drivers and day workers."[137] Uvarova and her group then returned to Samarkand, along with Vrevskii, and stayed at his home there for two weeks. Uvarova gives a detailed history of the region, its ancient canal system, the Zarafshan valley, and then describes its inhabitants – the most ancient residents, the Iranian Tajiks, and the Turkic Uzbeks, who came later.

Uvarova does not shy away from judgmental physical description (nor did any of the other writers discussed here, except perhaps for Apreleva), taking it as a given that "European" looks are the standard. She describes the Tajiks as attractive ("krasivyi") and with regular facial features ("s pravil'nymi chertami litsa"), stating that Uzbeks have "more yellow" skin and narrow eyes that taper in the corners, and a "more square" ("kvadtradnee") face. Early on she had described a "Kirghiz" as being far inferior to a Caucasian gorets – effeminate, yellow-skinned, with prominent cheekbones, and a "far from handsome face" ("daleko nekrasivoe litso").[138] "Besides these two main peoples [Tajiks and Uzbeks] in the Turkestan region also live Arabs, remaining from the once-great hordes which brought to the area the religion of Mohammad, Indians, Jews and Gypsies."[139] Uvarova describes the succession of power in Central Asia, from Alexander the

Great in the fourth century BCE, Turkish attacks in 571 CE, the arrival of the Arabs in the seventh century, the arrival of Genghis Khan, his successor Timur, down to Timur's grandson Ulug-bek. Samarkand, she notes, remains the capital of the Muslim world, a holy city, which strengthened its resistance to the "giaours," as she calls the Russians.[140] "Russian troikas honk and now flood the wide streets of the Tajik town, cutting down their honking only in the Russian part, thus not recognizing that in the Tajik side outside town they ring day and night, as if to changelessly and relentlessly remind the population of the conquerers and the subjugation/enslavement (poraboshchenie) of the region."[141] It is unclear how Uvarova regards this traffic activity; she indicates that the Russians have altered the local city structure and way of life; at one level, this seems to be viewed somewhat critically, but she is also full of praise for Kaufman's proclamation that Russian settlers should plant trees and gardens and names Korol'kov, Abramov, and Ivanov as generals who followed his lead in creating excellent gardens. Korol'kov's garden is singled out for special praise due to its taste and skill ("vkus i umenie";[142] Korol'kov's garden was also lavishly praised by Golovnina, as we have seen). Uvarova particularly enjoys relaxing under the branches of the *salix babylonica,* or weeping willow, dropping the Latin name into her text with scholarly satisfaction. Uvarova for the second time evokes *A Thousand and One Nights* when she praises the corner of Abramovskii Boulevard, enjoying the view of camels, melon sellers, bright khalats, and covered women; Gogol-style, she reduces some in her view to metonymies of their accoutrements: "sitting, bartering khalats and turbans."[143] From that vantage point, she can see part of the Afrasiab, and discusses excavations there, but declares as a professional that there is an absence of "real excavations" ("otsutstvie pravil'nykh raskopok") and that one can buy old items, but they are sold by people who do not know what they are.[144]

As Svetlana Gorshenina notes, the idea that the "natives" had to be taught by their European "masters" how to appreciate their own antiquities was widespread; Gorshenina also cites the passage from Uvarova about local collectors neither appreciating nor truly being interested in what they had collected. However, Gorshenina adds that this complaint also attests to the fact that local people had begun creating their own archeological collections.[145] As Gorshenina points out, the Russian military early on began to assert control over important historical sites, and local knowledge, while absolutely vital to Russians' learning even about the location of many sites, was not acknowledged by the Russians. Meanwhile the Russian-imported practice of turning of artefacts into something that could be bought and sold played a huge role in the fate of numerous ancient sites. Apreleva, too, points to this Russian reduction of all relationships to money as a major blind spot and an aspect of the degradation of community relations in Russian Turkestan.

Uvarova's comments on the Afrasiab lead to a description of how the older buildings in Samarkand were constructed, with small bricks. She notes that mosques are actually constituted by a combination of different buildings situated in a courtyard and speculates on the various reasons builders might have used the cupola form, one of which being that they are shaped like yurts.[146] In the second part of her article, Uvarova focuses far more on architectural specifics, first of Samarkand's masterpieces, then those of Bukhara and of Merv. At times, she writes in the second person, guide-book style, such as in her section on the Shakh-Zinde (Shah-i-Zinde), built by Tamerlane (Timur):

> You sit (vy sidite) and look … and only little by little do you begin to differentiate among the forms, the patterns, even the colors. Only then will you understand that only a great, powerful overlord (povelitel') could order such a building to be built, that only an artist-architect could build it with a mass of similar such artists, assistants, draughtsmen, chemists, and molders. Look around at all of these buildings, and in fact you will see that for each column, each capital, each arch, wall, belt – for each of these a separate form, a separate pouring was required: on the columns, either the year or the name of the master, on all the arches, belts, tombs – either the name of the founder, or the name of the deceased, or a devout saying, and everywhere each is particular, original.
>
> A love for text and [devout] sayings is brought to such a level that everything is covered with them: the necks of the cupolas, the arches, entire enormous walls; sayings and inscriptions are either poured in separate pieces (in small parts) or, created from lengthened tiles, a whole net of patterns that an untrained eye, unfamiliar with the Eastern alphabet, would be inclined to think was merely an Oriental ornament.[147]

Here Uvarova speaks as an archaeologist and scholar; she greatly admires the creativity, the glorification of text, and the exceptional level of craftsmanship as they merge together. It was of course also a common Western-received idea to proclaim that current inhabitants of Turkestan did not appreciate or understand the great works of their past, and her admiration for this Timurid construction is part of that trope. Her proclaimed admiration for the glorification of text, however, does not extend to the existence of the institutions of currently functioning mosques and madrassas. She comments on the pupils of the madrassa of Shir-Dar (Shir-Dor), one of the buildings on the Registan square, noting that they sit for hours "without moving, without an expression on their faces, without a sparkle in their eyes, as if without desires and even thoughts."[148] Uvarova associates this behaviour with an unquestioning service to Mohammad: "Such a madrassa represents an entire and quite large society, which cannot but support fanaticism, cannot but produce from its milieu people who are fully prepared for contemplative life and meek service to the prescriptions of Mohammad."[149] Uvarova writes extremely detailed descriptions of many of the most important buildings in the three cities in a scholarly tone; she notes, perhaps archly, of Samarkand's Bibi-Khanym mosque that it is "the opinion of Kal'" that the inscription supported the idea that the structure was dedicated to Timur's wife.[150] E.F. Kal', whom she called "our inseparable fellow traveler, assistant and teacher of Tashkent and the area ... a young, educated person, familiar with Eastern languages and having studied the area closely," was an assistant to Vrevskii.[151] Later in her account, describing the extensive ruins near the Imperial Murghab Estate near Merv, Uvarova politely but firmly questions both other scholars and General Komarov about their assessment of a building being 800–1,000 years old, asking rhetorically, "Isn't such an assessment too risky?"[152] Perhaps not surprisingly, Komarov was called an "amateur antiquarian" by one commentator and was associated with the buying and selling of artefacts.[153]

Uvarova also visited buildings outside Samarkand. One mosque had owned a Quran written on parchment, brought from Mecca and supposedly written by Osman (Uthman; known as the Uthman Quran); "it is now located in the St. Petersburg Public Library, to which it was sold for 100 roubles by the Mullahs."[154] Here again, rather than pointing to a reverence for text (since the Quran in question was a very ancient and authoritative one), she focused on its sale for 100 roubles, underscoring the notion that "natives" would sell their cultural heritage for money. The rationale for Russian control of the region is thereby justified by Uvarova, since the manuscript is now safely in St. Petersburg, where it is properly appreciated by those who, assumedly, truly value cultural treasures. Indeed, a merchant named Mirza Abdullah Bukhari, who was known as a Turkestani collector, viewed the Quran in 1887 in the St. Petersburg Public Library during a trip to Russia.[155]

Uvarova continues her tour of Russian conquest, taking note of the history of the nearby citadel, "destroyed and scattered after the treasonous siege in it of our garrison by the Samarkand population."[156] The siege of the Samarkand citadel occurred in 1868 after Kaufman had left only a small force to guard Samarkand as he led his troops on to Bukhara. The Russians who defended it were a weak force but put up a strong defence, in which Vereshchagin took part, receiving a medal for his heroic efforts.[157] Uvarova then lists a number of important buildings similar to the Samarkand mosques, listing their locations in nearby towns and noting that they were all built at the end of the fourteenth or beginning of the fifteenth century.

On 29 September, Uvarova and her group departed for Bukhara, travelling the thirteen versts from the Bukhara train station to the town in carriages "sent by our agent and consisting of four-person landaus and two similar carriages, which were "bad" but "gifts of our military governors."[158] She relates the funny story about how the emir of Bukhara, wanting to show off his new carriages, was taken in one to his palace, but everyone took the minister, sitting on the coach box, as the important person and paid no attention to the emir, sitting lower down in the landau. Now, she says, it is "not done" ("ne priniato") to ride on the coach box.[159] Once in Bukhara, they reached the agency (agentstvo, i.e., government office – since Bukhara was a protectorate and not under direct Russian control) and were greeted by V.O. Klemm, the secretary and "dragoman" of the Russian government office in Bukhara, and his wife.[160] Uvarova noted approvingly that Klemm had graduated from the Lazarevskii Institute of foreign languages in Moscow. Uvarova's disputing of scholars' claims and her praising (or wryly acknowledging) younger, well-prepared government officials are rhetorical moves which she seems to use to assert her own authority as an archaeologist and expert.

Again in authoritative style, Uvarova made note of the fact that near the city gates there were "traces of paganism" ("sledy iazychestva"), such as a small altar with offerings, "as in the Caucasus" ("kak na Kavkaze").[161] Uvarova and her group were not allowed in the main mosque, either because, as some members of the party thought, from a dislike of "giaours," or, according to others, because it was only open on Fridays.[162] Uvarova rather pointedly catches the mistake of "the translator from the agency," who claims that a madrassa, Mir-Arab, was built 783 years earlier, or about 1107 CE; Uvarova said that the building processes required were not known until later and that far more likely, the madrassa was built in 783 Hijri (the Islamic calendar year), or 1380 CE.[163] It is interesting that Uvarova decides to include these mistakes in her article, which serve to underscore her superior knowledge and status as an expert. She certainly could have left them out, but she underscores her expertise. She again returns to the subject of Islamic education: "The sheer number and great scale of the described madrassas proves that Bukhara until the current time serves as one of the main centers of Islamic propaganda and study; in the city, for a population of 100,000, there are up to 200 madrassas, into which pour and as a result from which are spread students and sowers of faith in the steppe and other Muslim centers."[164] Uvarova states that Bukhara is a far more typical Central Asian city than Samarkand or Tashkent: "it seems to us that who has not seen Bukhara, cannot have a clear understanding of the Central Asian city."[165] She goes on to describe the streets, the shops, the mosques, the canals, the people "bronzed as in Egypt, either silent with Eastern subservience (podobostrastiem), or noisy and prone to shouting, as is possible also only in the Orient (Vostok)."[166] The two Cossacks who accompanied them during the visit to the protectorate, she declares, did so more due to honour (pochet) than precaution, since the people, "even in the very crowded centers, behaved towards us, though with great curiosity, but in a completely friendly way, even gently."[167] By freight-passenger train, they travelled from Bukhara to Bairam-Ali, close to the Imperial Murghab Estate, founded in 1887, at which a dam had been built; Golovnina was to visit the estate in 1898. As Maya Peterson notes, "The estate was to serve as a model plantation for experimentation with seeds and modern agricultural techniques and thereby to 'plant culture among the native population.'"[168] Uvarova was interested mostly in the Bairam-Ali-Khan Fortress, the closest ruins to the estate, and proclaims that local officials should measure, draw, study, and describe the ruins of the fortress, especially since they have the personnel to do so.[169] She explores the extensive ruins around the Murghab Estate, which includes an entire town of graves, but notes that there are far more near the estate than she even mentions: "Describing the ruins of Bairam-Ali, Abdulla-khan, Iskander and Giaur-kal, we make no pretence of having described all of the ruins that surround the Murghab Estate; these ruins surround it on all sides, for several tens of versts and extend to places that are partly inhabited and now go along the irrigation canals, partly now collapsed and in general take up such an expanse that it is not only difficult to study them but even to generally travel around them in a more or less short time."[170] Uvarova declines to comment on the dam project itself, saying that much had already been written on the topic, but does describe a visit to Merv and some Turkmen there, noting that although they were once predators, they are now calm and suited, in the eyes of the Russians, for settlement. Uvarova praises the Turkmen for being so much improved from their days of pillage, calling them more self-confident than Tajiks and less sly than Uzbeks; she also praises their beautiful white teeth, their horsemanship and their horses.[171] Uvarova references more glancingly what Rossikova would say outright: that Russians, twenty-five years after the initial conquest, are still somewhat afraid of Turkmen, due to their violent past.[172] Uvarova describes Turkmen women weaving rugs, noting details of their attire; in her memoirs Uvarova declares that Merv rugs are the best.[173] Uvarova ends her account with her party's arrival in Baku on 6 October 1890.[174]

Uvarova works hard in the essay to establish and maintain an air of authority and expertise, specifically calling out others' (inevitably, men's) mistakes and giving some approving words to younger male officials, indicating her status as a senior expert and an adjudicator of the preparedness of junior officials for their jobs. She sees the purpose of the essay as multi-pronged: to describe a trip that she, a prominent archaeologist, was invited to take to the Turkestan Exhibition, to describe for those who could not attend the general experience of being in Central Asia and attending the exhibition, to describe from an archaeologist's point of view some of the main architectural and cultural treasures of the region, to give her viewpoint on Russia's relative success in "civilizing" the region, and to adjudicate how Russian officials are fulfilling their jobs, especially in terms of accumulating knowledge about the area and "properly" exploring it. It is clear that she is quite critical about the lack of "real excavations" at Afrasiab and the neglect, in her view, of vast quantities of meaningful ruins near the Murghab Estate; by praising both Klemm and Kal', she seems to implicitly criticize others whose preparation was not as extensive as theirs; she clearly also criticizes such figures as Komarov and others whom she finds both ignorant and neglectful of the scholarly imperative to explore many of the ruins, or who are simply treasure hunters who want to accumulate valuable items. However, given her high social position, and arguably her status as a woman, her critiques are somewhat veiled; either she trusts that what she says will be heeded or she is loath to perturb her close connections to the powerful, such as Vrevskii, Vishegradskii, and Witte.

According to Ekaterina Pravilova, Uvarova had strong views about the status of antiquities and became involved in some contentious arguments over religious antiquities in particular, especially in her role as president of the Moscow Archaeological Society. Uvarova, whom Pravilova calls "virulent," was particularly interested in transferring religious items she thought were poorly cared for into museums, but was also competitive about it.[175] In 1893, Pravilova notes, Uvarova rushed to the Kremlin to insist that a precious gospel from 1117 be rescued from a fire at the Archangel Cathedral, during which episode she was at first not recognized but "raised my voice and told them who I was" after which they brought the gospel, which was later moved to a safer place, although not to the Historical Museum where Uvarova wanted it moved.[176] On another occasion, when two men had been sent to buy, with permission, some religious antiquities from Murom's Annunciation Cathedral for the Russian Museum, Uvarova, whose estate was nearby, heard of some "speculators" trying to buy religious art and sent the police to arrest them. They were arrested but let go upon showing their references from the museum.[177] Uvarova lived an active professional life, departing for the Caucasus in 1917, and leaving Russia altogether in 1919, when she lived in Serbia and Slovenia until her death in 1924.

Anna Rossikova

The final traveller-writer discussed here is Anna Efimovna Rossikova (exact dates unknown), who was married to the well-known Russian zoologist (primarily entomologist and ornithologist) Konstantin Niko-laevich Rossikov (1854–?).[178] Rossikova wrote several articles about travel in the Caucasus and Central Asia, at least one short story under her own name, and according to some sources also wrote under the pseudonym "Sardar."[179] She was a member of the Caucasian section of the Russian Geographical Society and took part in a scholarly meeting on geography, ethnography and anthropology in 1890.[180] She wrote a pair of two-part articles about travelling by boat along the Amu-Darya River in 1898.[181] She begins the first of her two articles by drawing knowing attention to the fame and importance of the historically named Oxus, situating it as ancient but also now Russian, with its source designated as on "the border of Russian dominions and Afghanistan," in other words, on the border of the British Empire. Since the publication of John Wood's *Personal Narrative of a Journey to the Source of the River Oxus* in 1841, which was followed by other accounts as well as a famous poem by Matthew Arnold called *Sohrab and Rustum*, the Oxus had played a role in both the British and Russian imagination,[182] and Rossikova in her account claims it as being now essentially Russian: "The great river of the desert, the classical Oxus and Arab Dzhi-khun, begins almost on the border of Russian dominions and Afghanistan from the broad, high plateau of the Pamir, which is between the Tian-Shan in the north and the Hindu Kush in the south and reaches on average about 10 ½ t. f. [thousand feet] above sea level."[183] Because Rossikova begins with a description of the fame and history of the Amu-Darya, or Oxus, and because her article is written in educated Russian and published in a well-known journal, and perhaps because she expects readers to recognize her last name, she does not describe (except for briefly, in the second part of the second article) the reason for the trip or with whom she was travelling. Such phrases as "our Asian possessions"[184] and a positive description of the

Russian sections of the town of Chardzhou (present-day Turkmenabat, Turkmenistan) and its potential, due to the railroad, to be a prominent town in the region, make it clear that the writer is a member of the Russian upper classes who has come to describe a place and an experience that is new to her, if not to others, but with the novelty of travelling by means uncommon to her class – by small, locally made boat, a choice that eventually proves to be almost fatal.

In her account, Rossikova divides her attention among various topics, including the experience of boat travel, the sightseeing along the way, such as the appearance of ancient ruins, descriptions of people, plants, animals; she also addresses the river as an entity unto itself. She emphasizes the fact that during her trip in 1898, the Russians were celebrating twenty-five years since the conquest of Khiva.[185] With an eye on the Great Game rivalry, she also mentions such details as the fact that the Russian troops had moved from Chardzhou to the Afghan border and as a result there was less activity in the city.[186] Rossikova writes with pride about the twenty-five-year anniversary of the conquest; she worries whether the government has properly repaid the many sacrifices borne by the Russian people in the conquest of Central Asia and hopes that a new era will begin.[187] Rossikova ends her first two-part article with the announcement that when they arrived at Petro-Aleksandrovsk (present-day Turtkul, Uzbekistan) on 29 May, the town was hung with flags and lanterns in anticipation of the coming illuminations, celebrating "the twenty-fifth anniversary of the taking of Khiva and its founding," which had occurred on 28 May 1873.[188]

Unlike Golovnina or certainly Dukhovskaia, although similar to Apreleva (as a writer of fiction), Rossikova writes almost without divulging the participants or purpose of the trip. However, given that the reader discovers that, due to a terrifying and nearly fatal storm, an entire precious collection of insects was lost, entomology seemed to be the primary reason for the journey, although this fact comes to light only in the latter part of the second half of the second article. Rossikov, Rossikova's husband, published on locusts in Central Asia after their trip.[189]

By 1898, it was relatively easy to travel by rail to many parts of Turkestan, which the Rossikovs did in travelling to Khardzhui [Chardzhou/Turkmenabat], and many travellers had by then been to the region. However, travelling along the river by small boat was unusual; Rossikova describes how she and her party came to travel via "kaiuk," or Uzbek flat-bottomed boat. First, a long description indicates that the Amu-Darya is a "wandering" river, with banks that constantly change over time. Further, ship travel is said (by the local administration and by "leading people" to be infrequent and unreliable, hence travel by kaiuk is deemed preferable.[190] It was also the case, Rossikova mentions several times, that there had been severe flooding that spring (they were there beginning in late May) and roads were impassable.

It is clear from context that Rossikova's small Russian party, perhaps consisting only of herself and Rossikov, is more or less in charge, able to "order" the pilot, or darga, where to stop. Indeed, she avers, the darga is actually an elected position, decided by the crew, who pick the most experienced boatsman.[191] Rossikova, without giving anything away, notes numerous caveats about this travel at the beginning of her first article; although the larger boats travel infrequently and sometimes unpredictably, Russians, even those who travel on business, do not use them: "It turned out that, according to our personal experience, we were convinced that one should never blindly believe even knowledgeable people ... Traveling on the Amu-Darya by boat entails such deprivations, that hardly any Russian people travel that way willingly, even the leadership of the region, who are connected to the necessities of service, almost never cast a glance on such a distant region (dal'niuiu okrainu) of our Asiatic possessions."[192] Rossikova includes a footnote stating that maps of the river are so poor that a caravan route is shown on the wrong side of the river.

During the first part of the trip, from Chardzhou to Petro-Aleksandrovsk, there are ten local workers, Khivan Uzbeks, who row the boat, of whom one is also a cook. The boat carried goods owned by an Armenian merchant who was also part of the company; one of the "subplots" of the story is that he uses the "high position of the Russian travelers" to get customs officials at Khiva to process his wares quickly; in fact, they leave without the full required stamp because they grow impatient, having already waited three hours; Rossikova notes that sometimes merchants had to wait for days at a time.[193] On the second part of the trip, from Petro-Aleksandrovsk to Nukus, the group was smaller and so was the boat; there were only four crew members and no cargo, although there was a translator who also served as the party's cook.[194] Rossikova and her husband travelled back to Petro-Aleksandrovsk from Nukus on land, and her account includes elements of both directions of the travel, but the primary focus of the account is on river travel. Although Rossikova does not say so, it seems likely that because her husband, the entomologist and ornithologist, determined the style of travel partly in order to make observations, it was better, despite various inconveniences and discomforts, to take a smaller boat that could more easily be guided to observe the local fauna and flora, about which Rossikova herself provides much information, including scientific names of plants. She frequently lists names of animals, fish, birds, or plants, and describes in particular the sightings of birds, such as when they saw the first loon of the trip.[195]

Quite differently from Potanina, Golovnina, Apreleva, and even to some extent Praskov'ia Uvarova, who always retain a certain amount of respect and empathy for the local people who fall under the all-encompassing view of their colonial gaze – particularly women, with whom Golovnina, Potanina, and Apreleva, in particular, tend to identify – Rossikova's initial ethnographically styled description of a Turkmen family is somewhat dismissive and betrays little concern for the feelings of the hostess. Describing the poverty of the dwelling into which they have been invited, which is devoid of the rugs that richer families display – and despite noting that the Turkmen were extremely hospitable ("as are all Asiatic peoples"[196]) – when the hostess proffers food they find less than appetizing, such as "a gray mass called butter," airan (a milk product), and flour, "we refused, saying that we came not to eat, but to look at how the Turkmen live."[197] At this, the hostess, apparently hoping to offer something more appealing to her guests, sends for some fresh goats' milk (Rossikova does not record her response but notes that "the milk of livestock here is rarely tasty"); apparently the Russians do not partake, although the kaiuchki, the boat workers, are delighted with the offerings and "probably would have sat for quite some time, if we had not reminded them of the necessity of going farther."[198] Afterward, the Russians observe weaving taking place in another yurt, and the father of the family accompanies them back to the boat and asks for sugar for his youngest children. Golovnina, in a similar circumstance, describes the local nomad women much more empathetically, and partakes of the food offered, showing awareness of the difficulty of obtaining and preparing it and the trouble taken to treat her and her husband as honoured guests. Apreleva in her stories goes much further, on occasion creating characters, including those of local nomads, whose lives are almost entirely independent of Russians and focusing on them as human beings whose outer appearance and way of life is less important than their inner emotional life. Potanina, too, is very positive about local hospitality and describes local foods in detail. Rossikova writes somewhat more sensitively about women in her second two-part article, describing the hard lives of Uzbek women, but it is a rather impersonal description, even though she says that she was able, as a woman, to enter women's quarters. She also addresses, to an extent, the difficult lives of the "Kirghiz" and Karakalpak nomads, declaring that the women of the latter group often fled their husbands or killed themselves due to difficult conditions,[199] while the nomad women were some of the "freest Asiatic women," comparable to Russian women in terms of their social role within their own society.[200]

Rossikova is capable of making fairly sensitive observations about the overuse of the land and the increasing desertification that is occurring along the river, although she does not necessarily associate the numerous canals diverting water from the river with the latter. Rossikova sees the effects of Russian colonization on the use of the land primarily as good, but she acknowledges that the Turkmen, who were formerly nomads, if frightening ones, are suffering as they try to adapt to a mostly non-nomadic way of life in a land that she herself acknowledges several times is entirely dependent on water supply. She acknowledges the small size of their population and even says that their villages "look sad."[201]

The second of the two articles, "Po Amu-Dare ot Petro-Aleksandrovska do Nukusa" ("Along the Amu-Darya from Petro-Aleksandrovsk to Nukus"), is far more ethnographic in nature than the first. Rossikova begins once again with an extensive description of Central Asia and the areas near Khiva. In the second part of the article, the actual river trip continues. First and foremost in this article Rossikova focuses on the Ural Cossacks, who had been exiled to the region in 1875 for refusing to comply with new and repressive laws. The Ural Cossacks, always "eccentric and obstreperous," were originally the Iaik Cossacks, renamed after their participation in the Pugachev Rebellion, and were among the most troublesome for the Russian government to deal with.[202] They had their own longstanding methods of providing troops to the Russian government; they were among the wealthiest Cossacks due to their trade in sturgeon roe and were also Old Believers. Attempted reforms by the Russian government led to passive rebellion by the Ural Cossacks and resulted in the deportation of 2,500 of them without trial, 2,000 of them to the Amu-Darya region. The voisko was also assessed at the sum of 50,000 roubles to pay for the deportation. "The deportees repeatedly tried to avert their fate by refusing to cooperate. They would lie down on the road and on one occasion refused to mount camels that had been provided for their transportation. Some were persuaded to go along by others who believed that it was prophesied that they would go to the East to spread the Christian faith. On arriving near the Amu-Darya, they refused to build settlements, firm in their belief that they would be permitted to go home."[203] Rossikova praises the Cossacks for bringing a Russianizing influence to the Amu-Darya region despite their exiled status and their "fanatical" devotion to their Old Believer tradition – they refuse to eat together even with Orthodox Russians. Mostly they are literate, Rossikova notes with approval, and even women know how to read.[204] One of the more revealing exchanges occurs when Rossikova and her party encounter Ural Cossacks personally; these Cossacks are first mentioned in the first article and then are described in great detail in the second.[205] At first puzzled that the Cossack men, who are fishing, show so little interest in their boat, which is moored next to the bank, Rossikova's curiosity is at last satisfied when one Cossack comes over to her boat, although he actually comes over to talk to the rowers, which he does speaking "po-kirgizski."[206] Learning that there are Russians aboard, he inquires "with amazement" what captivity ("nevolia") brought them there.[207] Rossikova does not record her answer, but the Cossack tells his own tale of woe, indicating that twenty-five years before (coinciding, of course, with the twenty-five-year anniversary of the taking of Khiva, although Rossikova does not make the connection explicitly) the Ural Cossacks were exiled to the area because of a disagreement with the government, and although they are now free to return, they would feel just as foreign at home as they do in Central Asia and thus do not plan to go. "'They are Russianizing the area on our bones!' said our chance interlocutor, not without bitterness. Despite the incongruity of such an explanation, there was no possibility of dissuading the Uralian. To this day they are deeply convinced that they carry a heavy cross in the name of saving their homeland. All the Uralians, it turns out, are from the village Shi-mal', where they have their huts, wives and children ... 'We live a life of suffering,' our interlocutor said."[208] Rossikova goes on to claim that the Cossacks have made themselves at home and gained respect from the locals, with whom they live in peace after initial difficulties, but she appears deaf to understanding how the Cossacks feel about their treatment by the government, as well as to their intense self-awareness of themselves as having been forced to move to the region against their will and that this benefited the government.

Rossikova also spends a great deal of the second article describing the Uzbeks, saying they are the "ruling nationality ('natsional'nost') of the Khiva oasis."[209] She praises them for their "regular features" ("pravil'nye cherti"), their settled, agricultural ways and claims they are the hardest workers of the Khiva oasis.[210] She describes the difficulty of getting water raised up to the level of the fields and notes the typical scene of an "unhappy animal, usually a camel" that must continually walk in a circle, blindfolded, in order to haul up the water with a water wheel. She allies her point of view with Europeans such as a visiting Englishman who invented a machine to do the labour and thus prevent this cruelty to animals; however, it cost quite a bit more than the usual equipment and hence did not succeed. Rossikova goes on to say that twenty-five or thirty years before, it was human beings who were forced to do this labour, both prisoners and slaves, most of them Persian but some of them also Russians, taken prisoner by the Turkmen.[211] A trade in prisoners, she claims, took place until the Russian conquest, but "slavery and enslavement ('rabstvo i nevol'nichestvo') in Khiva and Bukhara are now destroyed."[212] Rossikova often cites the (presumably Russian or European) traveller, "puteshestvennik" (which is also what she calls herself), as in "many travelers will find that Uzbeks are the more open, honest people, and in relation to religion less fanatical and hypocritical," or "the safety of the Russian population will involuntarily stand out to every traveler."[213] Rossikova praises the local population for being averse to stealing and for not drinking alcohol. Rossikova's stereotyped expectations are fully entrenched, however; she states that "the hot climate makes them [the Uzbeks] susceptible to Oriental laziness and luxury"[214] and, in a generally sympathetic if impersonal description of Uzbek women and their difficult lives, notes that the Uzbek hostess lies on cushions in "lazy Oriental splendor" for whole days with her little children – a perplexing thought to anyone who has actually taken care of several small children at once.[215]

Rossikova says that she was able to visit women's quarters, as well as guest quarters for foreigners, and describes them as small, cramped, and fairly dirty.[216] However, they sometimes contained western furnishings, such as a bed and table. She describes Uzbek cooking and fruit orchards, noting that the Quran prescribes that husbands must provide their wives meat twice a week, usually Thursday and Sunday.[217] She declares that women fear the "coldness of a husband" ("kholodnost' muzha") and infertility most of all, and describes her disapproval of the young age at which girls are married off: "I saw women who were married at eleven and even ten years of age, and these were not exceptional cases. A woman grows up and is formed already in a state of marriage."[218] From this childish age, Rossikova declares, the woman begins a battle with "unseen, but always enemy forces" under whose yoke she will live all her life.

Rossikova also enters into the perennial Russian conversation about women covering their faces, noting that she has "more than once" ("ne raz") discussed this with Uzbeks and Sarts, and they all claim that it is women who insist on covering up, not men who require it.[219] In general, Rossikova sounds very distant when trying to sum up an entire group in an ethnographic manner, but less so when actually in conversation with individual people, although she never actually gives anyone's name, even that of her husband for that matter, except near the end of the second two-part article.

Rossikova also describes in detail the Karakalpaks, a Turkic ethnic group whose names means "black hat" and who Rossikova says used to live near Russians on the Volga and may be remnants of the Pechenegs.[220] Upon visiting a Karakalpak village, she says the inhabitants became frightened at the "unfamiliar faces and the carriage" and ran away, but later returned.[221] She emphasizes both in the first half of the article and in the second that Karakalpak women often ran away from their husbands or from an unwanted marriage, or killed themselves, often via hanging.[222]

The most dramatic episode of the trip occurs when a large storm breaks out on the river, swamping the boat with huge waves and high winds, and the group is in danger of drowning. Rossikova ascribes their survival to her husband, who took charge, galvanizing everyone into action, even the translator, who started bailing water. Even so, after another two and a half hours, they were losing hope, even sending out a message in a bottle to try to leave a record of their plight. Then the wind changed and they were able to reach land. Much of their baggage was gone, including most of their food and the precious entomological collection that had been gathered. Only some mutton, tea, and sugar remained. Perhaps because of the extremity of the experience, Rossikova and her group eagerly greeted some Karakalpak fishermen who had brought their boat nearby, bought two barbels (a type of fish) and a handful of salt from them, and compared notes about the storm. The fishermen told them that many people had drowned during the storm and that even the oldest people in their village did not recall that kind of severe storm occurring in June.[223]

Rossikova ends her second article on a solemn note, describing the poverty of the Karakalpaks and settled "Kirghiz" and the desperation of many women exacerbated by the poverty.[224] Rossikova seems to identify more closely with the local people after the storm, appreciating her commonality with others, but she also reaches her limit: "However interesting it was to become familiar with the region in all its fullness, after the terrible storm I no longer had the strength to battle with all the contingencies, and ended my trip along the Amu-Darya at Nukus."[225] After the terrifying episode on the river, there seemed to be a recognition on Rossikova's part that the environment's harshness had much to do with people's difficult lives, rather than in how "civilized" or "developed" they were as people. After the storm, when she was glad merely to be alive, she shared something in common with the Karakalpak fishermen and also appreciated their local knowledge and their ability to provide fish and salt, something her group needed. The wildness of the river during the storm was simply not controllable by anyone, and Rossikova, writing from the first person, states that she could no longer "battle against all the contingencies" of nature and weather and was no longer willing to travel by river. Interestingly, Rossikova ends her account at this point, and rather than recounting the return to Petro-Aleksandrovsk over land, she instead interpolates it into her overall description of the trip from the perspective of river travel. While it seems that travelogues were not usually expected to be overly polished pieces of prose, it stands out that her account ends with a kind of expression of defeat; it was more usual to describe a return to a point of entry to the region, a kind of orderly wrapping up such as that performed by Uvarova or, in the longer accounts, Golovnina or Dukhovskaia. Little more is known about Rossikova; she attended several meetings of the Congress of Naturalists and Physicians in 1889 in St. Petersburg, 1894 in Moscow, and 1901 in St. Petersburg.[226]

Conclusion

The definition of what it was to be a scientist, and to write "scientific" work, was broad in the late Russian nineteenth century, with genres overlapping in many cases with *belles lettres*, travel literature, and quasi-memoiristic writing. To paraphrase Fritjof Schenk, who noted that in memoirs, women were allowed a broader emotional (and arguably, more personal) range than men, this also seems to be true for the kind of writing engaged in by Potanina, Uvarova, and Rossikova, although Uvarova's written persona appeared to be quite unemotional except when describing her admiration for the skill utilized in Timurid building. Ol'ga Fedchenko left little of her own personal writing, but it is interesting to note the extent, as attested by Ivanov, to which she had to work to win over sceptical men, both as a scholar and as a woman, when she joined the expedition to Iskender-Kul. As a published scholar and authority later in life, however, she seemed to be well recognized. Uvarova, too, received official recognition, in her case as an archaeologist, but only after her husband died and she was able to become a member of the Imperial Moscow Archaeological Society (and then its president). Even as a recognized archaeologist, as late as her 1890 trip to Tashkent, she felt the need to remind (or inform) readers of her credentials; tellingly, she also signed herself as countess; her rank was as important as her profession. Potanina's writing varied with its audience; her essay on the Buriats was more typically ethnographic in nature, while her story about Dordzhi was oriented towards children but also towards explaining, in a way that resisted othering, what Buriat life was like. Several commentators noted that Potanina had many Buriat friends, and Buriat and "Kirghiz" students and acquaintances visited her in St. Petersburg, where she took them to see the cultural sights and taught them Russian.[227] These personal relationships, which existed on her own territory, so to speak, differentiated her from any of the other scientifically oriented writers addressed here, who met imperial "others" only on their travels and not when in Russia proper. The sensitivity of these women to other women in societies quite different from their own was variable, but significant; arguably the spectre of Russian inequality and violence towards women in Russia itself informed their views of women in other cultures, as did Russian women's quest for education and more rights.

Conclusion

The Russian women writers, travellers, and scientists who in the nineteenth century travelled to Central Asia and territories adjacent to it, both within and beyond the Russian sphere of influence in the region, were in many ways little different from their male equivalents in terms of outlook and ideology. They strongly supported Russia's civilizing and colonizing mission, but they also had to navigate, or simply submit to, the powerful discourses of male-dominated science and socially defined femininity, at times creating their own forms of writing and self-definition, and other times, as with Ol'ga Fedchenko, conforming to the dominant paradigm. In many cases they represented the "smaller lives and lesser figures" that Guelke and Morin argue make up much of the rhetorical fabric and practices of particular time periods.[1] At the same time, their literary, scholarly, and artistic contributions make evident the perspectives of the ruling class and the kind of cross-societal work that was needed to carry out a widely realized project of colonization, one that included the cultural contributions of women in a way that also stressed the apparent superiority of women's status in "European" culture.

Two writers as different as Varvara Dukhovskaia, who prided herself on her high position in society and her place in the pecking order as the wife of a general and governor-general, and Praskov'ia Uvarova, from a similarly prominent family and married to the well-known scholar Count Aleksei Uvarov, show on the one hand how similar perspectives on the Russian empire could be for the highborn, but also how the possibility of a career could make for an entirely different sense of a "woman's empire." Both women were married for about twenty-five years, after which they were widowed; Dukhovskaia considered that after her husband's death, there was nothing more to tell of her life, while after she was widowed, Uvarova was finally able to join, and then become the president of, the Moscow Archaeological Society, becoming a force to be reckoned with. Uvarova had already done archaeological work during her marriage, while Dukhovskaia considered her role as wife, hostess, and society lady (even when she hated the latter two positions) to be her métier, although she dreamed, it would seem, of a musical career, and published her writing. Both write with great authority born of high position, and of archeological knowledge, in the case of Uvarova, both move in the highest social and political circles, and both strongly advocate for Russia's civilizing mission. Dukhovskaia, however, writes almost exclusively of her own interactions with the world, while Uvarova intends to impress and educate her readers with her knowledge of history and architecture, not hiding her personal views but imagining an audience beyond her social peers.

Elena Apreleva, whose connection to Turgenev as a quite young woman certainly helped her launch her writing career, continued to pursue writing throughout her life. Having become a writer and editor before her marriage, she continued to publish during it. By embracing both a male and first-person plural narrator much of the time in her Central Asian stories, and by diverting focus from these narrators to the greatest extent possible, she decentred her own story from her narratives, and in many of them, also decentred Russians themselves, making many non-Russians the foci of her stories. She incorporated depictions of everyday Russians, Russian soldiers, and peasant transplants, and also created stories that did not include any Russian characters at all. Only a few stories incorporate overtly female perspectives, but by saying little about her male narrator and by telling stories mainly from a point of view of what appears to be a married couple, she includes perspectives of those who do not have power and by necessity usually does not delve into a male-only world. Some of her male characters are powerless, disadvantaged, or, in the case of Dr. Kallinik, in a kind of destructive exile that leads to suicide; she also effectively estranges Russian ways in many cases by presenting Russians as seen through non-Russian eyes. Tales of a young Muslim boy from Samarkand, of the music of a travelling bard, and of the effects of conquest on a nomad family all serve to shift perspective away from normalizing the Russian presence.

Elena Blavatskaia also spoke with the authority of a member of the nobility but emphasized concerns about the plight of the powerless and constantly professed Russian patriotism despite her American citizenship. Notably, she was a person who made her living through writing, with which she helped support her sister's family. While her travel writings emphasize spirituality, the traveller's body, which is so often downplayed in European travel writing, is a topic of discussion and often humour in her narratives, and the work of the many servants, bearers, and cooks who make travel possible is at least acknowledged by her. Her Russian audience was meant to understand that India was close to Russia spiritually and linguistically, and that knowledge of Indian spirituality was in accordance with the most modern ways of thinking. Although British imperial rule comes in for withering criticism, Blavatskaia defends Russia's treatment of her imperial subjects and Russia's expansion in Central Asia.

Iuliia Golovnina and Anna Rossikova, both participating in expeditions essentially as guests, emphasize moving through the challenging landscape, whether the Pamir Mountains or the Amu-Darya River. Each experiences either frightening moments – for Golovnina, as she rode a horse over a steep pass or crossed a swift river on a camel – or what was clearly abject terror, for Rossikova, as a powerful storm nearly sank her boat. Both have opportunities to meet local women, be served food by them, and to take note of their clothing, dwellings, and way of life. Both employ judgmental descriptions of local people (and Cossack exiles, in the case of Rossikova), as well as more intimate, less othering descriptions. Golovnina makes special note of how she and Nadezhda Barteneva managed their clothing and appearance during the trip, while Rossikova says nothing about the fact that she is a woman, except that it at times allows her in to visit women's quarters, and she notes with dismay the terrible inequalities women in some ethnic groups suffer in marriage. Both felt that what was unusual about their respective trips – the difficulty and severity of the Pamirs, the rarely experienced (by Russians) kaiuk boat trip – made them noteworthy. For Golovnina, of course, the lure of the *Ovis ammon polii* (Marco Polo) sheep also placed her trip in the context of Great Game hunting competitions; Rossikova also alludes to Great Game rivalries.

Finally, Ol'ga Fedchenko and Aleksandra Potanina were ultimately both full-fledged expedition members, scholars, and producers of recognized published work. Both travelled fairly early on to places that were either undergoing colonization or were under the control of foreign governments, and both faced real danger. Ol'ga Fedchenko took responsibility for editing the work that made her husband's name, mostly eliding her own work and participation in the process, but later continued as a professional botanist, publishing in her own name. Potanina took as a main objective to observe, meet, and describe the women of the places she visited. With a particular focus on the ethnographic details of these women and their lives – the paraphernalia of their everyday life, their clothing, their methods of cooking and maintaining a household, Potanina recorded what she saw but also encountered elements of women's lives that did not fit pre-conceived Western ideas or patterns of women's behaviour, such as the power and rituals of shamanesses and out-of-wedlock births that were greeted with approval. Two remarkable women, Maria Nalivkina, who lived among Uzbeks and co-wrote a study of them, and Lidiia Poltoratskaia, an early in-the-field photographer, have been studied elsewhere (in the case of Nalivkina) or deserve additional study.

While the women addressed here left disparate accounts about a broad range of places from Central Asia to India to China, their imperial consciousness is inscribed in their writings, artwork, and daily lives. Apparently secure in their own identity as representatives of a civilizing and scientific class, their view of the Russian empire was usually an endorsement of Russian practices and participation in them. Anglo-India may have loomed as rival, comparator, and sometimes threat, but these Russians usually felt they were more humane, more accepting of difference, and more aware of the negative consequences of empire than their chief rivals. However, these primarily upper-class women also noticed that Russian peasants lived far more poorly than their Central Asian counterparts, and in far more squalor, and suffered from the ills of alcoholism, theft, and cheating, and recognized that, by comparison, many Central Asian, Buriat, or Mongolian people lived better and arranged their lives in what the upper-class Russians found to be a superior way. This viewpoint was at times linked with the fear that Russian rule was bringing specifically Russian ills to Turkestan, a concern that was widespread among the writers and scholars. Even if their travel experiences were not greatly different from those of men, their attention to the less powerful was often evident, as was their interest in and ability to observe women's lives, which often highlighted social disparities, both cultural and colonial, in Central Asia and beyond.

Notes

Introduction

1 N.N. Karazin, *Na Dalekikh okrainakh*, "Где-то далеко на Востоке открылась какая-то страна. Туда нужны люди, туда их ищут и зовут, льготы разные обещают: уж не махнуть ли?. ." ch. 7, http://az.lib.ru/k/karazin_n_n /text_1872_na_dalekih_okrainah.shtml. English translation by Anthony W. Sariti, *In the Distant Confines*, AuthorHouse, 2007, 90.

2 Elena Andreeva, in her *Russian Central Asia in the Works of Nikolai Karazin, 1842–1908: Ambivalent Triumph* (Palgrave, 2021), also singles out this phrase, 188.

3 Karazin, *Na Dalekikh okrainakh*, ch. 10, *In the Distant Confines*, 117–18.

4 Some parts of several different chapters of this study previously appeared as "Russian Women Travelers in Central Asia," *Russian Review* 70 (January 2011): 1–19.

5 Sara Mills, *Gender and Colonial Space* (Manchester University Press, 2005), 16, describes women's participation in the British Empire in these terms.

6 Mills, *Gender and Colonial Space*, 13.

7 Mary Louise Pratt, *Imperial Eyes: Travel Writing and Transculturation* (Routledge, 1992), 29, cited in Mills, 95.

8 Sarah Mills, "Gender and Colonial Space," *Gender, Place and Culture: A Journal of Feminist Geography* 3, no. 2 (1996): 125–48, 140. See also Indira Ghose, *Women Travellers in Colonial India* (Oxford University Press, 1999), 139.

9 Mills, *Gender and Colonial Space*, 15.

10 Mills, *Gender and Colonial Space*, 16.

11 See Jeff Sahadeo, "Home and Away: Why the Asian Periphery Matters in Russian History," *Kritika: Explorations in Russian and Eurasian History* 16, no. 2 (Spring 2015, New Series): 375–88, 379; see also Adeeb Khalid, "Backwardness and the Quest for Civilization: Early Soviet Central Asia in Comparative Perspective," *Slavic Review* 65, 2 (2006): 231–5.

12 The Pamirs, a mountain range that forms part of the Himalayas, currently mostly in Tajikistan, were a contested border region among the Chinese, Russian, and British territories. See John F. Shroder, ch. 9, "Afghanistan Border Fixing," *Natural Resources in Afghanistan: Geographic and Geologic Perspectives on Centuries of Conflict,* 2014, 280–300.

13 M.P. Cherskaia, "Vospominaniia o Kolymskoi ekspeditsii 1892 g.," in I.D. Cherskii, *Neopublikovannye stat'i, pis'ma i dnevniki. Stat'i o I. D. Cherskom i A. I. Cherskom* (Irkutsk: Irkutskoe knizhoe izdatel'stvo, 1956). See also O.A. Val'kova, *Shturmuia tsitadel' nauki, zhenshchiny-uchenye Rossiiskoi imperii* (Moscow: Novoe Literaturnoe Obozrenie, 2019), 411–13. See also Tat'iana Danilova, *Bogini dalekikh stranstvii* (Veche), 2006.

14 Ol'ga Lobri, "Ot Astrakhani do Margelana (putevye nabroski) Avgust' 1895 goda," *Russkii vestnik* 259, no. 2 (1899): 639–49; 260, no. 4: 601–12; 605–7. Biography at http://book.uraic.ru/elib/authors/gorbunov/sl-11.htm.

15 *Muslim Women of the Fergana Valley: A 19th-century Ethnography from Central Asia,* Vladimir Nalivkin and Maria Nalivkina, edited by Marianne Kamp, translated by Mariana Markova and Marianne Kamp (Bloomington and Indianapolis: Indiana University Press, 2016). See in particular the editor's introduction.

16 Lidiia Poltoratskaia, *Al'bom tipov i vidov Zapadnoi Sibiri,* St. Petersburg, 1879, "Poezdka po Kitaiskoi granitse ot Altaia do Tarbagataia," *Russkii vestnik* 93, no. 6 (1871): 580–661; "Bremenskaia ekspeditsiia v Semipalatinskoi oblasti," *Priroda i okhota* 1, no. 3 (1879): 23–52. See also Elena Barkhatova, *Russkaia Svetopis': Pervyi vek fotoiskusstva 1839–1914,* Al'ians-Liki Rossii, St. Petersburg, 2009, 162, with photos by Poltoratskaia on 170–1, as well as Natalia Matkhanova and Natalia Aleksandrova, "First Ladies. The Province of Siberia, 19th Century," *Science, First Hand* 15, no. 3 (25 June 2007): 80–91. https://scfh.ru/en/papers/first-ladies-the-province-of-siberia-19th-century/.

17 Marie Ujfalvy-Bourdon, *De Paris À Samarkand: Le Ferghanah, Le Kouldja Et La Sibérie Occidentale: Impressions De Voyage D'une Parisienne* (Paris, 1876). *Voyage d'une parisienne dans l'Himalaya occidental* (Paris: Hachette, 1887).

18 Isabelle Mary Phibbs, *A Visit to the Russians in Central Asia* (London: K. Paul, Trench, Trübner & co., ltd., 1899).

19 Elizabeth and Nicholas Clinch, *Through a Land of Extremes: The Littledales of Central Asia* (Seattle: Mountaineers Books, 2011). See St. George Littledale, "A Journey across Central Asia," *The Geographical Journal* 3, no. 6 (June 1894): 445–72; "A Journey across the Pamir from North to South," *Proceedings of the Royal Geographical Society and Monthly Record of Geography, New Monthly Series* 14, no. 1 (January 1892): 1–35; "A Journey across Tibet, from North to South, and West to Ladak," *The Geographical*

Journal 7, no. 5 (May 1896): 453–78; and Frank Wallace, "Mr. St. George Littledale's Trophies," *Country Life* (11 February 1911), 196–7. In "A Journey across the Pamir from North to South," Littledale writes, for example, "Mrs. Littledale, the Persian interpreter, and two hunters and myself went forward to parley, and four or five of their men came forward to meet us" (18).

20 Robert Middleton and Huw Thomas, in *Tajikistan and the High Pamirs*, cite Sofiia Skerskaia, Mrs. Leslie Renton (a British woman), and Mrs. Edward Kivekes as women, along with Teresa Littledale, who preceded such travellers as the Golovnins to the Pamirs. *Tajikistan and the High Pamirs: A Companion and Guide* (Hong Kong: Odyssey Books & Guides, 2012), 481. See also chapter five.

21 A.S. Morrison, *Russian Rule in Samarkand 1868–1910* (Oxford, New York: Oxford University Press, 2008), see in particular the section "Russia's Aims in Turkestan," 30–6. Jeff Sahadeo notes that Governor-General Kaufman (served 1867–82) sought the extension of the railway to Tashkent immediately, wishing to integrate the empire and show colonial progress, but it was extended only for military reasons – to Samarkand in 1888, with permission to extend it to Tashkent given only in 1895. Jeff Sahadeo, *Russian Colonial Society in Tashkent, 1865–1923* (Bloomington: Indiana University Press, 2010), 120. See also Steven Marks, *Road to Power: The Trans-Siberian Railroad and the Colonization of Asian Russia 1850–1917* (Ithaca, NY: Cornell University Press), 1991, "Introduction."

22 Ian Campbell, "'Our Friendly Rivals': Rethinking the Great Game in Ya'qub Beg's Kashgaria, 1867–77," *Central Asian Survey* 33, no. 2 (2014): 199–214, citing manuscript article by Morrison, 200. https://spb.hse.ru /en/humart/history/news/137462123.html.

23 For Karazin, see Shafranskaia, *Turkestanskii tekst v russkoi kul'ture: Kolonial'naia proza Nikolaia Karazina*, 2016, Andreeva, *Russian Central Asia in the Works of Nikolai Karazin,* and Emily Laskin, diss., University of California, Berkeley, *Geopoetics and Geopolitics: Landscape, Empire, and the Literary Imagination in the Great Game* (2021). On Il'in, Laskin, "Liberty and License in Nikolai Il'in's *At a New Border*," (AATSEEL paper, 2019) and Elena Govor, *My Dark Brother: The Story of the Illins, a Russian-Aboriginal Family* (Australia: New South Wales Press), 2000.

24 On Russian travelogues to Persia, see Elena Andreeva, *Russia and Iran in the Great Game* (Routledge, 2007). A book called *Writing Travel in Central Asian History*, edited by Nile Green (Indiana University Press, 2014), while an excellent book, does not address any women writers.

25 Eleonora Shafranskaia, *Turkestanskii tekst v russkoi kul'ture: Kolonial' naia proza Nikolaia Karazina (istoriko-literaturnyi i kul'turno-etnograficheskii kommentarii)*, St. Petersburg: Self-published, 2016, and *Tashkentskii*

tekst v russkoi kul'ture (Moscow: Art House Media, 2010), Elena Andreeva, *Russian Central Asia in the Works of Nikolai Karazin, 1842–1908: Ambivalent Triumph* (Palgrave, 2021), and Emily Laskin, *Geopoetics and Geopolitics: Landscape, Empire, and the Literary Imagination in the Great Game.* PhD diss., University of California, Berkeley, 2021.

26 Sarah Mills, *Discourses of Difference: An Analysis of Women's Travel Writing and Colonialism* (London and New York: Routledge, 1991), 106.

27 The Andijan Uprising of 1898 occurred on 17 May, Old Style, when about 1,500 armed men, led by a Sufi sheikh, attacked Andijan. Although the Russian casualties were low, the uprising revealed dissatisfaction with tsarist rule. See Edward Dennis Sokol, *The Revolt of 1916 in Central Asia* (Johns Hopkins University Press, 2016), 51.

28 See, for example, Harsha Ram, *Imperial Sublime: A Russian Poetics of Empire* (Madison: University of Wisconsin Press, 2003), 131–2.

29 Hermann Kreutzmann, *Wakhan Quadrangle: Exploration and Espionage During and after the Great Game* (Wiesbaden, Germany: Harrassowitz Verlag, 2017), 35–40.

30 Yuri Slezkine, *Arctic Mirrors: Russia and the Small Peoples of the North* (Ithaca, NY: Cornell University Press, 1996), 53. (Quoted in John Slocum, "Who, and When, Were the *Inorodtsy*? The Evolution of the Category of 'Aliens' in Imperial Russia." *The Russian Review* 57 [April 1998]: 173–90, 176); see Slocum, 178–81, for discussion of inorodtsy as a juridical term. Slocum provides the translations for the terms on 177.

31 Slocum, "Who, and When, Were the *Inorodtsy*?" 183.

32 See Valerie Kivelson and Ronald Grigor Suny, *Russia's Empires* (Oxford, 2017), 166–7.

33 Kappeler, *The Russian Empire: A Multiethnic History* (London: Routledge, 2001), chs. 4–5, 114–70, "second class" quote from 169.

34 Kappeler, *Russian Empire*, 174–5.

35 Kappeler, *Russian Empire*, 183.

36 Kappeler, *Russian Empire*, 194; Morrison, *Russian Rule in Samarkand*, 30.

37 Kivelson and Suny, 211. Turkestan, a Persian word for "land of the Turks," is a Central Asian region that was controlled successively by Persia, Alexander the Great, the Arabs, the Mongol Empire, as well as China, with the western part of the region taken over by Russia until 1990 (see Matthew Kilburn, "Turkistan," entry in *Dictionary Plus History*, Oxford University Press, 2016.)

38 See M.G. Gerard, *Report on the Proceedings of the Pamir Boundary Commission* (Calcutta, Office of the Superintendant of Government Printing, India, 1897).

39 Morrison, "Killing the Cotton Canard," 136. See also Steven Marks, *Road to Power: The Trans-Siberian Railroad and the Colonization of Asian Russia 1850–1917* (Ithaca, NY: Cornell University Press, 1991), and Christian Wolmar, *To the Edge of the World: The Story of the Trans-Siberian Express, the World's Greatest Railroad* (Philadelphia and Great Britain: Perseus Books, 2013).

40 See Fritjof Schenk, "Imperiale Raumerschließung: Die Beherrschung der russischen Weite," *Osteuropa* 55, no. 3 (2005): 33–45.

41 See Jeff Sadaheo, "Visions of Empire: Russia's Place in an Imperial World," *Kritika: Explorations in Russian and Eurasian History* 11, 2 (Spring 2010): 381–409, Mark von Hagen, "Empires, Borderlands, and Diasporas: Eurasia as Anti-Paradigm for the Post-Soviet Era," *The American Historical Review* 109, no. 2 (2004): 445–68; Bruce Grant, *The Captive and the Gift: Cultural Histories of Sovereignty in Russia and the Caucasus: Culture and Society after Socialism* (Ithaca, NY: Cornell University Press, 2009); Alexander Etkind, *Internal Colonization Russia's Imperial Experience* (Oxford: Wiley, 2013); and Andreas Kappeler, *The Russian Empire*, esp. 321–2.

42 Alexander Morrison, "The 'Turkestan Generals' and Russian Military History," *War in History* 26, no. 2 (2019): 153–84, 145–5. See also his "Camels and Colonial Armies: The Logistics of Warfare in Central Asia in the Early 19th Century," *Journal of the Economic and Social History of the Orient* 57, no. 4 (2014): 443–85.

43 Morrison, "Turkestan Generals," 154.

44 Kappeler, *Russian Empire*, 298.

45 Scott C. Matsushita Bailey, *Travel, Science, and Empire: The Russian Geographical Society's Expeditions to Central Eurasia, 1845–1905*. PhD diss., University of Hawaii, Manoa, 2008, 275–7.

46 See, for example, Daniel Brower, *Turkestan and the Fate of the Russian Empire* (London: RoutledgeCurzon, 2003); Jeff Sahadeo, *Russian Colonial Society in Tashkent, 1865–1923* (Bloomington: Indiana University Press, 2007), A.S. Morrison, *Russian Rule in Samarkand 1868–1910: A Comparison with British India* (Oxford University Press, 2008), and Morrison's articles "Introduction: Killing the Cotton Canard and Getting Rid of the Great Game: Rewriting the Russian Conquest of Central Asia, 1814–1895," *Central Asian Survey* 33, no. 2 (2014): 131–42; "'Applied Orientalism' in British India and Tsarist Turkestan," *Comparative Studies in Society and History* 51, no. 3 (July 2009), 619–47; "Twin Imperial Disasters: The Invasions of Khiva and Afghanistan in the Russian and British Official Mind, 1839–1842," *Modern Asian Studies* 48, no. 1 (2014): 253–300. Sahadeo addresses the question of Russian women in Turkestan in particular, he writes: "Women, in elite society as in official ceremonies, continued to

serve as markers of European culture in Russian Tashkent. Central and local newspaper correspondents praised their efforts to uphold European civilization through the wearing of the latest fashions from St. Petersburg to Paris," 65, *Russian Colonial Society in Tashkent*.

47   H.P. Blavatsky, *From the Caves and Jungles of Hindostan*, translated by Boris de Zirkoff (Wheaton, IL: Theosophical Publishing House, 1975), 16.

48   Mills, "Gender and Colonial Space," 136. See also Anthony King, *Colonial Urban Development: Culture, Social Power and Environment* (London: Routledge, 1976).

49   Sahadeo, see in particular ch. 2, "Educated Society, Identity, and Nationality" and ch. 4, "Migration, Class and Colonialism."

50   *Central Asia: 130 Years of Russian Dominance, A Historical Overview*, 3rd edition, edited by Edward Allworth (Durham, NC: Duke University Press, 1994), 485–7.

51   Homi Bhabha, *The Location of Culture* (New York: Routledge, 1994), 153, cited in Éadaoin Agnew, *Imperial Women Writers in Victorian India: Representing Colonial Life, 1850–1910* (Palgrave, 2017), 11.

52   Sahadeo, in particular ch. 2, "Educated Society, Identity and Nationality."

53   Potanina, Aleksandra Viktorovna. *Iz puteshestvii po Vostochnoi Sibiri, Mongolii, Tibetu i Kitaiu; sbornik statei*. Moscow: Izdatel'stvo Geograficheskogo otdeleniia Imperatorskago obshchestva liubitelei estestvoznanie, antropologii i etnografii), 1895.

54   Sahadeo, *Russian Colonial Society in Tashkent*, 50.

55   I.I. Popov, "Pamiati N. M. Iadrintseva i A. V. Potaninoi," *Izvestiia Vostochno-Sibirskogo Otdeleniia Russkogo Geograficheskogo obshchestva* XXV, no. 1 (1894): 1–28, 3–4. Translated by the author. All translations by author unless otherwise indicated.

56   A.P. Fedchenko, *Puteshestvie v Turkestan* 1, part 2 (Izvestiia Imperatorskogo Obshchestva liubitelei Estestvozananiia, Antropologii i Etnografii), 1875, 50. http://books.e-heritage.ru/book/10084193.

57   See Inderpal Grewal, *Home and Harem: Nation, Gender, Empire and the Cultures of Travel* (Durham, NC: Duke University Press, 1996), and Indira Ghose, *Women Travellers in Colonial India* (Oxford: Oxford University Press, 1999). See also Vladimir Nalivkin and Maria Nalivkina, *Muslim Women of the Fergana Valley: A 19th-century Ethnography From Central Asia*, edited by Marianne Kamp.

58   Mills, "Gender and Colonial Space," 140.

59   See Alexis Hofmeister, "Imperial Case Studies: Russian and British Ethnographic Theories," *An Empire of Others: Creating Ethnographic Knowledge in Imperial Russia and the USSR*, edited by Roland Cvetkovski

and Alexis Hofmeister, 23–47. Budapest and New York: Central European University Press, 2014.

60 Aleksandra Viktorovna Potanina, "Iz stranstviia po Uriakhaiskoi zemle," *Iz puteshestvii po Vostochnoi Sibiri, Mongolii, Tibetu i Kitaiu; sbornik statei* (Moscow: Izdatel'stvo Geograficheskogo otdeleniia Imperatorskago obshchestva liubitelei estestvoznanie, antropologii i etnografii, 1895), 71.

61 See A.S. Morrison, *Russian Rule in Samarkand 1868–1910: A Comparison with British India* (Oxford: Oxford University Press, 2008), 35.

62 Mills, *Gender and Colonial Space*, 89, R. Granqvist, "Her Imperial Eyes: A Reading of Mary Wollstonecraft's 'Letters Written during a Short Residence in Sweden, Norway and Denmark,'" *Moderna Sprak* 91, no. 1 (1997): 16–24.

63 Iuliia D. Golovnina, *Na Pamirakh: Zapiski russkoi puteshestvennitsy* (Moscow, Tipo-litografiia T-va I. N. Kushener' i K, 1902), 31: "Впервые мысль о ней зародилась у насъ послѣ посѣщенія Николая Ивановича въ Москвѣ, при чемъ онъ съ такою любовью хвалилъ свой край, такъ убѣждалъ насъ, что путешествовать въ немъ можно безопасно и безъ особыхъ лишеній даже и съ дамами, что мы впервые подумали о такой поѣздкѣ серьезно." ("The first thought of this was conceived by us after a visit of Nikolai Ivanovich in Moscow, during which he praised his region with such love that he convinced us that traveling there could be safe and without any particular privations even with ladies, so that we for the first time thought of such a trip seriously.")

64 Iuliia Golovnina, *Na Pamirakh*, 60. Emphasis in the original.

65 Vladimir Nabokov, *The Gift*, translated by Scammell and Nabokov (New York: Vintage, 1991), 106–7; tellingly, the experience is described in a letter written by the mother. *Dar* (Ann Arbor, MI: Ardis, 1952), 119–20. My thanks to Jenifer Presto for pointing out this episode to me.

66 Mills, *Gender and Colonial Space*, 98.

67 See, for example, *Madame Blavatsky: The Mother of Modern Spirituality*, by Gary Lachman (London: Penguin, 2012); and J. Barton Scott, "Miracle Publics: Theosophy, Christianity, and the Coulomb Affair," *History of Religions* 49, no. 2 (2009): 172–96. doi:10.1086/649525. In the Russian context she is known as Blavatskaia, indicated for example by her signing a copy of her book *The Voice of the Silence* to Tolstoy under that name. An image of the page can be found at http://blavatskynews.blogspot .com/2010/02/hpbs-inscription-to-leo-tolstoys-copy.html. The correct Russian spelling is "Блаватская."

68 Sara Mills, *Gender and Colonial Space*, 84–6.

69 There is a lengthy list of texts to consult on the topic. A few important ones are Susan Layton, *Russian Literature and Empire* (Cambridge:

Cambridge University Press, 1994); Harsha Ram, *The Imperial Sublime: A Russian Poetics of Empire* (Madison: University of Wisconsin, 2006); Bruce Grant, *The Captive and the Gift: Cultural Histories of Sovereignty in Russia and the Caucasus* (Ithaca, NY: Cornell University Press, 2009); Monika Frenkel Greenleaf, *Pushkin and Romantic Fashion* (Stanford, CA: Stanford University Press, 1993); Olga Maiorova, *From the Shadow of Empire: Defining the Russian Nation through Cultural Mythology, 1855–1870* (Madison: University of Wisconsin Press, 2010); G.A. Gukovskii, *Pushkin i russkie romantiki* (Moscow, 1965); Oleg Proskurin, *Poeziia Pushkina, ili podvizhnyi palimpsest* (Moscow: Novoe Literaturnoe obozrenie, 1999); Boris Tomashevskii, *Pushkin*, 2 vols. (Moscow: 1956 and 1961); Stephanie Sandler, *Distant Pleasures: Alexander Pushkin and the Writing of Exile* (Stanford, CA: Stanford University Press, 1989); and Katya Hokanson, *Writing at Russia's Border* (Toronto: University of Toronto Press, 2008).

70 Ivan Turgenev, *Polnoe sobranie sochinenii* (Moscow: Nauka, 1986), ed. Alekseev, vol. 12, 296–7. See Nicholas G. Zekulin, "Turgenev's 'Kroket v Vindzore' ('Croquet at Windsor')," *New Zealand Slavonic Journal*, Ivan Sergeyevich Turgenev 1818–83 (1983): 85–103.

71 Sahadeo, *Russian Colonial Society in Tashkent*, 61.

72 M.E. Saltykov-Shchedrin, "Gospoda Tashkentsy. Chto takoe 'tashkentsy'?" in *Sobranie sochinenii v 20 tomakh* (Moscow: Khudozhestvennaia literatura, 1970), vol. 10, 22–40. Eleonora Shafranskaia, *Turkestanskii tekst v russkoi kul'ture: Kolonial'naia proza Nikolaia Karazina (istoriko-literaturnyi i kul'turno-etnograficheskii kommentarii)*, St. Petersburg: Self-published, 2016, 52–60.

73 Eleonora Shafranskaia, *Turkestanskii tekst v russkoi kul'ture: Kolonial'naia proza Nikolaia Karazina (istoriko-literaturnyi i kul'turno-etnograficheskii kommentarii)*, St. Petersburg: Self-published, 2016, 51.

74 Shafranskaia, *Turkestanskii tekst*, 51–3.

75 Shafranskaia, *Turkestanskii tekst*, 53.

76 Shafranskaia, *Turkestanskii tekst*, 52–60.

77 Morrison, *Russian Rule in Samarkand*, 126–32.

78 Hans Rogger, "The Skobelev Phenomenon: the Hero and his Worship," *Oxford Slavonic Papers*, no. 9, 1976: 46–78, 50.

79 For a discussion of this, see Anindita Banerjee, *We Modern People: Science Fiction and the Making of Russian Modernity* (Wesleyan University Press, 2012), 30–5.

80 Yuan Gao, "Captivity and Empire: Russian Captivity Narratives in Fact and Fiction," Nazarbaev University, Kazakhstan, MA in Eurasian Studies, 2016, 27–8. Reference is to Fyodor Dostoevsky, "Foma Danilov, a Russian Hero Tortured to Death," in *A Writer's Diary, Volume 2: 1877–1881,*

translated by Kenneth Lantz (Evanston, IL: Northwestern University Press, 1997), 820–5.

81 See Vahan Barooshian, *V. V. Vereshchagin: Artist at War* (Gainesville: University Press of Florida, 1993), 21–32. See also Oleg Tarasov, *Framing Russian Art* (Reaktion Books, 2011), ch. 4, "Between Industry and Art."

82 David Schimmelpenninck van der Oye, *Russian Orientalism: Asia in the Russian Mind from Peter the Great to the Emigration* (New Haven, CT: Yale University Press, 2010), 84.

83 Barooshian, *V. V. Vereshchagin*, 42–50; Mussorgsky was moved to write a composition in music by the same name in order to "resurrect" "Zabytyi." See Solomon Volkov, *St. Petersburg: A Cultural History* (Simon & Schuster, 1995), 102–6. Volkov also writes about the famous panorama of Kars, for which Mussorgsky also composed (104).

84 Blavatsky, *From the Caves*, 57, *Iz peshcher i debrei Indostana: Pis'ma na rodinu*, Chast' 1 (Moscow, 1883), letter 5, 64; Golovnina, *Na Pamirakh*, 12, Uvarova, *Byloe. Davno proshedshie schastlivye dni* (Moscow: izdatel'stvo im. Sabashnikovykh, 2005), 141, "Poezdka v Tashkent i Samarkand," 6 (part 1), Potanina, *Iz puteshestvii*, xxxvii, Elena Apreleva, *Sredne-aziatskie ocherki* (Shanghai, 1935), pages 12–13. Ol'ga Fedchenko was considered "one of the first European artists (perhaps only the second after V. V. Vereshchagin)" to depict Russian Turkestan (Val'kova, *Ol'ga Fedchenko*), 113.

85 F.B. Schenk, "'Ia tak ustala byt' pereletnoi ptitsei,' imperskoe prostrantstvo i imperskoe gospodstvo v avtobiografii Rossiiskoi dvorianki," *Vestnik Iuzhno-Ural'skogo gosudarstvennogo universiteta*. Seriia: Sotsial'no-gumanitarnye nauki 2, no. 14 (2014): 40–50. http://cyberleninka.ru /article/n/ya-tak-ustala-byt-pereletnoy-ptitsey-imperskoe-prostranstvo -i-imperskoe-gospodstvo-v-avtobiografii-rossiyskoy-dvoryanki.

86 These are "Zhenit'ba kapitana Narkizova" and "Zametki malen'kogo cheloveka."

87 See Hokanson, "Russian Women Travelers in Central Asia and India," *The Russian Review* 70 (January 2011): 1–19; and Jeanne Kay Guelke and Karen Morin, "Gender, Nature, Empire: Women Naturalists in Nineteenth Century British Travel Literature," *Transactions of the Institute of British Geographers, New Series* 26, no. 3 (2001): 306–26.

88 Guelke and Morin, "Gender, Nature, Empire," 323.

89 Clinch, *Through a Land of Extremes*, 100; Golovnina, *Na Pamirakh*, 2–3.

90 Dukhovskaia, *Turkestanskie vospominaniia*, 95–6; Dukhovskaia, *Diary*, 529–30. Uvarova published *Die Sammlungen des Kaukasischen Museums Band 1. Archaeologie* (Tiflis: Typographie der Kanzlei des Landeschefs, 1902), with Radde as a co-author.

91 Golovnina writes of staying with Korol'kov, *Na Pamirakh*, 24. Her book is also dedicated to Korol'kov. Uvarova writes of staying with Korol'kov

on page 14 of the first segment of her article. Golovnina describes Dukhovskoi's arrival into Tashkent (29) and her husband goes to see him at a ball (196).

92 There are many texts that treat the "woman question," see in particular Richard Stites, *The Women's Liberation Movement in Russia: Feminism, Nihilism, and Bolshevism, 1860–1930* (Princeton, NJ: Princeton University Press, 1978); and Natalia Pushkareva, *Women in Russian History From the Tenth to the Twentieth Century*, translated and edited by Eve Levin (New York: M. E. Sharpe, 1997).

93 Daniel Brower, *Turkestan and the Fate of the Russian Empire* (London: RoutledgeCurzon, 2003), 41–2.

94 Potanina, *Iz puteshestvii*, xxxiii.

95 Lermontov's *A Hero of Our Time* plays on Russian fears of the abduction of society women. Susan Layton notes that Elena Gan's story "A Recollection at Zheleznovodsk" ("Vospminanie Zheleznovodska"), in which a heroine is kidnapped by Caucasian tribesmen then nearly raped by a local prince only to cut her own throat and then ultimately wake up from the entire episode, which is revealed to be a dream, threatens to counter the heroic Russian male figure with both Russian cowards and far more forceful and erotically enticing Caucasian male figures. (Layton, 148–50). There was also a book, *Shamil's Prisoners* (*Plen u Shamilia*), about the real-life experiences of kidnapped Georgian princesses Chavchavadze and Orbeliani, who were held by Shamil in an attempt to exchange them for his son. (Layton, 153–5).

96 Ol'ga Valkova describes the fact that Ol'ga Fedchenko had hoped to meet the wives of the Khan of Khokand, but the visit was denied on the basis that the people would not like it. Val'kova, *Ol'ga Fedchenko*, 52, description of the denial in A.P. Fedchenko, *V Kokanskom khanstve*, 39–40 and 44.

97 Marianne Kamp, ed., *Muslim Women of the Fergana Valley*, 14–16.

98 See Oleg Tarasov, *Framing Russian Art* (Reaktion Books, 2011), ch. 4, "Between Industry and Art," and Maria Chernysheva, "'The Russian Gérôme?' Vereshchagin as a Painter of Turkestan," *RIHA Journal*, 18 September 2014.

99 Tarasov, *Framing Russian Art*, 288.

100 David Schimmelpenninck van der Oye, *Russian Orientalism*, 85.

101 Brower and Lazzerini, eds., *Russia's Orient: Imperial Borderlands and Peoples, 1700–1917* (Bloomington: Indiana University Press, 1999), xviii.

102 Brower and Lazzerini, *Russian Orientalism*, 313.

103 In particular, Mark Bassin, *Imperial Visions: Nationalist Imagination and Geographical Expansion in the Russian Far East 1840–1865* (Cambridge: Cambridge University Press, 1999), "Russia between Europe and Asia: The Ideological Construction of Geography," *Slavic Review* 50, no. 1 (Spring 1991): 1–17; Richard Wortman, *Scenarios of Power: Myth and*

Ceremony in Russian Monarchy, Vol. 1, *From Peter the Great to the Death of Nicholas I* (Princeton: Princeton University Press, 1995), and Vol. II, *From Alexander II to the Abdication of Nicholas II* (Princeton: Princeton University Press, 2001); Vera Tolz, *Russia's Own Orient: The Politics of Identity and Oriental Studies in the Late Imperial and Early Soviet Periods* (Oxford: Oxford University Press, 2011), Andreas Kappeler, *The Russian Empire: A Multi-Ethnic History* (London: Routledge, 2001).

104 In particular, Susan Layton, *Russian Literature and Empire: Conquest of the Caucasus from Pushkin to Tolstoy* (Cambridge: Cambridge University Press, 1995); Harsha Ram, *The Imperial Sublime: A Russian Poetics of Empire* (Madison: University of Wisconsin Press, 2003); Peter Scotto, "Prisoners of the Caucasus: Ideologies of Imperialism in Lermontov's 'Bela," *PMLA* 107 (1992): 246–60; Natan Eidel'man, *Byt' mozhet za khrebtom Kavkaza* (Moscow: Nauka, 1990); Iurii Lotman, "Problema Vostoka i Zapada v tvorchestve pozdnego Lermontova," *Lermontovskii sbornik* (Leningrad: Nauka, 1985), 5–22; Rebecca Gould, *Writers and Rebels: The Literature of Insurgency in the Caucasus* (New Haven, CT: Yale University Press, 2016); Leah Feldman, *On the Threshold of Eurasia: Revolutionary Poetics in the Caucasus* (Ithaca, NY: Cornell University Press, 2018).

105 In particular, Alexander Etkind, *Internal Colonization. Russia's Imperial Experience* (Cambridge, UK: Polity, 2011); David Schimmelpenninck van der Oye, *Toward the Rising Sun: Ideologies of Empire and the Path to War with Japan* (DeKalb: Northern Illinois University Press, 2006); David Schimmelpenninck van der Oye, *Russian Orientalism: Asia in the Russian Mind from Peter the Great to the Emigration* (New Haven, CT: Yale University Press, 2010); Susanna Lim, *China and Japan in the Russian Imagination, 1685–1922: To the Ends of the Orient* (London: Routledge, 2013); Edyta Bojanowska, *A World of Empires: The Russian Voyage of the Frigate Pallada* (Cambridge, MA: Harvard University Press, 2018).

106 Alexander Morrison, *The Russian Conquest of Central Asia: A Study in Imperial Expansion, 1814–1914.* Cambridge: Cambridge University Press, 2021, and *Russian Rule in Samarkand* (Oxford: Oxford University Press, 2008); "Introduction: Killing the Cotton Canard and Getting Rid of the Great Game: Rewriting the Russian Conquest of Central Asia, 1814–1895," *Central Asian Survey* 33, no. 2 (2014): 131–42; "'Applied Orientalism' in British India and Tsarist Turkestan," *Comparative Studies in Society and History* 51, no. 3 (July 2009), 619–47; "Twin Imperial Disasters. The Invasions of Khiva and Afghanistan in the Russian and British Official Mind, 1839–1842," *Modern Asian Studies* 48, no. 1 (2014): 253–300.

107 Jeff Sahadeo, *Russian Colonial Society in Tashkent, 1865–1923* (Bloomington: Indiana University Press, 2010); "Epidemic and Empire: Ethnicity, Class, and 'Civilization' in the 1892 Tashkent Cholera Riot," *Slavic Review* 64, no. 1 (Spring 2005): 117–39.

108 See in particular Adeeb Khalid, "Culture and Power in Colonial Turkestan," *Cahiers d'Asie centrale* 17, no. 18 (2009): Le Turkestan russe: une colonie comme les autres?: 413–47; Daniel Brower, *Turkestan and the Fate of the Russian Empire* (New York: Routledge, 2003); Daniel Brower, "Islam and Ethnicity: Russian Colonial Policy in Tashkent," in *Russia's Orient: Imperial Borderlands and Peoples, 1700–1917*, edited by Daniel Brower and Edward Lazzerini, 114–35 (Bloomington: Indiana University Press, 1999); Svetlana Gorshenina, "Russian Archaeologists, Colonial Administrators, and the 'Natives' of Turkestan: Revisiting the History of Archaeology in Central Asia," in *"Masters" and "Natives": Digging the Others' Past*, edited by Svetlana Gorshenina, Philippe Bornet, Michael Fuchs, and Claude Rapin, 31–86 (Berlin: DeGruyter, 2019); Svetlana Gorshenina, *The Private Collections of Russian Turkestan in the Second Half of the 19th and Early 20th Century* (Berlin: Klaus Schwarz Verlag, 2004); and Jennifer Keating, "'There Are Few Plants, but They Are Growing, and Quickly': Foliage and the Aesthetics of Landscape in Russian Central Asia, 1854–1914," *Studies in the History of Gardens & Designed Landscapes* 37, no. 2 (2016): 174–89.

109 See in particular Hermann Kreutzmann, *Wakhan Quadrangle: Exploration and Espionage during and after the Great Game* (Wiesbaden, Germany: Harrassowitz Verlag, 2017); Eleonora Shafranskaia, *Turkestanskii tekst v russkoi kul'ture: Kolonial'naia proza Nikolaia Karazina (istoriko-literaturnyi i kul'turno-etnograficheskii kommentarii)* (St. Petersburg: Self-published, 2016); Eleonora Shafranskaia, *Tashkentskii tekst v russkoi kul'ture* (Moscow: Art House Media, 2010); Nicholas Breyfogle, *Heretics and Colonizers: Forging Russia's Empire in the South Caucasus* (Ithaca, NY: Cornell University Press, 2005); Nathaniel Knight, "Vocabularies of Difference: Ethnicity and Race in Late Imperial and Early Soviet Russia," in *Kritika: Explorations in Russian and Eurasian History* 13, no. 3 (Summer 2012): 667–83; Nathaniel Knight, "Seeking the Self in the Other: Ethnographic Studies of Non-Russians in the Russian Geographical Society, 1845–1860," in *Defining Self: Essays on Emergent Identities in Russia, Seventeenth to Nineteenth Centuries*, edited by M. Branch (Helsinki: Finnish Literature Society, 2009): 117–38.

110 Alberto Masoero, "Territorial Colonization in Late Imperial Russia: Stages in the Development of a Concept," *Kritika: Explorations in Russian and Eurasian History* 14, no. 1 (Winter 2013, New Series): 59–91.

111 Charles Steinwedel, *Threads of Empire: Loyalty and Tsarist Authority in Bashkiria, 1552–1917* (Bloomington: Indiana University Press, 2016); Virginia Martin, *Law and Custom in the Steppe: The Kazakhs of the Middle Horde and Russian Colonialism in the Nineteenth Century* (London: Routledge, 2001).

112 Steven Marks, *Road to Power: The Trans-Siberian Railroad and the Colonization of Asian Russia 1850–1917* (Ithaca, NY: Cornell University Press, 1991); Christian Wolmar, *To the Edge of the World: The Story of the Trans-Siberian Express, the World's Greatest Railroad* (Philadelphia and Great Britain: Perseus Books, 2013); Claudia Weiss, "Representing the Empire: The Meaning of Siberia for Russian Imperial Identity," *Nationalities Papers* 35, no. 3 (July 2007): 339–456; Anindita Banerjee, "The Trans-Siberian Railroad and Russia's Asia: Literature, Geopolitics, Philosophy of History," *Clio* 34, nos.1–2 (2004–5): 19–40.

113 As her Russian Wikipedia page notes, "Своеобразие мемуаров, написанных В. Ф. Духовской, состоит в том, что многие описываемые ею события показываются с точки зрения представительницы высших великосветских кругов" – "The distinctiveness of the memoirs written by V. F. Dukhovskaia consists in the fact that many of the events she describes are shown from the point of view of a representative of the highest high society circles." https://ru.wikipedia.org/wiki/%D0%94 %D1%83%D1%85%D0%BE%D0%B2%D1%81%D0%BA%D0%B0%D1 %8F,_%D0%92%D0%B0%D1%80%D0%B2%D0%B0%D1%80%D0 %B0_%D0%A4%D1%91%D0%B4%D0%BE%D1%80%D0%BE%D0 %B2%D0%BD%D0%B0.

114 See, for example, Vera Tolz, *Russia's Own Orient: The Politics of Identity and Oriental Studies in the Late Imperial and Early Soviet Periods* (Oxford: Oxford University Press, 2011).

115 Pratt: "The travelers are chiefly present as a kind of collective moving eye on which the sights/sites register; as agents their presence is very reduced" (*Imperial Eyes*, 59).

116 Blavatsky, *From the Caves*, 510–12, *Russkii vestnik*. v. 180 (November–December 1885), 309–10.

117 Suzanne Marchand, *German Orientalism in the Age of Empire: Religion, Race, and Scholarship* (Cambridge: Cambridge University Press, 2009), 129; Marchand refers to Christian Lassen, in his *Indische Altertumskunde*, 1858. Lassen "used 'Arier' [Aryans] to refer to the lighter-skinned, ruling people of northern India, the people who, he argued, were 'the true subject of Indian history' – both, it seems because they defined its high culture and because they were the ones to leave the records." (Marchand, 128).

118 Peter van der Veer, *Imperial Encounters: Religion and Modernity in India and Britain* (Princeton, NJ: Princeton University Press, 2001), 127.

119 George Curzon, *Russia in Central Asia in 1889 and the Anglo-Russian Question* (London: Longmans, Green, and Co., 1889), 18 (first quotation) and Curzon, *The Pamirs and the Source of the Oxus* (London: The Royal Geographical Society, 1896), 78.

120 John MacKenzie, *The Empire of Nature: Hunting, Conservation and British Imperialism* (Manchester: Manchester University Press, 1988).
121 Ol'ga Val'kova, *Ol'ga Aleksandrovna Fedchenko: 1845–1921* (Moscow: Nauka, 2006), 125–9, in regard to Ol'ga Fedchenko. Val'kova, *Shturmuia tsitadel' nauki: zhenshchiny-uchenye Rossiiskoi imperii* (Moscow: Novoe Literaturnoe Obozrenie, 2019).

Chapter 1: Reinforcing the State at the Imperial Periphery: The Governor-General's Wife

1 V.F. Dukhovskaia, "Iz dnevnika russkoi zhenshchiny v Erzerume," *Russkii vestnik* 136, no. 8 (August 1878): 803–51, and 138, no. 11 (November 1878): 98–158.
2 V.F. Dukhovskaia, *Turkestanskie vospominaniia* (M. O. Vol'f, 1913); and V. F. Dukhovskaia, *Iz moikh vospominanii* (St. Petersburg: Golike and Vil'borg, 1900). The republished article was *Iz dnevnika russkoi zhenschiny v Erzerume vo vremia voennogo zaniatiia ego v 1878 g.* (Spb: tipografiia i khromolit. A Transhelia, 1879), 98 pages. In addition, Dukhovskaia took part in a volume issued for the benefit of sufferers of leprosy in Tashkent, *Turkestanskii literaturynyi sbornik v polzu prokazhennykh*, published by the Turkestan Red Cross (St. Petersburg: Tipografiia A. Benke, 1900), 315 pages, called "Otryvok iz moikh vospominanii. Cherez Velikii Okean. Iz San-Frantsisko v Iaponiu," 2–10.
3 V.F. Dukhovskaia (Barbara Doukhovskoy), *Diary of a Russian Lady: Reminiscences of Barbara Doukhovskoy (née Princesse Galitzine)* (London, J. Long, 1917).
4 Dukhovskaia, "Iz dnevnika russkoi zhenshchiny v Erzerume." The article is referenced in a footnote in *Iz moikh vospominanii*, 75. See also above for reference to republication of the *Russkii vestnik* article.
5 Dukhovskaia, *Diary*, 97–8.
6 Dukhovskaia, *Iz moikh vospominanii*, 122.
7 Dukhovskaia, *Iz moikh vospominanii*.
8 Some sources say Dukhovskaia died in 1913, but it is unclear if this may be a transposition of 1931. She published the English-language version of her memoirs in 1917, suggesting that she certainly lived at least until 1917, and probably longer. See entry in *Pisatel'nitsy Rossii*: http://book .uraic.ru/elib/Authors/Gorbunov/sl-5.htm.
9 Among them Jeff Sahadeo, *Russian Colonial Society in Tashkent*; Alexander Morrison, *Russian Rule in Samarkand*; and Seymour Becker, *Russia's Protectorates in Central Asia: Bukhara and Khiva, 1865–1924* (Cambridge, MA: Harvard University Press, 1968).
10 F.B. Schenk, "'Ia tak ustala byt' pereletnoi ptitsei,' imperskoe prostrantstvo i imperskoe gospodstvo v avtobiografii Rossiiskoi dvorianki," *Vestnik*

Iuzhno-Ural'skogo gosudarstvennogo universiteta. Seriia: Sotsial'no-gumanitarnye nauki 2, no. 14 (2014): 40–50. http://cyberleninka.ru/article/n/ya-tak-ustala-byt-pereletnoy-ptitsey-imperskoe-prostranstvo-i-imperskoe-gospodstvo-v-avtobiografii-rossiyskoy-dvoryanki.

11 Sara Mills, *Discourses of Difference: An Analysis of Women's Travel Writing and Colonialism* (London: Routledge, 1991), 36.

12 Schenk, "Ia tak ustala," 43.

13 The coronation of Alexander III occurred in 1883, Erzerum was taken by the Russians in the Russo-Turkish War in 1878, and the Andijan uprising occurred in 1898 in Andijan and two nearby cities; the uprising indicated local unrest and precipitated General Dukhovskoi's appointment to the governor-generalship of Turkestan.

14 Dukhovskaia, *Diary*, 383.

15 Schenk, "Ia tak ustala," 43.

16 Schenk, "Ia tak ustala," 44.

17 Dukhovskaia, "Iz dnevnika russkoi zhenshchiny v Erzerume," 105; corresponding description in Dukhovskaia, *Diary*, 116–17, omits this comparison, as well as other parts of the narrative.

18 Dukhovskaia, *Iz moikh vospominanii*, 124. There is a description of the same incident in Dukhovskaia, *Diary*, 139–40, where the admirer is named (Stenger, in the Russian version only "Sh" is given) and appears far more lovelorn than in the Russian version. In Pushkin's *Eugene Onegin*, the young Tatiana falls in love with the title character, Onegin, who declines to return her affection until later in the novel, when she has become a grande dame in society. She still loves him but declines to be disloyal to her husband on his behalf and remains extremely calm and self-possessed in his presence.

19 Dukhovskaia, "Iz dnevnika russkoi zhenshchiny v Erzerume," 107. English-language description is in Dukhovskaia, *Diary*, 117.

20 In none of the versions of this trip, both English and Russian, does she mention Pushkin (although she mentions Pushkin elsewhere), but she seems likely to have been aware of his *Journey to Arzrum*, which had described Pushkin's own arduous journey in 1829 from Tiflis to Kars and from Kars to Erzerum, like Dukhovskaia attempting to catch up with the Russian army, and like her emphasizing crossing the Arpachai River, which Russians typically considered the border between Russia and "Asia." In her telling, once she and another officer's wife step foot on "Asiatic soil" after crossing over the frozen Arpachai, "the border of Aleksandropol' with Asiatic Turkey," they are immediately told to go back because the Turkish sentry "looks at them suspiciously," fearing they might be trying to go to Kars (*Iz moikh vospominanii*, 74). This recalls Pushkin's own crossing of the Arpachai, which is in vain, since the Russians had already taken the territory. See Pushkin, *Journey to Arzrum*,

PSS 8, no. 1 (1948): 463. For a fuller discussion of Pushkin's *Journey to Arzrum*, see Katya Hokanson, *Writing at Russia's Border*, ch. 3, "Centring the Periphery: *Eugene Onegin*, 'Onegin's Journey,' and 'A Journey to Arzrum'," in particular 160–1.

21 Dukhovskaia, "Iz dnevnika," 804. Dukhovskaia, *Diary*, 92.

22 Dukhovskaia, *Iz moikh vospominanii*, 103.

23 Dukhovskaia, *Iz moikh vospominanii*, baptism on p. 99, stay in Molokan village on p. 111. The Molokans are a group of Christians who evolved from Eastern Christianity and, while called "dairy eaters" by others, call themselves Spiritual Christians, "dukhovnye khristiane."

24 Dukhovskaia, "Iz dnevnika," 833–4.

25 Dukhovskaia, *Diary*, 102.

26 Dukhovskaia, "Iz dnevnika," 154, *Diary*, 101–2 ("young giaour") and 152–4, meetings with Moussa-Pasha. The description of the riding costume ("amazonka") occurs in the first part of the article, Dukhovskaia, "Iz dnevnika," 825.

27 Edward Said famously quotes Benjamin Disraeli in an epigraph to his *Orientalism*; the quotation is from Disraeli's *Tancred, or The New Crusade* (New York: Routledge and Sons, 1877), 141.

28 Dukhovskaia, *Iz moikh vospominanii*, 396.

29 D.N. Shilov and Iu. A. Kuz'min, eds., *Chleny gosudarstvennogo soveta rossiiskoi imperii, 1801–1906, Bibliograficheskii spravochnik* (St. Petersburg: Isskustvo Rossii, 2007), 309–12, 310. One source claims that he was of the hereditary nobility, but without any substantiation: L.A. Vostrikov and Z.V. Vostokov, *Khabarovsk i khabarovchane: Ocherki o proshlom* (Khabarovskoe khnizhnoe izdatel'stvo, 1991, essay "Vtoroi general-gubernator," 62–73. They say: Преемник барона Корфа генерал-лейтенант Сергей Михаилович Духовской имел отличный послужной список. Потомственный дворянин, один из лучших выпускников 1-го кадетского корпуса, он получил высшее военное образование в Николаевской инженерной академии и академии Генерального штаба. (62) (Baron Korf's replacement Lt. General Sergei Mikhailovich Dukhovskoi had an excellent service record. A hereditary nobleman, one of the best graduates of the first cadet corps, he received his higher military education at the Nikolaevsk Engineering Academy and the academy of the General staff.) Dukhovskoi's article is "Russkie v Erzerume v 1878 godu," *Voennyi sbornik*, 1878, t. 124 no. 11: 131–49 (part one) and no. 12: 309–29 (part two).

30 Uwe Halbach, "The Circassian Question: Russian Colonial History in the Caucasus and a Case of "Long-distance Nationalism," *SWP Comments* 2014/C 37 (August 2014): 4 pages. http://www.swp-berlin.org /fileadmin/contents/products/comments/2014C37_hlb.pdf.

31 Shilov and Kuz'min, eds., *Chleny gosudarstvennogo soveta rossiiskoi imperii, 1801–1906, Bibliograficheskii spravochnik* (St. Petersburg, 2007), 309–12, p. 310, entries for 9 October 1862 and 6–10 August 1864.

32 "S. M. Dukhovskoi," *Niva* 18 (1893): 430–1, with a portrait on 432.

33 "The Andijan Uprising of 1898, in which a religious leader called the Dukchi Ishan led an uncoordinated attack by 2,000 of his followers on a Russian garrison, was the only significant rebellion in Central Asia before the First World War. While it generated significant alarm and paranoia among colonial officials, this was out of all proportion to its scale – only twenty soldiers were killed." Alexander Morrison, *The Russian Conquest of Central Asia*, 537–8.

34 Hans Rogger, "The Skobelev Phenomenon: the Hero and his Worship," *Oxford Slavonic Papers* 9 (1976): 46–78, 50.

35 Dukhovskaia, *Diary*, 136–7. Dukhovskaia, *Iz moikh vospominanii*, 116–18 approximately corresponds to these pages.

36 Dukhovskaia, *Iz moikh vospominanii*, 118.

37 L.A. Vostrikov and Z.V. Vostokov, *Khabarovsk i khabarovchane: Ocherki o proshlom* (Khabarovskoe khnizhnoe izdatel'stvo, 1991), essay "Vtoroi general-gubernator," 62–73, 63.

38 Dukhovskaia, *Iz moikh vospominanii*, 568.

39 Dukhovskaia, *Iz moikh vospominanii*, 568–9, the event appears in *Diary*, 456–7, but that lyrical passage is absent in the English.

40 Dukhovskaia, *Iz moikh vospominanii*, 570–1, *Diary*, 458.

41 Dukhovskaia, *Iz moikh vospominanii*, 488.

42 *Khabarovsk and Khabarovchane*, essay "Vtoroi general-gubernator," 62–73, 69.

43 Dukhovskaia, *Diary*, 520. In Dukhovskaia, *Turkestanskie vospominaniia*, 78.

44 Dukhovskaia, *Diary*, 520; Dukhovskaia, *Turkestanskie vospominaniia*, 78.

45 Dukhovskaia, *Diary*, 520; Dukhovskaia, *Turkestanskie vospominaniia*, 78.

46 Dukhovskaia, *Turkestanskie vospominaniia*, 78: "Но все это только лавры изъ зеленой бумаги; я тайно жаждала другихъ лавръ – настоящихъ, желала успеха среди другой, менее пристрастной публики, на эстраде другого концерта, не дилетантскаго." ("But all of this was only laurels of green paper; I secretly thirsted after other laurels – real ones, I wanted success among another, less partisan public, on the stage of another concert, not a dilettantish one.")

47 *Turkestanskii literaturynyi sbornik v polzu prokazhennykh*, published by the Turkestan Red Cross (St. Petersburg: Tipografiia A. Benke, 1900, 315 pages), 2–10.

48 Dukhovskaia, *Iz moikh vospominanii*, iii.

49 Dukhovskaia, *Iz moikh vospominanii*, 122–3. The episode is not mentioned in the *Diary*.

50 Dukhovskaia, *Iz moikh vospominanii*, 132.

51 Dukhovskaia, *Iz moikh vospominanii*, 148–9, *Diary*, 150–3.

52 Richard Wortman, *Scenarios of Power, Myth and Ceremony in Russian Monarchy* (Princeton, NJ: Princeton University Press, 2000), vol. 2, 197–8.
53 Dukhovskaia, *Diary*, 153; Dukhovskaia, *Iz moikh vospominanii*, 148–9.
54 Dukhovskaia, *Diary*, 362–3; Dukhovskia, *Iz moikh vospominanii*, 442–3.
55 Dukhovskaia, *Iz moikh vospominanii*, 443–4; Dukhovskaia, *Diary*, 362–4.
56 Wortman, *Scenarios*, vol. 2, 223.
57 Jeff Sahadeo, *Russian Colonial Society in Tashkent, 1865–1923* (Bloomington: Indiana University Press, 2010), 28.
58 Sahadeo, *Russian Colonial Society*, 29.
59 Sahadeo, *Russian Colonial Society*, 31.
60 Dukhovskaia compared herself to a bird of flight and a bird in a gilded cage.
61 Dukhovskaia, *Iz moikh vospominanii*, 444–5; Dukhovskaia, *Diary*, 364 (does not mention the servant or the cap of invisibility).
62 Dukhovskaia, *Turkestanskie vospominaniia*, 3.
63 Dukhovskaia, *Turkestanskie vospominaniia*, 3.
64 See Dukhovskaia, *Turkestanskie vospominaniia*, 14, for a mention of *A Thousand and One Nights*.
65 Dukhovskaia, *Turkestanskie vospominaniia*, 18–19 and 27, respectively.
66 Dukhovskaia, *Diary*, 372; Dukhovskaia, *Iz moikh vospominanii*, 455–6.
67 Dukhovskaia, *Diary*, 385; see also Dukhovskaia, *Iz moikh vospominanii*, 455–6.
68 Dukhovskaia, *Iz moikh vospominanii*, 479.
69 Sahadeo, *Russian Colonial Society*, 31.
70 Dukhovskaia, *Diary*, 490, a less fulsome description is in Dukhovskaia, *Turkestanskie vospominaniia*, 7.
71 See Dukhovskaia, *Turkestanskie vospominaniia*, 97.
72 Dukhovskaia, *Turkestanskie vospominaniia*, 76.
73 Dukhovskaia, *Diary*, 516; Dukhovskaia, *Turkestanskie vospominaniia*, 69.
74 Aleksei K. Kuropatkin, 1848–1925, was the governor of Transcaspia from 1890 to 1898, and from 1898 on was the minister of war.
75 Quotation from Dukhovskaia, *Diary*, 515, from Dukhovskaia, *Turkestanskie vospominaniia*, 69.
76 Dukhovskaia, *Diary*, 515.
77 Dukhovskaia, *Turkestanskie vospominaniia*, 70.
78 Bacha dancers (also written as batcha) were young boys who were dressed in feminine style and were a frequent topic of travellers' accounts, as well as depictions by such artists as Vereshchagin. See Maria Chernysheva, "'The Russian Gérôme'? Vereshchagin as a Painter of Turkestan," *RIHA Journal* 96 (18 September 2014). See also Shafranskaia, *Turkestanskii tekst*, 105–18.
79 Henri Moser, *À Travers L'asie Centrale: La Steppe Kirghize, Le Turkestan Russe, Boukhara, Khiva, Le Pays Des Turcomans Et La Perse, Impressions De*

Voyage (Paris: E. Plon, Nourrit, 1886), as well as Golovnina's *Na Pamirakh*, Apreleva's *Central Asian Sketches* and the works of Karazin.

80 Dukhovskaia, *Turkestanskie vospominaniia*, 70–1.

81 Dukhovskaia, *Turkestanskie vospominaniia*, 51.

82 Dukhovskaia, *Turkestanskie vospominaniia*, 14.

83 Dukhovskaia, *Turkestanskie vospominaniia*, 26. Jeff Sahadeo has defined "Sart" as follows: "a term used by Central Asian locals before the Russian conquest to designate the sedentary population of the region. Tsarist authorities employed the moniker to designate Turkic-speaking urban dwellers, and it eventually gained a pejorative connotation." Sahadeo, *Russian Colonial Society in Tashkent*, 237.

84 Dukhovskaia, *Turkestanskie vospominaniia*, 39.

85 Dukhovskaia, *Iz moikh vospominanii*, 83.

86 Dukhovskaia, *Iz moikh vospominanii*, 131.

87 Dukhovskaia, *Iz moikh vospominanii*, 129–31; Dukhovskaia, *Diary*, 142–4.

88 Dukhovskaia, *Iz moikh vospominanii*, 135.

89 Dukhovskaia, *Turkestanskie vospominanii*, 96.

90 These threats appear to have been made by Russian anarchists and those who opposed the Russian regime. See Dukhovskaia, *Iz moikh vospominanii*, 408, and Dukhovskaia, *Diary*, 327–8. Dukhovskaia says that the Dukhovskois' movements were public and published in the papers, so they had to reduce their visibility, in part by travelling under assumed names.

91 Dukhovskaia, *Diary*, 494; Dukhovskaia, *Turkestanskie vospominaniia*, 16.

92 Dukhovskaia, *Diary*, 152. The discovery that terrorists were making explosives that looked like oranges is discussed on page 148.

93 Dukhovskaia, *Diary*, 132; Dukhovskaia, *Iz moikh vospominanii*, 144.

94 Dukhovskaia mentions anarchists a number of times and names Sofiia Perovskaia (*Diary*, 143; *Iz moikh vospominanii*, 130) and Kobzev/Kobozev (*Diary*, 144; *Iz moikh vospominanii*, 131). She mentions the high birth of Perovskaia and the good manners of Kobzev with some incredulity.

95 Dukhovskaia, *Diary*, 502.

96 Dukhovskaia, *Turkestanskie vospominaniia*, 37.

97 Dukhovskaia, *Turkestanskie vospominaniia*, 37.

98 Iu. D. Golovnina, *Na Pamirakh: Zapiski russkoi puteshestvennitsy* (Moscow, 1902), 28–9.

99 Golovnina, *Na Pamirakh*, 194–5 (Golovnina's contemporanous spelling).

100 Dukhovskaia, *Turkestanskie vospominaniia*, 38.

101 Sahadeo, *Russian Colonial Society*, 67, 102. Fedorov served from 1870 to 1906. G.P. Fedorov, "Moia sluzhba v Turkestanskom krae (1870–1906 goda)," *Istoricheskii Vestnik* 6 (1912): 786–812; 10 (1913): 33–55; 11 (1913): 538–67; 12 (1913): 860–93.

102 Fedorov, ch. XIX, 863, http://www.vostlit.info/Texts/Dokumenty
     /M.Asien/XIX/1860-1880/Fedorov_G_P/text4.htm.
103 Fedorov, ch. XIX, 863–4.
104 Richard Pierce, *Russian Central Asia, 1867–1917: A Study in Colonial Rule*
     (Berkeley: University of California Press, 1960), 176.
105 Dukhovskaia, *Diary*, 498–500; Dukhovskaia, *Turkestanskie vospominaniia*, 28.
106 Dukhovskaia, *Turkestanskie vospominaniia*, 28. See Simon Sebag
     Montefiore, *The Romanovs: 1613–1918* (New York: Knopf, 2016); I.V.
     Zimin, "The 'Forgotten' Grand Duke (Nikolai Konstantinovich Romanov,
     1850–1928)," *Voprosy Istorii* 10 (2002): 131–9; Prince Michael of Greece,
     The White Night of St. Petersburg, translated by Franklin Philip (New York:
     Atlantic Monthly Press, 2004), https://www.rbth.com/history/328923
     -4-sex-scandals-romanovs; E.F. Shafranskaia, *Turkestanskii tekst v russkoi
     kul'ture: Kolonial'naia proza Nikolaia Karazina* (St. Petersburg: Self-
     published, 2016), 265; Jennifer Keating, "'There Are Few Plants, but They
     Are Growing, and Quickly': Foliage and the Aesthetics of Landscape
     in Russian Central Asia, 1854–1914," *Studies in the History of Gardens &
     Designed Landscapes* 37, no. 2 (2016): 174–89, 176.
107 Dukhovskaia, *Diary*, 499; Dukhovskaia, *Turkestanskia vospominaniia*, 28.
108 Dukhovskaia, *Turkestanskie vospominaniia*, 66–7, see same event in
     Dukhovskaia, *Diary*, 495.
109 Dukhovskaia, *Turkestanskie vospominaniia*, 99–100.
110 Hisao Komatsu, "The Andijan Uprising Reconsidered," in *Muslim
     Societies: Historical and Comparative Aspects*, edited by Sato Tsugitaka
     (London: RoutledgeCurzon, 2004): 29–61, 47.
111 Komatsu, "Andijan Uprising," 50.
112 Adeeb Khalid, "Culture and Power in Colonial Turkestan," *Cahiers d'Asie
     centrale* 17, no. 18 (2009): Le Turkestan russe: une colonie comme les
     autres?: 413–47, 424.
113 Dukhovskaia, *Diary*, 511.
114 Dukhovskaia, *Turkestanskie vospominaniia*, 58.
115 Dukhovskaia, *Diary*, 511; Dukhovskaia, *Turkestanskie vospominaniia*, 58.
116 Shilov and Kuz'min, eds., *Chleny gosudarstvennogo soveta rossiiskoi imperii,
     1801–1906, Bibliograficheskii spravochnik* (St. Petersburg, 2007), 309–12, 310.
117 Lev Tolstoy, *Polnoe sobranie sochinenii*, vol. 34, 116–25. See in particular
     Alexander Zholkovsky, "Before and after 'After the Ball,'" in *Text Counter
     Text. Rereadings in Russian Literary History* (Stanford, CA: Stanford
     University Press, 1994).
118 Dukhovskaia, *Diary*, 520–1; Dukhovskaia, *Turkestanskie vospominaniia*, 78.
119 See Dukhovskaia, *Diary*, 524–31; Dukhovskaia, *Turkestanskie
     vospominaniia*, 83–97.
120 Dukhovskaia, *Diary*, 524; See also Dukhovskaia, *Turkestanskie
     vospominaniia*, 84–5.

121 Dukhovskaia, *Diary*, 524. This element is discussed similarly in
Turkestanskie vospominaniia, although there it is an "Oriental potentate"
(vostochnyi vlastelin) and those who dismount are "the same kind of
people as all of them" (84).
122 Dukhovskaia, *Turkestanskie vospominaniia*, 102.
123 Dukhovskaia, *Turkestanskie vospominaniia*, 100–2; Dukhovskaia, *Diary*,
535 (taken from the Russian version and translated by the author). In
the English-language version, she makes it clear that it is the Tashkent
cathedral.
124 Dukhovskaia, *Turkestanskie vospominaniia*, 102; Dukhovskaia, *Diary*, 537.
125 Dukhovskaia, *Turkestanskie vospominaniia*, 102; Dukhovskaia, *Diary*, 537–8.
She does not mention the grand duke in the English version, only the tsar.

Chapter 2: Turkestan through Russian Eyes: Elena Apreleva's
Central Asian Sketches

 1 E. Ardov (E.I. Apreleva), "Uzun-Ada," in *Sredne-aziatskie ocherki*
(Shanghai: Tipografiia Izdatel'stva Slovo, 1935), 8–9 (epigraph) and 7.
"Ad" is the Russian word for hell, thus evoking Dante.
 2 *Russkie vedomosti, 1863–1913: Sbornik statei* (Moscow: tip. Russkikh
Vedomostei, 1913), 12–15 contains a biographical essay by Apreleva and
a list of her publications, including the original dates and volumes of the
Central Asian Sketches, and it also contains, on 161–3, Apreleva's essay,
"Iz vospominanii o sotrudnichestve v 'Russkikh vedomostiakh.'" The
Central Asian Sketches, as listed on 14–15, are (all in *Russkie vedomosti*):
"Uzun-Ada" (1898, no. 110); "Registan" (1898, no. 110); "Sail'" (1896, no.
112); "Aishe" (1898 no. 114); "Solimka," "Kapitan Narkizov" (1899, no.
238); "Turkestanets," "Gurimar," "Tri brata" (1899, no. 24); "Kerbalai
i Zogra" (1899, no. 41); "Dzhugut Khana" (1899, no. 55); "Golodnaia
step'" (1899, no. 289); "Ulanka sartenok" (1899, nos. 287, 289); "Brodiachii
muzikant" (1900, no. 78); "Na rybalke" (1900, no. 92); "Ne podvodi"
(1901, no. 332); "Doktor Kallinik" (1900, no. 326); "V gornom ushchele"
(1900, nos. 350, 355); "Pereselenka" (1901, no. 283); "Ishan" (1901, no.
352); "Zhenit'ba kapitana Narkizova" (1902, no. 61); "Na pokoi" (1905
no. 269 – note, despite concerted efforts, this one could not be found
and the year or number are likely incorrect); "Zametki malen'kogo
cheloveka" (1905, nos. 49, 56, 60); "General ot rezedy" (1906, nos. 59,
69); and "Ditia kochevnikov" (1906, nos. 125, 127). "Ditia kochevnikov"
was also published in *Dva Mira: Rasskazy dlia detei srednego vozrasta*
in 1909, republished in 1915 by the Glavnoe upravlenie Ministerstva
Prozveshcheniia dopushch. v uchenich. bibl. gorodskikh, po polzh. 1872,
i dvukhklassnikykh sel'skikh uchilishch, Petrograd, 1915. "Turkestanets"
was also published in *Vasil'ki. Literaturnyi-khudozhestvennyi sbornik* (St.

Petersburg, 1901), 7–13, with the subtitle "Iz sredne-aziatskikh ocherkov" and with the dateline "Gurimar: V otrogakh Tian-Shiana" (Gurimar: In the foothills of the Tian-Shan). There is also an essay called "travel impressions," "Ot Tashkenta do Moskvy" (*Russkie vedomosti*, 1906, no. 183). Except for the travel impressions, which are signed "E. Ardov-Apreleva," the other stories are all signed with her pseudonym, E. Ardov. The *Central Asian Sketches* as published by her sons in 1935 in Shanghai include eighteen of the stories, those listed above excluding the following: "V gornom ushchele," "Ishan," "Zhenit'ba kapitana Narkizova," "Na pokoi," "Zametki malen'kogo cheloveka," "General ot rezedy," and "Ditia kochevnikov." The 1935 volume does not include the travel essay.

3 Mary Zirin, "Elena Apreleva," in *An Encyclopedia of Continental Women Writers*, edited by Katharina M. Wilson (New York and London: Garland Publishing, 1991), vol. 1, 48. Ivan Fedorovich Blaramberg, *Erinnerungen aus dem Leben des Kaiserlich Russischen General-Lieutenant Johann von Blaramberg: Nach dessen Tagebüchern von 1811–1871*, 3 vols. (Berlin: Schroeder, 1872–5.

4 Marina Ledkovskaia-Astman, Charlotte Rosenthal, and Mary Fleming Zirin, *Dictionary of Russian Women Writers* (Westport, CT: Greenwood Press, 1994), 37–9 (entry on E. Ardov, pseudonym for Apreleva, written by Mary Zirin).

5 Tamara Zviguilsky, "Une disciple de Tourguéniev: Eléna Blaramberg-Ardov-Apréleva (1846–1923) Pour le cent cinquantenaire de sa naissance," *Exposition Les Frères Goncourt et Tourgueniev, Catalogue*, Musée Ivan Tourgueniev, 16, rue Ivan Tourguéniev, 78380 Bougival, 1996, 102–7. Reference to pseudonym is on 105.

6 Ivan Turgenev, *Polnoe sobranie sochinenii i pisem v dvadsati vos'mi tomakh, Pis'ma v trinadsat' tomakh. Pis'ma*, Moscow: Akademiia nauk, 1960–8, vol. 12, 52–3. The letter is to M.M. Stasiulevich, #4154, 31 December 1876/12 January 1877. The quote is: "Я полагаю, что, если это исправление ей удастся, роман этот стоит напечатать, потому что в нем есть нечто, как говорят французы: написано горячо, искренне – и не без таланта."

7 Ledkovskaia-Astman, Rosenthal, and Zirin, *Dictionary*, 38.

8 See https://s-t-o-l.com/kultura/kartiny-repina-priplyli/ and http://artpoisk.info/article/i_repin_v_abramceve/page/5/.

9 A.A. Khisamutdinov, in *Russkaia slovestnost' v Shankhae* (Vladivostok: Izdatel'stvo Dal'nevostochnogo universiteta, 2014) describes the sons' publication of Apreleva's book and notes that some of her children's stories were also published in Shanghai (56). See also https://russianemigrant.ru/book-author/apreleva-elena-ivanovna-ardov-e.

10 *Russkie vedomosti, 1863–1913*, 12–15.

11 https://knigovek.ru/ardov-e-bez-viny-vinovatye. "Ее романы, очерки и переводы имели успех. Однако современному читателю имя писательницы незнакомо, ее произведения почти не переиздавались." ("Her novels, sketches and translations were successful. However her name is unknown to the contemporary reader, her works have almost never been republished.")
12 Zirin, "Elena Apreleva," 48.
13 Two of the sketches in the collection, "Sail'" (first published in 1896), and "Gurimar" (first published in 1899), are not discussed here. "Sail'" describes a Russian couple's visit to the Afrasiab, an old fortification in Samarkand, to watch a game called *baiga* and partake in a Central Asian feast. "Gurimar" is about the family's move to the mountain area and their fear of both cholera in the cities and smugglers, who turn out to be anything but frightening. "Ishan" describes the life of a religious leader.
14 Ardov, *Sredne-aziatskie ocherki*, 14.
15 Apreleva's story "Turkestanets" was also published in *Vasil'ki. Literaturnyi-khudozhestvennyi sbornik* (St. Petersburg, 1901), 7–13, with the subtitle "Iz sredne-aziatskikh ocherkov" and with the dateline *"Gurimar: V otrogakh Tian-Shiana"* (Gurimar: In the foothills of the Tian-Shan).
16 At this juncture, the author has been unable to find out more information about the photographs. The website on Shanghai authors referenced in note 8 above notes that the black-and-white illustrations in the book are by B.I. Davydov.
17 See Katya Hokanson, "Russian Women Travelers in Central Asia and India," *The Russian Review* 70, no. 1 (January 2011): 15.
18 Apreleva, *Sredne-Aziatskie ocherki*, hereafter *Central Asian Sketches*, 14.
19 Apreleva, *Central Asian Sketches*, 9–10.
20 Apreleva, *Central Asian Sketches*, 10.
21 Apreleva, *Central Asian Sketches*, 14. See Figure 0.3., "Zabytyi."
22 Apreleva, *Central Asian Sketches*, 16.
23 Apreleva, *Central Asian Sketches*, 19–20.
24 Apreleva, *Central Asian Sketches*, 21.
25 Apreleva, *Central Asian Sketches*, 21.
26 As Hugo Stumm notes, "Tiura is the general expression by which the Central Asiatic nomads designate the Russian officers," *Russia in Central Asia: Historical Sketch of Russia's Progress in the East up to 1873, and of the Incidents Which Led to the Campaign against Khiva; with a Description of the Military Districts of the Caucasus, Orenburg, and Turkestan*, translated by J.W. Ozanne and H. Sachs (London: Harrison & Sons, 1885), 324, footnote.
27 Apreleva, *Central Asian Sketches*, 111.
28 Apreleva, *Central Asian Sketches*, 118.
29 Apreleva, *Central Asian Sketches*, 122.

30 Apreleva, *Central Asian Sketches*, 115–16.
31 Apreleva, *Central Asian Sketches*, 117.
32 Apreleva, *Central Asian Sketches*, 118.
33 Apreleva, *Central Asian Sketches*, 13.
34 Ol'ga Lobri, "Ot Astrakhani do Margelana (putevye nabroski) Avgust' 1895 goda," *Russkii vestnik* 259, no. 2 (1899): 639–49; 260, no. 4: 601–12; 605–7. Lobri also published "Iz Turkestanskikh vospominanii," *Russkii vestnik* 261, no. 5 (1899): 220–8.
35 "Turkestanets" was also published in *Vasil'ki. Literaturnyi-khudozhestvennyi sbornik* (St. Petersburg, 1901), 7–13, with the subtitle "Iz sredne-aziatskikh ocherkov" and with the dateline "Gurimar: V otrogakh Tian-Shiana" (Gurimar: In the foothills of the Tian-Shan).
36 Sahadeo, *Russian Colonial Society*, 64–5.
37 It is possibly notable that General Kaufman's wife's patronymic was Mavrikievna; see Sahadeo, *Russian Colonial Society*, 65.
38 Apreleva, *Central Asian Sketches*, 70.
39 Apreleva, *Central Asian Sketches*, 70.
40 Apreleva, *Central Asian Sketches*, 72.
41 Apreleva, *Central Asian Sketches*, 72–3.
42 Apreleva, *Central Asian Sketches*, 73–4.
43 Apreleva, *Central Asian Sketches*, 74.
44 Apreleva, *Central Asian Sketches*, 74–6.
45 Apreleva, *Central Asian Sketches*, 76.
46 Apreleva, *Central Asian Sketches*, 76. These are the last words of the story.
47 Sahadeo, *Russian Colonial Society*, 256, note 42, "Khalatnik is a derogatory term that refers to the wearer of a khalat, a robe used by the local population. M. A. Terent'ev, 3:292." The reference is to M.A. Terent'ev, *Istoriia zavoevaniia Srednei Azii*, 3 vols (St. Petersburg: Tipo-litografiia V. V. Komarova, 1906).
48 Sahadeo, *Russian Colonial Society*, 67, Федоров Г. *Моя служба в Туркестанском крае* (1870–1906) // Исторический вестник. 1913. Кн. 9–12. See also Sh. B. Mukhamedov, "Istoriia Russkogo Turkestana: Pravda i vymysel. Vzgliad istorika iz XXI veka," https://cyberleninka .ru/article/n/istoriya-russkogo-turkestana-pravda-i-vymysel-vzglyad -istorika-iz-xxi-veka.
49 Apreleva, *Central Asian Sketches*, 197–8.
50 Apreleva, *Central Asian Sketches*, 199.
51 On gardening, see Jennifer Keating, "'There Are Few Plants, but They Are Growing, and Quickly': Foliage and the Aesthetics of Landscape in Russian Central Asia, 1854–1914," *Studies in the History of Gardens & Designed Landscapes* 37, no. 2 (2016): 174–89.
52 Apreleva, *Central Asian Sketches*, 200.

53 Apreleva, *Central Asian Sketches*, 203.
54 Apreleva, *Central Asian Sketches*, 211.
55 Apreleva, *Central Asian Sketches*, 58.
56 Apreleva, *Central Asian Sketches*, 60. Bachas, or batchas, dancing boys, were attested in numerous travelogues, such as those of Henri Moser, Eugene Schuyler, K.K. Pahlen, and others. Henri Moser describes these dancing boys in his account *A Travers l'Asie Centrale* in a practice that is now recognized as frequently abusive. "Il y a des batchas dont le nom est dans toutes les bouches, comme ceux de nos grands artistes, et leur apparition dans une féte donne lieueà une allégresse générale. Quand ils traversent a cheval les bazaars, c'est à qui les comblèra de présents et de gracieux sourires; dans la vie publique, c'est lui qui représente l'élément féminin banni par le Coran. Parfois, pour ses danses, le batcha endosse le costume de la femme, et, ainsi vétu, il fait naitre des passions et des jalousies terribles qu'on a vues se terminer souvent par des querelles sanglantes et des coups de couteau; quand il danse et termine ses exercices choréographiques par un saut périlleux ou des pirouettes sur lui-méme d'une rapidité vertigineuse, on voit les indigènes, si calmes, si sobres dans leurs mouvements, sortir de cette apathie pour se livrer à un enthousiasme frénétique … nous ne sommes pas assez Orientaux pour saisir les nuances de cet exercise et apprécier le talent des danseurs." (There are batchas whose name is on everyone's lips, like those of our great artists, and their appearance at a fete gives rise to a general cheerfulness. When they traverse the bazaars on horseback, they are given presents and gracious smiles; in public life, it is they who represent the feminine element banned by the Quran. Sometimes, for his dances, the batcha assumes a woman's costume, and dressed thus, gives rise to passions and terrible jealousies which are often ended by bloody quarrels and blows of the knife; when he dances and ends his choreographic exercises with a perilous leap or with pirouettes of vertiginous rapidity, one sees the local people, so calm, so sober in their movements, leave this apathy to deliver themselves to a frenetic enthusiasm … we are not sufficiently Oriental to capture the nuances of this exercise and to appreciate the talent of the dancers.) Henri Moser, *A Travers L'Asie Centrale: la Steppe kirghize, le Turkestan russe, Boukhara, Khiva, le pays des Turcomans et la Perse, impressions de voyage*, 175–7. Current research relating to the topic includes Ellen Anna Philo Gorris, "Invisible Victims? Where Are Male Victims of Conflict-Related Sexual Violence in International Law and Policy?" *European Journal of Women's Studies* 22, no. 4 (2015): 412–27, as well as Diederik F. Janssen, "Age-Stratifying Homosexualities in the Social Sciences," *Sexuality & Culture* 21, no. 1 (March 2017): 300–22. Eleonora Shafranskaia discusses many aspects of typical Central Asian accounts in her *Turkestanskii tekst v russkoi kul'ture: Kolonial'naia proza Nikolaia Karazina*

(St. Petersburg: Self-published, 2016). Vereshchagin also depicted bachas, see Maria Chernysheva, "'The Russian Gérôme'? Vereshchagin as a Painter of Turkestan," *RIHA Journal* 96 (18 September 2014). See also Apreleva, *Russian Central Asia*, in particular 261–4.

57 Apreleva, *Central Asian Sketches*, 61.

58 Apreleva, *Central Asian Sketches*, 66–7.

59 Apreleva, *Central Asian Sketches*, 67–8.

60 Apreleva, *Central Asian Sketches*, 46.

61 Apreleva, *Central Asian Sketches*, 81.

62 Apreleva, *Central Asian Sketches*, 50.

63 Apreleva, *Central Asian Sketches*, 51.

64 Apreleva, *Central Asian Sketches*, 52.

65 Apreleva, *Central Asian Sketches*, 53.

66 Apreleva, *Central Asian Sketches*, 53.

67 Apreleva, *Central Asian Sketches*, 53.

68 Apreleva, *Central Asian Sketches*, 56.

69 Apreleva, *Central Asian Sketches*, 123–5.

70 Apreleva, *Central Asian Sketches*, 129. A.S. Morrison glosses dzhigit or jigit as "a Tatar word meaning simply 'a horseman' applied to the men who acted as a mixture of butler, bodyguard, messenger, and general dogsbody to Russian administrators." A.S. Morrison, *Russian Rule in Samarkand: 1868–1910, A Comparison with British India* (Oxford: Oxford University Press, 2008), 155, n. 95.

71 Apreleva, *Central Asian Sketches*, 134.

72 Apreleva, *Central Asian Sketches*, 134.

73 Apreleva, *Central Asian Sketches*, 135–6.

74 Apreleva, *Central Asian Sketches*, 138–40.

75 Apreleva, *Central Asian Sketches*, 140.

76 Apreleva, *Central Asian Sketches*, 41–2.

77 Ledkovskaia-Astman, Rosenthal, and Zirin, *Dictionary*, 38. The story is in Apreleva, *Central Asian Sketches*, 142–51.

78 Apreleva, *Central Asian Sketches*, 146.

79 Apreleva, *Central Asian Sketches*, 147.

80 Apreleva, *Central Asian Sketches*, 149.

81 Apreleva, *Central Asian Sketches*, 150.

82 Apreleva, *Central Asian Sketches*, 150.

83 Apreleva, *Central Asian Sketches*, 150.

84 See Harsha Ram, *The Imperial Sublime: A Russian Poetics of Empire* (Madison: University of Wisconsin Press, 2003).

85 I have previously discussed this story more briefly in "Russian Women Travelers in Central Asia and India," *The Russian Review* 70 (January 2011): 1–19, 17. The story is on 33–47 of *Central Asian Sketches*.

86 Apreleva, *Central Asian Sketches*, 34.

87 Shafranskaia, *Turkestanskii tekst*, 61.

88 Apreleva, *Central Asian Sketches*, 36.

89 Apreleva, *Central Asian Sketches*, 37.

90 Apreleva, *Central Asian Sketches*, 37.

91 Apreleva, *Central Asian Sketches*, 37.

92 Apreleva, *Central Asian Sketches*, 39.

93 Apreleva, *Central Asian Sketches*, 39–40.

94 Apreleva, *Central Asian Sketches*, 42–3.

95 Apreleva, *Central Asian Sketches*, 43.

96 Apreleva, *Central Asian Sketches*, 44.

97 Apreleva, *Central Asian Sketches*, 44.

98 Apreleva, *Central Asian Sketches*, 44–5.

99 Apreleva, *Central Asian Sketches*, 47.

100 Apreleva, *Central Asian Sketches*, 47.

101 Apreleva, *Central Asian Sketches*, 47.

102 Apreleva, *Central Asian Sketches*, 46.

103 N.N. Karazin, "Doktorsha," 1872, http://az.lib.ru/k/karazin_n_n /text_1872_doktorsha.shtml. Often the "twist," as with Pushkin's *Journey to Arzrum*, for example, is that the women in the harem are not that attractive or are completely uninterested in their visitor, or both.

104 *Russkie vedomosti*, 1900, Nos. 350, 355.

105 Apreleva, *Central Asian Sketches*, 90–101.

106 Apreleva, *Central Asian Sketches*, 98.

107 Apreleva, *Central Asian Sketches*, 100.

108 Apreleva, *Central Asian Sketches*, 100.

109 Apreleva, *Central Asian Sketches*, 99.

110 Apreleva, *Central Asian Sketches*, 91.

111 Apreleva, *Central Asian Sketches*, 101.

112 Apreleva, *Central Asian Sketches*, 100.

113 Apreleva, *Central Asian Sketches*, 176–92 ("Pereselenka,") and 152–65 ("Na rybalke").

114 Apreleva, *Central Asian Sketches*, 177.

115 Apreleva, *Central Asian Sketches*, 182.

116 Apreleva, *Central Asian Sketches*, 180.

117 Apreleva, *Central Asian Sketches*, 191.

118 Apreleva, *Central Asian Sketches*, 192.

119 Apreleva, *Central Asian Sketches*, 158–9.

120 Apreleva, *Central Asian Sketches*, 160.

121 Apreleva, *Central Asian Sketches*, 166–75.

122 Apreleva, *Central Asian Sketches*, 168.

123 Apreleva, *Central Asian Sketches*, 169–70.

124 Apreleva, *Central Asian Sketches*, 171–2.
125 Apreleva, *Central Asian Sketches*, 173.
126 Apreleva, *Central Asian Sketches*, 174.
127 Apreleva, *Central Asian Sketches*, 170.
128 This gradually became an increasing worry among the Russian Turkestan population: how much civilization were the Russians bringing? See Sahadeo, *Russian Colonial Society*, 72–3. Like Apreleva, Sahadeo describes alcoholism among the Russians as a major concern.
129 Apreleva, *Central Asian Sketches*, 170–1.
130 The influential writer N.N. Karazin was known for his positive portrayal of the "white shirt" Russian soldiers. See, for example, Elena Andreeva, *Russian Central Asia*, 105–7.
131 The original pagination is not available, the quotation is found on page 14 of the PDF copy.
132 Apreleva, *Central Asian Sketches*, 102–10.
133 Apreleva, *Central Asian Sketches*, 104–5.
134 Apreleva, *Central Asian Sketches*, 108–9.
135 Apreleva, *Central Asian Sketches*, 110.
136 Apreleva, *Central Asian Sketches*, 110.
137 Apreleva, *Central Asian Sketches*, 85–9.
138 Apreleva, *Central Asian Sketches*, 89.
139 Tolstoi, "Rubka lesa," *Polnoe Sobranie Sochinenii* (Moscow: Khudozhestvennaia literatura, 1928–58), vol. 3, 65–6. Translation from *The Portable Tolstoy*, edited by John Bayley. New York: Viking Press, 1978, 228–9.
140 Apreleva, *Sredne-aziatskie ocherki*, sons' foreword (1).
141 Apreleva, *Sredne-aziatskie ocherki*, foreword by author (5).

**Chapter 3: Propagandist of Russian Imperialism:
Madame Blavatsky in India**

 1 See his description of her in *The Memoirs of Count Witte* (Garden City, NY, and Toronto: Doubleday, Page & Company, 1921), 4–10. https://archive.org/stream/memoirsofcountwi00wittuoft /memoirsofcountwi00wittuoft_djvu.txt. Also available in Russian, *Vospominaniia*, 1911, http://az.lib.ru/w/witte_s_j/text_0010.shtml.
 2 See Gary Lachman, *Madame Blavatsky: The Mother of Modern Spirituality* (London: Penguin, 2012), particularly ch. 3, "Seven Years in Tibet?"
 3 My thanks to Bella Grigoryan for suggesting this interesting way of situating Blavatskaia.
 4 Maria Carlson, *"No Religion Higher than Truth": A History of the Theosophical Movement in Russia, 1875–1922* (Princeton, NJ: Princeton University Press, 1993), 43.

5 Carlson, *"No Religion,"* 10–11.
6 Mark Bevir, "The West Turns Eastward: Madame Blavatsky and the Transformation of the Occult Tradition," *Journal of the American Academy of Religion* 62, no. 3 (Autumn 1994): 747–67, 749.
7 Bevir, "The West Turns Eastward," 751.
8 K. Paul Johnson, *The Masters Revealed: Madame Blavatsky and the Myth of the Great White Lodge* (New York: SUNY Press, 1994), 4.
9 Bevir, "The West Turns Eastward," 754.
10 Carlson, *"No Religion,"* 11.
11 Carlson, *"No Religion,"* 12.
12 Bevir, "The West Turns Eastward," 756.
13 Bevir, "The West Turns Eastward," 758.
14 See Johnson, "Introduction."
15 Mark Bevir, "Annie Besant's Quest for Truth: Christianity, Secularism and New Age Thought," *Journal of Ecclesiastical History* 50, no. 1 (January 1999): 62–93, 87.
16 Suzanne Marchand, *German Orientalism in the Age of Empire: Religion, Race, and Scholarship* (Cambridge: Cambridge University Press, 2009), i.
17 Quoted in Edward Said, *Orientalism* (New York: Vintage, 1978), 77 (Reference to Raymond Schwab, *Vie d'Anquetil-Duperron, suivie des Usages civils, et religieux des Perses par Anquetil-Duperron* [Paris: Ernest Leroux, 1934], 10, 96, 4, 6.
18 Radda-Bai, *Iz peshcher i debrei Indostana; pis'ma na rodinu*, published in *Moskovskie vedomosti* from 30 November 1879 through January 1882. Second series: *Russkii vestnik* 11 (1885), 2–3, 8 (1886). See also *Iz peshcher i debreĭ Indostana: pis'ma na rodinu* / Radda-Bai (Moskva: v Univ. tip. [M. Katkov], 1883), which contains all of part 1 and some of part 2 of her narrative. The full Russian text of the second series is as follows: Letters I–II are in *Russkii vestnik*, vol. 180, Nov.–Dec. 1885, 270–323. Letter III is in *Russkii vestnik*, vol. 181, part 2, Feb. 1886, 772–92, and Letter IV is from 792 to 822 in the same volume. Letters V and VI are in *Russkii vestnik*, vol. 182, March 1886, 318–35 and 335–54, respectively, and Letter VII is on 684–718 of *Russkii vestnik*, t. 184, part 2 (Aug. 1886). An excellent translation of Blavatsky's narrative entitled *From the Caves and Jungles of Hindostan* was made by Boris de Zirkoff (Wheaton, IL: Theosophical Publishing House, 1975). De Zirkoff follows Blavatsky's text as taken from *Russkii vestnik*, which included the entire texts of the *Moskovskie vedomosti* letters along with some additional footnotes and one additional section, added by Blavatsky. Russian editions do not always contain her complete text. English translations are taken from this text unless otherwise indicated.
19 A Russian version of *Zagadochnye plemena na "Golubykh gorakh"* can be found at https://filosoff.org/blavatsky/tvorchestvo/zagadochnye

-plemena-na-golubyx-gorax/, and an English translation, called *The People of the Blue Mountains*, can be found at https://www.filosofiaesoterica .com/the-people-of-the-blue-mountains/.

20 For example, a disgruntled Muslim Seyd M. is quoted as follows: "They constantly prate to us about the tyranny and despotism of Russia. Do you know the answer to that from our Moslems, the descendants of the sultans, sardars, heroes and greatest statesmen of bygone centuries? They say: 'Yes, maybe the administrators of Russia are cruel, and its government hardly to be compared with the "benign" government of Her Majesty, the Empress of India. But when we read and hear on all sides that such-and-such a general in Russia is a *Moslem*, and such-and-such a one is an Armenian, and in spite of this is the Commander-in-Chief of a whole army, while here the lowliest English soldier would rather desert than consent to acknowledge a *native* as commander, even though the latter were of princely blood, and comparing our sad fate with the fate and the hopes of any man of a different faith or tribe faithful to Russia, a question arises in our souls: "Why are we the only ones to deserve such a humiliation, why do we find ourselves in a dark body? Realizing in silent despair the inescapable nature of our situation, why should we not envy at times the circumstances of our brother-Moslem in so-called *despotic* Russia!.."'" Blavatsky, *From the Caves*, 155. *Iz peshcher i debreĭ Indostana: pis'ma na rodinu* / Radda-Bai. H.P. Blavatsky (Helena Petrovna), 1831–91. Moskva: v Univ. tip. (M. Katkov), 1883, 133–4. Emphasis in the original.

21 Gita Dharampal-Frick et al., eds., *Key Concepts in Modern Indian Studies* (New York: NYU Press, 2015), "Caste": 37–42, 39.

22 Gita Dharampal-Frick et al., eds., *Key Concepts in Modern Indian Studies*, 39.

23 Gita Dharampal-Frick et al., eds., *Key Concepts in Modern Indian Studies*, 38–9.

24 *The Durbar of Lahore*, Letter V., 241, and footnote 1. The letters themselves ran from 30 November 1879 to January 1882 in the *Moscow Herald*, and then from 1883 to 1886 in the *Russian Herald*. See Carlson, *"No Religion,"* 51.

25 A reference to the same Seyd M., a young Muslim man who wears European clothes and was educated in England, but complains bitterly of the haughtiness and contempt of British officials in India. (154 and ff.) *Iz peshcher i debreĭ Indostana*, entire discussion 130–6.

26 Constance Frederica Gordon-Cumming, *From the Hebrides to the Himalayas: A Sketch of Eighteen Months' Wanderings in Western Isles and Eastern Highlands* (London: Sampson Low, Marson, Searle, and Rivington), 1876, 2 vols.

27 *The Letters of H. P. Blavatsky to A. P. Sinnett and Other Miscellaneous Letters*, transcribed, compiled, and with an introduction by A.T. Barker

(Pasadena, CA: Theosophical University Press, 1973) (facsimile edition first published 1925), 153. An excerpt of this quotation is also published in Blavatsky, *From the Caves*, xxxiii. Emphasis in the original.

28 John Murray (Firm) and Edward B Eastwick, *A Handbook for India: Being an Account of the Three Presidencies, And of the Overland Route* (London: J. Murray, 1859), quoted (accurately except for the exact title) with attribution, on page 215 of *From the Caves*. The quotations come from pages 83–4 of vol. 1 of the *Handbook*.

29 See, for example, Gary Lachman, *Madame Blavatsky: The Mother of Modern Spirituality* (London: Penguin, 2012), particularly ch. 3, "Seven Years in Tibet?"

30 Henry Steel Olcott, *Old Diary Leaves: The True Story of the Theosophical Society*. Second Series, 1878–83 (London: The Theosophical Publishing Society and Madras: Theosophist Office, 1900). H.P. Blavatsky and Vera Vladimirovna Johnston, *From the Caves and Jungles of Hindostan* (London: Theosophical Publishing Society, 1892).

31 Henry Steel Olcott, *Old Diary Leaves*, 34–8.

32 Blavatsky and Vera Vladimirovna Johnston, *From the Caves*, translator's preface (Johnston).

33 Suzanne Marchand, *German Orientalism in the Age of Empire: Religion, Race, and Scholarship* (Cambridge: Cambridge University Press, 2009), 129; Marchand is referring to Christian Lassen, in his *Indische Altertumskunde*, 1858. Lassen "used 'Arier' to refer to the lighter-skinned, ruling people of northern India, the people who, he argued, were 'the true subject of Indian history' – both, it seems because they defined its high culture and because they were the ones to leave the records" (Marchand, 128).

34 Vera Tolz, *Russia's Own Orient*, 61; V.V. Bartol'd, "Zadachi russkogo vostokovedeniia v Turkestane," in his *Sochineniia*, vol. 9, 529. On the subject of racialization of Orientalist studies, see also Marchand, *German Orientalism*. Bartol'd's full sentence reads: "Преувеличенное представление о культурных заслугах арийцев и варварстве турок не могло не отразиться на понимании научных задач России в Туркестане; в 1895 г., при открытии действий местного археологического кружка, высшим представителем русской власти в крае кружку было предложена задача изучить древнюю арийскую культуру края, уничтоженную варварами-турками и подлежащую восстановлению при господстве других арийцев – русских." ("The exaggerated perception of the cultural achievements of the Aryans and the barbarism of the Turks could not avoid having an impact on the understanding of Russia's scholarly tasks in Turkestan; in 1895 at the opening of the activity of the local archaeological kruzhok, the highest representative of Russian authority in the region gave the kruzhok the task of studying ancient Aryan culture of the area, which had been

destroyed by the barbarian Turks and underlying its resurrection through the control of other Aryans – Russians.")

35 Col. James Tod, 1782–1835, was an English officer of the East India Company and a scholar who wrote on the history and geography of India, especially Rajasthan, and is referenced throughout Blavatskaia's *From the Caves*. The tale of Collector Rous Peter, or Peters, as Blavatskaia calls him, is discussed in the third letter of Part II (526–46) of *From the Caves*, and in *Russkii vestnik*, vol. 180, Nov.–Dec. 1885, 270–84. See also Donald S. Lopez, "Orientalist vs. Theosophist," about Müller, Olcott, and Blavatsky, in *Imagining the East*, 37–57.

36 Edward Said notes, "There was general agreement too that, according to a strangely transformed variety of Darwinism sanctioned by Darwin himself, the modern Orientals were degraded remnants of a former greatness; the ancient or 'classical,' civilizations of the Orient were perceivable through the disorders of present decadence," *Orientalism*, 232–3.

37 Srinivas Aravamudan, *Guru English: South Asian Religion in a Cosmopolitan Language* (Princeton, NJ: Princeton University Press, 1995), 92.

38 Van der Veer, *Colonial Encounters*, 58.

39 I will not try here to adjudicate the thorny question of Blavatskaia's relationship to her "masters," but will point the reader to a number of texts that do address the topic. See, for example, K. Paul Johnson, *The Masters Revealed: Madame Blavatsky and the Myth of the Great White Lodge* (New York: SUNY Press, 1994); Lachman's *Madame Blavatsky*; Carlson's *"No Religion"*; Christopher Hutton, "Back to Blavatsky: The Impact of Theosophy on Modern Linguists" *Language and Communication* 18 (1998): 181–204; and a review by Steven Prothero, "Theosophy's Sinner/Saint: Recent Books on Madame Blavatsky," *Religious Studies Review* 23, no. 5 (July 1997): 257–651. Prothero reviews Carlson's *"No Religion,"* Cranston's *HPB: The Extraordinary Life and Influence of Helena Blavatsky*; Peter Washington's *Madame Blavatsky's Baboon: A History of the Mystics, Mediums, and Misfits Who Brought Spiritualism to America* (New York: Schocken Books, 1995); Johnson's *The Masters Revealed*; Joscelyn Godwin's *The Theosophical Enlightenment* (New York: SUNY Press, 1994); and Michael Gomes's *Theosophy in the Nineteenth Century: An Annotated Bibliography* (New York: Garland Publishing, 1994).

40 De Zirkoff, introduction to *From the Caves*, xi–x, quoting from *The Theosophist*, vol. V, Dec.–Jan., 1883–4, 64.

41 Gauri Viswanathan, *Outside the Fold: Conversion, Modernity, and Belief* (Princeton, NJ: Princeton University Press, 1998); Gauri Viswanathan, "The Ordinary Business of Occultism," *Critical Inquiry* 27, no. 1 (Autumn 2000): 1–20; Gauri Viswanathan, "In Search of Madame Blavatsky: Reading the Exoteric, Retrieving the Esoteric,"

Representations 141 (Winter 2018): 67–94; Pat Holden, ed., *Women's Religious Experience* (London and Totowa, NJ: Croom Helm and Barnes & Noble, 1983); Joy Dixon, *Divine Feminine: Theosophy and Feminism in England* (Baltimore: Johns Hopkins University Studies in Historical and Political Science; 119th Ser., 1, 2001); Peter Van Der Veer, *Imperial Encounters: Religion and Modernity in India and Britain* (Princeton, NJ: Princeton University Press, 2001); Stephen R. Prothero, *The White Buddhist: The Asian Odyssey of Henry Steel Olcott*, Religion in North America (Bloomington: Indiana University Press, 1996); Nicholas Goodrick-Clarke, *The Western Esoteric Traditions: A Historical Introduction* (Oxford and New York: Oxford University Press, 2008); James Webb, *The Occult Underground* (LaSalle, IL: Open Court, 1974); Helen Sword, *Ghostwriting Modernism* (Ithaca, NY: Cornell University Press, 2002); Alex Owen, *The Darkened Room: Women, Power, and Spiritualism in Late Victorian England*, New Cultural Studies Series (Philadelphia: University of Pennsylvania Press, 1990).

42 Radda-Bai, *Iz peshcher i debrei Indostana*, part 1 (supplement to the journal *Russkii vestnik*) (Moscow: Universitetskaia tipografiia [M. Katkov], 1883); Radda-Bai, *Iz peshcher i debrei Indostana*, part 2 (supplement to *Russkii vestnik*) (Moscow: Universitetskaia tipografiia [M. Katkov], 1883). Parts 3 and 4 were also published as a supplement to *Russkii vestnik* in 1886. Boris de Zirkoff states that the last part of Blavatskaia's second volume, ch. VII of part II, was published in vol. 184 in *Russkii vestnik* in August 1886, 684–718 (*From the Caves*, 660, footnote).

43 Blavatsky and Vera Vladimirovna Johnston, *From the Caves*.

44 Blavatsky and de Zirkoff, *From the Caves*, 1975.

45 Just how much money is not known, but she mentions that, due to her disagreement with Vsevolod Soloviev, who wrote the highly critical *The Modern Priestess of Isis*, that she expected to lose "a few thousand roubles a year." *The Letters of H. P. Blavatsky to A. P. Sinnett and other miscellaneous letters*, 193.

46 E.P. Blavatskaia, *Pis'ma druz'iam i sotrudnikam. Sbornik. Per. s angliiskogo P. Sh. Akhunov* (M: Sfera, 2002, 784 pp.), Primechaniia T. V Korzhen'iants. http://svitk.ru/004_book_book/13b/2917_blavatskaya-pisma _druzyam_i_sotrudnikam.php#_ftn415.

47 The relationship between Blavatskaia and Olcott was, by all accounts, platonic, although Olcott apparently fell under Blavatskaia's spell, at least for a time, but there was also, according to Stephen Prothero, significant tension between the two from the beginning; as Prothero puts it, "Blavatsky was its philosopher while Olcott was its ethicist. If spiritualism lacked a coherent, unifying philosophy, then it was Blavatsky's job to provide it; and if whiskey-drinkers, free-lovers, and

socialists had overtaken the spiritualist movement, then it was up to Olcott to restore moral order" (*The White Buddhist*, 51).

48 Olcott, *Old Diary Leaves*, 21.

49 See https://www.carloscardosoaveline.com/wp-content /uploads/2019/01/The-Aquarian-Theosophis_January2019.pdf.

50 Johnson, *Masters Revealed*, 122.

51 Olcott, *Old Diary Leaves*, 111. The parting of ways of Wimbridge and Bates with Olcott and Blavatskaia is referenced, among other places, on page 3 of a 13 September 1880 letter in the *Bombay Gazette*, titled "Tempest in a Teapot," http://www.blavatskyarchives.com/anonbgtt.htm.

52 Olcott, *Old Diary Leaves*, 56.

53 Vsevelod Sergyeevich Solovyoff, *A Modern Priestess of Isis*, abridged and translated on behalf of the Society for Psychical Research from the Russian, translated by Walter Leaf, with appendices (London: Longmans, Green and Co., 1895), 10.

54 Vsevelod S. Solov'iev, *Sovremennaia zhritsa Izidy: Moe znakomstvo s E. P. Blavatskoi i "Teosofskim obshchestvom,"* (Epizod "fin de siècle") (St. Petersburg: Tip. Obshchestvennaia pol'za), 1893), 5.

55 Carlson, *"No Religion,"* 51–2. Carlson cites page 279 of *Sovremennaia zhritsa Izidy*.

56 Witte, *Vospominaniia*, in "O predkakh," "Я помню, что когда я познакомился в Москве с Катковым, он заговорил со мной о моей двоюродной сестре Блавацкой, которую он лично не знал, но перед талантом которой преклонялся, почитая ее совершенно выдающимся человеком. В то время в его журнале 'Русский Вестник' печатались известные рассказы Блавацкой 'В дебрях Индостана', и он был очень удивлен, когда я высказал мое мнение, что Блавацкую нельзя принимать всерьез, хотя, несомненно, в ней был какой то сверхъестественный талант." ("I recall that when I met Katkov in Moscow, he talked to me about my cousin Blavatskaia, whom he did not know personally, but whose talent he was greatly impressed by, considering her an absolutely outstanding person. At that time he was publishing Blavatskaia's famous letters 'In the jungles of Hindostan' in his journal, *Russkii vestnik,* and he was quite surprised when I told him that in my opinion one could not take Blavatskaia seriously, although she had a preternatural talent.")

57 Esper Esperovich Ukhtomskii, *Puteshestvie na Vostok Ego Imperatorskogo Vysochestva Gosudaria Naslednika Tsesarevicha*, 1890–1. Avtor-Izdatel' E.E. Ukhtomskii. Illiustriroval N.N. Karazin, tom. 2, Leipzig, F.A. Brokgauz, 1895, 88–91. Emphasis in the original.

58 Andreas Renner, "Defining a Russian Nation: Mikhail Katkov and the 'Invention" of National Politics," *Slavonic and East European Review* 81, no. 4 (October 2003): 659–82, 661.

59 H.P. Blavatsky, *Collected Writings*, vol. 2, 1879–1880 (Wheaton, IL; Madras, India; and London, n.d.), 263–6.

60 Radda-Bai, *Iz peshcher*, 10. Blavatsky, *From the Caves*, 9–10. Russian quotations taken from Radda-Bai, *Iz peshcher*. H.P. Blavatsky (Helena Petrovna), 1831–91. Moskva: v Univ. tip. (M. Katkov), 1883, except for the second series, which will be given according to their appearance in *Russkii vestnik*. English taken from de Zirkoff translation, 1975.

61 Radda-Bai, *Iz peshcher*, 13; Blavatsky, *From the Caves*, 13.

62 On page 14 in both languages.

63 Both of the foregoing quotations occur on page 16 of each text.

64 Blavatsky and de Zirkoff, *From the Caves*, 154 in terms of the rejection of a business visit by an Indian Muslim to an English lady (see footnote 20 above), 316 for the "Refreshment Rooms" incident (Radda-Bai, *Iz peshcher*, 343–4), and 326 when Lady Cooper of Allahabad was shocked that Blavatskaia and her companions did not leave their cards with her (*Iz peshcher*, 356).

65 Éadaoin Agnew, *Imperial Women Writers in Victorian India: Representing Colonial Life, 1850–1910* (London: Palgrave, 2017), first quotation from page 9, second from page 184.

66 Blavatsky and de Zirkoff, *From the Caves*, 38; Radda-Bai, *Iz peshcher*, 35.

67 Blavatsky and de Zirkoff, *From the Caves*, "Deeds of long forgotten days,/ traditions of a distant era," 43, Radda-Bai, *Iz peshcher*, 39. Pushkin, PSS v. 4 (1937): 1–88, 7.

68 Blavatsky and de Zirkoff, *From the Caves*, 45; Radda-Bai, *Iz peshcher*, 41. (The English translation has "would have driven any Parisian woman frantic with envy.")

69 Blavatsky and de Zirkoff, *From the Caves*, 45–6; Radda-Bai, *Iz peshcher i debrei*, 41.

70 Blavatsky and de Zirkoff, *From the Caves*, 184; Radda-Bai, *Iz peshcher*, 159.

71 Blavatsky and de Zirkoff, *From the Caves*, 192, Radda-Bai, *Iz peshcher*, 165.

72 Olcott, *Old Diary Leaves*, vol. 2, 34–6.

73 Blavatsky and de Zirkoff, *From the Caves*, 188–9; Radda-Bai, *Iz peshcher*, 162–3.

74 Constance Gordon-Cumming, *From the Hebrides to the Himalayas*, vol. ii, 325.

75 Blavatsky and de Zirkoff, *From the Caves*, 191–2, Radda-Bai, *Iz peshcher*, 164–5.

76 Blavatsky and de Zirkoff, *From the Caves*, 202–6; Radda-Bai, *Iz peshcher*, 174–8. Gordon-Cumming also mentions the fossil of a "sivathere" in her book, on page 289.

77 Blavatsky and de Zirkoff, *From the Caves*, 217–18, Radda-Bai, *Iz peshcher*, 188–9.

78 Horace Hayman Wilson, *Works by the Late Horace Hayman Wilson*, M.A., F.R.S., Vol. II (London: Trübner & Co., 60, Paternoster Row, 1862); Wilson specifically says, "I have reason to believe, that the burning of widows was unknown to the Vedic period of Hindu religion or belief" (307).

79 Blavatsky and de Zirkoff, *From the Caves*, 232–3; Radda-Bai, *Iz peshcher*, 201–2. Emphasis in the original.

80 Blavatsky and de Zirkoff, *From the Caves*, 240, Radda-Bai, *Iz peshcher*, 208.

81 Mills, *Gender and Colonial Space*, 99; quoting Margaret Strobel, *European Women and the Second British Empire* (Bloomington: Indiana University Press, 1991), 51.

82 Mark Bevir, "Mothering India," *History Today* 56, no. 2 (February 2006): 19–25, 20.

83 Blavatsky and de Zirkoff, *From the Caves*, Letter 21, 250–9; Radda-Bai, *Iz peshcher*, 216–24.

84 Blavatsky and de Zirkoff, *From the Caves*, 253; Radda-Bai, *Iz peshcher*, 218–19.

85 Mary Louise Pratt remarks on the disembodied "imperial eyes" of Western travelers in *Imperial Eyes: Travel Writing and Transculturation* (London: Routledge, 1992), 59. Sara Mills notes the common awareness among female travellers about how they must appear to others, as distinct from the absence of such perceptions among male travellers (*Discourses of Difference*, 98).

86 Blavatsky and de Zirkoff, *From the Caves*, 252; Radda-Bai, *Iz peshcher*, 218. Olcott actually gives the weight of Blavataskaia (237 lbs.) and himself (170 lbs.) after their trip to Ceylon. (*Old Diary Leaves*, Second Series, 205).

87 Unsteady: Blavatsky and de Zirkoff, *From the Caves*, 309; Radda-Bai, *Iz peshcher*, 270; fakirs' avenue: Blavatsky, *From the Caves*, 311; Radda-Bai, *Iz peshcher*, 272.

88 Blavatsky and de Zirkoff, *From the Caves*, 313; Radda-Bai, *Iz peshcher*, 274.

89 Blavatsky and de Zirkoff, *From the Caves*, 325–6; Radda-Bai, *Iz peshcher*, 286–7.

90 Blavatsky and de Zirkoff, *From the Caves*, 316; Radda-Bai, *Iz peshcher*, 277. Emphasis in the original.

91 Arya Samajists: Hindu reform movement, led by Swami Dayananda Saraswati. The Theosophical Society was at first allied with the Arya Samaj. See Gary Lachman, *Madame Blavatsky: The Mother of Modern Spirituality* (London: Penguin, 2012), 170–5.

92 Olcott, *Old Diary Leaves*, 78. As both Carlson and Lachman note, Blavatskaia was understood to be a spy by the British.

93 Olcott, *Old Diary Leaves*, 81.

94 Olcott, *Old Diary Leaves*, 82–3.

95 Steven Prothero, *The White Buddhist*, 81.

96 See, for example, vols. 2 and 3 of Blavatskaia's *Collected Writings*.

97 See, for example, her third volume of collected writings, which contains numerous letters to the editor; one exchange concerned the falling out of Rosa Bates and Edward Wimbridge, on the one hand, with Olcott and Blavatskaia on the other. http://www.katinkahesselink.net/blavatsky/articles/v3/. A letter by Olcott (http://www.blavatskyarchives.com/olcottbg1880.htm_) also attests to discussion in the *Bombay Gazette* of the Theosophical Society, which he also discusses in his second volume of *Old Diary Leaves* (206–12).

98 Carlson, "No Religion," 40 and 214, respectively. See also *Russkie pisateli 1800–1917 biograficheskii slovar'* (Moscow, 1989), vol. 1, 272–3.

99 Prothero, *The White Buddhist*, 71.

100 Blavatsky and de Zirkoff, *From the Caves*, 368; Radda-Bai, *Iz peshcher*, 321–2.

101 Blavatsky and de Zirkoff, *From the Caves*, 374; Radda-Bai, *Iz peshcher*, 327. Emphasis in the original.

102 https://en.wikipedia.org/wiki/Suppression_of_the_Indian_Revolt_by _the_English. Alexander Morrison notes that this depiction is actually of the consequences of a Sikh rebellion, not the Sepoy Rebellion. *Russian Rule in Samarkand*, 169, note 142.

103 Blavatsky and de Zirkoff, *From the Caves*, 57; Radda-Bai, *Iz peshcher*, 64.

104 Patrick Brantlinger provides a brief, helpful account in *Rule of Darkness: British Literature and Imperialism, 1830–1914* (Ithaca, NY: Cornell University Press, 1988), 200–2.

105 Blavatsky and de Zirkoff, *From the Caves*, 376; Radda-Bai, *Iz peshcher*, 329.

106 Mike Davis, *Late Victorian Holocausts: El Niño Famines and the Making of the Third World* (New York: Verso, 2001), 25–58.

107 Blavatsky and de Zirkoff, *From the Caves*, 376–7; Radda-Bai, *Iz peshcher*, 329. The longer quotation, from Horace's *Satires*, reads: "Absentem qui rodit amicum, qui non defendit, alio culpante; hic niger est; hunc tu, Romane, caveto – He who attacks an absent friend, or who does not defend him when spoken ill of by another; that man is a dark character; you, Romans, beware of him." And in the words of a curator at the British Museum, "suggest[s] that the subject has betrayed a friend." https:// www.britishmuseum.org/research/collection_online/collection_object _details.aspx?objectId=3073434&partId=1.

108 On Rani of Jhansi, see Harleen Singh. *The Rani of Jhansi: Gender, History, and Fable in India* (Cambridge: Cambridge University Press, 2014).

109 Blavatsky and de Zirkoff, *From the Caves*, 386; Radda-Bai, *Iz peshcher*, 337–8. Emphasis in the original.

110 Blavatsky and de Zirkoff, *From the Caves*, 391; Radda-Bai, *Iz peshcher*, 342.

111 Blavatsky and de Zirkoff, *From the Caves*, 392–3; Radda-Bai, *Iz peshcher*, 344–5.

112 Blavatsky and de Zirkoff, *From the Caves*, footnote on 392–3; Radda-Bai, *Iz peshcher*, footnote on 344.

113 Madame [Emma] Coulomb, *Some Account of My Intercourse with Madame Blavatsky from 1872 to 1884; with a Number of Additional Letters and a Full Explanation of the Most Marvellous Theosophical Phenomena* (London: Elliot Stock, 1885), 104.

114 Blavatsky and de Zirkoff, *From the Caves*, 396; Radda-Bai, *Iz peshcher*, 346.

115 Blavatsky and de Zirkoff, *From the Caves*, 411; Radda-Bai, *Iz peshcher*, 360.

116 Blavatsky and de Zirkoff, *From the Caves*, 401–2; Radda-Bai, *Iz peshcher*, 350–1.

117 Blavatsky and de Zirkoff, *From the Caves*, 406; Radda-Bai, *Iz peshcher*, 355–6.

118 Blavatsky and de Zirkoff, *From the Caves*, 410; Radda-Bai, *Iz peshcher*, 359.

119 Blavatsky and de Zirkoff, *From the Caves*, 430; Radda-Bai, *Iz peshcher*, 378.

120 Gordon-Cumming, *From the Hebrides*, vol. ii, 7.

121 Blavatsky and de Zirkoff, *From the Caves*, 429–30; Radda-Bai, *Iz peshcher*, 377.

122 Blavatsky and de Zirkoff, *From the Caves*, 430; Radda-Bai, *Iz peshcher*, 378.

123 Gordon-Cumming, *From the Hebrides*, vol. ii, 1–2.

124 Blavatsky and de Zirkoff, *From the Caves*, 132; Radda-Bai, *Iz peshcher*, 112–13.

125 Blavatsky and de Zirkoff, *From the Caves*, 432; Radda-Bai, *Iz peshcher*, 380. It should be noted that Pushkin references Sadi in both "The Fountain of Bakchisarai" and *Eugene Onegin*.

126 Blavatsky and de Zirkoff, *From the Caves*, 436; Radda-Bai, *Iz peshcher*, 383. Tavernier is Jean-Baptiste Tavernier (1605–89), a gem merchant and traveller. Gordon-Cumming, *From the Hebrides*, 15.

127 Blavatsky and de Zirkoff, *From the Caves*, 436; Radda-Bai, *Iz peshcher*, 383.

128 "The Fountain of Bakhchisarai," translated by Walter Arndt, *Collected Narrative and Lyrical Poetry of Alexander Pushkin*, translated in the Prosodic Forms of the Original by Walter Arndt (New York: Ardis, 2009), 265. "Bakhchisaraiskii fontan" is in Pushkin, *Polnoe sobranie sochinenii v 16 tomakh*, 4:153–76 (1937), 169–70.

129 Blavatsky and de Zirkoff, *From the Caves*, 440; Radda-Bai, *Iz peshcher*, 387. Emphasis in the original.

130 Gordon-Cumming, *From the Hebrides*, vol. ii, 18–19.

131 Olcott, *Old Diary Leaves*, 208–9.

132 Blavatsky and de Zirkoff, *From the Caves*, 460; Radda-Bai, *Iz peshcher*, 406.

133 Blavatsky and de Zirkoff, *From the Caves*, 460; Radda-Bai, *Iz peshcher*, 406.

134 Blavatsky and de Zirkoff, *From the Caves*, 489; *Russkii vestnik* 180 (Nov.–Dec. 1885): Letters 1–2 of second part, 270–323, 290. Letters are divided into 270–304 (Letter I) and 304–23 (Letter II).

135 Blavatsky and de Zirkoff, *From the Caves*, 489–90; *Russkii vestnik* 180 (Nov.–Dec. 1885): 290–1.

136 Blavatsky and de Zirkoff, *From the Caves*, 494; *Russkii vestnik* 180 (Nov.–Dec. 1885): 295.

137 Blavatsky and de Zirkoff, *From the Caves*, 505–25; Olcott, *Old Diary Leaves*, Second Series, 71–2. He also alludes to "vulgar debauchery" in Bhurtpore. *Russkii vestnik* 180 (Nov.–Dec. 1885): 304–23.

138 Blavatsky and de Zirkoff, *From the Caves*, 510–12; *Russkii vestnik* 180 (Nov.–Dec. 1885): 309–10.

139 Blavatsky and de Zirkoff, *From the Caves*, 516–20; *Russkii vestnik* 180 (Nov.–Dec. 1885): 315–19. Emphasis in the original.

140 Blavatsky and de Zirkoff, *From the Caves*, 520; *Russkii vestnik* 180 (Nov.–Dec. 1885): 319.

141 Olcott, *Old Diary Leaves*, Second Series, 13. Both Olcott and Blavatskaia describe Moolji, a member of the Theosophical Society, as a frequent travelling companion after their arrival in India. Collector Peters is known as Collector Peter in most sources.

142 Blavatsky and de Zirkoff, *From the Caves*, 526. Letter III of the second series is on 526–46 (translation), and from 772–92 of *Russkii vestnik* 181, part 2 (Feb. 1886).

143 https://www.thehindu.com/news/cities/Madurai/enthralling-story-of-rubystudded-stirrups/article7160861.ece.

144 Blavatsky and de Zirkoff, *From the Caves*, 538–9; *Russkii vestnik* 181, part 2 (Feb. 1886): (Letters III and IV, 772–822), 783–5.

145 Blavatsky and de Zirkoff, *From the Caves*, 546; *Russkii vestnik* 181, part 2 (Feb. 1886): 791. Emphasis in the original.

146 Olcott, *Old Diary Leaves*, 71.

147 Letters V and VI, *Russkii vestnik* 182 (March 1886): 318–35 and 335–54, respectively.

148 Blavatsky and de Zirkoff, *From the Caves*, 639; *Russkii vestnik* 184, part 2 (Aug. 1886): Letter VII, 684–718, 700.

149 Blavatsky and de Zirkoff, *From the Caves*, 639–40; *Russkii vestnik* 184, part 2 (Aug. 1886): (Letter VI, 684–718), 700–1.

150 There are seven letters in all. Letters I–IV were printed in *Russkii vestnik* 153 (1881), as follows: I, 5–16; II, 16–38; III, 584–601; IV, 601–13. Letters V–VII were printed in *Russkii vestnik* 154 (1881), as follows: V, 171–84; VI, 185–98; and VII, 198–218. The entire Russian text can also be found at http://www.magister.msk.ru/library/blavatsk/india/blvlahor.htm.

151 The translated letters were printed as follows: *The Theosophist*, Theosophical Society (Madras, India) [Adyar, etc.: Theosophical Publishing House, etc.], Vol. 82 (1960): August 1960, Letter I, 289–302; Letter II, September 1960, 359–74; second half of Letter II, October 1960, 8–20; Letter III, November 1960, 81–101; Letter IV, December 1960, 148–63; 1961: vol. 83: Letter V, January 1961, 229–45; Letter VI, February 1961, 286–302; Letter VII, March 1961, 357–80. A note from Boris de Zirkoff notes that the English translation was based on a rough translation by Inga Sjöstedt and later revised by de Zirkoff and Irene Ponsonby, who had long been involved in editing Blavatskaia's *Collected Writings* (see page 289 of the August 1960 article). A PDF of this translation can also be found under "Durbar in Lahore" at http://www.iapsop.com/ssoc/1881__blavatsky___the_durbar_in_lahore.pdf. Quotations taken from the English translation will indicate letter and page number.

152 Olcott, *Old Diary Leaves*, 263–5.

153 Peter Hopkirk, *The Great Game: The Struggle for Empire in Central Asia* (New York: Kodansha, 1992), 370–401; Evgeny Sergeev, *The Great Game 1856–1907: Russo-British Relations in Central and East Asia* (Washington and Baltimore: Johns Hopkins University Press, 2013), 149–210, "The Climax of the Great Game, 1874–1885."

154 http://www.iapsop.com/ssoc/1881__blavatsky___the_durbar_in _lahore.pdf. Third letter, page 9., *Russkii vestnik* 153 (1881): 29. Translation slightly altered.

155 Blavatsky, "The Durbar in Lahore," Letter II, 10, *Russkii vestnik* 153 (1881): 30.

156 Blavatsky, "The Durbar in Lahore," Letter II, 12, *Russkii vestnik* 153 (1881): 31. Blavatskaia calls it "miatezh" in Russian.

157 Blavatsky, "The Durbar in Lahore," Letter II, 11, *Russkii vestnik* 153 (1881): 31.

158 Blavatsky, "The Durbar in Lahore," Letter III, 81, *Russkii vestnik* 153 (1881): 584.

159 Blavatsky, "The Durbar in Lahore," Letter III, 86, *Russkii vestnik* 153 (1881): 588–9.

160 Blavatsky, "The Durbar in Lahore," Letter III, 93, *Russkii vestnik* 153 (1881): 594.

161 Blavatsky, "The Durbar in Lahore," Letter III, 95, *Russkii vestnik* 153 (1881): 595.

162 Blavatsky, "The Durbar in Lahore," Letter III, 95, *Russkii vestnik* 153 (1881): 596.

163 Blavatsky, "The Durbar in Lahore," Letter III, 96, *Russkii vestnik* 153 (1881): 597.

164 Blavatsky, "The Durbar in Lahore," Letter III, 98, *Russkii vestnik* 153 (1881): 598.

165 Blavatsky, "The Durbar in Lahore," Letter III, 99, *Russkii vestnik* 153 (1881): 599.

166 Blavatsky, "The Durbar in Lahore," Letter III, 100–1, *Russkii vestnik* 153 (1881): 600.

167 Hopkirk, *The Great Game*, 380; Sergeev, *The Great Game*, 172–89.

168 Blavatsky, "The Durbar in Lahore," Letter IV, 149–50, *Russkii vestnik* 153 (1881): 602.

169 Blavatsky, "The Durbar in Lahore," Letter IV, 160, *Russkii vestnik* 153 (1881): 611.

170 Thomas Moore, *Lalla Rookh*, first published in 1817, 25–6, https://ebooks .adelaide.edu.au/m/moore/thomas/lalla-rookh/index.html.

171 Blavatsky, "The Durbar in Lahore," Letter IV, 159–60, *Russkii vestnik* 153 (1881): 610–11.

172 Blavatsky, "The Durbar in Lahore," Letter V, 232–3, *Russkii vestnik* 154 (1881): 174.

173 Blavatsky, "The Durbar in Lahore," Letter V, 234, *Russkii vestnik* 154 (1881): 176.

174 For the elephant with a ladder, see Blavatsky, "The Durbar in Lahore," Letter V, 233, and Gordon-Cumming, *From the Hebrides*, 89. For the objection to carving emeralds and setting stones in silver, see Gordon-Cumming, *From the Hebrides*, 90, and similarly, "The Durbar in Lahore," Letter V, 234 for Blavatskaia's objections to the same. Both writers also go from describing the animals to describing the people who accompany them. Gordon-Cumming describes the durbar (darbar) on pages 88–102.

175 Blavatsky, "The Durbar in Lahore," Letter V, 235, *Russkii vestnik* 154 (1881): 176–7.

176 Blavatsky, "The Durbar in Lahore," Letter V, 238–9, *Russkii vestnik* 154 (1881): 179.

177 Blavatsky, "The Durbar in Lahore," Letter V, 241 and footnote 1, *Russkii vestnik* 154 (1881): 181. The *Bombay Gazette* did indeed print a letter to the editor on 6 November 1880 entitled "A Challenge to Madame Blavatsky," criticizing Blavatsky. https://archive.org/details/dli.granth.28172. Emphasis in the original.

178 Blavatsky, "The Durbar in Lahore," Letter V, 241, *Russkii vestnik* 154 (1881): 181.

179 Blavatsky, "The Durbar in Lahore," Letter V, 242, *Russkii vestnik* 154 (1881): 182. To be clear, it is the young man who uses the term "darkies," not Blavatskaia.

180 Blavatsky, "The Durbar in Lahore," Letter V, 244–5, *Russkii vestnik* 15 (1881): 183–4.

181 Tolstoy, *PSS*, vol. 37, 245–58 in English, 259–72 in Russian.

182 References, respectively, in Blavatsky, "Durbar at Lahore," Letter VII, 364 (letter from St. Petersburg), 371 (Kaufman), and 366 (Blavatskaia feels guilty), *Russkii vestnik* 154 (1881): 205, 210, and 206.

183 Blavatsky, "The Durbar in Lahore," Letter VII, 374, *Russkii vestnik* 154 (1881): 213.

184 Blavatsky, "The Durbar in Lahore," Letter VII, 374, *Russkii vestnik* 154 (1881): 213.

185 Olcott, *Old Diary Leaves*, Second Series, 260.

186 Blavatsky, "The Durbar of Lahore," Letter VII, 378, *Russkii vestnik* 154 (1881): 216.

187 Hopkirk, *The Great Game*, 388.

188 Blavatsky, "The Durbar in Lahore," Letter VII, 380, *Russkii vestnik* 154 (1881): 217–18.

189 Blavatsky, "The Durbar in Lahore," Letter VII, 360, *Russkii vestnik* 154 (1881): 201.

190 Gordon-Cumming, *From the Hebrides*, 311, quotation is from Samuel Butler's (1612–80) "Hudibras."

Chapter 4: Hunting, Photography, and National Rivalry: *In the Pamirs*

1 Iu. D. Golovnina, *Na Pamirakh: Zapiski russkoi puteshestvennitsy* (Moscow, Tipo-litografiia T-va I. N. Kushener' i K, 1902). According to a commenter, Petr Golovnin, on an article on an online website http://www.fergananews.com/article.php?id=4962, Golovnina's maiden name was Nikiforova. http://www.fergananews.com/comments.php?id=4962. A second commenter, Natal'ia Fatieva (Golovnina), says that Golovnin was her grandfather, and Iuliia Golovnina was his first wife. "After his second marriage to my grandmother, Iu. D. became the godmother of their children (my father and his sister) and lived together with them until her death." Comments quoted in their entirety: "П.Головнин, 02.04.2007

Уважаемый господин Дубовицкий! Спасибо за интересное упоминание о Юлии Головниной. Её девичья фамилия Никифорова (в замужестве – за Давидом Николаевичем Головниным) Всего доброго. Петр Головнин, Петербург

Наталья Фатиева(Головнина), 11.11.2013

Давыд Николаевич Головнин-мой дед, а Юлия Дмитриевна-его первая жена, а не наоборот. После его второй женитьбы на моей бабушке Ю.Д. стала крестной их детей (моего отца и его сестры) и жила вместе с ними до самой своей кончины. Ее книга "На Памирах" 1902 года хранится в нашей семье. Буду рада связаться с кем-то из Головниных."

2 D.N. Golovnin, 1865–1929, notes that he had organized the expedition in the first part of his seven-part article (see note 9). A January 1912 article by him, "Sel'skoe khoziaistvo i kholodil'noe delo," reprinted in *Kholodil'naia tekhnika* 2 (2012): 63–7, contains a biography of Golovnin on page 67, indicating that he was related to the famous Golovnin family of explorers like Vasilii Golovnin, the famous naval explorer.

3 On page 189, Golovnina calls herself the "cashier" (*kassir*) of the trip; she includes a detailed explanation of preparations and expenses on pages 232–41.

4 Personal communication with museum staff by Heghine Hakobyan, University of Oregon Slavic librarian.

5 Golovnina, *Na Pamirakh*, 213. St. George and Teresa Littledale travelled extensively in Central Asia and elsewhere in the 1880s and 1890s. St. George Littledale, "A Journey across Central Asia," *The Geographical Journal* 3, no. 5 (June 1894): 445–72; and Nicholas Clinch and Elizabeth Clinch, *Through a Land of Extremes: The Littledales of Central Asia* (Seattle: The Mountaineers Books, 2011), see especially ch. 6 and 7, 103–29.

6 A. Markoff, "On the Afghan Frontier: A Reconnaissance in Shugnan," *Geographical Journal of the Royal Geographical Society* XVI, no. 6 (Dec. 1900): 666–79, 667. Markoff quotes memoirs by Adrian Georgievich Serebrennikov: "We forded the river Murgh-ab after parting from and receiving the good wishes of all our brother-officers remaining behind, and also-last but not least- those of the only lady on the Pamirs, Madame S. G. Skerskaya, who had, in spite of the weather, made one of our honorary escort up to this point" (667).

A letter from Vasilii Nikolaevich Zaitsev (also Zaitsov) mentions Sverskaia's wife. As G.G. Belogolovyi writes: "The replacement detachment of Captain Aleksandr Genrikhovich came to Murgab only on 29 June; a festive meeting of the detachments repeated to precision that of the year before, only this time the person who was meeting [the arrivals] was Zaitsev, but Skerskii was accompanied to the Pamir by his wife Sofiia Georgievna," who "traveled to the side in a man's outfit, burned and exhausted from the long crossing." Quotation from letter by Zaitsev of 9 July 1894, available at http://www.boris-belogolovy.ru/zaycev /zaycev17.html. Sven Hedin, in his *Through Asia*, also remarks on Mrs. Sverskaia in regard to his visit to Pamirskii Post in 1894: "Two other changes had been made since my former visit. The lonely fort, which one of my friends in Fergana called a paradise, because there were no women within its walls, was now honoured with the presence of the young wife of the new commandant, Madame Skersky. German by birth, and a lady of an exceptionally sweet and reliable disposition, she did the honours at table with exquisite charm. Tastes, as we know, differ; but in my opinion the fort was now infinitely more like paradise than it had been before. Threadbare tunics and dusty boots had given place to a more becoming exterior, whilst linen cuffs, blacking, and the little arts of the toilet-table afforded evidence of their existence: everything in fact bore witness to the ennobling presence of woman." Sven Hedin, *Through Asia*, vol. 1, translated by J.T. Bealby (London: Methuen & Co, 1898), 391–2. Quoted in Robert Middleton, *The Russians in the Great Game* (Bishkek, Kyrgyzstan: University of Central Asia, 2019), 43, although the quote given there is to a different edition of Hedin.

7 Robert Middleton and Huw Thomas, *Tajikistan and the High Pamirs: A Companion and Guide* (Hong Kong: Odyssey Books & Guides, 2012), 435. The Golovnins are also cited in Middleton, *Russians in the Great Game*, 51.

8 Middleton and Thomas, *Tajikistan and the High Pamirs*, 481.

9 M.M. Voskoboinikov, "Iz nabliudenii na Pamire (s 10 ris.)," *Zemlevedenie*, vol. 3, 1899 (published by the Obshchestvo liubitelei estestvozananiia, antropologii i etnografii [OLEAE]), 31–60. Includes photographs by Nadezhda Barteneva. D.N. Golovnin, "Ocherki okhoty na Pamirakh," *Priroda i okhota*, in seven parts: "Priroda Pamirov i moia ekspeditsiia," February 1901, kniga II-aia, 1–10; Part II, "Arkhar (Ovis polii, Blyth)," March 1901 kniga III-aia, 1–11; Part III, "Pervaia vstrecha s arkharami," April 1901, kniga IV-aia, 1–9; Part IV, "Okhota na arkharov v okrestnostiakh Bol'shoi Kara-Kul'," May 1901, kniga V-aia, 137–49; Part V, "Okhota na arkharov u perevala Kizil-Dzhiik," June 1901, kniga VI-aia, 95–104, Part VI, "Kiik (Capra Sibirica. Meyer)," July (?) 1901, kniga VII-aia, 21–9; Part VII, "Okhota na kiikov," August 1901, kniga VIII-aia, 1–14. Golovnin also published an additional, eighth article under "Ocherki okhoty na Pamirakh" in *Okhotnik i priroda*, which was not internally numbered, "Ocherki okhoty na Pamirakh po peru," September(?) 1901, kniga IX, 1–16, also available online at https://www.oir.su/anons/28 -08-2013-ocherki-okhoty-na-pamirakh-po-peru. A note on page 40 of the June 1901 issue of *Okhota i priroda* indicates that "Professor Golovnin, author of 'Essays about Hunting in the Pamirs,' at the current time has

left for a trip to the Sayan Mountains." Biography of M.M. Voskoboinikov (1873–1942) in G. Iu. Liubarskii, *Istoriia Zoologicheskogo muzeia MGU: Idei, liudi, struktury* (Moscow: Tovarishchestvo nauchnykh izdanii KMK, 2009), 506. Brief biography of David Nikolaevich Golovnin (1865–1929) in *Kholodil'naia tekhnika* 2 (2012): 67 (following a reprint of an article by him on pages 63–7; original article appeared in *Kholodil'noe delo* 1 [January 1912]: 7–11). Golovnin began as an engineering professor and became a specialist in refrigeration.

10　Lidiia Poltoratskaia, *Al'bom tipov i vidov Zapadnoi Sibiri, sniatykh L. K. Poltoratskoi*. St. Petersburg, 1879, "Poezdka po Kitaiskoi granitse ot Altaia do Tarbagataia," *Russkii vestnik* 93, no. 6 (1871): 580–661, "Bremenskaia ekspeditsiia v Semipalatinskoi oblasti," *Priroda i okhota* 1, no. 3 (1979): 23–52.

11　*Russkii vestnik* 277, no. 2 (February 1902): 641–2, review of *Na Pamirakh*. On the conventions of women's travel writing, see Sara Mills, *Discourses of Difference*, 110.

12　Golovnina, *Na Pamirakh*, 78.

13　Golovnina, *Na Pamirakh*, 101.

14　Golovnina, *Na Pamirakh*, 20.

15　George Curzon, *Russia in Central Asia in 1889, and the Anglo-Russian Question* (London and New York, Longmans, Green, and co., 1889), 29.

16　George Curzon, "The Pamirs and the Source of the Oxus," *The Geographical Journal: Including the Proceedings of the Royal Geographical Society* 8 (July–December 1896): 38. The article appeared in three parts: 32–54, 97–119, and 239–64.

17　Morrison, *The Russian Conquest of Central Asia*, 513–15.

18　Kate Teltscher, "'The Rubicon between the Empires': The River Oxus in the Nineteenth-Century British Geographical Imaginary," in *Writing Travel in Central Asian History*, edited by Nile Green (Bloomington: Indiana University Press, 2014), 135–212, 136–8. For a history of the conquest of the border area, see Alexander Morrison, *The Russian Conquest of Central Asia* (Cambridge: Cambridge University Press, 2021), 483–516.

19　Golovnina, *Na Pamirakh*, 204.

20　Vladimir K. Arsenyev, *Across the Ussuri Kray*, translated by Jonathan Slaght (Bloomington: Indiana University Press, 2016), 5, footnote 1. *Na Pamirakh* notes that the teams are not necessarily great hunters but that their experience (and fitness, it seems, since they are on foot) is invaluable in case of war (Golovnina, *Na Pamirakh*, 67).

21　Curzon writes, "The Alichur Pamir and Yeshil Kul in particular had been for many years the more or less disputed boundary-line between the Afghan and Chinese spheres of jurisdiction on the Pamirs, when, in the early summer of 1891, Colonel Yonoff was despatched by the Russian Government with a body of troops, facetiously christened the Hunting Detachment, nominally in order to shoot Ovis Poli, and to indulge in rifle-practice on the Pamirs (of all places in the world!); really to execute a demonstration over the entire region, to turn out any Chinese or Afghan soldiers who might be found, and to anticipate the proposed diplomatic annexation" (Curzon, *The Pamirs and the Source of the Oxus*, 46). Golovnina finds that Ionov's task was to rightfully claim the territory, and quoting Curzon above (in Russian translation) says he writes "with extreme irritation about this reconnaissance mission"; of course, he also misunderstands (perhaps wilfully) what a "hunting detachment" is in Russian military terms. Quoted in Golovnina, *Na Pamirakh*, footnote on page 205.

22 Golovnina, *Na Pamirakh*, notes to pages 204–6.

23 Golovnina, *Na Pamirakh*, 25.

24 Curzon, *Russia in Central Asia*, 29–30.

25 Clinch, *Through a Land of Extremes*, 117.

26 Dukhovskaia, *Turkestanskie vospominaniia*, 70–1.

27 Curzon, *Russia in Central Asia*, 431.

28 See, for example, Ralph Cobbold, *Innermost Asia: Travel and Sport in the Pamirs* (London: W. Heinemann, 1900), see esp. 261–79; and Charles Cumberland, *Sport on the Pamirs and Turkistan Steppes* (Edinburgh: Blackwood, 1895).

29 Younghusband, 289–98. Grombchevskii is discussed primarily on pages 238–54.

30 Curzon, *Russia in Central Asia*, 429–30.

31 Curzon, *The Pamirs and the Source of the Oxus*, 22–4. Nikolai Alekseevich Severtsov (1827–85), renowned naturalist and explorer.

32 Richard Pierce, *Russian Central Asia, 1867–1917: A Study in Colonial Rule* (Berkeley: University of California Press, 1960), ch. 14, "Native Rebellions," 221–33; and Alexander Morrison, *Russian Rule in Samarkand, 1868–1910, A Comparison with British India* (Oxford: Oxford University Press, 2008), 73–5, 193–5.

33 Golovnina, *Na Pamirakh*, 55. The photo of one of the participants in the rebellion appears on page 56.

34 Golovnin, "Ocherki okhoty na Pamirakh," Part One, 8.

35 Nikolai Alekseevich Severtsov (1827–85), renowned naturalist and explorer and brother-in-law of Lidiia Poltoratskaia (married to her husband's sister).

36 Golovnin, "Ocherki okhoty na Pamirakh," Part Two, 2–3.

37 R. Lydekker, *Wild Oxen, Sheep & Goats of All Lands Living and Extinct* (London: Rowland Ward, 1898), 191.

38 A Kyrgyz film about her appeared in 2014, *Queen of the Mountains*, or *Kurmanjan Datka*. https://www.imdb.com/title/tt2640460/.
39 Golovnina, *Na Pamirakh*, 44.
40 Golovnina, *Na Pamirakh*, 45–7.
41 Golovnina, *Na Pamirakh*, 38.
42 Traveller Stephen Graham described them as follows: "When the harvest has been taken in in Russia many peasants go on pilgrimage to shrines and many go out in quest of new land. The khodoki, or walkers, set out. A village or a family sends out a messenger to seek new land; this messenger is called a khodok. The khodoki are specially encouraged by the Government. The police will not allow a whole village to take to the road and go off all together in quest of land; they insist on the khodok going first and booking something in advance. Very great reductions are made in railway fares and great facilities are given to the khodoki, who go forth and look at all the valleys and irrigated levels at the disposal of the colonists during the year in question. They travel in twos and threes, one khodok being required for each three families." Stephen Graham, *Through Russian Central Asia* (New York: MacMillan, 1916), 149–50.
43 Voskoboinikov, "Iz nabliudenii," 34.
44 Golovnina, *Na Pamirakh*, viii.
45 See Geoffrey Wakeman, *Aspects of Victorian Lithography: Anastatic Printing and Photozincography* (Wymondham: Brewhouse Press, 1970).
46 *Marco Polo's Travels*, with an introduction by John Masefield (London: J. M. Dent and Sons, 1908): "In this plain there are wild animals in great numbers, particularly sheep of a large size, having horns, three, four, and even six palms in length. Of these the shepherds form ladles and vessels for holding their victuals; and with the same materials they construct fences for enclosing their cattle, and securing them against the wolves, with which, they say, the country is infested, and which likewise destroy many of these wild sheep or goats. Their horns and bones being found in large quantities, heaps are made of them at the sides of the road, for the purpose of guiding travellers at the season when it is covered with snow. For twelve days the course is along this elevated plain, which is named Pamer; and as during all that time you do not meet with any habitations, it is necessary to make provision at the outset accordingly. So great is the height of the mountains, that no birds are to be seen near their summits; and however extraordinary it may be thought, it was affirmed, that from the keenness of the air, fires when lighted do not give the same heat as in lower situations, nor produce the same effect in dressing victuals" ch. 29, "Of the Province of Vokhan, of an Ascent for Three Days, Leading to the Summit of a High Mountain, of a Peculiar Breed of Sheep Found There, of the Effect of the Great Elevation Upon Fires, and of the Savage Life of

the Inhabitants," 91. https://archive.org/stream/marcopolo00polouoft /marcopolo00polouoft_djvu.txt.
47 M.G. Gerard, T.H. Holdich, R.A. Wahab, A.W. Alcock, *Report on the Proceedings of the Pamir Boundary Commission*, Office of the Superintendant of Government Printing, Calcutta, India, 1897.
48 Also published under the title "Ocherki okhoty na Pamirakh" but without a number indicating it is the eighth part of the article.
49 Voskoboinikov, "Iz nabliudenii," 46.
50 Voskoboinikov, "Iz nabliudenii," 46.
51 Golovnina, *Na Pamirakh*, 107.
52 Golovnin, "Ocherki okhoty na Pamirakh," Part Six, 27.
53 Harriet Ritvo, *The Animal Estate: The English and Other Creatures in the Victorian Age* (Cambridge, MA, and London: Harvard University Press, 1987), 258–9.
54 Voskoboinikov, "Iz nabliudenii," 54.
55 Sara Mills, *Gender and Colonial Space* (Manchester: Manchester University Press, 2005), 95.
56 Gerard et al., *Proceedings*, see in particular pages 59–83 for a lengthy list of specific genus and species names.
57 Gerard et al., *Proceedings*, 18.
58 Gerard et al., *Proceedings*, 17–21.
59 Golovnin, "Ocherki okhoty na Pamirakh," Part One, 8.
60 Golovnin, "Ocherki okhoty na Pamirakh," Part One, 1–10, 7.
61 In contemporaneous literature by non-Russians, the inhabitants of the area were also called Kirghiz, for example, in Curzon's *The Pamirs and the Source of the Oxus* (1896, 22) and Younghusband's *The Heart of a Continent.* Alexander Morrison points out that Kirghiz/Kirgiz was the "generic term used by the Russians for both Qazaqs and Kyrgyz in Central Asia" (*The Russian Conquest of Central Asia: A Study in Imperial Expansion, 1814–1914*, Cambridge: Cambridge University Press, 2021, xxiii). Many of the nomadic pastoralists who lived in the Pamir Mountains were Kyrgyz (Morrison, 4).
62 Virginia Martin, *Law and Custom in the Steppe: The Kazakhs of the Middle Horde and Russian Colonialism in the Nineteenth Century* (London: Routledge, 2001), x.
63 O.A. Val'kova, in her very detailed book *Ol'ga Aleksandrovna Fedchenko: 1845–1921* (Moscow: Nauka, 2006), discusses the Golovnin expedition and Golovnina's book, but mistakenly leaves out the "n," hence referencing the name throughout as "Golovin/a" and not "Golovnin/a" (see, for example, 205–14). Val'kova does not, however, add to the information that is obtainable by reading the book itself, nor does she reference Golovnin's hunting articles. There is a reference to an article on

refrigeration that Golovnina translated from the German in the December 1912 issue of the journal *Kholodil'noe delo*, see http://www.alib.ru/5_holodilnmnnoe_delo_1912_g_12_dekabrnmn_w1t17991fd51d73f812bab32fd2cf9f6aa2d800.html. This issue also contained an article on the Aral Sea that used material from D.N. Golovnin's expedition there.

64 Credit to Valeriia Sobol for pointing this out.
65 Golovnin, "Ocherki okhoty na Pamirakh," 145, Part Four, "Okhota na arkharov v okrestnostiakh oz. Bol'shoi Kara-kul'," *Priroda i okhota*, June 1901, kniga 5-aia, 137–49.
66 Golovnina, *Na Pamirakh*, 60.
67 Golovnina, *Na Pamirakh*, 61–2.
68 Golovnina, *Na Pamirakh*, 59.
69 http://az.lib.ru/k/karazin_n_n/text_1872_doktorsha.shtml.
70 "Pamirskaia sluzhba Vasiliia Zaitsova," http://www.voskres.ru/army/library/belogoloviy.htm, article by Boris Belogolovyi. "Сменный отряд капитана Скерского Александра Генриховича пришёл на Мургаб только 29 июня; торжественная встреча отрядов повторила в точности прошлогоднюю, только теперь встречающим был Зайцев, а Скерского сопровождала на Памир жена Софья Георгиевна. Она ехала в сторонке верхом в мужском костюме, загорелая и усталая от длинного перехода." "The replacement detachment of Captain Aleksandr Genrikhovich Skerskii arrived in Murgab only on June 29; a solemn meeting of the detachments repeated with exactitude that of the previous year, only now the person meeting them was Zaitsev, and Skerskii was accompanied to the Pamir by his wife Sofiia Georgievna. She rode to the side in men's attire, burned and tired from the long crossing." Poltoratskaia describes wearing a beshmet and wide trousers, chembary, in "Poezdka po Kitaiskoi granitse," 640.
71 Golovnina, *Na Pamirakh*, 91.
72 Fermented mares' milk, long a staple of the Central Asian steppes.
73 Golovnina, *Na Pamirakh*, 64.
74 Golovnin, "Ocherki okhoty na Pamirakh," Part One, 8.
75 Golovnina, *Na Pamirakh*, 66.
76 Curzon, *Russia in Central Asia*, 18.
77 Curzon, *The Pamirs and the Source of the Oxus*, 29.
78 Golovnina, *Na Pamirakh*, 26, 113–14.
79 Golovnina, *Na Pamirakh*, 95, chocolate oil, page 84 men complain about having to carry soap and towels.
80 See Éadaoin Agnew, *Imperial Women Writers in Victorian India: Representing Colonial Life, 1850–1910* (London: Palgrave, 2017), 9–10; as well as Mills, *Discourses of Difference*.

81 Golovnina, *Na Pamirakh*, 171.
82 Golovnina, *Na Pamirakh*, 73.
83 Golovnina, *Na Pamirakh*, 198.
84 Golovnina spells it "tomasha," but it was more commonly spelled "tamasha" (*Na Pamirakh*, 191).
85 Golovnina, *Na Pamirakh*, 16–17.
86 Golovnina, *Na Pamirakh*, 17.
87 Mills, *Gender and Colonial Space*, 99.
88 See, for example, *Vassili Verestchagin, painter, soldier, traveler; autobiographical sketches*, translated from the German and the French by F.H. Peters with illustrations after drawings by the author (London: R. Bentley & Son, 1887), 104–5.
89 Golovnina, *Na Pamirakh*, 77. Apreleva also describes "barbarian" treatment of camels in her story "Sail'" (23–32) in her *Central Asian Sketches (Sredne-aziatskie ocherki)*, originally published separately in 1896.
90 Golovnina, *Na Pamirakh*, 113–15; Golovnin, "Ocherki okhoty na Pamirakh," Part Four, 149.
91 Golovnina describes the game on pages 97–101, with a footnote on page 97 noting that "baiga" includes races as well as the polo-like game. There is also a photograph of ulak on page 97. Apreleva's story "Sail'" also describes it, *Central Asian Sketches*, 23–32.
92 Golovnina, *Na Pamirakh*, 86.
93 Golovnina, *Na Pamirakh*, 132–5.
94 Golovnina, *Na Pamirakh*, 134, #46.
95 Both Golovnins gave measurements in feet, not atypically for the time for those writing with a science-based audience in mind, although they also mentioned versts. See G. Ia. Romanova, *Naimenovanie mer dliny v russkom iazyke* (Moscow: Nauka, 1975), 86–7. Voskoboinikov, however, uses metres in his account. The metric system was introduced in Russia in 1899, but only in the 1920s, in the Soviet period, was it fully implemented.
96 Golovnina, *Na Pamirakh*, 91.
97 Golovnina cites John Wood's *A Journey to the Source of the River Oxus* (London, 1872); Alexander Humboldt's *Asie Centrale* (Paris, 1843); T.E. Gordon, *The Roof of the World* (Edinburgh, 1876); Dr. Potagos, *Dix années de Voyages dans L'Asie Centrale* (Paris, 1885); Gabriel Bonvalot, *Du Caucase aux Indes à travers le Pamir* (Paris, 1889); Guillaume Capus, *Le toit du monde (Pamir)* (Paris, 1890); *Russia's March towards India by 'An Indian Officer,'* 2 vols. (London, 1894); Charles Dunmore, *The Pamirs; Being a Narrative of a Year's Expedition on Horseback and on Foot through Kashmir, Western Tibet, Chinese Tartary, and Russian Central Asia* (London, J. Murray, 1893); C.S. Cumberland, *Sport on the Pamirs* (London, 1895); G.N. Curzon's *The Pamirs and the Source of the Oxus* (London, 1896); and articles from journals, alongside Russian sources.

 98 Golovnina, *Na Pamirakh*, 3.
 99 Golovnin, "Ocherki okhoty na Pamirakh," Part Six, 21.
100 Golovnin, "Ocherki okhoty na Pamirakh," Part Six, 22.
101 Golovnin, "Ocherki okhoty na Pamirakh," Part Seven, reference to the guide carrying Golovnin's gun is on page 10, quotation about the guide retrieving the animal is on page 6.
102 Golovnina, *Na Pamirakh*, 90.
103 Harriet Ritvo, *The Animal Estate: The English and Other Creatures in the Victorian Age* (Cambridge, MA, and London: Harvard University Press, 1987), 248.
104 Ritvo, *Animal Estate*, 248.
105 Ritvo, *Animal Estate*, 258.
106 Ritvo, *Animal Estate*, 252–68.
107 Ritvo, *Animal Estate*, 272.
108 Ritvo, *Animal Estate*, 275.
109 Golovnina, *Na Pamirakh*, 131.
110 Golovnin, "Ocherki okhoty na Pamirakh," Part Four, 144.
111 Golovnin, "Ocherki okhoty na Pamirakh," Part Four, 146.
112 Golovnin, "Ocherki okhoty na Pamirakh," Part Five, 98.
113 Golovnina, *Na Pamirakh*, 131.
114 Ritvo, *Animal Estate*, 253.
115 Ritvo, *Animal Estate*, 252.
116 See https://www.skansen.se/en/biologiska-mus%C3%A9et.
117 T.N.V., "Na Pamirakh," *Priroda i okhota* 7 (1902): 57–9 (book review).
118 Katherine Hill Reischl, "Photography and the Crisis of Authorship: Tolstoy and the Popular Photographic Press," *Jahrbücher für Geschichte Osteuropas*, Neue Folge, Bd. 60, H. 4 (2012): 533–49, 547. Reischl notes in footnote 61 on the same page: "Авторское право на литературные, музыкальные, художественные и фотографические произведения принадлежать автору в течение всей его жизни, а наследникам или правопреемникам его в течение пятидесяти лет со времени автора." (Zapiski ob avtorskom prave fotografa gosudarstvennoi dume, 188). ["The author's right to literary, musical, artistic and photographic works belongs to the author during his entire life, and to his descendants or lawful successors for 50 years after the time of the author." – KH] The first copyright law in Russia, issued in 1828, was enacted to halt the unauthorized publication of literary works as part of the tsar's censorship statute. The author or translator was given exclusive right, to be succeeded by his/her heirs, to be protected for another twenty-five years after the author's death. This time tended to fifty years in 1857 in response to a request made by Pushkin's widow. In 1845 the Council extended copyright protection to musical works and a year later to the fine arts. By 1897 the laws were again under review. However, it was not until 1906 that a new draft of the statute, which would extend copyright to literature, music, works of

fine art, and photographs, was under discussion in the State Duma. It was passed by the Duma in 1909 and ratified by the tsar in 1911. "One major departure from previous practice was the rejection of the concept of copyright as 'property.' The law merely asserted that copyright was sui generis and subsists in literary, musical, artistic, and photographic works" (Newcity: *Copyright Law in the Soviet Union*, 6–9).

119 Curzon, "The Pamirs," 45 (head of Ovis polii from the side). The reading took place at the Royal Geographical Society on 18 February 1895. In the revised version of the article, published as *The Pamirs and the Source of the Oxus, Revised and Reprinted from 'The Geographical Journal' for July, August and September, 1896* (London: The Royal Geographical Society, 1896), 83 pages, a straight-ahead picture of the head of the sheep appears on page 31, the same one that also appears in Golovnina's book and on the first page of Golovnin's third article for *Priroda i okhota*.

120 Golovnin, "Ocherki okhoty na Pamirakh," Part Three, 1.

121 For this reason, I made the mistake of identifying this photograph as being by Barteneva in an earlier publication, "Russian Women Travelers in Central Asia and India," *The Russian Review* 70 (January 2011): 1–19.

122 Golovnina, *Na Pamirakh*, 59.

123 Golovnina, *Na Pamirakh*, 101.

124 Lidiia Poltoratskaia, *Al'bom tipov i vidov Zapadnoi Sibiri, sniatykh L. K. Poltoratskoi*. St. Petersburg, 1879, "Poezdka po Kitaiskoi granitse ot Altaia do Tarbagataia," *Russkii vestnik* 93, no. 6 (1871): 580–661; "Bremenskaia ekspeditsiia v Semipalatinskoi oblasti," *Priroda i okhota* 1, no. 3 (1879): 23–52. See also Elena Barkhatova, *Russkaia Svetopis': Pervyi vek fotoiskusstva 1839–1914* St. Petersburg: Al'ians Liki Rossii, 2009), 162 and 372, with photos by Poltoratskaia on pages 170–1, as well as Natalia Matkhanova and Natalia Aleksandrova, "First Ladies. The Province of Siberia, 19th Century," *Science, First Hand* 15, no. 3 (25 June 2007): 80–91. Also at https://scfh.ru/en/papers /first-ladies-the-province-of-siberia-19th-century/. Also see Elena Barkhatova and Natalia Matkhanova, "Ee prevoskhoditel'stvo fotograf," *Nauka iz pervykh ruk* 2, no. 26 (May 2009): 62–75.

125 Sergei Morozov, *Russkie Puteshestvenniki-fotografy* (Moscow: Gos. Izdatel'stvo Geograficheskoi literatury, 1953), 33–5. Sergei Morozov, *Russkaia khudozhestvennaia fotografiia 1839–1917* (Moscow: gosudarstvennoe izdatel'stvo iskusstvo, 1955), 48–9. Elena Barkhatova and Natalia Matkhanova, "Ee prevoskhoditel'stvo fotograf," 75.

126 Poltoratskaia, "Poezdka po Kitaiskoi granitse," 640.

127 Barkhatova and Matkhanova, "Ee prevoskhoditel'stvo fotograf," 73.

128 Poltoratskaia, "Bremenskaia ekspeditsiia," see page 38, in which she struggles to take pictures her husband requests, despite the wind and snow, and page 47, in which only one of two negatives turns out.

129 Poltoratskaia, "Bremenskaia ekspeditsiia," 44–6.

130 Poltoratskaia, "Bremenskaia ekspeditsiia," 40.

131 Poltoratskaia, "Bremenskaia ekspeditsiia," 40.

132 Peter E. Palmquist, "Pioneer Women Photographers in Nineteenth-Century California," *California History* 71, no. 1 (Spring 1992): 110–27, 111–12.

133 Anne Maxwell, *Women Photographers of the Pacific World, 1857–1930* (London: Routledge, 2020), 174.

134 Bronwyn A.E. Griffith, ed., *Ambassadors of Progress: American Women Photographers in Paris, 1900–1901* (Giverny, France: Musée d'Art Américain, in association with the Library of Congress, Washington, DC, 2001), 9–10. See also translations of reviews of the exhibit, 188–91.

135 Simone Natale, "Photography and Communication Media in the Nineteenth Century," *History of Photography* 36, no. 4 (2012): 451–6, 453. Internal quotation taken from Jeremy Foster, "Capturing and Losing the 'Lie of the Land': Railway Photography and Colonial Nationalism in Early Twentieth Century South Africa," in *Picturing Place: Photography and the Geographical Imagination*, edited by Joan M. Schwartz and James R. Ryan (London: I.B. Tauris 2003), 140–61.

136 Middleton, *Russians in the Great Game*, 42. See also Alexander Morrison, *Russian Conquest*, 503–5.

137 Golovnina, *Na Pamirakh*, 141.

138 Golovnina, *Na Pamirakh*. 141–2.

139 Gerard et al., *Report on the Proceedings of the Pamir Boundary Commission*, Office of the Superintendant of Government Printing, Calcutta, India, 1897, 3.

140 Gerard et al., *Proceedings*, 5–6.

141 Emily Laskin, "Writing Imperial Borderlands: Nikolai Grodekov's Ride Across Afghanistan," talk presented at 2017 Association for Slavic, East European and Eurasian Studies.

142 See Hokanson, "Russian Women Travelers in Central Asia and India," *The Russian Review* 70 (January 2011): 1–19.

143 Golovnina, *Na Pamirakh*, 88–9.

144 Golovnina, *Na Pamirakh*, 101–2.

145 Golovnina, *Na Pamirakh*, 121.

146 Golovnina, *Na Pamirakh*, 137–8.

147 Golovnina, *Na Pamirakh*, 138.

148 Golovnina, *Na Pamirakh*, 152.

149 Golovnin, "Ocherki okhoty na Pamirakh," Part One, 2–3.

150 Golovnin, "Ocherki okhoty na Pamirakh," Part Five, 97. See Mills, *Gender and Colonial Space*, 84–5.

151 Golovnina, *Na Pamirakh*, 160–2.

152 Golovnina, *Na Pamirakh*, 165–6.

153 Golovnina, *Na Pamirakh*, 168.

154 Golovnina, *Na Pamirakh*, 1.

155 "Sel'skoe khoziaistvo i kholodil'noe delo," reprint of D.N. Golovnin's article of January 1912 in *Kholodil'noe delo* (no. 1, 7–11), reprinted in *Kholodil'naia tekhnika* 2 (2012): 63–7, and containing a biography of Golovnin on page 67, which says that he published a journal called *Kholodil'noe delo na putiakh soobshcheniia*. http://www.holodteh.ru/UserFiles/File/Xt-2-12/63-67 .pdf. Another site notes that Golovnin had to leave Moscow for Krasnodar and then Baku after 1917, where he briefly published the above-named journal starting in 1923, and notes that he is from the famous Golovnin family, referring probably to the naval commander and explorer Vasilii Mikhailovich Golovnin, 1776–1831. http://www.holodcatalog.ru /entsiklopedii/obzory-i-analitika/zhurnalu-kholodilnaya-tekhnika-100 -let/. There is also a mention of an expedition to the Aral Sea undertaken by Golovnin (http://www.alib.ru/5_holodilnmnnoe_delo_1912_g_12 _dekabrnmn_w1t17991fd51d73f812bab32fd2cf9f6aa2d800.html), as well as an article translated from the German by "Iu. D. Golovnina." Golovnin is also mentioned several times in the article "Istoriia kholodil'noi promyshlennosti Rossii kontsa 19-nachala 20 vv" by Sergei Rogatko, https://statehistory.ru/5731/Istoriya-kholodilnoy-promyshlennosti -Rossii-kontsa-19-nachala-20-vv/.

156 Golovnina, *Na Pamirakh*, 183–4.

157 Golovnina, *Na Pamirakh*, 192.

158 The greenery was seen as a mark of civilization by the Russians, see Jennifer Keating's "'There Are Few Plants, but They Are Growing, and Quickly': Foliage and the Aesthetics of Landscape in Russian Central Asia, 1854–1914," *Studies in the History of Gardens & Designed Landscapes* 37, no. 2 (2012): 174–89.

159 Vasilii Grigor'evich Piankov, *Po Turkestanu: Ob"ezd Turkestanskim general-gubernatorom S. M. Dukhovskim Samarkandskoi i Ferganskoi oblastei v 1898 godu*, Tashkent, 1989, 192 pp. The visit to New Margelan is described on pages 126–39.

160 Golovnina, *Na Pamirakh*, 196–7.

161 On page 29, Golovnina describes getting advice from V.F. Oshanin (1844–1917), the biologist, geographer, and traveller, before the trip.

162 Golovnina, *Na Pamirakh*, 199.

163 Golovnina, *Na Pamirakh*, 201–2.

164 N.V.T., "Na Pamirakh," review of Golovnina's book *Priroda i okhota*, July 1902, kn. VII-aia, 57–9.

165 Voskoboinikov, "Iz nabliudenii," 51-2; Golovnina, *Na Pamirakh*, 126–31. Curzon discusses the cave with the optical illusion in *The Pamirs and the*

Source of the Oxus (book version, 1896), 49, and mentions that Francis Younghusband, a British officer, had already checked on this optical illusion for himself, which occurred in 1890 (Francis Younghusband, *The Heart of a Continent: a Narrative of Travels in Manchuria, across the Gobi Desert, through the Himalayas, the Pamirs, and Hunza, 1884–1894* (London: J. Murray, 1904), 266.

Chapter 5: In Pursuit of Imperial Knowledge: Ol'ga Fedchenko, Aleksandra Potanina, Praskov'ia Uvarova, and Anna Rossikova

1 Lidiia Poltoratskaia, *Al'bom tipov i vidov Zapadnoi Sibiri, sniatykh L. K. Poltoratskoi* (St. Petersburg, 1879); "Poezdka po Kitaiskoi granitse ot Altaia do Tarbagataia," *Russkii vestnik* 93, no. 6 (1871): 580–661; "Bremenskaia ekspeditsiia v Semipalatinskoi oblasti," *Priroda i okhota* 1, no. 3 (1879): 23–52. See also Elena Barkhatova, *Russkaia Svetopis': Pervyi vek fotoiskusstva 1839–1914* (St. Petersburg: Al'ians-Liki Rossii, 2009, 162 and 372, with photos by Poltoratskaia on pages 170–1, as well as Natalia Matkhanova and Natalia Aleksandrova, "First Ladies. The Province of Siberia, 19th Century," *Science, First Hand* 15, no. 3 (25 June 2007): 80–91. Also at https://scfh.ru/en/papers/first-ladies-the-province-of-siberia -19th-century/. Also see Elena Barkhatova and Natalia Matkhanova, "Ee prevoskhoditel'stvo fotograf," *Nauka iz pervykh ruk* 2, no. 26 (May 2009): 62–75, and Sergei Morozov, *Russkaia khudozhestvennaia fotografiia 1839– 1917* (Moscow: gosudarstvennoe izdatel'stvo iskusstvo, 1955), 33–5. See also "'Welcome to the Desert' with Alfred Brehm in Kazakhstan 1876– 2021," https://kasachstan-revisited.de/2021/03/03/saysay-magazine -travel-issue/?lang=en.
2 A.A. Golovlev, "Konstantin Nikolaevich Rossikov kak issledovatel' prirody severnogo Kavkaza," *Istoriia nauki: Samarskaia luka: problemy regional'noi i global'noi ekologii* 26, no. 2 (2017): 197–224, 201. See also Mary Zirin, "Rossikova, Anna Efimovna," *Mary Zirin's Bibliography of Pre-Revolutionary Writings by Women*, https://zlist.omeka.net/items/show/2513.
3 Ol'ga Val'kova, *Ol'ga Aleksandrovna Fedchenko: 1845–1921* (Moscow: Nauka), 2006, 125–9 in regard to Ol'ga Fedchenko. Val'kova, *Shturmuia tsitadel' nauki: zhenshchiny-uchenye Rossiiskoi imperii* (Moscow: Novoe Literaturnoe Obozrenie), 2019.
4 See, for example, N.K. Gudzii and E.A. Maimin, "Roman L. N. Tolstogo 'Voskresenie,'" *Tolstoy L. N. Voskresenie* (Akademiia Nauk SSSR; Moscow: Nauka, 1964), 483–545, 529.
5 Creese, "Ladies in the Laboratory," 73; see also Val'kova, *Ol'ga Aleksandrovna Fedchenko*, 133 and 144–52, the latter about both revolutionary siblings.

6 Val'kova, *Shturmuia tsitadel' nauki*, 255–7.

7 Val'kova, *Ol'ga Fedchenko*, 34–5.

8 Val'kova, *Ol'ga Fedchenko*, 40–54.

9 See O.A. Val'kova, *Shturmuia tsitadel' nauki*, esp. 196–380; Ol'ga Val'kova, "The Conquest of Science: Women and Science in Russia, 1860–1940," *Osiris*, Second Series 23, *Intelligentsia Science: The Russian Century, 1860–1960* (2008), 136–65; and Mary R.S. Creese with Thomas M. Creese, *Ladies in the Laboratory IV: Imperial Russia's Women in Science, 1800–1900, A Survey of Their Contributions to Research* (London: Rowman and Littlefield, 2015), esp. 71–86; and Ol'ga Val'kova, *Ol'ga Aleksandrovna Fedchenko*. See also Tatiana Danilova, *Bogini dalekikh stranstvii* (Moscow: Veche, 2006), 89–113.

10 Val'kova, *Shturmuia tsitadel' nauki*, 281.

11 Vereshchagin: Val'kova, *Shturmuia tsitadel' nauki*, 364; lithography, O.V. Maslova, ed., *Obzor Russkikh puteshestvii i ekspeditsii v sredniuiu aziu, Part II, 1856–1869*: (Tashkent: Izdatel'stvo Sagu, 1956), LI, "Ekspeditsiia A. P. Fedchenko i O. A. Fedchenko v Turkestanskii krai 1868–1871," 70–89, 72.

12 See, for example, O.E. Knorring, "Pamiati Ol'gi Aleksandrovny Fedchenko," *Izvestiia glavnogo botanicheskogo sada RSFSR*, Vol. XXIII, vyp. 2: 91–5, 95.

13 Knorring, "Pamiati," 91.

14 See https://mytashkent.uz/2013/12/31/pavil-on-turkestanskogo-kraya-na-politehnicheskoj-vy-stavke-1872-goda-v-moskve/.

15 Val'kova, *Shturmuia tsitadel' nauki*, 275–6.

16 Val'kova, *Shturmuia tsitadel' nauki*, 349.

17 Val'kova, *Shturmuia tsitadel' nauki*, 336.

18 Val'kova, *Shturmuia*, 312–57.

19 Val'kova, *Shturmuia*, 354.

20 "A Fedtschenko's Reisen in Turkestan, 1868–71," 205 (my translation from the German). *Mittheilungen aus Justus Perthes' Geographischer Anstalt Uber Wichtige Neue Erforschungen Dem Gessamtgebiete der Geographie* (Gotha: Justus Perthes) 20 (1874): 201–6. "Am 20. Juli öffnete sich vom Gipfel des Passes Isfairam im Süden die Aussicht auf das riesige, von A. Fedtschenko Trans-Alai-Kette benannte Schneegebirge. Dieser reizende Anblick war wirklich überraschend … Von der Aussicht, die sich hier den Augen der Reisenden bot, können alle möglichen Beschreibungen nur einen schwachen Begriff geben. Diese undendliche, bis 60 Werst lange Steppe mit dem Flusse Kisil su in der Mitte and der riesigen Schneekette im Hintergrund, in der einige Gipfel bis 25,000 F. erreichen, war das Schönste, was Fedtschenko während seiner ganzen Reise in Turkestan gesehen hatte. Eine Abbildung dieser Aussicht, so wie diejenigen vieler anderer der interessantesten Aussichten werden in der jetzt unter

der Presse befindlichen 'Reise nach Turkestan on A. P. Fedtschenko' (Russisch) publicirt [*sic*]" (206).

21 I.V. Mushketov, *Geologicheskoe i orograficheskoe opisanie po dannym sobrannym vo vremia puteshestvii s 1874 po 1880 g.* (Spb., Tipgrafiia M. M. Stasiulevicha, Vas. Ostrov, 2. lin., 7., 1886), 220–1, Fedchenko, *V Kokanskom khanstve*, 139, in Vol. 1, Part II of A.P. Fedchenko's *Puteshestvie v Turkestan*, "V kokanskom khanstve," Izvestiia Imperatorskogo Obshchestva liubitelei Estestvozananiia, Antropologii i Etnografii, Tom XI, Vyp. 7, 1875, 176 pp.

22 Curzon, "The Pamirs and the Source of the Oxus," *The Geographical Journal: Including the Proceedings of the Royal Geographical Society* 8 (July–December 1896): 251–2. The article appeared in three parts: pages 32–54, pages 97–119, and pages 239–64.

23 Fedchenko's illustrations accompanied Vol. 1, Part II of A.P. Fedchenko's *Puteshestvie v Turkestan*, as well as *Vidy Russkogo Turkestana po risunkam s natury Ol'gi Aleksandrovny Fedchenko* (Izdatel'stvo Obshchestva liubitelei estestvoznaniia, antropologii i etnografii, published in 1880 or 1881). Full title: Виды русского Туркестана по рисункам с натуры О.А. Федченко, исполненные гг. Саврасовым в Москве, Лоран, Сисери, Сабатье и Лемерсье в Париже. М.: Изд. О-ва любителей естествознания, антропологии и этнографии, б.г. 13 л. The illustrations listed in the publication, with lithographs by Savrasov, are 1. Rigistan [sic], glavnaia ploshchad' v Samarkande, 2. Shakh Zinda, v okstrestnostiakh Samarkand, 3. Bibi Khanym, mechet' vremeni Timura, 4. Vnutrennost' Gur Emira (grobnitsy Timura), 5. Ishrat' Khana, razvaliny uveselitel'nogo dvortsa Timura, 6. Gory Aksai Tau, k iugu ot Samarkanda, 7. Razvaliny kreposti Karatiube, 8. Mogila sviatogo v Urgute, 9. Varzaminor, v verkhoviakh Zaravshana, 10. Iskander Kul', 11. Kadzhraga, v doline Iagnau, 12. Anzob na reke Iagnob, 13. Diusebai. kolodez v Kizil-Kumakh 14. Rastitel'nost' v Kizil-Kumakh. The volume can be downloaded at https://archive.org /details/vidy_russkogo_turkestana/page/n13/mode/2up.

24 Mushketov, *Turkestan*, 528, "Gory Aksai-tau ili Kara-tiube u Samarkanda," fig. 29. See also Val'kova, *Shturmuia tsitadel' nauki*, 361–2.

25 Val'kova, *Ol'ga Aleksandrovna Fedchenko*, 114.

26 Vahan Barooshian, *V. V. Vereshchagin: Artist at War* (Gainesville: University Press of Florida, 1993), 21–32.

27 Both can be seen at https://rus-turk.livejournal.com/304498.html.

28 See, for example, Anthony Parton's review of Averil King's *Isaak Levitan: Lyrical Landscape,* "A Sense of Place." *Apollo* 175, no. 595 (2012): 96–7. Parton notes that Levitan "studied landscape painting under Alexei Savrasov (1830–97), who was the first to reject the traditional Italianate approach to landscape in favour of the unique qualities of the Russian

countryside. Levitan inherited his teacher's mantle." N.M. Moleva describes in her book on Korovin Savrasov's emphasis to his pupils on painting with feeling: "glavnoe chuvstvuite" was his constant refrain, as well as the idea of painting a landscape as a whole. *Konstantin Korovin: Zhizn i tvorchestvo,* ed. Moleva (Moscow: Izdatel'stvo akademii khudozhestv SSSR, 1963), 17.

29 Val'kova, *Ol'ga Fedchenko,* 26, 109–10.

30 Val'kova, *Ol'ga Fedchenko,* 110, reproduction of lithograph in Fedchenko, *V Kokanskom khanstve,* 136–7.

31 Val'kova, *Shturmuia tsitadel' nauki,* 325–30, quotation from A. Iu. Davydov, 330. *Protokly zasedanii Imperatorskogo Obshchestva liubitelei estestvoznaniia, antropologii i etnografii s. sentiabria 1874 g. po oktiabr' 1876 g,* Izvestiia OLEAE. 1876. T. XXIV: 27–33, quotation on 29.

32 Val'kova notes that the OLEAE had a strict policy of producing scholarship in Russian, and that A.P. Fedchenko had determined that *Puteshestvie v Turkestan* would be published in Russian. *Shturmuia tsitadel' nauki,* 314, 335.

33 Vera Tolz, *Russia's Own Orient: The Politics of Identity and Oriental Studies in the Late Imperial and Early Soviet Periods* (Oxford: Oxford University Press, 2011), 12–13.

34 Val'kova, *Shturmuia tsitadel' nauki,* 287.

35 A.P. Bogdanov, *Materialy dlia istorii nauchnoi i prikladnoi deiatel'nosti v Rossii po zoologii i soprikasaiushchimsia s neiu otrasliam znaniia za poslednee tridtsatipiatiletie (1850–1887 g.)* T. 1 (Moscow, 1888): unpaginated as far as I can determine.

36 G. Iul', "Ocherk geografii i istorii verkhov'ev Amu-Dar'i," perevod s angliiskogo O. A. Fedchenko s dopolneniami i primechaniami A. P. Fedchenko, N. V. Khanykova, G. Iul'ia," *Izvestiia Russkogo Geograficheskogo obshchestva* IX, no. 6 (1873): Prilozhenie, 1–82. See also Val'kova, *Shturmuia tsitadel' nauki,* 296. Yule's essay was published in the second edition of John Wood's *A Journey to the Source of the River Oxus* (London: John Murray), 1872.

37 A.P. Bogdanov, *Materialy dlia istorii nauchnoi i prikladnoi deiatel'nosti v Rossii po zoologii i soprikasaiushchimsia s neiu otrasliam znaniia za poslednee tridtsatipiatiletie (1850–1887 g.)* T. 1 (Moscow, 1888): n.p.; and Val'kova, *Ol'ga Aleksandrovna Fedchenko,* 129.

38 Ivanov quotes his own diary in which he says "'Botanika' (the pseudonym of O.A. in my diary)" – hence while "botanika" in Russian typically means botany, and a botanist is a botanik, Ivanov called Ol'ga Fedchenko "botanika." D.L. Ivanov, "Iz lichnykh vospominanii ob O. A. Fedchenko," *Izvestiia glavnogo botanicheskogo sada RSFSR* XXIII, no. 2 (1924): 99–104, 101. On Ivanov's observations, see also Val'kova,

Shturmuia tsitadel' nauki, 270–7. I. Ikramov describes Grebenkin in his article, "Iskanderskaia voennaia ekspeditsiia i nachala izucheniia verkhnego Zarafshana" ("Iskandarkul military expedition and the sources of the Zarafshan upper Stretches study"), *Uchenye zapiski Khuzhandskogo gosudarstvennogo universiteta im. akademika B. Gafurova. Gumanitarnye nauki* 1, no. 21 (2010): 133–43.

39 Ivanov, "Iz lichnykh," 100.

40 D.L. Ivanov, "Iz lichnykh," 100–1.

41 Ivanov, "Iz lichnykh," 100.

42 Ivanov, "Iz lichnykh," 101.

43 Ivanov, "Iz lichnykh," 101.

44 Ivanov, "Iz lichnykh," 101–2.

45 V. Iversen, "Otchet o poezdke na Moskovskuiu politekhnicheskuiu vystavku," *Trudy Imperatorskogo vol'nogo ekonomicheskogo obshchestva* (Spb: Tipografiia tovarishchestva 'Obshchestvennaia Pol'za,' 1 (1873): 507–25, 521–5.

46 *Vsemirnaia illiustratsiia* VIII, no. 194 (1872): 214. Some of the mannequins and the row of shops are depicted in Karazin's illustration on page 181, "Turkestanskii otdel. Bazar i manekeny mestnykh tipov."

47 N. Karazin, "Turkestanskii otdel. Glavnyi zal," *Vsemirnaia illiustratsiia* VIII, no. 194 (1872): 180. Engraved by K. Veierman. Depictions of the Turkestan pavilion are on pages 180–1, and an article about it is on page 214.

48 Georg Lohde, "Alexis Fedtschenko. Ein Nachruf," *Berliner Entomologische Zeitschrift* (Berlin, 1873), 236–8, 238. Translation mine.

49 Val'kova, *Shturmuia*, 514–15.

50 Val'kova, *Shturmuia*, 284.

51 Creese, "Ladies in the Laboratory," 74.

52 See Val'kova, *Shturmuia* and *Ol'ga Fedchenko*; and Creese, "Ladies in the Laboratory," 73–4.

53 V.M. Zarin and E.A. Zarina, *Puteshestviia A. V. Potaninoi* (Moscow: Geografgiz, 1950), 47.

54 Aleksandra Viktorovna Potanina, *Iz puteshestvii po Vostochnoi Sibiri, Mongolii, Tibetu i Kitaiu; sbornik statei* (Moscow: Izdatel'stvo Geograficheskogo otdeleniia Imperatorskago obshchestva liubitelei estestvoznaniia, antropologii i etnografii, 1895); *Rasskazy o Buriatakh, ikh vere i obichaiakh* (Moscow, Tipografiia K. L. Men'shova, 1912). See also Val'kova, *Shturmuia tsitadel' nauki*, 409–11, and V.M. Zarin and E.A. Zarina, *Puteshestviia A. V. Potaninoi* (Moscow: Geografgiz, 1950).

55 For Potanin's life, see sources on Potanina as well as Vladimir Afanas'evich Obruchev, *Grigorii Nikolaevich Potanin: Kratkii ocherk ego*

zhizni i deiatel'nosti (Moscow, tip. I. N. Kushnerev i K, 1916). Available at http://elib.tomsk.ru/purl/1-6097/.

56 V.M. Zarin and E.A. Zarina, *Puteshestviia A. V. Potaninoi* (Moscow: Geografgiz, 1950). V. Obruchev, "Velikii Pervootkryvatel' Azii Grigorii Potanin," *Armeiskii sbornik: Nauchno-metodicheskii zhurnal MO RF* (Moscow: Redaktskionno-izdatel'skii tsentr MO RF, 2008), no. 12, 56–9. See also Tatiana Danilova, *Bogini dalekikh stranstvii* (Moscow: Veche, 2006), 114–64.

57 Zarins, *Puteshestviia A. V. Potaninoi*, 47; P.P. Semenov, *Istoriia poluvekovoi deiatel'nosti Imperatorskogo Russkogo Geograficheskogo Obshchestva 1845–1895* (St. Petersburg: Tip. Bezobrazov, 1896), Part II, otdel iv, 554.

58 Scott C. Matsushita Bailey, *Travel, Science, and Empire: The Russian Geographical Society's Expeditions to Central Eurasia, 1845–1905*. PhD diss., University of Hawaii, Manoa, 2008, 271, 298.

59 Val'kova, *Shturmuia*, 270.

60 Potanina, *Iz puteshestvii*, xxvii.

61 Potanina, *Iz puteshestvii*, xxxiii.

62 *Iz puteshestvii*, xxvii–xxvi. See also N.V. Serebrennikov, "G. N. Potanin i L. N. Tolstoi," *Vestnik Tomskogo gosudarstvennogo universiteta: Istoriia* 2, no. 14 (2011): 65–6.

63 Potanina, *Iz puteshestvii*; see also Val'kova, *Shturmuia tsitadel' nauki*, 270, 407–11.

64 A recent article about her interest in Tuvan people can be found at https://www.tuva.asia/journal/issue_7/2136-mongush-z-m.html.

65 In her collection *Iz puteshestvii*, 229–72, see also D. Ulymzhiev, "Dordzhi Banzarov – the First Buryat Scholar," *Mongolian Studies* 16, Index and Reviews Issue (1993): 55–7.

66 Potanina, *Iz puteshestvii*, "O kitaiskoi zhenshchine," 192–216, 198.

67 Potanina, *Iz puteshestvii*, 194.

68 Potanina, *Iz puteshestvii*, 202.

69 Both in *Iz puteshestvii*, 273–7 and 278–90, respectively.

70 Potanina, *Iz puteshestvii*, 217–28.

71 Sergei Ol'denburg, "Pamiati Aleksandry Viktorovny Potaninoi," *K Svetu: Nauchno-literaturnyi sbornik*, ed. Ek. P. Letkova and V.D. Batiushkov (St. Petersburg, publication of Komitet Obshchestva dostavleniia sredstv S.-Peterburgskim vyshchim zhenskim kursam, 1904), 220–6. "Dordzhi" is in *Iz puteshestvii*, 229–72. See also N.M. Iadrintsev, "Podvizhnitsa nauki: (Pamiati A. V. Potaninoi), *Knizhki Nedeli* 1., no. 1 (January 1894): 113–24.

72 *Entsiklopedicheskii slovar' Brokgauza i Efrona* IIa (1891): 881–2.

73 Potanina, *Iz puteshestvii*, 244.

74 Zarins, *Puteshestviia*, 12.

75 Potanina, *Iz puteshestvii*, "Dordzhi, buriatskii mal'chik" 230.

76 Sergei Ol'denburg, "Pamiati Aleksandry Viktorovny Potaninoi," 225.

77 Zarins, *Puteshestviia*, 51.

78 See Potanina, *Iz puteshestvii*, 61 and 63 re: camels, and Zarins, *Puteshestviia*, 74 for yaks, 71 for mules.

79 Semenov, *Istoriia poluvekovoi deiatel'nosti*, 561.

80 Potanina, *Iz puteshestvii*, xxii, Zarins, *Puteshestviia A. V. Potaninoi*, 34, 74.

81 Potanina, *Iz puteshestvii*, 64.

82 *Iz puteshestvii*, xx, original text is "Podvizhnitsa nauki: (Pamiati A. V. Potaninoi), *Knizhki Nedeli* 1., no. 1 (January 1894): 113–24.

83 Semenov, *Istoriia poluvekovoi deitatel'nosti*, 558.

84 I.I. Popov, "Pamiati N. M. Iadrintseva i A. V. Potaninoi," *Izvestiia Vostochno-Sibirskogo Otdeleniia Russkogo Geograficheskogo obshchestva* XXV, no. 1 (1894): 1–28, 3–4.

85 Zarins, *Puteshestviia*, 50.

86 Potanina, "Iz stranstviia po Uriankhaiskoi zemle," *Iz puteshestvii*, 48. Bailey also draws attention to this passage, *Travel, Science, and Empire*, 295.

87 Potanina, "Iz stranstviia po Uriankhaiskoi zemle," *Iz puteshestvii*, 52–3.

88 Potanina, "Iz stranstvii a po Uriankhoiskoi zemle," *Iz putshestvii*, 53.

89 Potanina, "Iz stranstvii a po Uriankhoiskoi zemle," *Iz putshestvii*, 54–7.

90 Vaccines were typically made with calf lymph.

91 Potanina, *Iz puteshestvii*, 71.

92 Potanina, *Iz Puteshestvii*, "O kitaiskoi zhenschine," 192–216, *Russkoe bogatstvo* no. 7 (July 1887): 57–114, published under "Belletristika."

93 Potanina, *Iz puteshestvii*, 205–6 and ff.

94 Potanina, *Iz puteshestvii*, 211.

95 Potanina, *Iz puteshestvii*, "Utai," 165–77.

96 Potanina, *Iz puteshestvii*, 169. For Skassi, see S.V. Dmitriev, "Etnografiia Tadzhikov v trudakh rossiiskikh uchenykh XIX-nachala XX v.," in *Tadzhiki: Istoriia, kul'tura, obshchestvo*, Rossiiskaia akademiia nauk, Muzei antropologii i etnografii im. Petra Velikogo (Kunstkamera), Institut ismailitskikh issledovanii (St. Petersburg, 2014), 64–96, 70. Skassi participated in the 1970 Fedchenko trip to Iskender-kul.

97 Potanina, *Iz puteshestvii*, 170.

98 Potanina, *Iz puteshestvii*, 177.

99 Potanina, *Iz puteshestvii*, 19–20.

100 Potanina, *Iz puteshestvii*, 40.

101 V.M. Zarin and E.A. Zarina, *Puteshestviia A. V. Potaninoi* (Moscow: Geografgiz, 1950), 9–10.

102 G.N. Potanin, *Ocherki Severo-zapadnoi Mongolii: Rezul'taty puteshestvia ispolnennogo v 1876–1877 godakh po porucheniu Imperatorskogo Russkogo Geograficheskogo Obshchestva, Vol. 1: Dnevnik Puteshestviia i materialy dlia fizicheskooi geografii i topografii s z. Mongolii* (St. Petersburg: Tipografiia V. Bezobrazova i Komp., 1881), iii.

103 Potanin, *Ocherki Severo-zapadnoi Mongolii*, iii.
104 Potanin, *Ocherki Severo-zapadnoi Mongolii*, v.
105 Potanina, *Iz puteshestvii*, XXXVI.
106 Potanina, *Iz puteshestvii*, XXXVII.
107 Zarins, *Puteshestviia A. V. Potaninoi*, 81.
108 Maria Tagangaeva, "Visualizing (Post)-Soviet Ethnicity. Fine Art of Buryatia," *Anthropology & Archaeology of Eurasia* 54, no. 3 (2015): 24–57, 45.
109 https://1baikal.ru/en/o-bajkale/istoriya-regiona/the-guiding-light-of -grigory-potanin1.
110 Vladimir Petrovich Nalivkin and Maria Vladimirovna Nalivkina, *Ocherk byta zhenshchiny osedlogo tuzemnogo naseleniia Fergany* (Kazan': tipografiia Imperatorskogo universiteta, 1886). For a complete translation with a scholarly introduction, see Vladimir Nalivkin and Maria Nalivkina, eds., *Muslim Women of the Fergana Valley: A 19th-century Ethnography from Central Asia*, translated by Mariana Markova and Marianne Kamp (Bloomington: Indiana University Press, 2016).
111 *Muslim Women of the Fergana Valley*, editor's introduction by Marianne Kamp. For the Narodniks and reference to Chernyshevsky, see pages 14–15; the editor also singles out Chernyshevsky-like commentary directed towards the reader on pages 18–19 and makes note of the Nalivkins' matter-of-fact approach towards prostitution on page 21.
112 See, for example, V.G. Aksareeva, "Gendernyi vzgliad na memuary Praskov'i Sergeevny Uvarovoi," *Vestnik Udmurtskogo Universiteta: Istoriia i filologia* (2009, 2nd edition): 138–47, 145. It is also mentioned by Rosamund Bartlett in her *Tolstoy: A Russian Life* (Ch. 6, Literary Duellist and Repentant Nobleman, 137–8), as well as in N.N. Gusev, *Lev Nikolaevich Tolstoi. Materialy k biografii's 1855 po 1869 god* (Moscow, 1957).
113 Uvarova, "Poezdka v Tashkent i Samarkand," *Russkaia Mysl'* 12, no. 11, section 2 (1891): 1–19 (first part of the article), no. 12, section 2 (1891): 1–25 (second part of the article). Reprinted in *Turkestanskii sbornik* 438 (1907): 62–84.
114 Uvarova, "Poezdka v Tashkent i Samarkand," first part, 1–2.
115 Nikolai Karazin, 1842–1908, *Na Dalekhikh okrainakh*, translated by Anthony W. Sariti (AuthorHouse, [1875], 2007 as *In the Distant Confines*). Elena Andreeva translates it as *In the Outlying Districts* in *Russian Central Asia in the Works of Nikolai Karazin* (Palgrave: 2021), 4.
116 Apreleva, *Central Asian Sketches*, 111–22.
117 Apreleva, *Central Asian Sketches*, 7–14.
118 Uvarova, "Poezdka v Tashkent i Samarkand," first part, 6. See Fig. 0.3.
119 Barooshian, *V. V. Vereshchagin*, 44–9; and I. Zilbershtein, "Vystavka khudozhnika V. V. Vereshchagina," *Literaturnoe nasledstvo* 73, no. 1

(Moscow, Nauka, 1964): 294, also at https://www.booksite.ru
/vereschagin/0_10.html.

120 Julie Hessler, "A Thaw to the East: India in the Soviet Imagination,"
book chapter in progress, Olga Maiorova, "Severed Heads on Display:
Visualizing Central Asia (1868–1872)," forthcoming in *Picturing Russian
Empire*, edited by Valerie Kivelson and Joan Neuberger.

121 Uvarova, "Poezdka v Tashkent i Samarkand," first part, 3.

122 Uvarova, "Poezdka v Tashkent i Samarkand," first part, 5.

123 Uvarova, "Poezdka v Tashkent i Samarkand," first part, 7.

124 Uvarova, "Poezdka v Tashkent i Samarkand," first part, 7–8.

125 Uvarova, "Poezdka v Tashkent i Samarkand," first part, 8.

126 Uvarova, *Byloe: Davno proshedshie schastlivye dni* (Moscow: izdatel'stvo im.
Sabashnikovykh), 2005, 140.

127 Daniel Brower, *Turkestan*, 84–5.

128 Uvarova, *Byloe*, 140.

129 Uvarova, *Byloe*, 142.

130 Uvarova, *Byloe*, 141–2.

131 Photo by Paul Nadar, available at https://rus-turk.livejournal
.com/330628.html.

132 N. Maev, *Turkestanskaia vystavka predmetov sel'skogo khoziaistva i
promyshlennosti v Tashkente, 1890 g.* (putevoditel' po vystavke i ee
otdelam) (Tashkent, tipo-litografiia S. I. Lakhtina, 1890), 163.

133 http://www2.culture.gouv.fr/public/mistral/memsmn_fr?ACTION=C
HERCHER&FIELD_1=PAYS&VALUE_1=ouzbekistan&FIELD_5=AUTP&V
ALUE_5=Nadar. See also Anne-Marie Bernard and Claude Malécot, eds.,
L'odyssée De Paul Nadar Au Turkestan, 1890: Photographies De Paul Nadar
(Paris: Ed. du Patrimoine, 2007).

134 Inessa Kouteinikova, "Tashkent in St. Petersburg: The Constructed
Image of Central Asia in Russia's Nineteenth-Century Ethnographic
Exhibitions," in Francine Giese, *À L'orientale: Collecting, Displaying
and Appropriating Islamic Art and Architecture in the 19th and Early 20th
Centuries* (Leiden and Boston: Brill, 2020), 151–62, 154.

135 Kouteinikova, "Tashkent in St. Petersburg," 156.

136 Jeff Sahadeo notes that Cherniaev closed the library and sold off much
of its contents in an attempt to "reverse trends associated with his
predecessor [Kaufman] and the Great Reform Era," *Russian Colonial
Society in Tashkent*, 66. It was later reopened.

137 Uvarova, "Poezdka v Tashkent i Samarkand," first part, 10.

138 Uvarova, "Poezdka v Tashkent i Samarkand," first part, 4–5.

139 Uvarova, "Poezdka v Tashkent i Samarkand," first part, 11.

140 Uvarova, "Poezdka v Tashkent i Samarkand," first part, 13.

141 Uvarova, "Poezdka v Tashkent i Samarkand," first part, 15.

142 Uvarova, "Poezdka v Tashkent i Samarkand," first part, 14.

143 Uvarova, "Poezdka v Tashkent i Samarkand," first part, 14.

144 Uvarova, "Poezdka v Tashkent i Samarkand," first part, 15.

145 Svetlana Gorshenina, "Russian Archaeologists, Colonial Administrators, and the 'Natives' of Turkestan: Revisiting the History of Archaeology in Central Asia," in *"Masters" and "Natives": Digging the Others' Past*, edited by Philippe Bornet Gorshenina, Michael Fuchs, and Claude Rapin (Berlin: DeGruyter, 2019), 31–86, 51.

146 Uvarova, "Poezdka v Tashkent i Samarkand," first part, 17.

147 Uvarova, "Poezdka v Tashkent i Samarkand," second part, 4–5. (The pagination of the second part also begins with "1.")

148 Uvarova, "Poezdka v Tashkent i Samarkand," second part, 10.

149 Uvarova, "Poezdka v Tashkent i Samarkand," second part, 10.

150 Uvarova, "Poezdka v Tashkent i Samarkand," second part, 6.

151 Uvarova, "Poezdka v Tashkent i Samarkand," first part, 7. E.F. Kal' (1861–91) was the author of *Persidskie, arabskie i tiurkskie rukopisi Turkestanskoi Publichnoi Biblioteki* (Tashkent, 1889). Svetlana Gorshenina notes that Kal' was also a collector of manuscripts and archaeological pieces, see *Private Collections of Russian Turkestan*, 105.

152 Uvarova, "Poezdka v Tashkent i Samarkand," second part, 20. A.V. Komarov (1830–1904) was a general and participant in the conquest of Turkestan. Gorshenina in her *Private Collections of Russian Turkestan* notes (quoting A. A. Semenov) that Komarov would make the Cossacks pick up items on the surface of ancient sites after it rained, 39–40. He had begun "collecting" in the Caucasus and particularly specialized in coins (Gorshenina, 105–6).

153 Svetlana Gorshenina, "Russian Archaeologists," 50.

154 Uvarova, "Poezdka v Tashkent i Samarkand," second part, 11. This Quran was known as the Samarkand Kufic Quran or the Uthman Quran, written in the eighth or ninth century. It was subsequently returned to Tashkent and remains there today. E.A. Rezvan, "On the Dating of an 'Uthmanic Qur'an' from St. Petersburg," *Manuscripta Orientalia* 6, no. 3 (2000): 19–22. See also http://news.bbc.co.uk/2/hi/asia-pacific/4581684.stm.

155 Gorshenina, "Russian Archaeologists," 62.

156 Uvarova, "Poezdka v Tashkent i Samarkand," second part, 12.

157 Alexander Morrison, *Russian Rule in Samarkand*, 21–3.

158 Uvarova, "Poezdka v Tashkent i Samarkand," second part, 12.

159 Uvarova, "Poezdka v Tashkent i Samarkand," second part, 12.

160 Klemm is mentioned by Isabelle Phibbs in *A Visit to the Russians in Central Asia* (London: K. Paul, Trench, Trübner & co., 1899), 47 and 49, while George Dobson calls him "a great linguist, speaking no less than ten languages." Dobson, *Russia's Railway Advance into Central Asia: Notes*

of a Journey from St. Petersburg to Samarkand (London, 1890), Chapter X, "Samarkand to Bokhara," 243.

161 Uvarova, "Poezdka v Tashkent i Samarkand," second part, 13.

162 Uvarova, "Poezdka v Tashkent i Samarkand," second part, 13.

163 Uvarova, "Poezdka v Tashkent i Samarkand," second part, 14.

164 Uvarova, "Poezdka v Tashkent i Samarkand," second part, 15.

165 Uvarova, "Poezdka v Tashkent i Samarkand," second part, 16.

166 Uvarova, "Poezdka v Tashkent i Samarkand," second part, 16.

167 Uvarova, "Poezdka v Tashkent i Samarkand," second part, 16.

168 Maya Peterson, *Pipe Dreams: Water and Empire in Central Asia's Aral Sea Basin* (Cambridge: Cambridge University Press, 2019), 66.

169 Uvarova, "Poezdka v Tashkent i Samarkand," second part, 17.

170 Uvarova, "Poezdka v Tashkent i Samarkand," second part, 22.

171 Uvarova, "Poezdka v Tashkent i Samarkand," second part, 23–4.

172 Anna Efimovna Rossikova, "Sredi pustyni po velikoi sredne-aziatskoi reke Amu-dar'e," (iz puteshestvii letom 1898 g. v Russkii Turkestan) *Nauchnoe obozrenie* 10–12 (1899): 1780–806 (no. 10, October 1899), 2201–19 (no. 12, December 1899); no. 12, 2204.

173 Uvarova, "Poezdka v Tashkent i Samarkand," second part, 24, *Byloe*, 142.

174 Uvarova, "Poezdka v Tashkent i Samarkand," second part, 25.

175 See Ekaterina Pravilova, *A Public Empire: Property and the Quest for the Common Good in Imperial Russia* (Princeton, NJ: Princeton University Press, 2014), esp. 148–165. "Virulent" appears on page 339, note 4.

176 Pravilova, *A Public Empire*, 153–4.

177 Pravilova, *A Public Empire*, 349–50, note 136.

178 See A.A. Golovlev, "Konstantin Nikolaevich Rossikov kak issledovatel' prirody severnogo Kavkaza," *Istoriia nauki: Samarskaia luka: problemy regional'noi i global'noi ekologii* 26, no. 2 (2017): 197–224. Golovlev deduces that Rossikova was a close relative of Rossikov's, most likely his wife, as she was referred to as such in at least one source, see 200–1. However, since Rossikova states in her *Russkii vestnik* article of 1901 that Rossikov is her husband (646), there is no question.

179 A.E. Rossikova, "V gorakh i ushchel'iakh Kurtatii i istokov reki Tereka" (Iz putevykh vospominanii o gornoi Osetii), *Zapiski Kavkazskogo otdela imperatorskogo Russkogo geograficheskogo obshchestva* XVI (1894): 301–56; "Puteshestvie po tsentral'noi chasti gornoi Chechni, *Zapiski Kavkazskogo otdela imperatorskogo Russkogo geograficheskogo obshchestva* (Tiflis: Tipografiia Gruzinskogo izdatel'skogo tovarishchestva, 1896), kn. XVIII, 139–228; Rossikova, "Sredi pustyni"; and Rossikova, "Po Amu-Dar'e ot Petro-Aleksandrovska do Nukusa," *Russkii vestnik* 8 (1901): 562–88, vol. 10, 630–56, also reprinted in *Turkestanskii sbornik* 439 (1907): 25–52. According to Bregel's *Bibliography of Islamic Central Asia,*

Part II, 839, Rossikova also wrote "Les russes dans l'Asie centrale: Une excursion a' Khiva," *La revue scientifique* 13 (1878): 289–98, but this information is incorrect; "S Amu-Dar'i," *Turkestanskie Vedomosti* 13 (1883); and "Na Aral'skom more i Syr-Dar'e: Iz dnevnika," *Kronshtadtskii vestnik* 140 (1883) and 46 (1884). Rossikova published "Belyi Tur (Osetinskaia legenda)" in *Kavkazskii vestnik, ezhemesiachnyi nauchno-literaturnyi zhurnal* 5 (May 1900): 25–43. For references to her pseudonym, see, for example, https://doxie-do.livejournal.com/294655.html, http://book.uraic.ru /elib/authors/gorbunov/sl-16.htm, and https://daimand.ru/vyazanie /antonina-odinets-kniga-vyazanie-i-shite-otzivi.php.

180 See http://book.uraic.ru/elib/authors/gorbunov/sl-16.htm, as well as Golovlev, "Konstantin Nikolaevich Rossikov," 2–1, 224.

181 Rossikova, "Sredi pustyni"; and "Po Amu-Dar'e ot Petro-Aleksandrovska do Nukusa," *Russkii vestnik* 8 (1901): 562–88, vol. 10, 630–56, also reprinted in *Turkestanskii sbornik* 439 (1907): 25–52.

182 Kate Teltscher, "'The Rubicon between the Empires': The River Oxus in the Nineteenth-Century British Geographical Imaginary," in *Writing Travel in Central Asian History*, edited by Nile Green (Bloomington: Indiana University Press, 2014, 135–212.

183 Rossikova, "Sredi pustyni," 1780.

184 Rossikova, "Sredi pustyni," 1784.

185 Rossikova, "Sredi pustyni," 1785.

186 Rossikova, "Sredi pustyni," 1782.

187 Rossikova, "Sredi pustyni," 1785.

188 Rossikova, "Sredi pustyni," 2219.

189 According to Golovlev, "Konstantin Nikolaevich Rossikov," Rossikov published "Pereletnaia ili aziatskaia sarancha. Prichiny gibeli saranchi v ee gnezdilishchakh i novyi sposob ee unichtozheniia," in *Trudy biuro po entomologii Uchenogo komiteta Glavnogo upravleniia zemleustroistva i zemledeliia, izdavaemye pod redaktsii zavedyvaiushchego biuro* (Ministerstvo zemledeliia i gosudarstvennykh imuschchest. Department zemledeliia), T. IV (St. Petersburg: Tipografiia V. Demakova, 1899), a. 37 pp.; and "Primenenie parizhskoi zeleni dlia istrebleniia saranchi," in *Trudy biuro po entomologii Uchenogo komiteta Glavnogo upravleniia zemleustroistva i zemledeliia, izdavaemye pod redaktsii zavedyvaiushchego biuro* (Ministerstvo zemledeliia i gosudarstvennykh imuschchest. Department zemledeliia) t. I, no. 2 (St. Petersburg: Tipografiia V. Demakova, 1899), b. 15 pp.

190 Rossikova, "Sredi pustyni," 1783. See a reference to such a boat in Vladimir Sergeevich Trubetskoi. *A Russian Prince in the Soviet State* (Evanston, IL: Northwestern University Press, 2006), 120.

191 Rossikova, "Sredi pustyni," 1783.

192 Rossikova, "Sredi pustyni," 1783–4.

193 Rossikova, "Sredi pustyni," 2218.

194 Rossikova, "Po Amu-Dar'e," 630–34.

195 Rossikova, "Sredi pustyni," 2214.

196 Rossikova, "Sredi pustyni," 2206.

197 Rossikova, "Sredi pustyni," 2206.

198 Rossikova, "Sredi pustyni," 2206.

199 Rossikova, "Po Amu-Dar'e," 655.

200 Rossikova, "Sredi pustyni," 1801.

201 Rossikova, "Sredi pustyni," 2205.

202 Robert McNeal, *Tsar and Cossack, 1855–1914* (New York: St. Martin's Press, 1987), 42.

203 McNeal, *Tsar and Cossack*, 47.

204 Rossikova, "Po Amu-Dar'e," 567–8.

205 For background, see McNeal, *Tsar and Cossack*, 44–8.

206 Rossikova, "Po Amu-Dar'e," 635–6.

207 Rossikova, "Po Amu-Dar'e," 636.

208 Rossikova, "Po Amu-Dar'e," 636–7.

209 Rossikova, "Po Amu-Dar'e," 570.

210 Rossikova, "Po Amu-Dar'e," 571.

211 Rossikova, "Po Amu-Dar'e," 571.

212 Rossikova, "Po Amu-Dar'e," 572.

213 Rossikova, "Po Amu-Dar'e," 572.

214 Rossikova, "Po Amu-Dar'e," 573.

215 Rossikova, "Po Amu-Dar'e," 575.

216 Rossikova, "Po Amu-Dar'e," 575.

217 Rossikova, "Po Amu-Dar'e," 576.

218 Rossikova, "Po Amu-Dar'e," 577.

219 Rossikova, "Po Amu-Dar'e," 578.

220 Rossikova, "Po Amu-Dar'e," 585.

221 Rossikova, "Po Amu-Dar'e," 586.

222 Rossikova, "Po Amu-Dar'e," 587–8 and 655.

223 Rossikova, "Po Amu-Dar'e," 652.

224 Rossikova is cited in David Richardson and Sue Richardson, *Qaraqalpaqs of the Aral Delta* (Munich: Prestel, 2012).

225 Rossikova, "Po Amu-Dar'e," 656.

226 Golovlev, "Konstantin Nikolaevich Rossikov," 200–1; Val'kova, *Shturmuia tsitadel' nauki*, 754–5.

227 Potanina, *Iz puteshestvii*, xxxvii.

Conclusion

1 Jeanne Kay Guelke and Karen Morin, "Gender, Nature, Empire: Women Naturalists in Nineteenth Century British Travel Literature," *Transactions of the Institute of British Geographers, New Series* 26, no. 3 (2001): 306–26.

Bibliography

Agnew, Éadaoin. *Imperial Women Writers in Victorian India: Representing Colonial Life, 1850–1910*. London: Palgrave, 2017.

Aksareeva, V.G. "Gendernyi vzgliad na memuary Praskov'i Sergeevny Uvarovoi," *Vestnik Udmurtskogo Universiteta: Istoriia i filologia* (2009, 2nd ed.): 138–47.

Aleksandrova, Natalia, and Natalia Matkhanova. "First Ladies: The Province of Siberia, 19th Century," *Science, First Hand* 15, no. 3 (2007): 80–91.

Allworth, Edward, ed. *Central Asia: 130 Years of Russian Dominance, A Historical Overview*. 3rd ed. Durham, NC, and London: Duke University Press, 1994.

Andreeva, Elena. *Russia and Iran in the Great Game*. London: Routledge, 2007.

Andreeva, Elena. *Russian Central Asia in the Works of Nikolai Karazin, 1842–1908: Ambivalent Triumph*. London: Palgrave, 2021.

Anonymous. *Russia's March towards India by 'An Indian Officer.'* 2 vols. London: S. Low, Marston & co, 1894.

Aravamudan, Srinivas. *Guru English: South Asian Religion in a Cosmopolitan Language*. Princeton, NJ: Princeton University Press, 1995.

Ardov, E. (E.I. Apreleva). *Sredne-aziatskie ocherki*. Shanghai: Tipografiia Izdatel'stva Slovo, 1935.

Arndt, Walter. *Collected Narrative and Lyrical Poetry of Alexander Pushkin*. Translated in the Prosodic Forms of the Original by Walter Arndt. New York: Ardis, 2009.

Arsenyev, Vladimir K. *Across the Ussuri Kray*. Translated by Jonathan Slaght. Bloomington: Indiana University Press, 2016.

Bailey, Scott C. Matsushita. *Travel, Science, and Empire: The Russian Geographical Society's Expeditions to Central Eurasia, 1845–1905*. PhD diss., University of Hawaii at Manoa, 2008.

Banerjee, Anindita. "The Trans-Siberian Railroad and Russia's Asia: Literature, Geopolitics, Philosophy of History." *Clio* 34, nos. 1–2 (2004–5): 19–40.

Banerjee, Anindita. *We Modern People: Science Fiction and the Making of Russian Modernity*. Middletown, CT: Wesleyan University Press, 2012.

Barkhatova, Elena. *Russkaia Svetopis': Pervyi vek fotoiskusstva 1839–1914*. St. Petersburg: Al'ians-Liki Rossii, 2009.

Barkhatova, Elena, and Natalia Matkhanova. "Ee prevoskhoditel'stvo fotograf," *Nauka iz pervykh ruk* 2, no. 26 (May 2009): 62–75.

Barooshian, Vahan. *V. V. Vereshchagin: Artist at War*. Gainesville: University Press of Florida, 1993.

Bartlett, Rosamund. *Tolstoy: A Russian Life*. Boston: Houghton-Mifflin, 2011.

Bartol'd, V.V. *Sochineniia*. Vols. 1–9. Moscow: Nauka, 1963–77.

Bassin, Mark. *Imperial Visions: Nationalist Imagination and Geographical Expansion in the Russian Far East 1840–1865*. Cambridge: Cambridge University Press, 1999.

Bassin, Mark. "Russia between Europe and Asia: The Ideological Construction of Geography." *Slavic Review* 50, no. 1 (Spring 1991): 1–17.

Becker, Seymour. *Russia's Protectorates in Central Asia: Bukhara and Khiva, 1865–1924*. Cambridge, MA: Harvard University Press, 1968.

Belogolovyi, B.G. "Pamirskie pis'ma kapitana Zaitsova." http://www.boris-belogolovy.ru/zaycev/zaycev17.html.

Belogolovyi, B.G. "Pamirskaia sluzhba Vasiliia Zaitsova." http://www.voskres.ru/army/library/belogoloviy.htm.

Bernard, Anne-Marie, and Claude Malécot, eds. *L'odyssée De Paul Nadar Au Turkestan, 1890: Photographies De Paul Nadar*. Paris: Ed. du Patrimoine, 2007.

Berry, Thomas E. *Spiritualism in Tsarist Society and Literature*. Baltimore: Edgar Allan Poe Society, 1985.

Bevir, Mark. "The West Turns Eastward: Madame Blavatsky and the Transformation of the Occult Tradition." *Journal of the American Academy of Religion* 62, no. 3 (Autumn 1994): 747–67.

Bevir, Mark. "Annie Besant's Quest for Truth: Christianity, Secularism and New Age Thought." *Journal of Ecclesiastical History* 50, no. 1 (January 1999): 62–93.

Bevir, Mark. "Mothering India." *History Today* 56, no. 2 (February 2006): 19–25.

Bevir, Mark. "Theosophy, Cultural Nationalism, and Home Rule." In *Imagining the East*, edited by Tim Rudbøg and Erik Sand, 321–43. Oxford: Oxford University Press, 2020.

Bhabha, Homi. *The Location of Culture*. New York: Routledge, 1994.

Bharath, Stéphanie Roy. "John Edward Saché in India." *History of Photography* 35, no. 2 (2011): 180–92.

Blaramberg, Ivan Fedorovich. *Erinnerungen aus dem Leben des Kaiserlich Russischen General-Lieutenant Johann von Blaramberg: Nach dessen Tagebüchern von 1811–1871*. 3 vols. Berlin: Schroeder, 1872–5.

Blavatsky, H.P. *From the Caves and Jungles of Hindostan*. Translated by Vera Johnston. London: Theosophical Publishing Society, 1892.

Blavatsky, H.P. *The Letters of H. P. Blavatsky to A. P. Sinnett and Other Miscellaneous Letters*. Transcribed, compiled, and with an introduction by A.T. Barker. Pasadena, CA: Theosophical University Press, 1973.

Blavatsky, H.P. *From the Caves and Jungles of Hindostan, Collected Writings*. Translated by Boris de Zirkoff. Wheaton, IL: Theosophical Publishing House, 1975.

Blavatsky, H.P. *Pis'ma druz'iam i sotrudnikam. Sbornik*. Per. s angliiskogo P. Sh. Akhunov. M: Sfera, 2002.

Blavatsky, H.P. *The Durbar in Lahore. The Theosophist*. Theosophical Society (Madras, India) [Adyar, etc.: Theosophical Publishing House, etc.], Vol. 82 (1960): August 1960, Letter I, pp. 289–302; Letter II, September 1960, 359–74; second half of Letter II, October 1960, 8–20; Letter III, November 1960, 81–101; Letter IV, December 1960, 148–63; 1961: Vol. 83: Letter V, January 1961, 229–45; Letter VI, February 1961, 286–302; Letter VII, March 1961, 357–80. http://www.iapsop.com/ssoc/1881_blavatsky___the _durbar_in_lahore.pdf.

Blavatsky, H.P. *Durbar v Lagore*. There are seven letters in all. Letters I–IV were printed in *Russkii vestnik* vol. 153, 1881, as follows: I, 5–16; II, 16–38; III, 584–601; IV, 601–13. Letters V–VII were printed in *Russkii vestnik* vol. 154, 1881, as follows: V, 171–84; VI, 185–98; and VII, 198–218. http://www .magister.msk.ru/library/blavatsk/india/blvlahor.htm.

Blavatsky, H.P. *Iz Peshcher i debrei Indostana*. published in *Moskovskie vedomosti* from 30 November 1879 through January 1882. Second series: *Russkii vestnik* 11 (1885), 2–3, 8 (1886). See also *Iz peshcher i debreĭ Indostana: pis'ma na rodinu*/Radda-Bai (Moskva: v Univ. tip. (M. Katkov), 1883), which contains all of part 1 and some of part 2 of her narrative. The full Russian text of the second series is as follows: Letters I–II are in *Russkii vestnik*, vol. 180, Nov.–Dec. 1885, 270–323. Letter III is in *Russkii vestnik*, vol. 181, part 2, Feb. 1886, 772–92, and Letter IV is from 792 to 822 in the same volume. Letters V and VI are in *Russkii vestnik* vol. 182, March 1886, 318–35 and 335–54, respectively, and Letter VII is on 684–718 of *Russkii vestnik*, t. 184 part 2 (Aug. 1886).

Blavatsky, H.P., Boris De Zirkoff, and Dara Eklund. *Collected Writings*. 16 vols. Madras, India, and Wheaton, IL: Theosophical Publishing House; Theosophical Press, 1950–91.

Bogdanov, A.P. *Materialy dlia istorii nauchnoi i prikladnoi deiatel'nosti v Rossii po zoologii i soprikasaiushchimsia s neiu otrasliam znaniia za poslednee tridtsatipiatiletie (1850–1887 g.)*. Moscow: T. 1., 1888.

Bogdanov, M.N. *Ocherki prirody Khivinskogo oazisa i pustyni Kizyl-Kum*. Tashkent: F. V. Bazilevskii, 1882.

Bojanowska, Edyta. *A World of Empires: The Russian Voyage of the Frigate Pallada*. Cambridge, MA: Harvard University Press, 2018.

Bonvalot, Gabriel. *Du Caucase aux Indes à travers le Pamir*. Paris: E. Plon, Nourrit et C., 1889.

Brantlinger, Patrick. *Rule of Darkness: British Literature and Imperialism, 1830–1914*. Ithaca, NY: Cornell University Press, 1988.

Bregel, Yuri. *Bibliography of Islamic Central Asia*. 3 vols. Bloomington: Indiana University Press, 1995.

Breyfogle, Nicholas. *Heretics and Colonizers: Forging Russia's Empire in the South Caucasus*. Ithaca, NY: Cornell University Press, 2005.

Brower, Daniel. "Islam and Ethnicity: Russian Colonial Policy in Tashkent." In *Russia's Orient: Imperial Borderlands and Peoples, 1700–1917*, edited by Daniel Brower and Edward Lazzerini, 114–35. Bloomington: Indiana University Press, 1999.

Brower, Daniel. *Turkestan and the Fate of the Russian Empire*. London: RoutledgeCurzon, 2003.

Burfield, Diana. "Theosophy and Feminism: Some Explorations in Nineteenth Century Biography." In *Women's Religious Experience: Cross-Cultural Perspectives*, edited by Pat Holden, 27–56. London: Croom Helm, 1983.

Campbell, Ian. "'Our Friendly Rivals': Rethinking the Great Game in Ya'qub Beg's Kashgaria, 1867–77." *Central Asian Survey* 33, no. 2 (2014): 199–214.

Capus, Guillaume. *Le toit du monde (Pamir)*. Paris: Hachette, 1890.

Carlson, Maria. *"No Religion Higher than Truth": A History of the Theosophical Movement in Russia, 1875–1922*. Princeton, NJ: Princeton University Press, 1993.

Chernysheva, Maria. "'The Russian Gérôme?' Vereshchagin as a Painter of Turkestan." *RIHA Journal* (18 September 2014).

Cherskaia, M.P. "Vospominaniia o Kolymskoi ekspeditsii 1892 g." In *Neopublikovannye stat'i, pis'ma i dnevniki. Stat'i o I. D. Cherskom i A. I. Cherskom*, edited by I.D. Cherskii, 300–9. Irkutsk: Irkutskoe knizhnoe izdatel'stvo, 1956.

Clinch, Elizabeth, and Nicholas Clinch. *Through a Land of Extremes: The Littledales of Central Asia*. Seattle: Mountaineers Books, 2011.

Cobbold, Ralph. *Innermost Asia: Travel and Sport in the Pamirs*. London: W. Heinemann, 1900.

Coulomb, Madame [Emma]. *Some Account of My Intercourse with Madame Blavatsky from 1872 to 1884; with a Number of Additional Letters and a Full Explanation of the Most Marvellous Theosophical Phenomena*. London: Elliot Stock, 1885.

Cranston, Sylvia. *HPB: The Extraordinary Life and Influence of Helena Blavatsky*. New York: Putnam, 1983.

Creese, Mary R.S., with Thomas M. Creese. *Ladies in the Laboratory IV: Imperial Russia's Women in Science, 1800–1900, A Survey of Their Contributions to Research*. London: Rowman and Littlefield, 2015.

Cumberland, Charles. *Sport on the Pamirs and Turkistan Steppes*. Edinburgh: Blackwood, 1895.

Curzon, George. *Russia in Central Asia in 1889 and the Anglo-Russian Question*. London: Longmans, Green, and Co., 1889.

Curzon, George. *The Pamirs and the Source of the Oxus*. The Geographical Journal: Including the Proceedings of the Royal Geographical Society 8 (July–December 1896): 251–2. The article appeared in three parts: pages 32–54, pages 97–119, and pages 239–64. London: The Royal Geographical Society, 1896.

Danilova, Tat'iana. *Bogini dalekikh stranstvii*. Moscow: Veche, 2006.

Davis, Mike. *Late Victorian Holocausts: El Niño Famines and the Making of the Third World*. London and New York: Verso, 2001.

Dharampal-Frick, Gita, Monika Kirloskar-Steinbach, Rachel Dwyer, and Jahnavi Phalkey, eds. *Key Concepts in Modern Indian Studies*. New York: NYU Press, 2015.

Dickinson, Sara. "The Russian Tour of Europe before Fonvizin: Travel Writing as Literary Endeavor in Eighteenth-Century Russia." *Slavic and East European Journal* 45, no. 1 (2001): 1–29.

Dickinson, Sara. *Breaking Ground Travel and National Culture in Russia from Peter I to the Era of Pushkin*. Studies in Slavic Literature and Poetics, vol. 45. Amsterdam and New York: Rodopi, 2006.

Dixon, Joy. *Divine Feminine: Theosophy and Feminism in England*. Johns Hopkins University Studies in Historical and Political Science; 119th Ser., 1. Baltimore: Johns Hopkins University Press, 2001.

Dmitriev, S.V. "Etnografiia Tadzhikov v trudakh rossiiskikh uchenykh XIX-nachala XX v." In *Tadzhiki: Istoriia, kul'tura, obshchestvo*, Rossiiskaia akademiia nauk, Muzei antropologii i etnografii im. Petra Velikogo (Kunstkamera), Institut ismailitskikh issledovanii (St. Petersburg, 2014): 64–96.

Dobson, George. *Russia's Railway Advance into Central Asia: Notes of a Journey from St. Petersburg to Samarkand*. London: W. H. Allen and Company, 1890.

Dostoevsky, Fyodor. *A Writer's Diary, Volume 2: 1877–1881*. Translated by Kenneth Lantz. Evanston, IL: Northwestern University Press, 1997.

Dukhovskaia, Varvara (Barbara Doukhovskoy). "Iz dnevnika russkoi zhenshchiny v Erzerume v 1878 godu," *Russkii vestnik* 136, no. 8 (August 1878): 803–51, and 138, no. 11 (November 1878): 98–158.

Dukhovskaia, Varvara (Barbara Doukhovskoy). *Iz dnevnika russkoi zhenschiny v Erzerume vo vremia voennogo zaniatiia ego v 1878 g*. Spb: tipografiia i khromolit. A Transhelia, 1879.

Dukhovskaia, Varvara (Barbara Doukhovskoy). *Iz moikh vospominanii*. St. Petersburg: Golike and Vil'borg, 1900a.

Dukhovskaia, Varvara (Barbara Doukhovskoy). "Otryvok iz moikh
vospominanii. Cherez Velikii Okean. Iz San-Frantsisko v Iaponiu."
Turkestanskii literaturynyi sbornik v polzu prokazhennykh, 2–10. St. Petersburg:
Tipografiia A. Benke, 1900b.

Dukhovskaia, Varvara (Barbara Doukhovskoy). *Turkestanskie vospominaniia.*
St. Petersburg: Izdanie T-va M. O. Vol'f, 1913.

Dukhovskaia, Varvara (Barbara Doukhovskoy). *Diary of a Russian Lady:
Reminiscences of Barbara Doukhovskoy (née Princesse Galitzine).* London: J.
Long, 1917.

Dukhovskoi, Sergei Mikhailovich. "Russkie v Erzerume v 1878 godu." *Voennyi
sbornik*, 1878, t. 124 No. 11: 131–49 and No. 12: 309–29. St. Petersburg: Tip.
V. A. Poletiki, 1878.

Dunmore, Charles. *The Pamirs; Being a Narrative of a Year's Expedition on
Horseback and on Foot through Kashmir, Western Tibet, Chinese Tartary, and
Russian Central Asia.* London: J. Murray, 1893.

Eidel'man, Natan. *Byt' mozhet za khrebtom Kavkaza.* Moscow: Nauka, 1990.

Etkind, Alexander. *Internal Colonization Russia's Imperial Experience.* Oxford:
Wiley, 2013.

Fedchenko, A.P. *Puteshestvie v Turkestan*, T. 1, part 2. Izvestiia Imperatorskogo
Obshchestva liubitelei Estestvozananiia, Antropologii i Etnografii, 1875.
http://books.e-heritage.ru/book/10084193.

Fedchenko, O.A. "A Fedtschenko's Reisen in Turkestan, 1868–71." In
*Mittheilungen aus Justus Perthes' Geographischer Anstalt Uber Wichtige Neue
Erforschungen Dem Gessamtgebiete der Geographie*, Vol. 20, 201–6. Gotha:
Justus Perthes, 1874.

Fedchenko, O.A. *Vidy Russkogo Turkestana po risunkam s natury Ol'gi
Aleksandrovny Fedchenko, ispolnennye gg. Savrasovym v Moskve, Loran, Siseri,
Sabat'ie i Lemers'ie v Parizhe.* Moscow: Izdatel'stvo Obshchestva liubitelei
estestvoznaniia, antropologii i etnografii, published in 1880 or 1881.

G. Iul' (Henry Yule). "Ocherk geografii i istorii verkhov'ev Amu-Dar'i,"
perevod s angliiskogo O. A. Fedchenko s dopolneniami i primechaniami
A. P. Fedchenko, N. V. Khanykova, G. Iul'ia," *Izvestiia Russkogo
Geograficheskogo obshchestva* IX, no. 6 (1873): 1–82.

Fedorov, G.P. "Moia sluzhba v Turkestanskom krae (1870–1906 goda)."
Istoricheskii Vestnik 6 (1912): 786–812; 10 (1913): 33–55; 11 (1913): 538–67; 12
(1913): 860–93.

Feldman, Leah. *On the Threshold of Eurasia: Revolutionary Poetics in the
Caucasus.* Ithaca, NY: Cornell University Press, 2018.

Foster, Jeremy. "Capturing and Losing the 'Lie of the Land': Railway
Photography and Colonial Nationalism in Early Twentieth Century South
Africa." In *Picturing Place: Photography and the Geographical Imagination*, edited
by Joan M. Schwartz and James R. Ryan, 140–61. London: I.B. Tauris, 2003.

Gao, Yuan. *Captivity and Empire: Russian Captivity Narratives in Fact and Fiction*. MA thesis in Eurasian Studies, Nazarbaev University, 2016.

Gerard, M.G. *Report on the Proceedings of the Pamir Boundary Commission*. Calcutta: Office of the Superintendant of Government Printing, 1897.

Ghose, Indira. *Women Travellers in Colonial India*. Oxford: Oxford University Press, 1999.

Godwin, Joscelyn. *The Theosophical Enlightenment*. New York: SUNY Press, 1994.

Golovlev, A.A. "Konstantin Nikolaevich Rossikov kak issledovatel' prirody severnogo Kavkaza," *Istoriia nauki: Samarskaia luka: problemy regional'noi i global'noi ekologii* 26, no. 2 (2017): 197–224.

Golovnin, D.N. "Ocherki okhoty na Pamirakh," *Priroda i okhota*, in seven parts: "Priroda Pamirov i moia ekspeditsiia," February 1901, kniga II-aia, 1–10; Part II, "Arkhar (Ovis polii, Blyth)," March 1901, kniga III-aia, 1–11; Part III, "Pervaia vstrecha s arkharami," April 1901, kniga IV-aia, 1–9; Part IV, "Okhota na arkharov v okrestnostiakh Bol'shoi Kara-Kul'," May 1901, kniga V-aia, 137–49; Part V, "Okhota na arkharov u perevala Kizil-Dzhiik," June 1901, kniga VI-aia, 95–104, Part VI, "Kiik (Capra Sibirica. Meyer)," July (?) 1901, kniga VII-aia, 21–9; Part VII, "Okhota na kiikov," August 1901, kniga VIII-aia, 1–14.

Golovnin, D.N. "Ocherki okhoty na Pamirakh po peru," (September?) 1901, kniga IX, 1–16.

Golovnin, D.N. "Sel'skoe khoziaistvo i kholodil'noe delo." January 1912 article reprinted in *Kholodil'naia tekhnika* 2 (2012): 63–7. Followed by biography of Golovnin, 67.

Golovnina, Iuliia D. *Na Pamirakh: Zapiski russkoi puteshestvennitsy*. Moscow: Tipo-litografiia T-va I. N. Kushener' i K, 1902.

Gomes, Michael. *Theosophy in the Nineteenth Century: An Annotated Bibliography*. New York: Garland Publishing, 1994.

Goodrick-Clarke, Nicholas. *The Western Esoteric Traditions: A Historical Introduction*. Oxford and New York: Oxford University Press, 2008.

Golitsyn, Prince N.N., ed. *Bibliograficheskii slovar' russkikh pisatel'nits*. St. Petersburg: Tipografiia V. S. Balasheva, 1889.

Gorbunov, Iu. A., ed. "Pisatel'nitsy Rossii. Materialy dlia bibiograficheskogo slovaria." https://www.uralstalker.com/nashi-proekty/samoobrazovatelnaya -biblioteka-yuniya-gorbunova/pisatelnicy-rossii-materialy-dlya -biobibliograficheskogo-slovarya/.

Gordon, T.E. *The Roof of the World: Being the Narrative of a Journey over the High Plateau of Tibet to the Russian Frontier and the Oxus Sources on Pamir*. Edinburgh: Edmonston and Douglas, 1876.

Gordon-Cumming, Constance Frederica. *From the Hebrides to the Himalayas: A Sketch of Eighteen Months' Wanderings in Western Isles and Eastern Highlands*. 2 vols. London: Sampson Low, Marson, Searle, and Rivington, 1876.

Gorris, Ellen Anna Philo. "Invisible Victims? Where Are Male Victims of Conflict-Related Sexual Violence in International Law and Policy?" *European Journal of Women's Studies* 22, no. 4 (2015): 412–27.

Gorshenina, Svetlana. *The Private Collections of Russian Turkestan in the Second Half of the 19th and Early 20th Century.* Berlin: Klaus Schwarz Verlag, 2004.

Gorshenina, Svetlana. "Russian Archaeologists, Colonial Administrators, and the 'Natives' of Turkestan: Revisiting the History of Archaeology in Central Asia." In *"Masters" and "Natives": Digging the Others' Past*, edited by Svetlana Gorshenina, Philippe Bornet, Michael Fuchs, and Claude Rapin, 31–86. Berlin: DeGruyter, 2019.

Gould, Rebecca. *Writers and Rebels: The Literature of Insurgency in the Caucasus.* New Haven, CT: Yale University Press, 2016.

Govor, Elena. *My Dark Brother: The Story of the Illins, a Russian-Aboriginal Family.* Australia: New South Wales Press, 2000.

Graham, Stephen. *Through Russian Central Asia.* New York: MacMillan, 1916.

Granqvist, Raoul. "Her Imperial Eyes: A Reading of Mary Wollstonecraft's 'Letters Written during a Short Residence in Sweden, Norway and Denmark.'" *Moderna Sprak* 91, no. 1 (1997): 16–24.

Grant, Bruce. *The Captive and the Gift: Cultural Histories of Sovereignty in Russia and the Caucasus: Culture and Society after Socialism.* Ithaca, NY: Cornell University Press, 2009.

Green, Nile, ed. *Writing Travel in Central Asian History.* Bloomington: Indiana University Press, 2014.

Greenleaf, Monika. *Pushkin and Romantic Fashion: Fragment, Elegy, Orient, Irony.* Stanford, CA: Stanford University Press, 1993.

Grewal, Inderpal. *Home and Harem: Nation, Gender, Empire and the Cultures of Travel.* Durham, NC: Duke University Press, 1996.

Griffith, Bronwyn A.E., ed. *Ambassadors of Progress: American Women Photographers in Paris, 1900–1901.* Musée d'Art Américain Giverny, France, in association with the Library of Congress, Washington, DC, 2001.

Gudzii, N.K., and E.A. Maimin. "Roman L. N. Tolstogo 'Voskresenie,'" In *Tolstoy L. N. Voskresenie*, 483–545. Akademiia Nauk SSSR. Moscow: Nauka, 1964.

Guelke, Jeanne Kay, and Karen Morin. "Gender, Nature, Empire: Women Naturalists in Nineteenth Century British Travel Literature." *Transactions of the Institute of British Geographers, New Series* 26, no. 3 (2001): 306–26.

Gukovskii, G.A. *Pushkin i russkie romantiki.* Moscow: Khudozhestvennaia literatura, 1965.

Gusev, N.N. *Lev Nikolaevich Tolstoi. Materialy k biografii's 1855 po 1869 god.* Moscow, 1957.

Halbach, Uwe. "The Circassian Question: Russian Colonial History in the Caucasus and a Case of "Long-distance Nationalism" *SWP Comments*

2014/C 37, August 2014. http://www.swp-berlin.org/fileadmin
/contents/products/comments/2014C37_hlb.pdf.

Hedin, Sven. *Through Asia*. Vol. 1. Translated by J.T. Bealby. London: Methuen & Co, 1898.

Hessler, Julie. "A Thaw to the East: India in the Soviet Imagination." Chapter of a book in progress.

Hofmeister, Alexis. "Imperial Case Studies: Russian and British Ethnographic Theories." In *An Empire of Others: Creating Ethnographic Knowledge in Imperial Russia and the USSR*, edited by Roland Cvetkovski and Alexis Hofmeister, 23–47. Budapest and New York: Central European University Press, 2014.

Hokanson, Katya. *Writing at Russia's Border*. Toronto: University of Toronto Press, 2008.

Hokanson, Katya. "Russian Women Travelers in Central Asia and India." *The Russian Review* 70 (January 2011): 1–19.

Holden, Pat., ed. *Women's Religious Experience*. London and Totowa, NJ: Croom Helm and Barnes & Noble, 1983.

Hopkirk, Peter. *The Great Game: The Struggle for Empire in Central Asia*. New York: Kodansha, 1992.

Humboldt, Alexander. *Asie Centrale*. Paris: Gide, 1843.

Hutton, Cristopher. "Back to Blavatsky: The Impact of Theosophy on Modern Linguists." *Language and Communication* 18 (1998): 181–204.

Iadrintsev, N.M. "Podvizhnitsa nauki: (Pamiati A. V. Potaninoi)." *Knizhki Nedeli* 1, no. 1 (January 1894): 113–24.

Ikramov, I. "Iskanderskaia voennaia ekspeditsiia i nachala izucheniia verkhnego Zarafshana" ("Iskandarkul military expedition and the sources of the Zarafshan upper Stretches study"). *Uchenye zapiski Khuzhandskogo gosudarstvennogo universiteta im. akademika B. Gafurova. Gumanitarnye nauki* 1, no. 21 (2010): 133–43.

Ivanov, D.L. "Iz lichnykh vospominanii ob O. A. Fedchenko." In *Izvestiia glavnogo botanicheskogo sada RSFSR*, Vol. XXIII, vyp. 2: 99–104. Leningrad, 1924.

Iversen, V. "Otchet o poezdke na Moskovskuiu politekhnicheskuiu vystavku." *Trudy Imperatorskogo vol'nogo ekonomicheskogo obshchestva* (Spb: Tipografiia tovarishchestva 'Obshchestvennaia Pol'za'), 1873, t. 1: 507–25.

Janssen, Diederik F. "Age-Stratifying Homosexualities in the Social Sciences." *Sexuality & Culture* 21, no. 1 (March 2017): 300–22.

Johnson, K. Paul. *The Masters Revealed: Madame Blavatsky and the Myth of the Great White Lodge*. New York: SUNY Press, 1994.

Kal', E.F. *Persidskie, arabskie i tiurkskie rukopisi Turkestanskoi Publichnoi Biblioteki*. Tashkent, 1889.

Kappeler, Andreas. *The Russian Empire: A Multiethnic History*. Translated by Alfred Clayton. London: Routledge, 2001.

Karazin, N.N. *Na Dalekikh okrainakh.* http://az.lib.ru/k/karazin_n_n
  /text_1872_na_dalekih_okrainah.shtml. Translation: *In the Distant Confines.*
  Translated by Anthony W. Sariti. Bloomington, IN: AuthorHouse, 2007.

Karazin, N.N. "Doktorsha." 1972. http://az.lib.ru/k/karazin_n_n/text_1872
  _doktorsha.shtml.

Karazin, N.N. "Turkestanskii otdel. Glavnyi zal." (illustration) in *Vsemirnaia
  illiustratsiia* VIII, no. 194 (1872): 180.

Keating, Jennifer. "'There Are Few Plants, but They Are Growing, and
  Quickly': Foliage and the Aesthetics of Landscape in Russian Central Asia,
  1854–1914." *Studies in the History of Gardens & Designed Landscapes* 37, no. 2
  (2016): 174–89.

Khalid, Adeeb. "Culture and Power in Colonial Turkestan." *Cahiers d'Asie
  centrale* 17, no. 18 (2009): 413–47.

Khalid, Adeeb. "Backwardness and the Quest for Civilization: Early Soviet
  Central Asia in Comparative Perspective." *Slavic Review* 65, no. 2 (2006):
  231–5.

Khisamutdinov, A.A. *Russkaia slovestnost' v Shankhae.* Vladivostok: Izdatel'stvo
  Dal'nevostochnogo universiteta, 2014.

King, Anthony. *Colonial Urban Development: Culture, Social Power and
  Environment.* London: Routledge, 1976.

Kivelson, Valerie, and Ronald Grigor Suny. *Russia's Empires.* New York:
  Oxford University Press, 2017.

Knight, Nathaniel. "Vocabularies of Difference: Ethnicity and Race in Late
  Imperial and Early Soviet Russia." *Kritika: Explorations in Russian and
  Eurasian History* 13, no. 3 (Summer 2012): 667–83.

Knight, Nathaniel. "Seeking the Self in the Other: Ethnographic Studies of
  Non-Russians in the Russian Geographical Society, 1845–1860." In *Defining
  Self: Essays on Emergent Identities in Russia, Seventeenth to Nineteenth
  Centuries,* edited by M. Branch, 117–38. Helsinki: Finnish Literature
  Society, 2009.

Knorring, O.E. "Pamiati Ol'gi Aleksandrovny Fedchenko." *Izvestiia glavnogo
  botanicheskogo sada RSFSR* XXIII, vyp. 2: 91–5. Leningrad, 1924.

Komatsu, Hisao. "The Andijan Uprising Reconsidered." In *Muslim Societies:
  Historical and Comparative Aspects,* edited by Sato Tsugitaka, 29–61.
  London: RoutledgeCurzon, 2004.

Kouteinikova, Inessa. "Tashkent in St. Petersburg: The Constructed Image of
  Central Asia in Russia's Nineteenth-Century Ethnographic Exhibitions."
  In *À L'orientale: Collecting, Displaying and Appropriating Islamic Art and
  Architecture in the 19th and Early 20th Centuries,* edited by Francine Giese,
  151–62. Leiden and Boston: Brill, 2020.

Kreutzmann, Hermann. *Wakhan Quadrangle: Exploration and Espionage During
  and After the Great Game.* Wiesbaden, Germany: Harrassowitz Verlag, 2017.

Lachman, Gary. *Madame Blavatsky: The Mother of Modern Spirituality*. London: Penguin, 2012.

Laskin, Emily. "Writing Imperial Borderlands: Nikolai Grodekov's Ride across Afghanistan." Association for Slavic, East European and Eurasian Studies conference paper, 2017.

Laskin, Emily. "Liberty and License in Nikolai Il'in's *At a New Border*." Association of American Teachers of Slavic and East European Langues conference paper, 2019.

Laskin, Emily. *Geopoetics and Geopolitics: Landscape, Empire, and the Literary Imagination in the Great Game*. PhD diss., University of California, Berkeley, 2021.

Lassen, Christian. *Indische Altertumskunde*. Osnabrück: Zeller, 1858.

Layton, Susan. *Russian Literature and Empire*. Cambridge: Cambridge University Press, 1994.

Ledkovskaia-Astman, Marina, Charlotte Rosenthal, and Mary Fleming Zirin. *Dictionary of Russian Women Writers*. Westport, CT: Greenwood Press, 1994.

Lermontov, M. Iu. *Sobranie sochinenii v chetyrekh tomakh*. Moscow: Khudozhestvennaia literatura, 1975.

Lim, Susanna. *China and Japan in the Russian Imagination, 1685–1922: To the Ends of the Orient*. London: Routledge, 2013.

Littledale, St. George. "A Journey across the Pamir from North to South." *Proceedings of the Royal Geographical Society and Monthly Record of Geography, New Monthly Series* 14, no. 1 (January 1892): 1–35.

Littledale, St. George. "A Journey across Central Asia." *The Geographical Journal* 3, no. 6 (June 1894): 445–7.

Littledale, St. George. "A Journey across Tibet, from North to South, and West to Ladak." *The Geographical Journal* 7, no. 5 (May 1896): 453–78.

Liubarskii, G. Iu. *Istoriia Zoologicheskogo muzeia MGU: Idei, liudi, struktury*. Moscow: Tovarishchestvo nauchnykh izdanii KMK, 2009.

Lobri, Ol'ga. "Iz Turkestanskikh vospominanii." *Russkii vestnik* 261, no. 5 (1899): 220–8. Biography at http://book.uraic.ru/elib/authors /gorbunov/sl-11.htm.

Lobri, Ol'ga. "Ot Astrakhani do Margelana (putevye nabroski) Avgust' 1895 goda." *Russkii vestnik* 259, no. 2 (1899): 639–49; 260, no. 4: 601–12.

Lohde, Georg. "Alexis Fedtschenko. Ein Nachruf," *Berliner Entomologische Zeitschrift* (Berlin 1873): 236–8.

Lotman, Iurii. "Problema Vostoka i Zapada v tvorchestve pozdnego Lermontova," In *Lermontovskii sbornik*, 5–22. Leningrad: Nauka, 1985.

Lydekker, R. *Wild Oxen, Sheep & Goats of All Lands Living and Extinct*. London: Rowland Ward, 1898.

MacKenzie, John. *The Empire of Nature: Hunting, Conservation and British Imperialism*. Manchester: Manchester University Press, 1988.

Maev, N. *Turkestanskaia vystavka predmetov sel'skogo khoziaistva i promyshlennosti v Tashkente, 1890 g.* (putevoditel' po vystavke i ee otdelam). Tashkent: tipo-litografiia S. I. Lakhtina, 1890.

Maiorova, Olga. *From the Shadow of Empire: Defining the Russian Nation through Cultural Mythology, 1855–1870.* Madison: University of Wisconsin Press, 2010.

Maiorova, Olga. "Severed Heads on Display: Visualizing Central Asia (1868–1872)." In *Picturing Russian Empire*, edited by Valerie Kivelson and Joan Neuberger, forthcoming.

Marchand, Suzanne. *German Orientalism in the Age of Empire: Religion, Race, and Scholarship.* Cambridge: Cambridge University Press, 2009.

Markoff, A. "On the Afghan Frontier: A Reconnaissance in Shugnan." *Geographical Journal of the Royal Geographical Society* XVI, no. 6 (December 1900): 666–79.

Marks, Steven. *Road to Power: The Trans-Siberian Railroad and the Colonization of Asian Russia 1850–1917.* Ithaca, NY: Cornell University Press, 1991.

Martin, Virginia. *Law and Custom in the Steppe: The Kazakhs of the Middle Horde and Russian Colonialism in the Nineteenth Century.* London: Routledge, 2001.

Maslova, O.V., ed. *Obzor Russkikh puteshestvii i ekspeditsii v sredniuiu aziu, Part II, 1856–1869.* Section LI, "Ekspeditsiia A. P. Fedchenko i O. A. Fedchenko v Turkestanskii krai 1868–1871," 70–89. Tashkent: Ministerstvo vyshego obrazovaniia SSSR: Sredneaziatskii gosudarstvennyi universitet imeni V. I. Lenina (Izdatel'stvo SAGU), 1956.

Masoero, Alberto. "Territorial Colonization in Late Imperial Russia: Stages in the Development of a Concept." *Kritika: Explorations in Russian and Eurasian History* 14, no. 1 (Winter 2013, New Series): 59–91.

Maxwell, Anne. *Women Photographers of the Pacific World, 1857–1930.* London: Routledge, 2020.

McNeal, Robert. *Tsar and Cossack, 1855–1914.* New York: St. Martin's Press, 1987.

Middleton, Robert. *The Russians in the Great Game.* Bishkek, Kyrgyzstan: University of Central Asia, 2019.

Middleton, Robert, and Huw Thomas. *Tajikistan and the High Pamirs: A Companion and Guide.* Hong Kong: Odyssey Books & Guides, 2012.

Mills, Sarah. *Discourses of Difference: An Analysis of Women's Travel Writing and Colonialism.* London and New York: Routledge, 1991.

Mills, Sarah. "Gender and Colonial Space." *Gender, Place and Culture: A Journal of Feminist Geography* 3, no. 2 (1996): 125–48.

Mills, Sarah. *Gender and Colonial Space.* Manchester: Manchester University Press, 2005.

Moleva, N.M., ed. *Konstantin Korovin: Zhizn i tvorchestvo.* Moscow: Izdatel'stvo akademii khudozhestv SSSR, 1963.

Montefiore, Simon Sebag. *The Romanovs: 1613–1918*. New York: Knopf, 2016.

Moore, Thomas. *Lalla Rookh: An Oriental Romance*. New York: Thomas Y. Crowell & Company, 1817.

Morozov, Sergei. *Russkie Puteshestvenniki-fotografy*. Moscow: Gos. Izdatel'stvo Geograficheskoi literatury, 1953.

Morozov, Sergei. *Russkaia khudozhestvennaia fotografiia 1839–1917*. Moscow: gosudarstvennoe izdatel'stvo iskusstvo, 1955.

Morrison, A.S. *Russian Rule in Samarkand 1868–1910: A Comparison with British India*. Oxford and New York: Oxford University Press, 2008.

Morrison, A.S. "'Applied Orientalism' in British India and Tsarist Turkestan." *Comparative Studies in Society and History* 51, no. 3 (July 2009): 619–47.

Morrison, A.S. "Camels and Colonial Armies: The Logistics of Warfare in Central Asia in the Early 19th Century." *Journal of the Economic and Social History of the Orient* 57, no. 4 (2014): 443–85.

Morrison, A.S. "Introduction: Killing the Cotton Canard and Getting Rid of the Great Game: Rewriting the Russian Conquest of Central Asia, 1814–1895." *Central Asian Survey* 33, no. 2 (2014): 131–42.

Morrison, A.S. "Twin Imperial Disasters: The Invasions of Khiva and Afghanistan in the Russian and British Official Mind, 1839–1842." *Modern Asian Studies* 48, no. 1 (2014): 253–300.

Morrison, A.S. The 'Turkestan Generals' and Russian Military History." *War in History* 26, no. 2 (2019): 153–84.

Morrison, A.S. *The Russian Conquest of Central Asia: A Study in Imperial Expansion, 1814–1914*. Cambridge: Cambridge University Press, 2021.

Moser, Henri. *À Travers L'asie Centrale: La Steppe Kirghize, Le Turkestan Russe, Boukhara, Khiva, Le Pays Des Turcomans Et La Perse, Impressions De Voyage*. Paris: E. Plon, Nourrit, 1886.

Mukhamedov, Sh. B. "Istoriia Russkogo Turkestana: Pravda i vymysel. Vzgliad istorika iz XXI veka." https://cyberleninka.ru/article/n/istoriya -russkogo-turkestana-pravda-i-vymysel-vzglyad-istorika-iz-xxi-veka.

Murray, John (Firm), and Edward B. Eastwick. *A Handbook for India: Being an Account of the Three Presidencies, and of the Overland Route*. London: J. Murray, 1859.

Mushketov, I.V. *Geologicheskoe i orograficheskoe opisanie po dannym sobrannym vo vremia puteshestvii s 1874 po 1880 g*. Spb.: Tipografiia M. M. Stasiulevicha, Vas. Ostrov, 2. lin., 7, 1886.

Nabokov, Vladimir. *The Gift*. Translated by Michael Scammell and Vladimir Nabokov. New York: Vintage, 1991.

Nalivkin, Vladimir, and Maria Nalivkina. *Muslim Women of the Fergana Valley: A 19th-century Ethnography from Central Asia*. Edited by Marianne Kamp, translated by Mariana Markova and Marianne Kamp. Bloomington: Indiana University Press, 2016.

324   Bibliography

Natale, Simone. "Photography and Communication Media in the Nineteenth Century." *History of Photography* 36, no. 4 (2012): 451–6.

Newcity, Michael A. *Copyright Law in the Soviet Union*. New York and London: Praeger Publishers, 1978.

Nikolaev, P.A. *Russkie pisateli 1800–1917. Biograficheskii slovar'*. 4 vols. Moscow: Sovietskaia entsiklopedia (vol. 1), Bol'shaia rossiiskaia entsiklopedia (vol. 2), 1989.

Obruchev, V.A. *Grigorii Nikolaevich Potanin: Kratkii ocherk ego zhizni i deiatel'nosti*. Moscow: tip. I. N. Kushnerev i K, 1916.

Obruchev, V.A. "Velikii Pervootkryvatel' Azii Grigorii Potanin." *Armeiskii sbornik: Nauchno-metodicheskii zhurnal MO RF* (Moscow: Redaktskionno-izdatel'skii tsentr MO RF) 12 (2008): 56–9.

Olcott, Henry Steel. *Old Diary Leaves: The True Story of the Theosophical Society*. Second Series, 1878–83. London, The Theosophical Publishing Society; Madras: Theosophist Office, 1900.

Ol'denburg, Sergei. "Pamiati Aleksandry Viktorovny Potaninoi." In *K Svetu: Nauchno-literaturnyi sbornik*, edited by Ek. P. Letkova and V.D. Batiushkov, 220–6. St. Petersburg, publication of Komitet Obshchestva dostavleniia sredstv S.-Peterburgskim vyshchim zhenskim kursam, 1904.

Owen, Alex. *The Darkened Room: Women, Power, and Spiritualism in Late Victorian England*. New Cultural Studies Series. Philadelphia: University of Pennsylvania Press, 1990.

Pahlen, Konstantin Konstanovich, Richard A. Pierce, and N.J. Couriss. *Mission to Turkestan, Being the Memoirs of Count K.K. Pahlen, 1908–1909*. London and New York: Oxford University Press, 1964.

Palmquist, Peter E. "Pioneer Women Photographers in Nineteenth-Century California." *California History* 71, no. 1 (Spring 1992): 110–27.

Parton, Anthony. "A Sense of Place." *Apollo* 175, no. 595 (2012): 96–7.

Paul, N.C. *A Treatise on the Yoga Philosophy*. Benares, India: Recorder Press, 1851.

Peterson, Maya. *Pipe Dreams: Water and Empire in Central Asia's Aral Sea Basin*. Cambridge: Cambridge University Press, 2019.

Phibbs, Isabelle Mary. *A Visit to the Russians in Central Asia*. London: K. Paul, Trench, Trübner & co., ltd., 1899.

Piankov, Vasilii Grigor'evich, *Po Turkestanu: Ob"ezd Turkestanskim general-gubernatorom S. M. Dukhovskim Samarkandskoi i Ferganskoi oblastei v 1898 godu*. Tashkent, 1989.

Pierce, Richard. *Russian Central Asia, 1867–1917: A Study in Colonial Rule*. Berkeley: University of California Press, 1960.

Polo, Marco. *Marco Polo's Travels*. With an introduction by John Masefield. London: J. M. Dent and Sons, 1908.

Poltoratskaia, Lidiia Konstantinovna. "Poezdka po Kitaiskoi granitse ot Altaia do Tarbagataia." *Russkii vestnik* 93, no. 6 (1871): 580–661.

Poltoratskaia, Lidiia Konstantinovna. *Al'bom tipov i vidov Zapadnoi Sibiri, sniatykh L. K. Poltoratskoi.* St. Petersburg, 1879.

Poltoratskaia, Lidiia Konstantinovna. "Bremenskaia ekspeditsiia v Semipalatinskoi oblasti." *Priroda i okhota* 1, no. 3 (1879): 23–52.

Popov, I.I. "Pamiati N. M. Iadrintseva i A. V. Potaninoi." *Izvestiia Vostochno-Sibirskogo Otdeleniia Russkogo Geograficheskogo obshchestva* XXV, no. 1 (1894): 1–28.

Potagos, Panagiotes (Dr. Potagos). *Dix années de Voyages dans L'Asie Centrale et l'Afrique équatoriale.* Translated by M.M. Adolphe Meyer, Jules Blancard, and Laur. Labadie. Paris: Ernest Leroux, 1885.

Potanin, G.N. *Ocherki Severo-zapadnoi Mongolii: Rezul'taty puteshestvia ispolnennogo v 1876–1877 godakh po porucheniu Imperatorskogo Russkogo Geograficheskogo Obshchestva, Vol. 1: Dnevnik Puteshestviia i materialy dlia fizicheskooi geografii i topografii s z. Mongolii.* St. Petersburg: Tipografiia V. Bezobrazova i Komp., 1881.

Potanina, Aleksandra Viktorovna. *Iz puteshestvii po Vostochnoi Sibiri, Mongolii, Tibetu i Kitaiu; sbornik statei.* Moscow: Izdatel'stvo Geograficheskogo otdeleniia Imperatorskago obshchestva liubitelei estestvoznanie, antropologii i etnografii, 1895.

Potanina, Aleksandra Viktorovna. *Rasskazy o Buriatakh, ikh vere i obichaiakh.* Moscow: Tipografiia K. L. Men'shova, 1912.

Pratt, Mary Louise. *Imperial Eyes: Travel Writing and Transculturation.* London: Routledge, 1992.

Pravilova, Ekaterina. *A Public Empire: Property and the Quest for the Common Good in Imperial Russia.* Princeton, NJ: Princeton University Press, 2014.

Prince Michael of Greece. *The White Night of St. Petersburg.* Translated by Franklin Philip. New York: Atlantic Monthly Press, 2004.

Proskurin, Oleg. *Poeziia Pushkina, ili podvizhnyi palimpsest.* Moscow: Novoe Literaturnoe obozrenie, 1999.

Prothero, Steven R. *The White Buddhist: The Asian Odyssey of Henry Steel Olcott.* Religion in North America. Bloomington: Indiana University Press, 1996.

Prothero, Steven R. "Theosophy's Sinner/Saint: Recent Books on Madame Blavatsky." *Religious Studies Review* 23, no. 5 (July 1997): 257–61.

Protokly zasedanii Imperatorskogo Obshchestva liubitelei estestvoznaniia, antropologii i etnografii s. sentiabria 1874 g. po oktiabr' 1876 g, Izvestiia OLEAE. 1876. T. XXIV: 27–33.

Pushkareva, Natalia. *Women in Russian History from the Tenth to the Twentieth Century.* Translated and edited by Eve Levin. Armonk, NY: M. E. Sharpe, 1997.

Pushkin, Aleksandr Sergeevich. *Polnoe sobranie sochinenii v 16 tomakh.* Moscow: Akademiia nauk, 1937–59.

Ram, Harsha. *Imperial Sublime: A Russian Poetics of Empire*. Madison: University of Wisconsin Press, 2003.

Reischl, Katherine Hill. "Photography and the Crisis of Authorship: Tolstoy and the Popular Photographic Press." *Jahrbücher für Geschichte Osteuropas* 60, no. 4 (2012): 533–49.

Renner, Andreas. "Defining a Russian Nation: Mikhail Katkov and the 'Invention' of National Politics." *Slavonic and East European Review* 81, no. 4 (October 2003): 659–82.

Richardson, David, and Sue Richardson. *Qaraqalpaqs of the Aral Delta*. Munich: Prestel, 2012.

Ritvo, Harriet. *The Animal Estate: The English and Other Creatures in the Victorian Age*. Cambridge, MA, and London: Harvard University Press, 1987.

Rogger, Hans. "The Skobelev Phenomenon: The Hero and his Worship." *Oxford Slavonic Papers* 9 (1976): 46–78.

Romanova, G. Ia. *Naimenovanie mer dliny v russkom iazyke*. Moscow: Nauka, 1975.

Rossikov, K.N. "Pereletnaia ili aziatskaia sarancha. Prichiny gibeli saranchi v ee gnezdilishchakh i novyi sposob ee unichtozheniia." *Trudy biuro po entomologii Uchenogo komiteta Glavnogo upravleniia zemleustroistva i zemledeliia, izdavaemye pod redaktsii zavedyvaiushchego biuro* (Ministerstvo zemledeliia i gosudarstvennykh imuschchest. Department zemledeliia) IV, no. 1: 1–37. St. Petersburg: Tipografiia V. Demakova, 1899.

Rossikov, K.N. "Primenenie parizhskoi zeleni dlia istrebleniia saranchi." *Trudy biuro po entomologii Uchenogo komiteta Glavnogo upravleniia zemleustroistva i zemledeliia, izdavaemye pod redaktsii zavedyvaiushchego biuro* (Ministerstvo zemledeliia i gosudarstvennykh imuschchest. Department zemledeliia) I, no. 2: 1–15. St. Petersburg: Tipografiia V. Demakova, 1899.

Rossikova, Anna Efimovna. "Na Aral'skom more i Syr-Dar'e: Iz dnevnika." *Kronshtadtskii vestnik* 140 (1883); 46 (1884).

Rossikova, Anna Efimovna. "S Amu-Dar'i." *Turkestanskie Vedomosti* 13 (1883).

Rossikova, Anna Efimovna. "V gorakh i ushchel'iakh Kurtatii i istokov reki Tereka." (Iz putevykh vospominanii o gornoi Osetii). In *Zapiski Kavkazskogo otdela imperatorskogo Russkogo geograficheskogo obshchestva*, kn. XVI, 301–56. Tiflis: Tipografiia Gruzinskogo izdatel'skogo tovarishchestva, 1894.

Rossikova, Anna Efimovna. "Puteshestvie po tsentral'noi chasti gornoi Chechni." In *Zapiski Kavkazskogo otdela imperatorskogo Russkogo geograficheskogo obshchestva*, kn. XVIII, 139–228. Tiflis: Tipografiia Gruzinskogo izdatel'skogo tovarishchestva, 1896.

Rossikova, Anna Efimovna. "Sredi pustyni po velikoi sredne-aziatskoi reke Amu-dar'e." (iz puteshestvii letom 1898 g. v Russkii Turkestan). *Nauchnoe obozrenie* 10–12 (1899): 1780–806; no. 10 (October 1899): 2201–19; no. 12 (December 1899).

"Rossikova, Anna Efimovna." *Mary Zirin's Bibliography of Pre-Revolutionary Writings by Women.* https://zlist.omeka.net/items/show/2513.

Rossikova, Anna Efimovna. "Belyi Tur (Osetinskaia legenda)." *Kavkazskii vestnik, ezhemesiachnyi nauchno- literaturnyi zhurnal* 5 (May 1900): 25–43.

Rossikova, Anna Efimovna. "Po Amu-Dar'e ot Petro-Aleksandrovska do Nukusa," *Russkii Vestnik* 8 (1901): 562–88; 10: 630–56; also reprinted in *Turkestanskii sbornik* 439 (1907): 25–52.

Russkie vedomosti, 1863–1913: Sbornik statei. Moscow: tip. Russkikh Vedomostei, 1913.

Rudbøg, Tim, and Erik Sand. *Imagining the East: The Early Philosophical Society.* Oxford: Oxford University Press, 2020.

"S. M. Dukhovskoi," Niva 18 (1893): 430–1, with a portrait on 432.

Sahadeo, Jeff. "Epidemic and Empire: Ethnicity, Class, and 'Civilization' in the 1892 Tashkent Cholera Riot." *Slavic Review* 64, no. 1 (Spring 2005): 117–39.

Sahadeo, Jeff. *Russian Colonial Society in Tashkent, 1865–1923.* Bloomington: Indiana University Press, 2010.

Sahadeo, Jeff. "Visions of Empire: Russia's Place in an Imperial World." *Kritika: Explorations in Russian and Eurasian History* 11, no. 2 (Spring 2010): 381–409.

Sahadeo, Jeff. "Home and Away: Why the Asian Periphery Matters in Russian History." *Kritika: Explorations in Russian and Eurasian History* 16, no. 2 (Spring 2015, New Series): 375–88.

Said, Edward. *Orientalism.* New York: Vintage, 1978.

Saltykov-Shchedrin, M.E. *Sobranie sochinenii* v 20 tomakh. Moscow: Khudozhestvennaia literatura, 1970.

Sandler, Stephanie. *Distant Pleasures: Alexander Pushkin and the Writing of Exile.* Stanford, CA: Stanford University Press, 1989.

Schenk, Fritjof. "Imperiale Raumerschließung: Die Beherrschung der russischen Weite." *Osteuropa* 55, no. 3 (2005): 33–45.

Schenk, Fritjof. "'Ia tak ustala byt' pereletnoi ptitsei,' imperskoe prostrantstvo i imperskoe gospodstvo v avtobiografii Rossiiskoi dvorianki." *Vestnik Iuzhno-Ural'skogo gosudarstvennogo universiteta.* Seriia: Sotsial'no-gumanitarnye nauki 2, no. 14 (2014): 40–50.

Schimmelpenninck van der Oye, David. *Russian Orientalism: Asia in the Russian Mind from Peter the Great to the Emigration.* New Haven, CT: Yale University Press, 2010.

Schimmelpenninck van der Oye, David. *Toward the Rising Sun: Ideologies of Empire and the Path to War with Japan.* DeKalb: Northern Illinois University Press, 2006.

Schuyler, Eugene. *Turkistan: Notes of a Journey in Russian Turkistan, Khokand, Bukhara, and Kuldja*. 2 vols. New York: Scribner, Armstrong & Co., 1876.

Schwab, Raymond. *Vie d'Anquetil-Duperron, suivie des Usages civils, et religieux des Perses par Anquetil-Duperron*. Paris: Ernest Leroux, 1934.

Schwab, Raymond. *The Oriental Renaissance: Europe's Rediscovery of India and the East, 1680–1880*. Translated by Gene Patterson-Black and Victor Reinking. New York: Columbia University Press, 1984.

Scott, J. Barton. "Miracle Publics: Theosophy, Christianity, and the Coulomb Affair." *History of Religions* 49, no. 2 (2009): 172–96.

Scotto, Peter. "Prisoners of the Caucasus: Ideologies of Imperialism in Lermontov's 'Bela.'" *PMLA* 107 (1992): 246–60.

Semenov-Tian-Shanskii, P.P. *Istoriia poluvekovoi deiatel'nosti Imperatorskogo Russkogo Geograficheskogo Obshchestva 1845–1895*. 3 vols. St. Petersburg: Tip. Bezobrazov, 1896.

Serebrennikov, N.V. "G. N. Potanin i L. N. Tolstoi." *Vestnik Tomskogo gosudarstvennogo universiteta: Istoriia* 2, no. 14 (2011): 65–6.

Shafranskaia, Eleonora. *Tashkentskii tekst v russkoi kul'ture*. Moscow: Art House Media, 2010.

Shafranskaia, Eleonora. *Turkestanskii tekst v russkoi kul'ture: Kolonial'naia proza Nikolaia Karazina (istoriko-literaturnyi i kul'turno-etnograficheskii kommentarii)*. St. Petersburg: Self-published, 2016.

Shilov, D.N., and Iu. A. Kuz'min, eds. *Chleny gosudarstvennogo soveta rossiiskoi imperii, 1801–1906, Bibliograficheskii spravochnik*. 309–11. St. Petersburg: Isskustvo Rossii, 2007.

Shroder, John. F. "Afghanistan Border Fixing." In *Natural Resources in Afghanistan: Geographic and Geologic Perspectives on Centuries of Conflict*, 281–300. Amsterdam: Elsevier, 2014.

Slezkine, Yuri. *Arctic Mirrors: Russia and the Small Peoples of the North*. Ithaca, NY: Cornell University Press, 1996.

Slocum, John. "Who, and When, Were the *Inorodtsy*? The Evolution of the Category of "Aliens" in Imperial Russia." *The Russian Review* 57 (April 1998): 173–90.

Sokol, Edward Dennis. *The Revolt of 1916 in Central Asia*. Baltimore: Johns Hopkins University Press, 2016.

Solovyov, Vsevolod Sergeevich. *Sovremennaia zhritsa Izidy: Moe znakomstvo s E. P. Blavatskoi i "Teosoficheskom obshchestvom." (Epizod 'fin de siècle')*. St. Petersburg: Tipografiia Obshchestva "Obshchestvennaia pol'za," 1893.

Solovyov, Vsevolod Sergeevich. *A Modern Priestess of Isis*. Abridged and translated on behalf of the Society for Psychical Research from the Russian of Vsevolod Sergyeevich Solovyoff by Walter Leaf, Litt.D. London: Longmans, Green and Co. and New York: 15 East 16th Street, 1895.

Steinwedel, Charles. *Threads of Empire: Loyalty and Tsarist Authority in Bashkiria, 1552–1917*. Bloomington: Indiana University Press, 2016.

Stites, Richard. *The Women's Liberation Movement in Russia: Feminism, Nihilism, and Bolshevism, 1860–1930*. Princeton, NJ: Princeton University Press, 1978.

Strobel, Margaret. *European Women and the Second British Empire*. Bloomington: Indiana University Press, 1991.

Stumm, Hugo. *Russia in Central Asia: Historical Sketch of Russia's Progress in the East up to 1873, and of the Incidents Which Led to the Campaign against Khiva; with a Description of the Military Districts of the Caucasus, Orenburg, and Turkestan*. Translated by J.W. Ozanne and H. Sachs. London: Harrison & Sons, 1885.

Sword, Helen. *Ghostwriting Modernism*. Ithaca, NY: Cornell University Press, 2002.

Tagangaeva, Maria. "Visualizing (Post)-Soviet Ethnicity. Fine Art of Buryatia." *Anthropology & Archaeology of Eurasia* 54, no. 3 (2015): 24–57.

Tarasov, Oleg. *Framing Russian Art: From Early Icons to Malevich*. London: Reaktion Books, 2011.

Teltscher, Kate. "'The Rubicon between the Empires': The River Oxus in the Nineteenth-Century British Geographical Imaginary." In *Writing Travel in Central Asian History*, edited by Nile Green, 135–212. Bloomington: Indiana University Press, 2014.

Terent'ev, M.A. *Istoriia zavoevaniia Srednei Azii*. 3 vols. St. Petersburg: Tipolitografiia V. V. Komarova, 1906.

Tolstoy, L.N. *Polnoe sobranie sochinenii v 90 tomakh*. Moscow: Khudozhestvennaia literatura, 1928–58.

Tolstoy, L.N. *The Portable Tolstoy*, edited by John Bayley. New York: Viking Press, 1978.

Tolz, Vera. *Russia's Own Orient: The Politics of Identity and Oriental Studies in the Late Imperial and Early Soviet Periods*. Oxford: Oxford University Press, 2011.

Tomashevskii, Boris. *Pushkin*. 2 vols. Moscow and Leningrad: Akademiia nauk, 1956 and 1961, respectively.

Trubetskoi, Vladimir Sergeevich. *A Russian Prince in the Soviet State*. Evanston, IL: Northwestern University Press, 2006.

Turgenev, Ivan. *Polnoe sobranie sochinenii i pisem v dvadsati vos'mi tomakh, Pis'ma v trinadsat' tomakh*. Moscow: Akademiia nauk, 1960–8.

Turkestanskii literaturnyi sbornik v polzu prokazhennykh. Published by the Turkestan Red Cross. St. Petersburg: Tipografiia A. Benke, 1900.

Turkin, N.V. (N.V.T.). "Na Pamirakh." *Priroda i okhota* 7 (1902): 57–9.

Ujfalvy-Bourdon, Marie. *De Paris À Samarkand: Le Ferghanah, Le Kouldja Et La Sibérie Occidentale: Impressions De Voyage D'une Parisienne*. Paris: Hachette, 1876.

Ujfalvy-Bourdon, Marie. *Voyage d'une parisienne dans l'Himalaya occidental.* Paris: Hachette, 1887.

Ukhtomskii, Esper Esperovich. *Puteshestvie na Vostok Ego Imperatorskogo Vysochestva Gosudaria Naslednika Tsesarevicha 1890–1891.* Avtor-Izdatel' E. E. Ukhtomskii. Illiustriroval N. N. Karazin, tom. 2. Leipzig: F. A. Brokgauz, 1895.

Ulymzhiev, D. "Dordzhi Banzarov – the First Buryat Scholar." *Mongolian Studies* 16, Index and Reviews Issue (1993): 55–7.

Uvarova, Praskov'ia. "Poezdka v Tashkent i Samarkand." *Russkaia Mysl'* 12, no. 11, section 2 (1891): 1–19; no. 12, section 2: 1–25.

Uvarova, Praskov'ia. *Byloe. Davno proshedshie schastlivye dni.* Moscow: izdatel'stvo im. Sabashnikovykh, 2005.

Val'kova, O.A. *Ol'ga Aleksandrovna Fedchenko: 1845–1921.* Moscow: Nauka, 2006.

Val'kova, O.A. "The Conquest of Science: Women and Science in Russia, 1860–1940." *Osiris* 23, *Intelligentsia Science: The Russian Century, 1860–1960* (2008): 136–65.

Val'kova, O.A. *Shturmuia tsitadel' nauki, zhenshchiny-uchenye Rossiiskoi imperii.* Moscow: Novoe Literaturnoe Obozrenie, 2019.

van der Veer, Peter. *Imperial Encounters: Religion and Modernity in India and Britain.* Princeton, NJ: Princeton University Press, 2001.

Vereshchagin, Vasilii. *Vassili Verestchagin, Painter, Soldier, Traveler; Autobiographical Sketches.* Translated from the German and the French by F. H. Peters with illustrations after drawings by the author. London: R. Bentley & Son, 1887.

Viswanathan, Gauri. *Outside the Fold: Conversion, Modernity, and Belief.* Princeton, NJ: Princeton University Press, 1998.

Viswanathan, Gauri. "The Ordinary Business of Occultism." *Critical Inquiry* 27, no. 1 (Autumn 2000): 1–20.

Viswanathan, Gauri. "In Search of Madame Blavatsky: Reading the Exoteric, Retrieving the Esoteric." *Representations* 141 (Winter 2018): 67–94.

Volkov, Solomon. *St. Petersburg: A Cultural History.* New York: Simon & Schuster, 1995.

von Hagen, Mark. "Empires, Borderlands, and Diasporas: Eurasia as Anti-Paradigm for the Post-Soviet Era." *The American Historical Review* 109, no. 2 (2004): 445–68.

Voskoboinikov, M.M. "Iz nabliudenii na Pamire (s 10 ris.)." *Zemlevedenie* 3 (1899): 31–60.

Vostrikov, L.A., and Z.V. Vostokov. *Khabarovsk i khabarovchane: Ocherki o proshlom.* Khabarovsk: Khabarovskoe khnizhnoe izdatel'stvo, 1991.

Wakeman, Geoffrey. *Aspects of Victorian Lithography: Anastatic Printing and Photozincography.* Wymondham, UK: Brewhouse Press, 1970.

Wallace, Frank. "Mr. St. George Littledale's Trophies." *Country Life* (11 February 1911), 196–7.

Washington, Peter. *Madame Blavatsky's Baboon: A History of the Mystics, Mediums, and Misfits Who Brought Spiritualism to America*. New York: Schocken Books, 1995.

Webb, James. *The Occult Underground*. LaSalle, IL: Open Court, 1974.

Weiss, Claudia. "Representing the Empire: The Meaning of Siberia for Russian Imperial Identity." *Nationalities Papers* 35, no. 3 (July 2007): 339–456.

Wilson, Horace Hayman. *Works by the Late Horace Hayman Wilson*. M.A., F.R.S., Vol. II. London: Trübner & Co., 60, Paternoster Row, 1862.

Witte, Sergei. *Vospominaniia*, 1911. http://az.lib.ru/w/witte_s_j/text_0010 .shtml.

Witte, Sergei. *The Memoirs of Count Witte*. Garden City, NY, and Toronto: Doubleday, Page & Company, 1921.

Wolmar, Christian. *To the Edge of the World: The Story of the Trans-Siberian Express, the World's Greatest Railroad*. Philadelphia and Great Britain: Perseus Books, 2013.

Wood, John. *A Journey to the Source of the River Oxus*. London: John Murray, Albemarle Street, 1872.

Wortman, Richard. *Scenarios of Power: Myth and Ceremony in Russian Monarchy*. Vol. 1: *From Peter the Great to the Death of Nicholas I*. Princeton, NJ: Princeton University Press, 1995.

Wortman, Richard. *Scenarios of Power: Myth and Ceremony in Russian Monarchy*. Vol. II: *From Alexander II to the Abdication of Nicholas II*. Princeton, NJ: Princeton University Press, 2001.

Yule, Henry. "Geography of the Valley of the Oxus." In *A Journey to the Source of the River Oxus*, 2nd edition, by John Wood, xix–xc. London: John Murray, 1872.

Zarin, V.M. and E.A. Zarina. *Puteshestviia A. V. Potaninoi*. Edited by V.V. Obruchev. Moscow: Gosudarstvennoe izdatel'stvo geograficheskoi literatury, 1950.

Zekulin, Nicholas G. "Turgenev's 'Kroket v Vindzore' ('Croquet at Windsor')." *New Zealand Slavonic Journal*, Ivan Sergeyevich Turgenev 1818–1883 (1983): 85–103.

Zholkovsky, Alexander. "Before and After 'After the Ball.'" In *Text Counter Text: Rereadings in Russian Literary History*. Stanford, CA: Stanford University Press, 1994.

Zilbershtein, I. "Vystavka khudozhnika V. V. Vereshchagina." *Literaturnoe nasledstvo* 73, no. 1 (1964).

Zimin, I.V. "The 'Forgotten' Grand Duke (Nikolai Konstantinovich Romanov, 1850–1928)." *Voprosy Istorii* 10 (2002): 131–9.

Zirin, Mary. "Elena Apreleva." In *An Encyclopedia of Continental Women Writers*, edited by Katharina M. Wilson, 48. New York and London: Garland Publishing, 1991.
Zviguilsky, Tamara. "Une disciple de Tourguéniev: Eléna Blaramberg-Ardov-Apréleva (1846–1923) Pour le cent cinquantenaire de sa naissance." *Exposition Les Frères Goncourt et Tourgueniev, Catalogue*, Musée Ivan Tourgueniev, 16, rue Ivan Tourguéniev, 78380 Bougival, 1996, 102–7.

Index